Benjamin Norton Bugbey

Sacramento's Champagne King

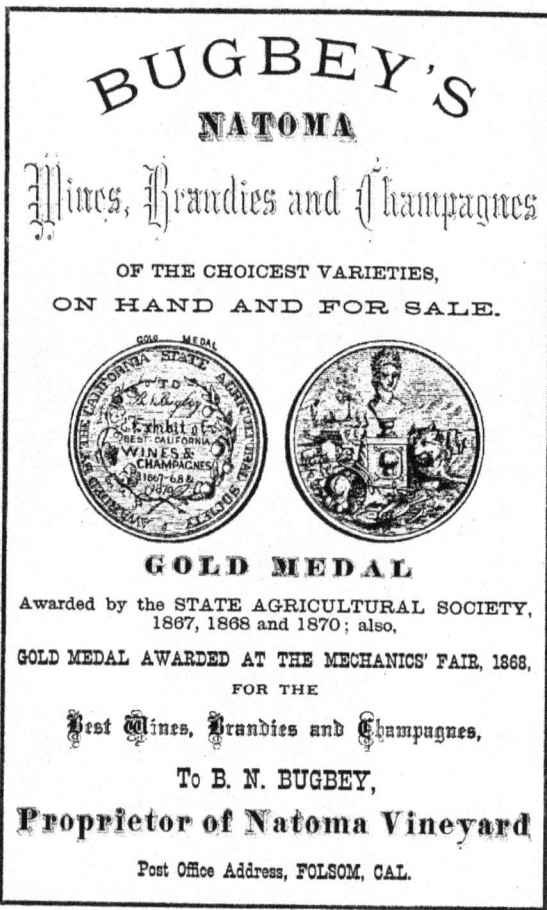

1871 Sacramento City & County Directory

© 2019 Copyright Kevin Knauss, Granite Bay, CA

Published by Kevin Knauss October 2019

Edited by Bonnie Osborn

Author: Kevin Knauss

Library of Congress Control Number: 2019905633

ISBN: 978-0-9978188-6-4

Acknowledgments

This book could not have been written without the professional services and generous assistance from the following organizations and institutions.

The Bancroft Library, UC Berkeley

California Digital Newspaper Collection

California State Archives

California State Library

Center for Sacramento History

Community Memorial Museum of Sutter County

El Dorado County Historical Museum

Folsom, El Dorado & Sacramento Historical Railroad Association, Inc.

Folsom Historical Society & Museum

Mechanics' Institute Library & Chess Room

Old City Cemetery Committee Inc. of the Historic Sacramento Cemetery

The Society of California Pioneers

UC Davis Shields Library, Special Collections

Table of Contents

Table of Images	9
Introduction	12
Chapter 1: California 1849 – 1852	15
Early Mining	15
Sacramento	16
Connecticut	17
Chapter 2: Migration, Furniture, & Farming 1849 – 1856	19
Connecticut To California	19
Hampden Mining and Trading Company	19
Return from Connecticut	22
Gold River Farming	24
Folsom Roots	26
Chapter 3: The Legend of Lawman Bugbey 1856 - 1861	33
Constable B. N. Bugbey	34
Wild West Round Up of Folsom Robbers	35
Chapter 4: Path to Sheriffalty	42
Nomination for Sheriff	43
Settlers' Association	45
Chapter 5: Sheriff Bugbey 1861 - 1864	49
Administration	49
Ex-Officio Tax Collector	51
Sacramento Floods	53
Law Enforcement	54
The Chinese Assault	55
Sheriff's Sales	58
Social Affairs	59
Law Suits	61
Woodliff v Bugbey	62

Benjamin Norton Bugbey

White v Bugbey	62
Woods v Bugbey	62
Peterie v Bugbey and Beck	64
1863 McClatchy vs. Bugbey	65
Chapter 6: Natoma Vineyard Begins to Grow 1863 - 1865	**70**
Mining to Farming	70
South Fork American River	71
Natoma Vineyard Topography, Soil	73
Natoma Vineyard	75
Bugbey Vineyardist & Promoter	76
Political Party Civil War	82
Chapter 7: Natoma Expansion, Scandals, Tragedy 1866 - 1869	**87**
Land Speculator	87
California Vineyard Expansions, Impending Glut	88
Mediocre California Wine	91
Mechanics' Institute	93
Fire At The Winery	94
Bigler Assessor Appointment	95
Registry Fraud	101
Campaign Trail	103
Natoma Vineyard Visitors	105
An Unfortunate Accident	108
Chapter 8: Wine, Brandy, Champagne, Music 1869 - 1872	**115**
Martinette McGlashan	115
Period of Expansion	116
Syebgub or Private Cuvee de Amotan	118
Fiher Zagos Questioned	119
Hugo Yanke-Mansfeldt	120
Musical Marketing	122
Natoma Vineyard & Winery Detailed	125

Benjamin Norton Bugbey

Big Investment	128
The Big Brandy Gamble	129
Sacramento Philanthropy	131
Natoma Water & Mining Company	132
Fire & Politics	133
New Folsom Home, C. T. H. Palmer	134
California State Fair Gold Medal Statements	136
Vine Growers' Association	141
Lobbying for Land Relief	142
Death of Peter McGlashan	144
Economic Changes	144
Chapter 9: Public Land Survey System & The Natoma Canal	157
Public Land Survey System	157
Land Patent & Preemption	158
Section 16 State Property	158
Natoma Vineyard Section 16	159
Water Ditch Provision	160
Bugbey Preemption & Acquisitions	161
Stroup Agreement	161
California State Purchase	162
CPRR Land Purchases	162
Henry Mette Land Swap	163
Brown's Ravine Flume	163
NWM Co. v Bugbey	164
Genesis of Natoma Ditch	164
Bugbey Protests Condemnation	165
Bugbey Wins First Round	166
Bugbey Sues NWM Co.	167
Bugbey Wins Second Round	167
Chapter 10: Natoma Vineyard 1873 – 1876	170

Natoma Vineyard Mortgage	170
Folsom Property Sales and Transfers	170
Slow Demise of Natoma Vineyards	171
National Monetary Policy	173
Republican Politics	173
Mortgage Default	174
Natoma Vineyard Mortgage Default	174
Natoma Vineyard Public Auction	176
More Debt Lawsuits	176
Strong v Bugbey, November 1874	177
Folsom Property Ordered Sold	178
Duroc Vineyard Sold	178
American Water and Mining Company	179
Eucalyptus Tree Experiment	179
Chapter 11: Bugbey Crash & Return 1877 – 1879	184
The Crash, Attempted Murder	184
Exile To San Francisco	185
U.S. Supreme Court Victory	186
Emma Bugbey	187
Rev. Elias W. Wible	187
Wible Axle Promoter	188
Nettie Divorces Benjamin	188
Invitation to Execution	189
Folsom Lamblett Murder	190
Julia Wible Courtship	192
Chapter 12: The Reinvention of Benjamin Bugbey, 1880 – 1885	195
New Family Saves Folsom Property	195
Butter Cooler	196
Slickens Debris Trial	198
Testimony Expert Witness Bugbey	199

Benjamin Norton Bugbey

Cross Examination by A. P. Catlin	199
Bugbey's Almond Orchard	203
James Lansing Murder	204
Final Folsom Fire	205
Bugbey's Railroad Refrigerator Car	206
Patching & Darning Tool	209
Bugbey Leaves Folsom For Sacramento	209
Real Estate Sales	210
The Miracle Worker	211
Mike Bryte	213
Sacramento Home	213
Chapter 13: Return to Law Enforcement 1886 U.S. Commissioner	**218**
Moses Drew	218
Commissioner Bugbey	220
Nicolaus Mob Drive Out Chinese	220
Anti-Chinese Movement	221
U. S. Commissioner Duties	222
Constitutional Questions	223
Judge Lorenzo Sawyer	224
Habeas Corpus	225
U. S. Supreme Court Opinion	226
Chinese Slavery Arrests	227
Bugbey Assaulted By Defense Attorney	229
Chinese Confidants	230
Bugbey's Above-Ground Railroad	230
Chinese are not Colored People	231
Slavery Not A Federal Crime	231
Chinese Target Bugbey	232
Gout You Arrested	233
Bugbey Helps Chinese Woman Escape	234

Exit U.S. Commissioner	235
Chapter 14: Back to Farming & Mining 1887 - 1892	242
Sutter County Kirkville Ranch	242
Pioneer Raisin Farmer Disputed	244
Shasta County Little Nellie Mine	246
Insolvent Debtor	247
Under Sheriff Bugbey	248
Contempt of Court	250
Judge A. P. Catlin	251
Bugbey on Human Nature	251
Republican Politics	252
Chapter 15: Independent Candidate for Sheriff 1892 - 1894	256
1892 Independent Candidacy	256
No Alcohol	257
Raging Against the Political Machine	258
Old Pete The Drunk	259
County Constable	260
1894 Equal Rights Candidate for Sheriff	260
Progressive Socialist	261
Bugbey's Manifesto of Jubilee Government	262
Special Privileges to None	263
Henry George	264
Bugbey Articulates the Problem	265
Jubilee is the Remedy	267
Specific National Proposals for Change	269
Bugbey: The Reformed Capitalist	270
Chapter 16: The Silver Republican Tax Collector 1898	279
Silver Republicans	279
Fusionists	280
Campaign for Tax Collector	281

Benjamin Norton Bugbey

Legal Battle to get on Ballot	281
Hiram Johnson	282
Bugbey Wins Legal Questions	282
Bugbey Finally Wins an Election	283
Hiram Johnson Attempts to Derail Bugbey	283
Sheriff Blocks Bugbey	284
Splendid Showing Collecting Taxes	285
More Battles with Board of Supervisors	286
Chapter 17: Retirement of a Pioneer 1902 - 1914	291
60 Years A Sacramento Pioneer	291
Historic Sacramento Cemetery Plot	292
Thoughts on Benjamin Norton Bugbey	295
Agriculture	295
Political Ambitions	296
Social Progressive	297
Evolution	297
Bibliography	300
Books, Published Documents	300
Congressional Acts	303
Court Cases	303
Images	304
Maps	304
Music	304
Archive and Online Material	305
Bugbey	306
Ann Johns	309
McGlashan	309
Wible	310
Yanke – Mansfeldt	310
Index	311

Benjamin Norton Bugbey

Table of Images

Figure 1: 1853 – Furniture & Upholstery Wareroom advertisement, Fifth and K Streets, Sacramento. CDNC. 23

Figure 2: 1857 - Map indicating Bugbey's farm along the American River. U. C Davis G4363, S26-465,1857, U61, No. 3. 25

Figure 3: 1862 - Announcement of locations Sheriff Bugbey would be available for residents to pay and county taxes in Sacramento County. CDNC 52

Figure 4: 1862 - Sheriff's Sale announcement for the auction of plant material in Sacramento. CDNC 58

Figure 5: 1864 - Choice grape vine cuttings advertisement for Bugbey's Fiher Zagos varietal. CDNC 79

Figure 6: 1866 - Natoma Vineyard Raisins advertised in the Marysville Daily Appeal. CDNC 82

Figure 7: 1868 - Bugbey's Natoma wine and brandy advertisement. CDNC 88

Figure 8: 1867 - $500 Reward offered by Bugbey for the arrest and conviction of the arsonist who set fire to his wine storeroom. CDNC . 94

Figure 9: 1869 - Raisins, cuttings, wines, and brandy advertisement for Natoma Vineyard in California Farmer and Journal of Useful Sciences. CDNC 105

Figure 10: 1869 - Natoma Vineyard, Residence of B. N. Bugbey, photographed by J. A. Todd of Sacramento. Natoma Vineyard, Residence of B. N. Bugbey, photographer J. A Todd, Sacramento, Natoma vineyard views, Calif. photographed by J.A. Todd, BANC PIC 1905.01574--A. 106

Figure 11: 1869 - Bugbey's new home in center of photograph with vineyard employees, Bugbey, and two women. Natoma Vineyard, Residence of B. N. Bugbey, photographer J. A Todd, Sacramento, Natoma vineyard views, Calif. photographed by J.A. Todd, BANC PIC 1905.01574--A. 107

Figure 12: Mary Jane Bugbey grave marker on the Bugbey obelisk monument in the Historic Sacramento Cemetery. Author's collection. 110

Figure 13: 1870 - Illustration of B. N. Bugbey from the sheet music for "Bugbey's Champagne Galop". John Hopkins, The Lester S. Levy Sheet Music Collection. 116

Figure 14: 1870 - Bugbey's Natoma wines, brandies, and champagne advertisement. CDNC 118

Figure 15: 1870 – "Bugbey's Champagne Galop" sheet music cover. John Hopkins, The Lester S. Levy Sheet Music Collection. 123

Figure 16: 1871 - "Bugbey's Champagne Waltz" sheet music cover. Note the similarities to J. A. Todd's photograph of the Natoma Vineyard from 1869. The Lester S. Levy Sheet Music Collection.....125

Figure 17: 1871 - Full page advertisement in the Sacramento directory for Bugbey's Natoma Vineyard products featuring images of Gold Medal awards. Located through Ancestry.com 137

Figure 18: 1866 - Government Land Office map, Section 16, T10N, R8E, noting B. N. Bugbey's Wine Distillation, Old House, and New House, along with the Natoma Ditch. 160

Figure 19: 1874 - Natoma Vineyard Sheriff's Sale advertisement. CDNC 175

Figure 20: 1876 - Eucalyptus and lime trees advertisement by Bugbey. CDNC 180

Figure 21: Bundock's terra cotta butter refrigerator that Bugbey was representing in the 1880s. CDNC 197

Figure 22: 1883 - Railroad freight car refrigerator illustration patented by B. N. Bugbey..208

Figure 23: 1886 - Real Estate advertisement in the Pacific Rural Press, listing properties that B. N. Bugbey had for sale in Northern California. CDNC 211

Figure 24: 1982 - Campaign advertisement for Bugbey's first run as an independent for Sacramento County Sheriff. CDNC 257

Figure 25: 1894 - Illustration of B. N. Bugbey from his second run as an independent candidate for Sacramento County Sheriff. CDNC 263

Figure 26: 1894 - Photograph of B. N. Bugbey used for newspaper illustration for is 1894 campaign. Courtesy of the El Dorado County Historical Museum..272

Figure 27: 1906 - Profile of B. N. Bugbey as the last supporter of wearing a shawl for warmth during the winter. CDNC 291

Figure 28: Bugbey grave marker obelisk monument in the Historic Sacramento Cemetery. The smaller headstone to the right marks the grave of his third wife Julia. Author's collection. 293

Figure 29: Wine cellar of B. N. Bugbey's house on the hill at the Natoma Vineyard, it is above Folsom Lake and can still be viewed. Author's collection..298

Benjamin Norton Bugbey

Introduction

Who was Benjamin Norton Bugbey? You can be forgiven if you have lived most of your life in Sacramento and never heard of Mr. B. N. Bugbey. There are no parks, imposing buildings, or major thoroughfares named after him. But beginning in the 1850s, the name B. N. Bugbey would have been familiar to many of the residents of Sacramento City and surrounding towns. He was the constable of Granite Township, which included Folsom City. He was the Sheriff of Sacramento County and later in life the county tax collector. He was the first person to grow raisins in a large-scale operation. He had acres of vineyards that allowed him to produce wine, brandy, and champagne which he sold across the country.

His name has become a mere footnote in Sacramento history, in spite of his numerous accomplishments and personal failings. He fully embraced the wide-open expanse and opportunities that California offered. He also witnessed the radical transformation of the western frontier from a Wild West territory to, in his opinion, a state controlled by large corporations and monopolies that he abhorred as enslaving the common man. He battled those forces in a lawsuit that was appealed all the way to the U.S. Supreme Court, where he was vindicated. He sparred with Hiram Johnson over technical aspects of state and county law and prevailed. He developed modest wealth as a businessman, only to see his enterprise crumble before his eyes. He oversaw and assisted in the execution of men for murder. His perspective colored by the events surrounding the Civil War, the human condition, guilt, innocence, and freedom weighed heavily on his mind. He railed against party politics and political machines, only to leverage the same system to gain an elected position. He was a writer and a speaker. He was a friend or acquaintance of virtually all the major business and political figures who emerged during California's infancy. He did not go out of his way to vilify any man, but was the object of others' derision. He lived a long life and had a quiet death.

Bugbey's life was extraordinary in many ways. His life story is also similar to those of other California pioneers of the 19th century. He is worthy to be remembered and studied not only from the perspective of the economic and political times he lived in and how that shaped and changed his belief system, but also for the similarities and challenges all people face in the 21st century. While Bugbey was keenly interested in state and national politics, he kept his focus on the Sacramento region. He thought in a national perspective, but acted locally to further his notions of equality and freedom.

He came to California in 1849 seeking gold, lived in Folsom, and died in Sacramento.

Benjamin Norton Bugbey

Bugbey was a man of the second half of the 19th century brought to California, as so many were, by the prospect of gold. He quickly realized that gold mining was short-lived and not an occupation that would create a stable income. He turned his attention to opportunities in agriculture and commerce that were developing with the steady increase of population in California.

In spite of the many successes Bugbey enjoyed, he also had his share of the sorts of tragedies that befell many early pioneers in California. He lost his wife in a riding accident at Mormon Island. He lost his homes, possessions and business to fire. He lost elections and he lost his land. At one point, he would confess that he lost his mind.

Bitterness at these losses never seemed to permanently overtake Bugbey. He persevered in life. With the optimism and grit that imbued so many men and women who trekked to California, he found or made other opportunities. As a constable and sheriff, Bugbey saw plenty of despair, murders, and suicides among his fellow community members.

Bugbey was a man who dropped between the cracks of history for various regions. His vineyard was in El Dorado County. He had a home in Folsom, but spent most of his time in Sacramento on business. Consequently, he never played a prominent role in any one region. He was a minor character in the development of each of the regions and the state. His legacy was also lost to fire, bankruptcy, and eventually to Folsom Lake. He was a pioneer in the literal and figurative sense of the word and context. He was a vigorous promoter of all that he believed in from politics, business, agriculture, and most importantly, himself.

What is the attraction to B. N. Bugbey? For better or worse, I can identify and empathize with many of Bugbey's personality traits such as his sense for adventure, his optimism, and the adversities he faced. His life mirrors the challenges many men face from career, marriage, business, insecurities, and the way in which one's world view changes with experience and age. He had a desire to be successful and gain recognition. He did some dumb things he later regretted. He lost people very close to him. He had periodic epiphanies about life, getting sober, etc. His world view matured as the events of the nation – Civil War – and his most consuming personal challenges – fighting corporations – shaped his life. He did not become bitter. He sought a better way.

He was a Douglas Democrat who could embrace the notion of turning a blind eye to slavery as long as it was not expanded. But he became a Union man during the Civil War. Political identity was important to Bugbey. He was a reader, learner, studier. He reflected on the Emancipation Proclamation as it related not only to black Americans, but Chinese immigrants as well. And then by logical extension, if all men were created equal, and women were among

God's creatures, should they not have equality and the right to vote as well?

He shared some of the common struggles of the Chinese in California. He was denigrated and ostracized because of his previous political party and votes. He was sneered at for hiring Chinese workers. While the injury to Bugbey was not as great as what the Chinese suffered, he could nonetheless commiserate with them as those in power had worked to derail some of his political ambitions. The personal and political wounds were deepened by the fact that some of those who attacked him were also his fellow sojourners on the trip from the East Coast to California. The powerful were too powerful.

He became a radical, expressing support for nationalizing railroads, telegraphs, and woman's suffrage. He hated political bosses. He ran for elected office in 1898 at the age of 71 and won! He only stopped pushing the political ball up the hill when the weight of taking care of his ailing wife, and his own infirmities, forced him to accept the inevitable of living a quieter life.

I stumbled across Bugbey when doing research about land ownership under the footprint of Folsom Lake. As I reviewed an 1866 Government Land Office map, I noticed not one home attributed to B. N. Bugbey, but two homes. Who was this man that could afford two homes overlooking the South Fork of the American River surrounded by acres of vineyards? A quick search on the California Digital Newspaper Collection website listed hundreds of entries for Bugbey beginning in 1853 and ending in 1914.

The more I dug into Bugbey's history the more I was amazed by this California pioneer. Not only was his life story interesting to me, he was an interesting man. He never started a railroad, but he knew the men who did. While lasting personal fortune eluded him, he did commission two pieces of music, built a large winery, oversaw the execution of murderers as Sheriff, tried to kill the Granite Township Constable, was a U. S. Commissioner, helped Chinese women escape bondage, and forever split the elected position of Tax Collector from Sheriff in Sacramento County.

Benjamin Norton Bugbey

Chapter 1: California 1849 – 1852

Early Mining

The light from the rising sun over the Sierra Nevada mountains made the inside of the white canvass tent glow. A young Benjamin Norton Bugbey woke up on a warm summer morning to the sounds of the American River flowing below his camp. On the opposite side of the river to his left was Mormon Island and to his right was Beal's Bar. He had staked his tent on a flat spot above the confluence of the north fork and the south fork of the American River.[1]

It was the summer of 1849 and Bugbey had only arrived in California a few months earlier. The morning melody was a collage of different dialects and languages from people all over the world. The sound of gold mining rockers could be heard working in the American River below. There was a sense of industriousness as the miners set about to find their fortunes in the river bed. They had come to California for an adventure, to find their treasure, and hopefully, to get rich. These young, ambitious men, with whom Bugbey would include himself, set up their crude living facilities among the Native American Nisenan people who already called the region their home.

On the long voyage from New York to Sacramento, many of the men talked about the methods, tools, and machines for placer mining, but none of them had ever done it. That is the situation in which Bugbey found himself. There was the theoretical side of mining, and then there was the practical side of doing the work. The work was hard. The river was cold, and days could be blisteringly hot. There was not a direct correlation between the amount or intensity of work a man did and the amount of gold he would ultimately find. Actually, finding gold seemed to be governed in large measure by luck, the accident of being in the right place at the right time.

Bugbey went to work, overwhelmed with a sense of adventure and the adrenaline of a young man looking to strike it rich. But, while he worked, he also kept his eyes and ears open for the next opportunity. He was truly living in a new world surrounded by men who all had but one goal, and that was to survive another day. The mines were populated with people from all over the world, working to earn a living and hoping to get rich.

As he walked from his campsite down the steep trail that led to the North Fork of the American River to start his day as a placer miner, young Bugbey was planting roots in the region. Northern California, the American River, Folsom, and Sacramento City would become his home. He would closely align his identity with the men, culture, and experience that he found as a '49er.

By the time Bugbey arrived in the gold fields, there were already thousands of men sloshing in the river, turning over rocks, and picking at the earth looking for gold. There were a couple of Native American villages nearby and Bugbey would see the women pounding acorns in the grinding holes they had carved out of the huge granite boulders poking out of the landscape. While some of the Native American men continued to fish in the river or hunt deer, rabbits and ducks, their way of life was rapidly being obliterated by miners and mining activity. Some of the Native American men had gone to work for Captain Beal, across the river from Bugbey's camp as part of the gold mining crew.

Always looking for a better mining spot, Bugbey would travel up the North Fork of the American River and prospect at Little Oregon Bar and as far north as Condemned Bar. He then wandered down to Big Gulch on the American River and then crossed over the river to the south side to mine at Negro Bar.[2]

Sacramento

When the autumn rains arrived, Bugbey headed west to Sacramento to spend the winter. The city of Sacramento was still rather primitive with limited options for entertainment. California was also wrestling with organizing both local and state government. With an abiding interest in politics, which Bugbey would pursue his whole life, he got involved in the campaign to elect P. B. Cornwall to the State Assembly and constitutional convention.[3]

Pierre Barlow Cornwall had arrived in California in 1848. He formed a political partnership with Sam Brannan and other men who were attempting to organize Sacramento as the premier point of entry on the Sacramento River to the gold fields in the foothills. Cornwall arrived in California $8,000 in debt, but in a short period of time, through selling goods to miners, shipping, and Sacramento real estate, had become a wealthy man. Bugbey most likely was attracted to Cornwall's entrepreneurial spirit.[4]

Before winter had officially ended Bugbey returned to the mining districts on the American River. He may have been driven out of Sacramento early after the devastating floods of January 1850 hit the ill-prepared community. The prospect of being cold and wet on a hill overlooking a rain swollen American River may have been preferable to the devastation and death visited upon the fledging town of Sacramento. He met up with a man who was operating a trading post at Rock Springs mid-way between Beal's Bar and Condemned Bar on the North Fork of the American River. Perhaps taking note of the success P. B. Cornwall and other merchants were having, he acquired the rudimentary trading post from George Champlin in May 1850.[5]

Benjamin Norton Bugbey

While he was selling dry goods and mining equipment to prospectors, Bugbey also had time to organize the Rock Bar Company in 1850.[6] He then shifted from placer mining in the river to drift mining above Negro Bar under what was to become the town of Folsom. In the process of drift mining, the miners would tunnel into the side of the hill and separate dirt from the cobble stones. They left the cobble rocks in the tunnel and hauled out the pay dirt to be washed.

He noted in his 1881 testimony during the lawsuit of People vs. The Gold Run Ditch Company that the drift mine was under block 40 in the town of Folsom. The town of Folsom had not yet been laid out by Theodore Judah in 1850. Bugbey, who would reside in Folsom for many years, was familiar with the layout of the town as he served as the Constable for five years in the late 1850s. [Block 40 of the original town layout would put Bugbey's drift mine north of Sutter Street most likely on undeveloped land adjacent to the City of Folsom Transportation Corporation Yard on Leidesdorff Street.]

Connecticut

It was also in 1850 that Bugbey received a letter notifying him that his father had died on October 8th, 1849[7]. His father, Eleazer Wales Bugbey, was only 56 years old and left his wife, Hannah Norton, and several children. It was reported he died of a fever after being ill for 28 days in Somers, Tolland County, Connecticut. Eleazer was born in Lanesborough, Massachusetts, but made his family home in Connecticut.[8] Eleazer served in the War of 1812[9] and had been named as Post Master of West Stafford in 1845[10].

In 1829, two years after Benjamin was born, Eleazer was part of a group of Methodist Episcopal ministers who negotiated a lease with the First Congregational Church of Stafford to hold meetings every other week. The Methodists had worked hard to establish a congregation in Stafford for years and this gave Eleazer an opportunity to preach while farming in the area.[11] Benjamin Bugbey would return to the roots of his childhood and the religious guidance of his father years later in California after he had strayed from the path of righteousness.

He waited until the fall of 1851 to return to Connecticut. It would be one of only two visits to the land where he was reared and that he had left behind. Bugbey boarded the steamer Independence on October 4th. He crossed through Central America at Nicaragua and then boarded the ship Prometheus for New York. The ship stopped at Havana, and Bugbey was able to explore the large stone fortress, Morro Castle, built by the Spanish in 1589. He was impressed by the huge fortress with four-story stone walls, cannons, lighthouse, observation turret, and two sets of doors with a drawbridge mechanism to span a dry moat. He felt no illustration to date had ever done it justice.[12]

Many '49ers were returning home after not finding their pot of gold in California. Bugbey never expressed any sentiment that, upon leaving California, he would not return. From all accounts he had become enamored with the opportunities that California offered, even if he had not found the vast quantities of gold that was being reported in 1848.

---

[1] *The People of the State of California vs The Gold Run Ditch and Mining Company, In the Superior Court of the State of California, in and for the County of Sacramento*, testimony of B. N. Bugbey, December 9th and 10th, 1881, Sacramento, Ca, California State Archives microfilm MF2:9 (46) Roll 4, Pages 4558 – 4599

[2] Ibid.

[3] *A Volume of Memoirs and Genealogy of Representative Citizens of Northern California Including Biographies of Many of Those Who Have Passed Away*, (Chicago Standard Genealogical Publishing Company 1901).

[4] Eifler, Mark A., *Gold Rush Capitalists Greed and Growth in Sacramento*, (University of New Mexico Press, 2002).

[5] *A Memorial and Biographical History of Northern California, Illustrated, Containing a History of this Important Section of the Pacific Coast from the Earliest Period of Its Occupancy...and Biographical Mention of Many of Its Most Eminent Pioneers and Also of Prominent Citizens of Today*, (The Lewis Publishing Company, Chicago, 1891).

[6] *A Volume of Memoirs and Genealogy of Representative Citizens of Northern California Including Biographies of Many of Those Who Have Passed Away*, (Chicago Standard Genealogical Publishing Company 1901).

[7] Connecticut Town Death Records, pre-1870 (Barbour Collection), Somers Vital Records

[8] Ibid.

[9] War of 1812 Pension Application Files Index, 1812 - 1815

[10] U.S., Appointments of U.S. Postmasters, 1832 – 1971, Eleazer W Bugbey, 14 October 1844, West Stafford, Tolland, Connecticut

[11] Grobel, Kendrick, *The First Church of Stafford, Connecticut known as "The Stafford Street Congregational Church" from its birth, 1723, to its Death, 1892*, Kendrick Grobel, Th. D. Pastor of the Congregational Church of Stafford Springs, Conn. (Published by the The Women's Council of the Congregational Church, Stafford Springs, 1942).

[12] *A Volume of Memoirs and Genealogy of Representative Citizens of Northern California Including Biographies of Many of Those Who Have Passed Away*, (Chicago Standard Genealogical Publishing Company 1901).

Benjamin Norton Bugbey

Chapter 2: Migration, Furniture, & Farming 1849 – 1856

Connecticut To California

News headlines about the California gold discovery and the ease of striking it rich in the waters of the American River, were commonplace in East Coast newspapers by late 1848. Shortly thereafter, numerous advertisements printed in papers in Massachusetts, where Bugbey was living and working at the time, announced the formation of mining companies and ships setting sail for California. It would have been hard for a 21-year-old with just a small thirst for adventure not to read these ads and day dream about California.

At the time, Bugbey had several options for traveling to California. He could either join a party of men to walk across the country to the West Coast, or he could hitch a ride on a sailing vessel. He chose a third option of reducing travel time with part sea travel and part overland trek.[1] Bugbey was working in Quincy, Massachusetts, when he first heard about California gold. Convinced that California was calling his name, he went back to Connecticut and started preparing for his big adventure.

He recognized the challenges he would face in California, the primitive conditions, high prices, and lack of easily accessible implements for living and mining. He put together the necessary tools and equipment to take with him for an extended stay in California.[2]

Hampden Mining and Trading Company

Bugbey also joined the Hampden Mining and Trading Company, which would charter the vessel John Castner. Hampden County, Massachusetts, is just north of Connecticut and very close to Stafford, where Bugbey's family was faming. Springfield, Massachusetts, was one of the largest urban areas in that part of the region and would have been a magnet for men to gather and formulate plans for traveling to California. Several men from the surrounding towns joined the company.[3]

The plan was to take a ship to Point Isabel, Mexico, disembark and travel over the mountain range to Mazatlán, where the company would catch another ship up the coast to California. The Hampden Mining and Trading Company secured passage on the schooner John Castner and set sail on January 29, 1849.[4] One of the members of the mining company[5] was Asa Bement Clarke, who published an account of his expedition to California in 1852.⁶ Bement chronicles most of the trip that Bugbey endured on his trek to California.

The schooner landed on Brazos Island on February 21st, and the group started making its way up to Brownsville, which was right across the Rio Grande from Matamoras, traveling by boat. The area was suffering from an outbreak of cholera that would kill several of the men in the company. By February 26th, they had reached Reynoso. On February 28th, they landed six miles from Camargo and set up camp. The rest of the journey would be on mule-back and foot.⁷

They crossed the Rio San Juan at Camargo on a ferry with two teams of oxen pulling their equipment. At the beginning of March more men were sick with cholera, a scorching sun and persistent wind and dust adding to their misery. On March 2nd, the company voted to split into three divisions, apportioning the property of the company under each division's responsibility.⁸

By the 18th of March, they had reached Monterey, Mexico. On March 25th, most of the company had made it to a little town called Parras, about midway on the journey to Mazatlán. At this point, with many men suffering extreme hardships and not looking forward to another sea voyage, the Hampden Mining and Trading Company dissolved into two groups. One group, with which Bugbey was associated, decided to continue onto Mazatlán. Asa B. Clarke and his group decided not to travel to Mazatlán because of a tall mountain range that had to be crossed and the reportedly high number of men waiting in Mazatlán for a ship up to California.⁹

Clarke decided to head north, up to Chihuahua and into New Mexico, to get to California. It would take him another three months to reach California, enduring an illness that forced him to rest for weeks and the most miserable desert conditions imaginable. In August of 1849, Clarke finally got to some gold mining spots along the Stanislaus and Tuolumne Rivers. He retreated to San Francisco when the rain came and spent the winter in a rented room on Clay Street.¹⁰

By contrast, once on the Pacific Coast, Bugbey and the second group of men would get another sailing vessel to resume the voyage to California. The company was able to secure passage on the French ship Olympia and sail up to San Francisco. They landed in California on June 12, 1849.¹¹

While Bugbey may have had to wait weeks for a ship to transport him from Mazatlán to California, he also avoided the agony of trying to cross the vast expanse of desert that nearly took Clarke's life. Clarke would prospect for gold along the Yuba River and open up a mercantile businesses in Marysville and Sacramento in 1850. In March of 1851 he left California and returned to the East Coast.¹²

Bugbey made the journey to California with several men who, like Bugbey, decided to make California their home. Among the pioneers from the Hampden Mining and Trading Company were Israel Luce and James McClatchy.[13]

Israel Luce was born in Ithaca, New York in 1824. He learned the marble cutting trade in Troy, New York. He later became experienced in marble monument work in Pittsfield, Massachusetts. He signed on to the Hampden Mining and Trading Company in 1848 for the journey west. He arrived ahead of Bugbey and went up to Coloma to mine for gold. He built the Nine Mile House along the American River and ran that for a while. He also mined below Cape Horn in Colfax.[14]

As early as December 1850, Luce was importing Vermont marble and advertising tombs and headstones on reasonable terms. He had set up his office on Seventh Street between J and K in Sacramento.[15]

In 1885 Luce was asked to visit a marble deposit near the Carson and Colorado Railroad Company's line by Owen's Lake, California. The deposit was of such high quality that Luce became the superintendent of the new formed Inyo Marble Company.[16]

Like Bugbey, Luce came to California a Democrat but switched to the Republican Party during the Civil War. He died suddenly in October 1898 in Sacramento.[17]

Bugbey arrived in California with another adventure seeker by the name of James McClatchy. McClatchy was born in 1824 and immigrated to New York from Ireland at an early age. Like virtually all of the young men who came to California in 1849, McClatchy tried gold mining with little success. He then returned to his chosen profession of journalism. Before traveling to California, McClatchy worked for newspaper publisher Horace Greeley and would go on to write articles for the New York Tribune from California.[18]

In California, McClatchy settled in as the city editor for the Daily Bee in 1857. In 1863 he would defeat Bugbey for the Republican nomination for Sacramento County Sheriff. This ended McClatchy's position as editor-in-chief of the Daily Bee and Bugbey's position as sheriff. McClatchy would go on to win the office of sheriff and spark minor squabbles with Bugbey over the collection of taxes. At that time, the sheriff was also the ex-officio tax collector for local, county and state taxes.

After his stint as sheriff, McClatchy moved briefly to San Francisco but returned shortly to purchase an interest in the Daily Bee. He was one of the founding members of the Association of California Pioneers, of which Bugbey was also a member. McClatchy was also a member of the Land Reform Club of New York, along with Horace Greeley before he came to California. He carried his philosophy of progressive policies to keep public land within the reach of settlers and away from the monopolizing influence of large corporations with him to California.[19]

Benjamin Norton Bugbey

McClatchy and Bugbey would become members of several of the same organizations and would be involved in many political and philanthropic causes together. But it was an uneasy friendship. Bugbey would often complain that the Daily Bee was distorting the truth of some of his business dealings.

James McClatchy died in 1883. Bugbey would go on to echo some of McClatchy's philosophy of land reform in later years, when Bugbey ran as an independent candidate for sheriff in 1894.

Return from Connecticut

Word eventually reached Bugbey that his father had died in fall of 1849. He returned to Connecticut to pay his respects to his father in 1851.

On June 23, 1852, Bugbey, with his new bride, Mary Jane Wells, stepped off the steamer Columbia at San Francisco. Their first ship from the East Coast had landed them in Panama. After crossing over the isthmus, they boarded the Columbia in Panama City and set sail again on June 4th. The steamer made a brief stop in Acapulco and then headed to San Francisco with over 100 passengers bound for the Golden State.[20] Bugbey's second arrival in California was just over three years from when he first set foot in California in 1849.

Upon his return to California in 1852, he brought with him two things. First were his connections to East Coast goods, and second was Mary Jane Wells, his new wife.[21] Bugbey's days as a full-time placer miner were over. With a new bride he set out to engage in business that would provide a proper home for him and Mary Jane. He tried his hand at hotel management, eventually purchasing the Monte Cristo Hotel on the Coloma Road 18 miles east of Sacramento in 1852.[22]

The hotel business seemed not to be Bugbey's calling, and he opened up a furniture store on the corner of 5th and K Streets in Sacramento in April of 1853.[23] He advertised it as a Furniture & Upholstery Wareroom. His connections with East Coast merchants had arrived in the form of furniture and bedding.

Benjamin Norton Bugbey

Figure 1: 1853 – Furniture & Upholstery Wareroom advertisement, Fifth and K Streets, Sacramento. CDNC.

"The undersigned begs respectfully to announce to the citizens of Sacramento and vicinity, that he has just received a well selected stock of good in the above line, and being connected with some of the best houses in the Eastern markets, he offers inducements that cannot be surpassed by any place of business in the country. B. N. Bugby."[24]

In June of 1853 he would add barber and dentist chairs to the list of furniture for sale, along with cabinet and upholstery work done to order.[25]

It's curious that Bugbey had his name printed as Bugby without the 'e.' As he changed the advertisement several times during its five-month run, he could have easily corrected the spelling of his last name if it was a typesetting error, but he didn't. Perhaps he was trying to establish his name without the 'e' for other reasons. But he was referred to as Bugbey in a March 1853 story about the delegates to the local Democratic party convention.[26]

His decision in 1853 to use Bugby as his last name contributed to later references of that spelling in stories about his duties as Constable of Granite Township. Regardless of the motivations for initially dropping the e in his name, he may have wanted to re-establish the original spelling in light of the crimes of another person. Ed Bugby made the newspapers for his escape from the Jackson jail in Amador County. Edward Bugby, who had served time in the State Prison, was arrested for robbing a saloon keeper in Drytown.[27] He was also known to Sacramento law enforcement as a thief and swindler. His crimes, escape, and capture routinely made it into the local papers.[28] It was probably best that Bugbey worked to reassert the correct spelling of his name to avoid any confusion with a local thief.

Once he became Sheriff of Sacramento County most references to his last name, excluding the occasional typographical error, were correctly printed as Bugbey. Unfortunately, the incorrect spelling would reappear after he went into retirement. The way Bugbey would sign his name with cursive penmanship, the 'e' would be hard to detect in his signature. Consequently, his name in newspaper stories would be once again be Bugby.

By the end of July 1853, Bugbey discontinued advertising his furniture business. More furniture import stores were opening, and constant private sales of used furniture helped depress prices. In a thumbnail biography of Bugbey[29] published in 1901, the reasons given for the closure of the store were the numerous fires and floods that plagued early Sacramento, and increased competition in the Sacramento market for such goods. However, 1853 was a relatively calm period in the city's history in relation to floods and fires, so most likely it was the growing competition that hastened the demise of the business.

Gold River Farming

As the furniture business withered, Bugbey decided to return to his father's occupation and become a farmer. He found a plot of land between Salisbury Station and the American River 16 miles east of Sacramento [approximately where the community of Gold River in Rancho Cordova is today, at the foot of the Fair Oaks Bridge]. The farm was north of the Coloma Road, nine miles to the west of Negro Bar.[30] Fresh vegetables were in higher demand than furniture, and they had a larger market. Crop prices were still relatively high, as production farming was still in its infancy in the 1850s.

Bugbey went into the farming business with his wife and partner T. H. Houghtaling. They purchased the property in 1853 or 1854. The Bugbey's farm, originally part of the Rancho Rio de Los Americanos land grant to William Alexander Leidesdorff, Jr., had not been officially surveyed. Sacramento County Sheriff William S. White, who sold the land at public auction, entered the property description using the metes and bounds property system.

At a stake on the bank of the American River about sixteen miles from Sacramento City and nearly opposite the sixteen mile house on the Coloma Road, from which stake a white oak tree about six inches in diameter bears east by compass and eight units distance running thence south forty° east forty chains to a stake. Thence north forty-nine° east forty-one chains and thirty-five links to a stake on the bank of the American River. Thence along the bank of said river with its meandering to the place of beginning, being the south east quarter of section thirteen, township four together with certain other real estate...[31] - Sacramento County Deed book document 18571218, pages 148 and 159, 1857, B. N. Bugby

From the landmarks of Coloma Road, Sixteen Mile House, Salisbury Station, and distance from Sacramento, Bugbey's farming operation would be in the vicinity of today's Gold River in Rancho Cordova. This would have put it within the Rancho Rio de Los Americanos land grant. Mexican land grants were not originally included in the government land surveying system. It's unclear why the description lists section 13 of township four. Township 4 of the Mount Diablo base meridian would have put the property 24 miles to the south. But the description clearly states the property was on the American River. A map of the Rancho Rio de Los Americanos[32] land grant drawn in 1857 does indicate the general location of Bugbey's first foray into farming in California.

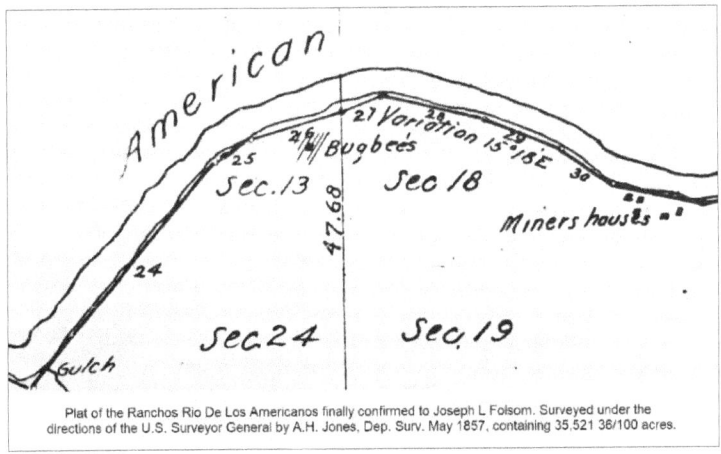

Figure 2: 1857 - Map indicating Bugbey's farm along the American River. U. C Davis G4363, S26-465,1857, U61, No. 3

Leidesdorff had received the Rancho Rio de Los Americanos land grant from the Mexican government in 1844. It was approximately 35,500 acres, with the northern boundary being the American River. The land grant also extended east to encompass what would become the city of Folsom. Leidesdorff died on May 18, 1848, just as the Gold Rush was getting underway.

The greatest restriction on successful farming in the Central Valley in the 1850s was access to water during the growing season. Below Negro Bar, south of the American River, the foothills and bluffs give way to a more level landscape. In some places along the river, the bank might only have been 3 or 4 feet above the water line. Depending on the topography, it was possible to cut a ditch from the river to divert water for farming. This had already been done in several places along the American River. John Sutter powered a grist mill on the south side of the American River by digging a trench that powered a water wheel. Afterward, the water was returned to the river.[33] Bugbey had some experience with cutting water canals along the river. He was involved with a mill race to a flour mill on the north side of the American River in 1852.[34] He and his partner most likely fashioned some sort of system to divert water from the river and onto their farm.

Bugbey's farm was not too far from a little stage coach stop called Salisbury Station, later to become a stop on the Sacramento Valley Railroad line. On his new California farming adventure, he grew vegetables. He could either cart his produce to Sacramento or up to Negro Bar and sell vegetables to the miners.

Bugbey's location at Salisbury Station allowed him to watch as the new Sacramento Valley Railroad (SVRR) was being built between Sacramento and the bluff above Negro Bar. He had read that the man who engineered the path for the Sacramento Valley Railroad, Theodore Judah, had also been hired by Captain Folsom, now the owner of the Leidesdorff Land Grant (Rancho Rio de Los Americanos), to lay out a new town above the American River. The proposed town of Granite City would be a station stop for the SVRR as it crossed the American River and travelled north to Marysville.

Folsom Roots

After Leidesdorff died in 1848, Captain Joseph Libby Folsom stepped in. Captain Folsom, who was stationed in the San Francisco region, was familiar with Leidesdorff's Rancho Rio de Los Americanos and set about to acquire it. There was much controversy and litigation over the acquisition of the Leidesdorff property by Folsom. In 1854 Folsom hired Theodore Judah, who had been brought out west to engineer a railroad from Sacramento up to the gold mining regions near Negro Bar, to design a town at the eastern edge of the Rancho Rio de Los Americanos land grant. Folsom was an officer of the Sacramento Valley Railroad, so he was familiar with its proposed route and economic potential for the region. The town Judah laid out was named Granite City and was perched on the bluffs above Negro Bar and the American River.

On July 19, 1855, Joseph Folsom died at Mission San Jose. In February 1856, the executors of Folsom's estate, Halleck, Peachy, and Van Winkle, changed the name of Granite City to Folsom.[35] It was also in February of 1856 that the Sacramento Valley Railroad made its first run from Sacramento to the new town of Folsom. Before the completion of the SVRR out to Folsom, the executors of Folsom's estate had already started selling lots in the town that Theodore Judah had helped design.

It wasn't too hard to figure out that this new town of Folsom would become a real business center. The railroad would be bringing people and goods up from Sacramento to the mines or to catch stage coaches east. Even though the placer mining was waning by the mid-1850s, hard rock mining and other activities were beginning to take root in the Sierra foothills. Bugbey decided to stake his future in the emerging town of Folsom by purchasing some lots[36] and building the first frame house there in February 1856.[37]

The auction of the Folsom lots was held on January 16, 1856, at the offices of J. B. Starr, Esq., on Front Street in Sacramento. The terms of the sale were one half cash, and one half in 90 days, with interest at the rate of one percent per month until maturity, and after maturity an interest rate of two percent monthly until paid. High bidders for the lots could also pay the full amount for the lot on that day.[38]

Bugbey made sure he was at that auction. He was the high bidder for lots 3 & 4 in Block 40, and lots 1 through 8 in Block 44. Bugbey's winning bid for all the property was $43.[39] With the purchase of lots in the new town of Folsom, Bugbey was setting his path to return to the California mining region he fell in love with when he first came west to mine for gold.

The move to Folsom was not entirely voluntary. The farming business the Bugbey's and partner T. W. Houghtaling entered together faltered, and the returns did not meet the partners' obligations. In 1855 they were sued by Robert Allen for $560. Judgment was rendered in August 1856 that the property they owned was to be sold to satisfy the debt.[40]

In any event, Bugbey's first farming experiment was not a total success compared to later endeavors. He and Mary Jane were now headed to the hills above the American River, the site of his first California mining venture.

The Folsom lot purchases in 1856 were not random. The lots in Block 40, on the western end of Sutter Street, were on the site where Bugbey had worked a drift mine in 1850[41] before departing for Connecticut. Over the next several years in the late 1850s, Bugbey would buy and sell various lots, all revolving around mining the bluff above Negro Bar. In one transaction, he sold 12 lots on Figueroa, Sutter, and Leidesdorff Streets for $4,000 in February 1857.[42]

Bugbey, acting almost as the sort of land speculator that he would come to detest later in life, would purchase lots at steep discounts from other men. In August 1859, Bugbey bought the mining rights for lots 1 – 8 in block 40 from James Jenkins, Henry

Benjamin Norton Bugbey

Middendorf, and William McLaughlin for $120[43]. The deed very specifically applied to drift mining under the new town of Folsom.

> ...three feet in width on the outside of the fence now enclosing said lots also a passage way from said lots to the brow of the bank fronting on Negro Bar. For tunneling mining or any other purpose at a point to be chosen by said party of the second part under or above ground, granting the said party of the second part full permission to work in the tunnel of the parties of the first part himself or by proxy and take from thence material sufficient to fill up certain excavations made by said parties of the first part do hereby agree to in no wise interfere or cause any other person so to do with the above described premises under penalty of forfeiting the full value of the land and improvements. The above described premises being a portion of the mining claim belonging unto the said parties of the first part.[44] – Sacramento County Land Deeds Document 18570202, page 104, February 2, 1857

As an illustration of how small the community of Folsom was at the time, in June 1859 Bugbey bought out the interest of P. R. Young in the mining claim on lots 1 through 8 in Block 40.[45] P. R. Young was the Justice of the Peace in Granite Township and would later attest to the real estate transaction between Bugbey and the other men for the same lots.[46]

The bluff and hills above Negro Bar on the American River were not deserted. There were approximately 200 structures dotting the hills, most being the cabins of squatters. The town lots had been auctioned off from as low as $1 up to $400. With the arrival of the railroad, the lots had jumped in value from $55 to $4,500.[47] The '49er philosophy of land and mining claims still prevailed amongst the mining population - a way of life in which you pitched your tent and laid claim to the public land that most suited your interest at will.

Increasingly, the transient mining population in Folsom was coming into conflict with organized government, just as it had in Sacramento with the settlers' riots years earlier. Without good law enforcement, there were bound to be serious conflicts. Just as the Native Americans had been pushed off the land, now the gold miners, most of whom were just barely squeezing out a living, were being forced off the ground they had been calling home.

Bugbey saw the conflicts and he witnessed the robberies of local miners by gangs of men roaming the foothill region. He also saw an opportunity to move from farming vegetables to law enforcement. With a young wife and new house, the steady paycheck of a law enforcement officer would be welcome. Folsom was situated in Granite Township. Townships were unincorporated areas within Sacramento

County. Each township elected its own constable for local law enforcement at the time.

In October 1856 the Board of Supervisors created Granite Township, which was formerly part of Mississippi Township.[48] (These townships were not the same as the federal Public Land Survey System of townships and ranges that was used to map land and sold to settlers). The new township was bounded by the American River to the north, Natoma Township to the east, Lee Township on the south and Brighton Township on the west. The principal urban areas were Alder Creek, Folsom and Salisbury Station. It contained over 22 square miles of territory.

The primary purpose of the townships was local law enforcement, with an elected Constable and Justice of the Peace to handle as many judicial matters locally as possible. Townships were also election precincts and used by the political parties at the county level as representative districts for delegates to conventions.

In November of 1856, Bugbey ran for, and won, the election for Granite Township Constable, with 401 votes out of 1,304 cast. His nearest competitor was William Moody, who received 296 votes.[49] With this modest electoral victory, Bugbey would weave his life in and out of politics and law enforcement for the better part of his life in Sacramento.

If Bugbey considered himself a California '49er first, he thought of himself as a Folsom pioneer second. He identified his residence more with Folsom than any other place he lived. When he was elected Sacramento County Sheriff, he kept his primary residence in Folsom. When his Natoma Vineyard was thriving in El Dorado County, where he had built two other homes, he still called Folsom home. It was only in the bitter depths of financial and personal hardship that he would leave the Folsom region that had crystalized his dreams of gold mining and becoming a Californian.

---

[1] Haskins, C. W., *The Argonauts of California, Being The Reminiscences of Scenes and Incidents that Occurred in California in early mining days by a Pioneer.* (Fords, Howard & Hulbert, New York, 1890).

[2] *A Volume of Memoirs and Genealogy of Representative Citizens of Northern California Including Biographies of Many of Those Who Have Passed Away*, (Chicago Standard Genealogical Publishing Company 1901).

[3] Pioneer Valley History Network, *Western Massachusetts Pioneers Spreadsheet*

https://pioneervalleyhistorynetwork.org/project/gold-rush-stories/

[4] Haskins, C. W., *The Argonauts of California, Being The Reminiscences of Scenes and Incidents that Occurred in California in early mining days by a Pioneer.* (Fords, Howard & Hulbert, New York, 1890).

[5] Passenger list of John Castner transcribed from handwritten entry: Capt. Somers, Capt. Harding, F. E. Foot, B. F. Barker, J. Hedges Jr., J. M. Folwer, Chas. Briggs, L. Grover,

Hy. Arnold, B. A. Baggby [B. N. Bugbey], D. Sizer, D. W. Sinclair, Dl. Houghton, E. W. Burke, D. B. Clapp, H. C. Pitman, Dr. F. K Robertson, Geo. Craven, A. H. Dodge, Wm. P. Adams, At Stone, A. Green, W. A. Dunbar, R. W. Whitmore, Ira Holten, J. D. Smith, S. S. Warner, T. H. Brown, Hy. Stanford, J. J. Mitchell, Hy. Wilson, T. Shepard, Israel Luce, S. S. Clark, R. H. Brown, S. S. Brooks, J. P. Newland, S. L. Hunz, P. McFarland, H. J. Kercher, Moses Searls, G. P. Duncan, A. B. Clark, F. F. Hunt, Rt. Lucky, J. Doherty, J. Cameron, M. B. Fondo, J. S. Manard, Ed. Manard, P. Herron, A. Terry, P. Monk, N. B. Morris, Dr. Lutteroth, N. C. Nichols, J. A. Minel, J. H. Holles, M. Levy, Dr. Taylor, Wm. Reynolds, J. O. Phelps, M. Chole, D. S. Glass, J. B. Pons, H. Darling, E. Loverich, J. H. Richards, L. T. Coggswell, W. Mason, Wm. Bennett, N. Newhouse, B. Buckingham, C. Brown, Jas. McClochy [James McClatchy], F. Crocket, W. S. Slocum, W. M. Kurtz, Ed. Jeffreyes, J. C. Briggs, James Schofield, N. C. Nichols, S. Cauldwell, N. Morehouse, John Smith, W. A. Handson. From – "Name Index of the California Pioneers, Members of the Overland Companies and Ship Passenger Lists" given in C. W. Haskins, *The Argonauts of California, Being The Reminiscences of Scenes and Incidents that Occurred in California in early mining days by a Pioneer.* (Fords, Howard & Hulbert, New York, 1890). California Chapter Daughters of the American Revolution, San Francisco, 1958.

[6] Clarke, Asa Bement, *Travels in Mexico and California: Comprising a Journal of a Tour from Brazos Santiago, through Central Mexico, by way of Monterey, Chihuahua, the Country of the Apaches, and the River Gila, to the Mining Districts of California,* (Boston: Wright & Hasty, Printers, 1852).

[7] Ibid.

[8] Ibid.

[9] Ibid.

[10] Ibid.

[11] *A Volume of Memoirs and Genealogy of Representative Citizens of Northern California Including Biographies of Many of Those Who Have Passed Away,* (Chicago Standard Genealogical Publishing Company 1901).

[12] Clarke, Asa Bement, *Travels in Mexico and California: Comprising a Journal of a Tour from Brazos Santiago, through Central Mexico, by way of Monterey, Chihuahua, the Country of the Apaches, and the River Gila, to the Mining Districts of California,* (Boston: Wright & Hasty, Printers, 1852).

[13] Haskins, C. W., *The Argonauts of California, Being The Reminiscences of Scenes and Incidents that Occurred in California in early mining days by a Pioneer.* (Fords, Howard & Hulbert, New York, 1890).

[14] Sacramento Daily Union, Volume 96, Number 52, 12 October 1898, CDNC

[15] Sacramento Transcript, Volume 2, Number 47, 18 December 1850, CDNC

[16] Minerals Yearbook, *Inyo Mountains, Inyo County, California – the Inyo Marble Company Marble Quarry (Marble)*, United States Bureau of Mines, Geological Survey (U.S.) 1886, "Structural Materials - Pacific Coast," pp. 545. http://quarriesandbeyond.org/states/ca/quarry_photo/ca-inyo_photos_2.html

[17] Sacramento Daily Union, Volume 96, Number 52, 12 October 1898, CDNC

[18] Sacramento Daily Union, Volume 18, Number 56, 26 October 1883, CDNC

[19] Ibid.

[20] Rasmussen, Louis J., *San Francisco Ship Passenger Lists, Volume IV, June 17, 1852 to*

Benjamin Norton Bugbey

January 6, 1853. California State Library

Ship: Columbia. Type: Steamer. From: Panama. Arrived: June 23, 1852. Captain: William L. Dall. Passage: 17 days from Panama, via Acapulco, Mexico. Left Panama on June 4th, 1852, at 11:00 PM with part of the mails and passengers brought to Aspinwall by the Illinois. On June 12, 1852, at 12M., passed steamship Independence, 20 miles south of Acapulco, Mexico, found considerable excitement at Acapulco in consequence of the American Consul having struck his flag, having been thrown into prison by the authorities. June 13th, at 6:00AM, left Acapulco. Same day at noon, George McGregor, a seaman belonging to the ship, fell overboard and was drowned. Lieut. ____Stevens, of the Coast Survey, and Mr. ____Lecount, of Cook and Lecount are on board. Cargo 113 packages of unspecified merchandise and 4 packages of segars.

[21] Ibid.

[22] *A Volume of Memoirs and Genealogy of Representative Citizens of Northern California Including Biographies of Many of Those Who Have Passed Away*, (Chicago Standard Genealogical Publishing Company 1901).

[23] Sacramento Daily Union, Volume 88, Number 52, 20 October 1894, CDNC

[24] Sacramento Daily Union, Volume 5, Number 622, 22 March 1853, CDNC

[25] Sacramento Daily Union, Volume 5, Number 699, 20 June 1853, CDNC

[26] Sacramento Daily Union, Volume 4, Number 616, 15 March 1853, CDNC

[27] Sacramento Daily Union, Volume 9, Number 1397, 17 September 1855, CDNC

[28] Sacramento Daily Union, Volume 9, Number 1398, 18 September 1855, CDNC

[29] *A Volume of Memoirs and Genealogy of Representative Citizens of Northern California Including Biographies of Many of Those Who Have Passed Away*, (Chicago Standard Genealogical Publishing Company 1901).

[30] Ibid.

[31] Sacramento County Deed Book 18571218, pages 148 and 159, 1857. *Chain is a unit of measure 66 feet long and comprised off 100 links. 80 chains equal one mile.

[32] *Plat of the Rancho Rio De Las Americanos finally confirmed to Joseph L. Folsom, U. S. Surveyor General by A. H. Jones, Dep. Surveyor, May 1857*. U. C Davis G4363, S26-465,1857, U61, No. 3

[33] Stapp, Cheryl Anne, *Before The Gold Rush, The Sinclairs of Rancho Del Paso 1840 – 1849*. (Cheryl Anne Stapp 2017)

[34] *A Volume of Memoirs and Genealogy of Representative Citizens of Northern California Including Biographies of Many of Those Who Have Passed Away*, (Chicago Standard Genealogical Publishing Company 1901).

[35] Folsom Historical Society, Images of America Folsom California. (Arcadia Publishing 2004).

[36] Sacramento County Deed Book 18580719, pages 361, 362, 16 January 1856.

[37] Sacramento Daily Union, Volume 88, Number 52, 20 October 1894, CDNC

[38] Sacramento Daily Union, Volume 10, Number 1488, 1 January 1856, CDNC

[39] Sacramento County Deed Book 18580719, pages 361, 362, January 16, 1856.

[40] Sacramento County Deed Book document 18571218, pages 148, 149, August 13, 1856.

Benjamin Norton Bugbey

[41] *The People of the State of California vs The Gold Run Ditch and Mining Company, In the Superior Court of the State of California, in and for the County of Sacramento*, testimony of B. N. Bugbey, December 9th and 10th, 1881, Sacramento, Ca, California State Archives microfilm MF2:9 (46) Roll 4, Pages 4558 – 4599

[42] Sacramento County Deed Book 18570202, page 104, February 2, 1857

[43] Sacramento County Deed Book 18590811, pages 348, 349, and 350, August 11, 1859

[44] Ibid.

[45] Sacramento County Deed Book 18590618 page 169, June 13, 1859.

[46] Sacramento County Deed Book 18590811, pages 348, 349, and 350, August 11, 1859

[47] Daily Alta California, Volume 7, Number 35, 5 February 1856, CDNC

[48] Davis, Win. J., *An Illustrated History of Sacramento County, California*, (The Lewis Publishing Company, Chicago, 1890).

[49] Sacramento Daily Union, Volume 12, Number 1757, November 12, 1856, CDNC

Chapter 3: The Legend of Lawman Bugbey 1856 - 1861

Benjamin Bugbey was not an imposing man. He stood 5 feet and 8 inches tall[1]. In 1856, when he was elected the first Granite Township Constable, he was just 29 years old. His hair was already starting to thin on top, but he could sport a full beard. He had blue eyes and a clear voice full of conviction. Upon his return to Sacramento, he was still looking for his career path. He didn't have huge ambitions and was not driven by greed. He was looking for an occupation that would make for a comfortable living in the new town of Folsom.

With his election as constable, the very modest wages the position paid would allow him to dabble in real estate and mining on the side. While Bugbey was active in local politics, he had never expressed, at least by his actions, any particular desire to enter into law enforcement. When the squatters' riots broke out in Sacramento in the winter of 1850, he had already left the city to return to the mines. However, he undoubtedly heard of the chaos and deaths in Sacramento as a result of the confrontation between squatters in the city and the property owners.

At first glance, the newly created town of Folsom would seem to have been on the same path of confrontation. The rolling foothills above Negro Bar were dotted with mining camps and shacks. Suddenly, imaginary lines were drawn in the form of a city grid. The lots were sold to the highest bidder, irrespective of the claims of any miner who might happen to be calling that patch of land home. In order for Folsom to grow and thrive, the squatters had to be pushed off so the new owners could build homes and businesses.

Bugbey had invested in the new shining city on the hill. Perhaps he saw an inevitable clash between squatters and new lot owners on the horizon. Becoming Constable of Granite Township might have been his attempt to help keep peace and let the new town thrive. Bugbey was himself a bridge between the placer gold mining of the past and the suburban town lot living of the present.

Whatever the reason, Folsom never had the riots between squatters and land owners that Sacramento did. But it had its own brand of lawlessness instigated by men who were no longer earning a living from mining. Small gangs of men who robbed other miners had long been a problem in the gold fields. Now this new township of Granite had a man dedicated to eradicating burglaries and highway robbery.

As new homes and businesses sprang up, thieves took advantage of the new dwellings. Bugbey was not immune to the criminal acts. After tracking down a house thief in Alder, Bugbey found property that had been stolen from his wife, Mary Jane, in the man's possession.[2]

In 1857 the town of Folsom was full of activity, sounds and smells. New little frame homes were being built. There was the sound of hand saws and men pounding nails. The American River could be heard coursing over granite outcroppings below the town. There was the sound of miners down by the water and possibly next door to a home that was being built. The gold mines were immigration central for people all over the world. It would not have been uncommon to hear different dialects and languages from Asia and Europe while hiking over the hills of this growing little community.

Horse-drawn wagons and stagecoaches clattered through town. Then there was the "steam horse" that was helping Folsom grow; the cars and locomotives of the Sacramento Valley Railroad could be heard rolling on the rails and blowing their steam whistles. There was the ever-present fog of wood smoke from the train, homes and restaurants, along with the smell of food cooking in the air.

It must have been quite a mixing bowl of sounds, smells, energy, and people that Bugbey woke up to every morning. He, like so many other men and women in town, was a worker. In order to survive, one had to work. Since coming to California in 1849, Bugbey had diligently pursued whatever activity he was engaged in. First it was mining, then running a trading outpost, then back to mining. He managed hotels, sold furniture, and grew vegetables on a farm. He had worked at all of these different occupations over the course of seven years since of coming to Sacramento.

Constable B. N. Bugbey

His latest endeavor as Constable of Granite Township would occupy a good portion of his time. Even though Granite Township had been cleaved from the much larger Mississippi Township in 1856, it was still a large tract of land to patrol. It drew its name in part from the large granite outcroppings along the American River, and for Granite City that was rechristened Folsom. The American River was the northern and partial western boundary of the township. It then encompassed land 8 miles to the south and then to the west to Salisbury Station.[3] Granite Township was over 22 square miles[4] of mostly open prairie. The main towns were Folsom, Alder Creek, Salisbury's Station, and Prairie City.

The office of Constable was similar to being a Sheriff's Deputy, with a defined territory to service. The Constable was empowered to arrest people, bring them before the Justice of the Peace, escort people accused of crimes to the main jail, and serve summons issued by local courts. Even though Granite Township did not have nearly the population of Sacramento City, Bugbey was nonetheless kept busy. He had no deputies to help him. There were plenty of demands on Bugbey's time for law enforcement and court services.

If Bugbey exhibited any partiality to the ethnicity of a man under suspicion of committing a crime, it was not reported in the local papers. He arrested men who were white, black, Hispanic, and Chinese during his tenure as Constable. There were arrests for stealing horses and saddles, residing in a house of ill-fame, gambling, maliciously shooting an ox, burglary, counterfeit silver coins, drunken brawls, knife attacks and murder. Bugbey also learned how to use his pistol. When attempting to arrest an escaped convict, the man started to withdraw a revolver from his pants pocket. Bugbey was quicker and shot the man in the shoulder.[5]

A few of Bugbey's law enforcement activities made it into the local newspapers.

- 1856 Served a summons to E. Anthony.[6]
- 1857 Escorted accused horse thief to the Sacramento jail.[7]
- 1857 Arrested a Chinese man for burglary.[8]
- 1857 Arrested three Chinese for residing in a house of ill-fame.[9]
- 1857 Arrested Chinese a man for illegal gaming.[10]
- 1857 Arrested a man for malicious mischief in shooting an ox.[11]
- 1857 Tracked down a house thief in Alder Creek.[12]
- 1859 Arrested a man for stealing 16 cows and attempting to sell them for $300 and a gold watch
- 1860 Arrested a man for murder.[13]
- 1860 Shot an escaped convict in the shoulder who was attempting draw his own pistol on Bugbey.[14]
- 1860 Involved in the apprehension of a man passing counterfeit silver coins.[15]
- 1860 Arrested a man accused of stealing saddles from Henry & Gage in Placerville.[16]
- 1860 Arrested a Chinese man accused of a knife attack on a fellow Chinese immigrant.[17]

He also oversaw the arrest of many men involved in drunken brawls, knife fights, and murders in Granite Township.

Wild West Round Up of Folsom Robbers

Bugbey's reputation as a tenacious lawman was secured with the apprehension of several outlaws. It was a series of events worthy of a screenplay for a Hollywood movie about the Wild West. There was the young constable, outgunned by a gang of highway robbers in a growing 1850s gold rush town, a secret plan to bring in extra lawmen, deputies slipping into town incognito on the railroad, the surprise arrest, daring escape, and finally a shootout in the hills above Folsom. The capture of a notorious gang of thieves would help propel Bugbey to be elected Sheriff of Sacramento County.

Even though the heady days of the placer gold rush were over, Folsom was a town that was thriving with the arrival of the Sacramento Valley Railroad. While some men, many of them immigrants, continued the arduous task of separating gold from dirt, usually for as little as 50 cents a day, other men found work driving wagons, in construction, or on the railroad. Still others, preferring a more carefree lifestyle, supplemented their incomes with robbing miners and merchants who were making an honest living. Since there was strength in numbers, many of the robbers formed loose associations or gangs.

These gangs preyed on the Chinese and other immigrants, vulnerable because of their lack of language skills and aversion to reporting crimes lest they be asked to leave their shacks or cabins. Since these immigrant miners typically were not living in town, but usually staying in a tent or shack next to their mining claims along the river or tributaries, they were isolated and easy targets for criminals. However, Mr. Meyers, who had come over from France to mine in California, did report a burglary: A gang of men broke into his miners' shack on Mississippi Bar and stole $180 in gold.[18] Another tactic of the thieves was to rob miners and merchants along the roads between Folsom and the mining areas.

Along the American River, just north of Folsom, the canyon gets very steep and narrow. People traveling along the river between Folsom and communities such as Mormon Island or McDowell Hill on the South Fork of the American River would climb out of the river canyon where it was intersected by a ravine that emptied an ephemeral creek into the river. The ravine was wooded and narrow with many good hiding spots. It became a favorite place for gangs of thieves to intercept travelers and acquire their valuable possessions. After so many robberies of travelers along this road in the ravine, it became known as Robber's Ravine.

Two of the outlaws were Tom Bell and Bill Scott, who each led separate groups of men in committing these highway or trail robberies.[19]

The loose knit gangs, each numbering about a dozen men, were robbing miners and stealing from cabins throughout Granite Township. By himself, Bugbey couldn't round up all the men to face charges. If he were to arrest each man associated with the gangs one by one over several weeks, other members of the gang would undoubtedly be tipped off, and they would evaporate. The best way to clean up the

Benjamin Norton Bugbey

scourge of criminal conduct plaguing the area was to have a coordinated plan with other deputies.

The major hurdle was getting authorization for Sacramento Sheriff's deputies to work with him. The only ways to make the 22-mile trip from Folsom to Sacramento were on horseback, in a buggy, or on the train. Even though the train trip from Sacramento only took an hour, it still cost money. Bugbey had to gain the cooperation of the County Sheriff to let him work with some of the deputies who were primarily assigned to patrol the City of Sacramento. The goal was to apprehend as many of the gang members over a short, two- to three-day time frame, so that word of the coordinated round up would have less chance to circulate among the thieves.

Bugbey recruited Sheriff Deputies Daniel Gay and Charles O'Neil in his plan. On a warm July day in 1857, Bugbey and his cohorts put their dragnet for criminals into action. It was a Wednesday evening when Gay and O'Neil traveled up to Folsom in the baggage car of the SVRR train to hide their arrival. They all dressed down so as not to alert people they were officers. The night was uneventful, as they did not encounter any of the gang members. The next morning, while scouting across the rolling dry foothills around Folsom for one of the gang members, Frank Ewing, officers Gay and O'Neil encountered another escaped state convict by the name of Ned Waldo. Gay drew his revolver, and Waldo acquiesced and was taken into custody without incident.[20]

Continuing, Gay and O'Neil found Frank Ewing's house, but Ewing ran out the back door, jumped into the American River, and swam to the other side, which was El Dorado County. They decided not to pursue Ewing but instead marched Waldo back to Folsom. Both deputies and prisoner got onboard the train back to Sacramento to deposit Waldo in the jail. But the work was not finished.

Deputy O'Neil got off the train at the Alder Creek Station and returned to Folsom on the next train, leaving Gay to continue on to Sacramento with his prisoner. That evening, having turned Waldo over to the jailers, Gay returned to Folsom via horse and buggy arriving about 8 o'clock.[21]

As Gay arrived back in Folsom, O'Neil and Bugbey succeeded in arresting Mountain Scott and A. Clark while the pair were in a store buying boots. Gay and Bugbey then visited a local dance hall, where they arrested Jack P. O'Hara and Limers Weed. The suspects were taken back to the Temperance house where O'Neil had assumed the duties of temporary jailer for the growing number of apprehended gang members.[22]

The team of lawmen got word that two other gang members were at a dance hall in Sacramento. O'Neil stayed with the prisoners while Bugbey and Gay travelled by train to Sacramento. There the duo found and arrested John Wright, manager of a dance hall on L Street, between 3rd and 4th streets, and J. W. Gafford. The arrest was made near daybreak on Friday morning as the festivities of the dance hall were winding down. Bugbey and Gay then stopped by the jail to pick up Waldo and took all three men back to Folsom.[23]

Seven prisoners were brought before Justice of the Peace Scofield of Granite Township. The charges related to the robbing of the French man by the name of Meyers, who was mining at Mississippi Bar on the American River.[24] As the arraignment of seven individuals is quite a show in a little town, it attracted a lot attention from the locals. One man who came to watch the proceedings was Charles Hamilton, who happened to be one of the gang members. Officer O'Neil, who was in attendance, offered Mr. Hamilton a seat, which he gladly accepted. When the proceeding concluded, and as Mr. Hamilton was preparing to leave, Officer O'Neil placed the handcuffs on him.[25]

With all the prisoners taken to the Sacramento jail, Officer Gay returned to Folsom on the Friday afternoon train. O'Neil was to telegraph the lawmen up in Folsom if he learned of any news about the remaining gang members. On Saturday morning, Gay and Bugbey arrested two men by the names of Jackson and Henry Berry, who kept a den near Robber's Ravine.[26]

After being arrested, Jackson wanted to get his coat from his house. Gay and Bugbey accompanied him to the house, where his wife was cooking dinner. Jackson then requested that he be allowed to eat, since he had no food all day. The two lawmen agreed to the request. When Jackson was done with dinner, he hugged his wife and bolted out the back door, lawmen in pursuit. Gay ran out the front door to intercept the fugitive. Jackson presented a pistol in the direction of Gay. Bugbey fired his pistol three times at Jackson, who was not hit. Gay's gun misfired twice.[27]

Jackson continued to run through the chaparral into a wooded area. He stopped and took aim at Bugbey. Gay stopped, set, and pulled the trigger, and the gun successfully fired, hitting Jackson in the leg below the knee.[28]

Jackson tumbled down, and the lawmen rushed over to him, assuming him incapacitated. As they neared the downed man, Jackson reared up, pointed his gun at Gay and fired. Even though the officer had been working for the past four days straight, weary from all the arrests and travel, he was able to quickly react and move behind a tree.[29] As both Bugbey and Gay had their pistols trained on Jackson, and he was in terrible pain from a shattered leg, he threw his weapon aside and surrendered upon the commands of the officers.

Gay bound up the badly bleeding leg of Jackson. They procured a buggy and arrived back in Sacramento around 5 o'clock with both prisoners. At 11 o'clock that night, O'Neil arrested another of

Benjamin Norton Bugbey

the gang members, Joe Burrows, at a house on the alley between M and N Streets, east of 2nd Street.[30]

Within a period of four days, the three officers arrested eleven felons and only lost one to escape. Bugbey was widely praised for organizing the successful plan. Gay and O'Neil were praised for their efforts but had their pay docked by the Council for being out of Sacramento City.[31] No good deed goes unpunished.

While Bugbey was credited with eliminating some of the less desirable elements of the Wild West in and around Folsom, he was also acknowledged for his integrity and adherence to the rule of law and due process afforded accused criminals under the constitution. One of the examples reported in the local newspapers centered on a murder in Brighton Township. William Price and Robert Poole were working at the ranch of Frank Favor. In an earlier altercation, Poole felt that Price had insulted one of his friends and chided Price over the incident. Poole also indicated that if he had a gun Price would not be alive. Even though Price, a young man of 22[32], apologized, Poole ordered Price to leave the ranch, or he would kill him.

Price then offered Poole a pistol for an impromptu duel. Poole refused to duel but continued his admonitions that Price leave the ranch within one hour in an aggressive manner. Price snapped, drew one of his guns and fired at Poole. More gunshots ensued, until Poole fell to the ground with a fatal gunshot. A fellow ranch hand who witnessed the altercation and fatal shots advised Price to leave immediately. Price was last seen fleeing toward Folsom.[33]

Five days later, in mid-August, Price was captured above Placerville. El Dorado County authorities turned Price over to Constable Bugbey, who presented him to the Justice of the Peace in Brighton Township. The return of Price to the neighborhood of the crime incited many of the local residents. There was an attempt to organize a vigilante group of residents to wrest control of Price from Bugbey so they could lynch Price on the spot. The Sacramento Union noted it was the "boldness and firmness of Officer Bugbey," along with the presence of Officer McClory and Coroner Murray, that probably quelled the attempt to lynch Price.[34]

In addition to his law enforcement duties, Bugbey was also the township's lost and found department. He advertised in the local papers about a horse that was brought to him that might have been stolen.

TAKEN UP — A SORREL HORSE, about 15 hands high, white stripe on face, branded ADS on left hip, Spanish brand on right hip, letter A on right side of neck, right hind hoof cracked ; supposed to be stolen. Inquire of B. N. BUGBEY, Constable at Folsom.[35]

Benjamin Norton Bugbey

With no administrative staff, Bugbey had to learn about bookkeeping and government bureaucracy the hard way. The auditor for Sacramento County rejected some of Bugbey's expense claims that he had submitted. Of the $224.04 for the July 1859 expense reimbursement submitted by Bugbey, the $14.40 mileage expense for searching for persons to arrest was rejected. The auditor noted there was no law to authorize payment for such services.[36] Another expense claim was rejected for Bugbey's time spent in court proceedings. The auditor noted that the Constable's Fee Bill expressly exempts payment for such court proceeding services.[37]

The tussle between Sacramento County and Bugbey over expense claims would settle into a familiar pattern over the years. Instead of just accepting how the Supervisors or auditor told him to proceed, Bugbey always seemed to push the envelope of accepted claims and expenses.

The position of Constable during that time came up for re-election annually. Bugbey was re-elected every year he ran for the office. As the country entered a period of civil war in the spring of 1861, Bugbey was nominated for Sacramento County Sheriff by the Union Democrat Party. A new chapter in Bugbey's life was about to begin.

---

[1] 1892 Sacramento County Voter Registration

[2] Sacramento Daily Union, Volume 14, Number 2079, 24 November 1857

[3] Sacramento City and County Directory for 1868, by Robert E. Draper

[4] Official Map of Sacramento County, California. Compiled by Fred. A. Shepherd, Sacramento, Cal. 1885.

[5] Sacramento Daily Union, Volume 19, Number 2919, 4 August 1860

[6] Sacramento Daily Union, Volume 12, Number 1779, 8 December 1856

[7] Sacramento Daily Union, Volume 12, Number 1836, 13 February 1857

[8] Sacramento Daily Union, Volume 12, Number 1853, 5 March 1857

[9] Sacramento Daily Union, Volume 13, Number 1890, 17 April 1857

[10] Sacramento Daily Union, Volume 13, Number 1901, 30 April 1857

[11] Sacramento Daily Union, Volume 14, Number 2028, 25 September 1857

[12] Sacramento Daily Union, Volume 14, Number 2079, 24 November 1857

[13] Sacramento Daily Union, Volume 19, Number 2824, 14 April 1860

[14] Sacramento Daily Union, Volume 19, Number 2919, 4 August 1860

[15] Sacramento Daily Union, Volume 20, Number 2966, 28 September 1860

[16] Sacramento Daily Union, Volume 19, Number 2949, 8 September 1860

[17] Daily Alta California, Volume 12, Number 3901, 18 October 1860

Benjamin Norton Bugbey

[18] Sacramento Daily Union, Volume 13, Number 1981, 1 August 1857
[19] Sacramento Union, Number 40, 10 December 1911
[20] Sacramento Daily Union, Volume 13, Number 1982, 3 August 1857
[21] Ibid.
[22] Ibid.
[23] Ibid.
[24] Sacramento Daily Union, Volume 13, Number 1981, 1 August 1857
[25] Sacramento Daily Union, Volume 13, Number 1982, 3 August 1857
[26] Ibid.
[27] Ibid.
[28] Daily Alta California, Volume 9, Number 101, 31 July 1857
[29] Ibid.
[30] Ibid.
[31] Sacramento Daily Union, Volume 13, Number 1982, 3 August 1857
[32] Sacramento Daily Union, Volume 19, Number 2928, 15 August 1860
[33] Sacramento Daily Union, Volume 19, Number 2929, 16 August 1860
[34] Sacramento Daily Union, Volume 19, Number 2932, 20 August 1860
[35] Sacramento Daily Union, Volume 21, Number 3139, 19 April 1861
[36] Sacramento Daily Union, Volume 17, Number 2588, 14 July 1859
[37] Ibid.

Benjamin Norton Bugbey

Chapter 4: Path to Sheriffalty

Politics and political parties played an important part in Bugbey's life and identity. He was active in politics from the 1850s through the early 1900s. He had very definite views on how government should operate and the nature of the Constitution. His political positions would evolve over time, as he became disgusted with party politics and witnessed some of the deficiencies of government.

After Bugbey settled in California he identified himself as more of a Northern Democrat. Since California had been admitted to the Union as a free state, the issue of slavery or black suffrage was rarely broached in local political party meetings. A central tenant of Bugbey's political philosophy revolved around individual rights, settlers' rights, and the Jeffersonian concept that a strong nation and economy began with the people who worked the land should also own the land. He also subscribed to the companion philosophy that a concentration of wealth and control in the hands of powerful corporations undermined the health of society.

One of Bugbey's first official involvements in politics was as a delegate to the Democratic County nominating convention in 1853[1]. But his participation in party politics dwindled while he was trying to earn a living farming outside of Sacramento.

Once Bugbey had established himself in Folsom and was elected the Constable of Granite Township, he had the opportunity to become active again in politics. He was not averse to voicing his opinion when he thought the system or the process was unfair. As a delegate from Granite Township at the 1857 County Democratic nominating convention, it was noted that many of nominees were from the city of Sacramento. Bugbey rose and objected to the fact that so many of the nominees were from the city. Because Granite Township had nine delegates, they were entitled to some nominations.[2] He expressed the sentiments of many of the rural delegates that if the convention did not give any nominees to the rural communities, they cannot expect the support of the rural voters. Bugbey was promptly shut down with a loud cry, "You are out of order."[3]

With the nation beginning to fracture over the question of slavery and the impending presidential election cycle, the Sacramento County Democrats appended their name to the Douglas Democrats. Bugbey was a delegate to the Douglas County Convention in September 1860, held in Sacramento.[4] The Douglas Democrat wing of the Democratic Party supported Stephen Douglas for president over Abraham Lincoln and opposed the re-election of fellow Democrat William Gwin to the United States Senate.

It was also during this period that Bugbey started to form political alliances, although they would later be shattered with Civil

War politics. He publicly supported P. J. Hopper as a candidate for Assembly[5] over E. D. Hoskins, both of whom he knew. Peter J. Hopper was a local Folsom attorney who notarized several of Bugbey's land transactions, as recorded in the Sacramento County Book of Deeds. Hopper would also become the publisher of the Folsom Telegraph newspaper.[6]

Nomination for Sheriff

With the onset of the Civil War in April of 1861, the Douglas Democrats renamed themselves the Union Democrats. This was to show solidarity for the cause of holding the Union together. The Civil War also scrambled some of the old allegiances and put more emphasis on candidates that supported the Union and not the rebellious Confederacy. The Union Democrats passed two resolutions at their June 1861 convention in Sacramento to make it clear they were for the Union:

1. That at this time, when the country is resisting with all its might, a war of invasion and distraction, indifference is impossible to the patriot, and neutrality is cowardice, If not premeditated disloyalty.

2. That the people of California in the past have been most anxious for peace throughout the land, and will hail with joy an honorable adjustment in the future; at the same time, they are, above all things, for the Union, the country, and the flag, against all assailants - no matter who they are, whence they come, or with what power armed.

The resolutions were an attempt to dispel any sympathies for or connections with the Democrats of the southern United States who had seceded from the Union.[7]

It was also at the 1861 county convention that Bugbey's nomination for County Sheriff started to gain steam. Most of his support was in the eastern part of Sacramento County where Folsom and Granite Township were located.[8]

Six men were nominated to be candidates for Sheriff: John Rooney of Brighton, John Madden, James Lansing, Sylvester Marshall, John Hunt of Sacramento, and Bugbey of Folsom. Each candidate came to the front of the convention, paid his $5 assessment to cover the costs of the convention, and made a short speech. Bugbey's speech, as those of most nominees, spoke more to party politics than to requirements of the office they were seeking.

Mr. President and gentlemen of the Convention, I appear before you as one of several candidates for the office of Sheriff of this county. If, in making your selection, you should favor me with your choice, I should work for and endeavor to secure the election of the whole ticket, and whether nominated or not, I pledge you my word of honor to support the ticket and work for the nominees of this Convention. I believe I have never been behind in working for the Democratic ticket, and I never voted any other ticket. I cheerfully concur in the resolutions which you have re-indorsed.[9] - Sacramento Daily Union, Volume 21, Number 3199, 28 June 1861

There were 122 delegates at the convention, including proxies, and the votes were evenly split between the six men. After 24 rounds of balloting, the convention adjourned for the evening to resume the consideration of the Sheriff candidate the next day.[10]

When the convention resumed the next day, there were another 26 rounds of balloting with no winner. The necessary number of votes to nominate was 61. Bugbey was consistently garnering between 30 and 34 votes per ballot, the most of any of the candidates. Rooney, who had only garnered 17 votes on the 51st ballot, decided to pull out of the contest. After the 53rd ballot, the president of the convention, Mr. Coffroth, stated that they should stop balloting. Peter Hopper objected, citing that the Republicans would take advantage of their disorganization and inability to nominate a candidate for Sheriff.[11]

The balloting continued, and on the 57th vote of the convention, Bugbey had received 53 votes. It was apparent that Bugbey was going to win, so before the 58th ballot, one of the delegates, McManus, suggested they nominate Bugbey by acclamation. The motion was put to a vote and carried unanimously.[12] At the age of 33, Benjamin Norton Bugbey was nominated to be the Union Democrat County candidate for Sacramento County Sheriff.

The Sacramento Daily Union noted the contentious battle for the Sheriff candidacy and that nominees Lansing and Marshal were instrumental in moving votes toward Bugbey. The newspaper wasn't overly enthusiastic about Bugbey's candidacy.

[Bugbey] has been a Constable for several years in Folsom and is represented by those who know him well to be a man of firmness, a good officer and a popular man. He has been somewhat noted for several years past for his large bills of costs against the county. We do not think that he is the strongest man that could have been nominated, though stronger than some whose names were before the Convention.[13]
- Sacramento Daily Union, Volume 21, Number 3201, 1 July 1861

There was little time to revel in the victory of being nominated as the Union Democratic candidate for Sheriff, as the human costs of the Civil War descended upon California. It was reported that George Bugbey, Benjamin's younger brother and a member of the First Connecticut Regiment, was killed while stationed in Vienna, Virginia.[14] Bugbey would receive word that his brother had not been killed but had suffered a near-fatal injury from being shot. Surgery recovered multiple pieces of bone fragment and resulted in George Bugbey losing the use of one arm.[15]

Settlers' Association

In addition to the two major political parties, California also had an active Settlers' Committee that acted as a political party at times. The Settlers' Committee was a derivative of the Settlers' Association formed in the summer of 1850 in opposition to land speculators in Sacramento.[16] Specifically, the Settlers' Association objected to Sacramento land being sold to speculators when John Sutter's original land grant from the Mexican government was in dispute

As the City of Sacramento was forming, numerous settlers began squatting on property within the newly laid out city. Some of the property lots on which they squatted had been sold by early speculators led by Samuel Brannan. It was the settlers' contention that the land, by virtue of the Treaty of Guadalupe Hidalgo between the U.S. and the Mexican government, was now owned by the U.S. Furthermore, under the Preemption Act of 1841, settlers or squatters could lay claim to the land before the land was offered to the general public.[17]

In 1849, one gentleman who tested this supposition was newly arrived immigrant Z. M. Chapman. He started building a house on property near Sacramento city proper with the intention of claiming 160 acres through the preemption process. Pierre B. Cornwall visited Chapman on behalf of the landowner, Priest, Lee & Company, telling Chapman to stop building the house and to vacate the property.[18]

A trial ensued that inflamed the passions of both land speculators and settlers. The immigrants who were camping in Sacramento organized the Sacramento City Settlers' Association. The land speculators and the settlers continued to argue over land ownership. The Sacramento Common Council passed a city ordinance forbidding anyone to erect a tent, shanty or house on land to which they did not hold title. John F. Madden did just that, at the corner of Second and N streets; he was arrested and subsequently represented by attorney J. H. McKune, who was representing the Settlers' Association in litigation.[19]

After losing at trial, McKune appealed the Madden decision. Because California was not yet a state, and Congress had failed to set up any territorial government, the judge felt there was no court to which he could refer an appeal.[20] In June of 1850, the speculators, aided by the Law and Order Association, began demolishing cabins, shacks and homes built on properties to which they were confident they held legal title.

James McClatchy, who had travelled over land and sea with Bugbey and would later become the editor of the Sacramento Bee, was a vocal proponent for the Settlers' Association. In the heat of the 1850 summer and the battle for land control, McClatchy proclaimed that although he was a law-abiding citizen, if these speculators were ready to fight, so was he.[21]

By early August, the settlers felt they had been pushed into a corner. The local government and courts, controlled by the land speculators, were having success at pushing them off land to which they felt they had a right. One of the Settlers' Association leaders, Charles Robinson, began working with another settler to organize a militia. Tensions rose when Mayor Hardin Bigelow rode out to Madden's cabin to encourage him to vacate the lot. The Settler's Association was out in force, and both sides backed down.[22]

The next day James McClatchy and another member of the Settlers' Association were arrested for interfering with the Sheriff in his duties to remove Madden from his cabin. McClatchy was jailed in the prison brig at the foot of I Street, along with McKune. Robinson and militia organizer John Maloney began marching their Settlers' Militia through the city. Mayor Bigelow, following the militia on horseback, was joined by Sheriff McKinney. At Fourth and J Street, Maloney inexplicably ordered the militia to open fire on the Mayor and Sheriff. Bigelow and Robinson were wounded. Maloney was shot dead. Sheriff McKinney was not shot during that showdown but was later shot and killed in Brighton while on a mission to round up more squatters.[23]

The Settlers' Association was essentially crushed, but not its members' spirits. Many of the men involved with the Settlers' Association continued on with the Settlers' Committee, endorsing candidates for elected office they felt represented their perspective on land rights. The Settlers' Committee was not supportive of miners in a broad sense. They felt mining interests were no different than men and companies that speculated in land. In the eyes of the Settlers' Committee, those who cultivated the land and made improvements were the people who imbued California, and the nation, with its greatness.[24]

In August of 1861, the Settlers' Committee of Sacramento gave their endorsement to Bugbey for Sheriff. Possibly not known to them at the time was that Bugbey had been a supporter of Pierre Cornwall, who attempted to evict a settler from land in 1850. Although Bugbey had been a farmer out by Salisbury Station, his first occupation was as a miner, and he had purchased lots in Folsom to continue mining. All of Bugbey's past history would seem to make him a less than ideal Sheriff candidate, from the settlers' point of view.

However, three of the Settlers' Committee members were James Lansing, John Madden, and John Rooney. Madden had been involved with the original Setters' Association. All three men had been nominated for Sheriff, with Bugbey, at the earlier Union Democratic County Convention. Most likely, the stronger bonds of the Union Democrat Party, along with the fact that Bugbey was an original '49er, helped overcome any objections other members may have had about Bugbey's views about land rights in California.

At this point Bugbey had not expressed any deeply held views about land ownership. His support and actions suggest he favored an orderly process for distributing land rights over major philosophical concepts about agrarianism. His success since moving to Folsom was rooted in the foundation of land speculators dividing up land and selling it to the highest bidder, regardless of who was mining or squatting on the land at the time.

Even though Folsom was a smaller version of Sacramento in terms of land being subdivided and sold, in which Bugbey was participating, rural residents in the county counted Bugbey as one of them. It didn't hurt that Bugbey had a track record of law and order from his time as Constable of Granite Township.

Bugbey's support in the eastern part of the county, along with the Settlers' Committee endorsement, helped push him to victory. The final election results were Bugbey: 2,186, Schwartz: 1,109, and Watson: 430.[25] Newly elected Sheriff Bugbey got down to work, appointing W. M. Hoag as Under Sheriff, and B. B. Redding, G. C. Haswell, James Lansing, Edward Christy, and S. W. Griffith as deputies.[26]

---

[1] Sacramento Daily Union, Volume 4, Number 616, March, 15, 1853, CDNC

[2] Sacramento Daily Union, Volume 13, Number 1960, July, 8 1857, CDNC

[3] Ibid.

[4] Sacramento Daily Union, Volume 19, Number 2945, September, 4 1860, CDNC

[5] Sacramento Daily Union, Volume 20, Number 2998, November 5, 1860, CDNC

[6] Davis, Win. J., *An Illustrated History of Sacramento County, California*, (The Lewis Publishing Company, Chicago, 1890).

[7] Sacramento Daily Union, Volume 21, Number 3199, June 28, 1861, CDNC

[8] Sacramento Daily Union, Volume 21, Number 3195, June 24, 1861, CDNC

[9] Sacramento Daily Union, Volume 21, Number 3199, June 28, 1861, CDNC

[10] Ibid.

[11] Sacramento Daily Union, Volume 21, Number 3201, July 1, 1861, CDNC

[12] Ibid.

[13] Ibid.

[14] Sacramento Daily Union, Volume 21, Number 3220, July 24, 1861, CDNC

15 Sacramento Daily Union, Volume 21, Number 3252, August 30, 1861, CDNC

16 Eifler, Mark, *Gold Rush Capitalists Greed and Growth in Sacramento*, (University of New Mexico Press, 2002, 1st edition).

17 Sacramento Daily Union, Volume 9, Number 1356, July 31, 1855, CDNC

18 Eifler, Mark, *Gold Rush Capitalists Greed and Growth in Sacramento*, (University of New Mexico Press, 2002, 1st edition).

19 Ibid.

20 Ibid.

21 Ibid.

22 Ibid.

23 Ibid.

24 Sacramento Daily Union, Volume 9, Number 1356, July 31, 1855, CDNC

25 Sacramento Daily Union, Volume 21, Number 3258, September 6, 1861, CDNC

26 Sacramento Daily Union, Volume 22, Number 3285, October 8, 1861, CDNC

Benjamin Norton Bugbey

Chapter 5: Sheriff Bugbey 1861 - 1864

The Sacramento County Sheriff at this time had the twin responsibilities of law enforcement and tax collections. This dual office function would remain until the end of the 19th century, when Bugbey, who ran solely for the office of tax collector in 1898, forced the tax collector duties to be split from the Sheriff's office. In the intervening years, it was the tax collector duties that ultimately created the biggest headaches for Bugbey. If a property owner failed to pay taxes, and property was ordered forfeited by the court order to pay the taxes, it was Bugbey who had to seize the property. He also ran into numerous problems collecting taxes targeted specifically at the Chinese immigrant community.

Numerous lawsuits were filed against Sheriff Bugbey on the grounds that he illegally seized property or improperly sold it at auction. These lawsuits were not unique to Bugbey's tenure as Sheriff, nor were the challenges of collecting taxes only applicable to Bugbey. All Sheriffs, before and after Bugbey, faced the same lawsuits and administrative challenges. Bugbey rarely equivocated over whether his actions were within the law. But the lawsuits did force him to spend more time defending his actions in civil court than he would have liked.

Bugbey's time as Sheriff and tax collector was an accelerated course in law enforcement, taxes, the judicial system and politics. He was also introduced to some of the most powerful men in the state as he served on committees for different events. Even though he spent the bulk of his time in Sacramento, he always maintained his home in Folsom.

Administration

Salaries and expenses were always chief concerns for the Sacramento County Board of Supervisors. As Sheriff, Bugbey was paid a salary of $4,000 per year plus mileage. Under Sheriff William Hoag earned $1,880 a year, and Deputies B. B. Redding, James Lansing, G. O. Haswell, Ed Christy, and S. W. Griffith were paid $1,500 on an annual basis. For a comparison to other county positions, William Shattuck, president of the Board of Supervisors, was paid $3,000 annually, and County Judge C. Clark earned $5,000 per year.[1]

Similar to his expense reimbursement requests when he was the Constable of Granite Township, Bugbey's Sheriff expenses were also questioned by the Board of Supervisors. In one instance Bugbey billed the county for $1,100 for travel to Tucson, Arizona, to bring back a prisoner.[2]

Under the regulations of 1862, the maximum fixed distances for a reimbursement of $0.20 per mile, one way, was set at 55 miles to Stockton and 155 miles to San Quinten. Bugbey was given the benefit of the doubt that he was fulfilling his legal obligations to travel to Tucson to arrest the individual and bring the prisoner back to Sacramento, but it was not a unanimous decision of the board to pay the expenses.[3]

Travel expenses for deputies were also scrutinized by the board. Deputies were employed during trials for summoning jurors and witnesses. Specifically, Grand Juries were routinely organized for criminal indictments. Instead of always relying on residents and merchants close to the court house, Bugbey instructed his Deputies to travel further out into the county to summon residents to be Grand Jurors. This made perfect sense to some of the supervisors, to the degree that residents near the court house should not be overly burdened with jury duty. The extra expense, it was suggested, was worth having the entire county represented in such court proceedings.[4]

As ex-officio tax collector, Bugbey, like all other Sheriffs, was able to keep a portion of the tax to offset his expenses. He was able to retain a 10% commission on the collection of most taxes he brought into the county treasury. One of the taxes for which Bugbey received a commission was the foreign miner's tax. The commissions were intended to be an added inducement for the Sheriff to be aggressive with collecting these sorts of taxes. The previous Sheriff collected $11,000 per year, while Bugbey's foreign miner tax collections totaled closer to $19,000 per year. Part of the increase was due to the fact that Sacramento County had an increase of 25 percent to 30 percent in the number of Chinese miners while Bugbey was Sheriff.[5]

James McClatchy, who was elected Sacramento County Sheriff in 1863 after Bugbey lost the nomination, was not impressed with his predecessor's administration or bookkeeping. Bugbey had been awarded the meal contract to prepare and serve food to the county prisoners but sold the contract to P. F. Murphy. McClatchy did not think the resulting contract was valid and refused Murphy entry to the jail with the meals. McClatchy instead provided his own meals to the prisoners.[6]

Sheriff McClatchy also complained that Bugbey had left the business license records in such disarray he had no idea when the former licenses were issued or when they expired. The Board of Supervisor passed a directive to have Bugbey turn over the license book as required by law.[7]

After Bugbey was no longer Sheriff, but had submitted his last expense reimbursements, some of the county supervisors questioned his honesty and integrity with respect to the commissions due him for tax collections. The board instructed the Auditor and District Attorney to

Benjamin Norton Bugbey

examine all of Bugbey's fees and expenses as Sheriff and Tax Collector beginning in May 1863.[8]

At issue was the bookkeeping of the tax collection commission or fee, and whether it should be withheld before the Sheriff deposited the money to the county treasury, or if the Sheriff should be reimbursed after an accounting of the receipts. Newly elected Sheriff McClatchy was wrestling with some of the same issues as the county tried to standardize its practices. It probably did not help that Bugbey seemed to be a bit of a sloppy bookkeeper.

Regardless, the resolution calling into question Bugbey's honesty by having his tax receipts audited was quickly disputed and found to have no merit. Supervisor Hollister offered a resolution to clear Bugbey of any mischief concerning tax collections while he was Sheriff.

Whereas, It appearing to this Board that ex-Sheriff Bugbey, in his collection of moneys for the county, always made prompt and correct payment of such moneys into the county treasury at such times as were required by law, with the exception of what he supposed to be his commissions as Tax Collector; be it, therefore, Resolved, That in certain resolutions passed by this Board on the 2nd and 4th days of May, in regard to said ex-Sheriff Bugbey, it was not the intention of this Board to censure any of his acts in regard to the collection and payment of moneys into the county treasury, as it was held by this Board, the question having never before been raised in regard to the Sheriff being entitled to retain fees as Tax Collector in the manner in which he did, and he is fully exonerated from any intention of wrongdoing in the premises. Be it further resolved, that, in consideration of the fact that said Bugbey, having been allowed claims against the county in sums much greater than the amount supposed to be due from him to the county, it is the sense of this Board that the District Attorney be ordered, and by this resolution is hereby ordered, to proceed no further against said Bugbey; but that an agreed case between said District Attorney and the attorneys of James McClatchy be had, and the decision and arbitration governing such case shall also govern and determine as between the rights of the county and said Bugbey in regard to moneys hereinbefore mentioned, retained by him as Tax Collector.[9] - Sacramento Daily Union, Volume 27, Number 4095, May 6, 1864, CDNC

Ex-Officio Tax Collector

As the county office with the most organized staff that circulated throughout the city and county, it seemed appropriate at the time for the Sheriff's department to also collect taxes and licenses.

Sacramento County was dependent on the collections of these taxes and fees in order to maintain the city and county. The city in particular was having severe growing pains, as they were under a constant threat of flooding during the winter, increased demand for higher quality drinking water in the summer, and problems surrounding sewage disposal. In order to set a firm tone of tax payment compliance, Bugbey sent out his deputies to immediately start collecting license fees. The Sacramento Daily Union noted, "…it will be found advisable to pay up promptly when called on."[10]

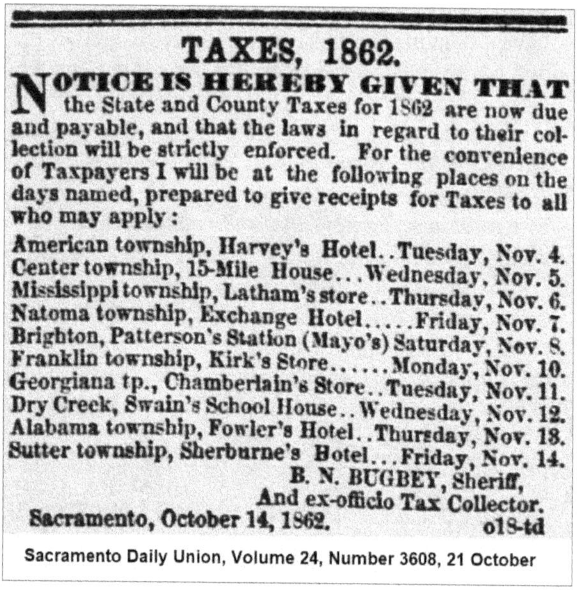

TAXES, 1862.

NOTICE IS HEREBY GIVEN THAT the State and County Taxes for 1862 are now due and payable, and that the laws in regard to their collection will be strictly enforced. For the convenience of Taxpayers I will be at the following places on the days named, prepared to give receipts for Taxes to all who may apply:

American township, Harvey's Hotel..Tuesday, Nov. 4.
Center township, 15-Mile House...Wednesday, Nov. 5.
Mississippi township, Latham's store..Thursday, Nov. 6.
Natoma township, Exchange Hotel.....Friday, Nov. 7.
Brighton, Patterson's Station (Mayo's) Saturday, Nov. 8.
Franklin township, Kirk's Store......Monday, Nov. 10.
Georgiana tp., Chamberlain's Store..Tuesday, Nov. 11.
Dry Creek, Swain's School House..Wednesday, Nov. 12.
Alabama township, Fowler's Hotel..Thursday, Nov. 13.
Sutter township, Sherburne's Hotel..Friday, Nov. 14.

B. N. BUGBEY, Sheriff,
And ex-officio Tax Collector.
Sacramento, October 14, 1862.   o18-td

Sacramento Daily Union, Volume 24, Number 3608, 21 October

Figure 3: 1862 - Announcement of locations Sheriff Bugbey would be available for residents to pay and county taxes in Sacramento County. CDNC

By the end of October 1861, Bugbey had deposited over $25,000 in taxes and licensing fees into the city and country treasuries.[11] In an effort to facilitate the payment as ex-officio tax collector of state and county taxes, Bugbey would undertake tours of the county to collect tax payments. In 1862, he advertised the 10 different locations and dates he would be available for local residents to come and pay their taxes. His first stop was Harvey's Hotel in American Township on November 4th.[12]

Then, from November 5th through the 14th, he announced stops at the 15 mile House in Center Township, Latham's Store in Mississippi Township, Exchange Hotel in Natoma Township,

Patterson's Station in Brighton, Kirk's Store in Franklin Township, Chamberlain's Store in Georgianna Township, Swain's School House in Dry Creek, Fowler's Hotel in Alabama Township, and, finally, Sherbune's Hotel in Sutter Township. Bugbey would take similar tours of the county for the next two years to collect taxes.[13]

Sheriff Bugbey didn't waste any time auctioning off property for unpaid taxes either. He held his first public auction of property forfeited for unpaid taxes in November 1861.[14] Sheriff Bugbey was listed on over 200 real estate transactions in the Sacramento County Deed Books as the seller of property that had been ordered sold by the courts to satisfy a judgment against the owner. Over 50 percent of these sales were due to delinquent taxes.

The great flood of 1861 – 1862, which resulted in significant property loss, combined with the subsequent taxes assessed to rebuild and strengthen the levees around Sacramento, also contributed to the necessity for Bugbey to hold numerous Sheriff's Sales to sell property for unpaid taxes. Some Sacramento residents were financially wiped out because of the great flood and could not meet their tax burden.

Sacramento Floods

As Bugbey was setting up his Sheriff's office and settling into the new job, storm clouds gathered over Northern California, and it began to rain in early December. The rain didn't stop. Sacramento would experience its worst flooding in its young life. The heavy rains would last through March 1862.[15]

On December 9, 1861, the little levee on the American River east of 30th Street failed. That led to the failure of a small levee protecting the central city. Sacramento was now a bathtub of flood water. To drain the water, the city breached the southern levee at 5th and R streets.[16] The rush of water out of the city, along with incoming water to the northeast, created strong enough water currents to push houses off of the foundations. Many people lost their lives, and there was significant property damage.

On April 9, 1862, Gov. Leland Stanford signed the Levee Law, which created a Board of City Levee Commissioners, along with the power to impose a levee tax on property to fund raising and strengthening the levees around the city.[17] Work on the new levees commenced almost immediately, but revenue from the levee tax was lagging. In July, a contract for $7,311 had been awarded to build the levee from 6th and H Streets out to 31st Street.[18] Unfortunately Bugbey had only collected $2,800 in levee tax revenue.[19] Contractors were demanding cash for their progress payments for work on the levee construction. They had between 1,000 and 1,500 men working on the levee project, with many of them earning $40 per month.[20]

By late July, with the intention of raising cash for the county, it was announced that Sheriff Bugbey would start filing lawsuits for non-payment of delinquent state and county licenses.[21] This must have been a terrible strain on Sacramento City residents, who had been decimated by the floods that had visited the city only eight months earlier. By August Bugbey was able to report to the Board of Supervisors that he had collected $10,173 in levee tax the previous week.[22]

Undoubtedly, there were a number of residents who lost their property to delinquent levee tax payments if they were unable to sell their properties to someone else.

Law Enforcement

The Sheriff's department performed the regular law enforcement duties such as investigating burglaries, murders, assaults, suicides, and drunken brawls. Sheriff Bugbey also had a couple counterfeiting and fraud cases. By default, Bugbey became a mental health professional, as he had to determine the mental capacity of some men and women who were exhibiting confusion and delirium. Some of these folks were escorted by Bugbey to Stockton, where there was a facility for the mentally incapacitated. Bugbey and his deputies also had to escort prisoners to different jurisdictions and men convicted of crimes to the state prison.

Even though Bugbey escorted convicted men down to the state prison at San Quentin for long prison terms, it was still the local counties who had to enforce any sentence of death. Bugbey inherited the death sentence of Louis Kahl. Kahl was convicted of strangling Catherine Gerken to death at her home at 2nd and L streets in Sacramento on January 4, 1861. He was found guilty and sentenced to death by Judge J. H. McKune. Kahl's case was appealed to the State Supreme Court, who let the verdict stand. An appeal for reprieve was even made to the Governor, but it was denied.

Kahl, who was only 23 years old, maintained his innocence, even as he stood on the gallows flanked by Bugbey. He made a lengthy statement proclaiming his innocence recounting witness testimony and the timeline of events. He thanked the attorneys, Mr. Coffroth and Mr. Curtis, who had defended him. He also said goodbye to his jailers, Warden Harris, Chief Watson, Deputy Sheriff Lansing and Lindsey. Then he turned to Sheriff Bugbey and said, "I know you are only performing your duty, and I have no hard feelings toward you for it."[23]

Louis Kahl fell through the trap door of the gallows erected on the second floor of the county jail at seven minutes past 1 o'clock on November 29th, 1861. He was pronounced dead 10 minutes later.[24]

At the end of Bugbey's term as Sheriff in 1863, he again found himself in the role of executioner. This time it was George N. Symonds, who had been convicted of murdering B. F. Russell on the night of July 11, 1860, near Benson's Ferry. District Court Judge McKune sentenced him to death for the murder. While generally calm in demeanor, Symonds expressed bitterness over his wife living with J. W. Knaggs, who happened to be one of the officers who arrested him for the murder.

On December 4, the evening before the execution, Sheriff Bugbey visited Symonds in his cell. Symonds had always maintained his innocence and blamed his situation on the influence of bad company he kept. That evening Bugbey asked Symonds if he still denied his guilt. Bugbey wanted Symonds to confess in order to remove any later doubt that he might have executed an innocent man. Symonds is reported to have told Bugbey that he should have no guilt about putting an innocent man to death; he was only doing his job.

The next day, while standing on the trap door of the gallows constructed on the second floor the jail house, Symonds stated that if there were any published confessions of guilt attributed to him, they were entirely fictitious. Bugbey then adjusted the rope around Symonds neck, and after a few prayers and a hymn, he touched the lever that opened the trap doors allowing Symonds to be hanged.[25]

The Chinese Assault

In the rough and tumble frontier town of Sacramento, where the liquor flowed freely and gambling was ubiquitous, a little use of excessive force by a law enforcement officer was seen as a virtue for curtailing crime. But the Sacramento community did have its limits for acceptable force when arresting or interrogating individuals. Sheriff Bugbey crossed the line into the realm of excessive force on at least one occasion.

As the tax and license collector for Sacramento County, Sheriff Bugbey was also in charge of collecting the Foreign Miner's Tax of 1852 from Chinese miners. In April of 1862, the California Legislature passed another tax on Chinese immigrants titled "An Act to protect free white labor against competition with Chinese coolie labor, and discourage the immigration of the Chinese into the State of California." It levied a $2.50 police tax on each Chinese person, male and female, over the age of 18 years of age[26]. As with most tax collections, the Sheriff got to keep a percentage of the collection. In this case it was 20 percent.

In Sacramento City, a large bulk of the Chinese immigrants lived along I Street, which was also the southern border of China Slough. This body of water was fed by the Sacramento River to the west and was originally named Sutter's Lake. When Chinese immigrants started building little shanties on stilts on the shoreline of the waterbody, it became known as China Slough.[27]

In early June of 1862, Sheriff Bugbey and one of his deputies went to the Chinese community along I Street to collect the new police tax. This may have been the first or second time Bugbey and his deputies went to collect the police tax, since it had only become law less than two months earlier. In addition to language challenges, many Chinese may never have heard of this new tax that they were expected to pay on a monthly basis.

Chinese immigrant Chew Yew resisted paying the police tax to Sheriff Bugbey and Deputy S. S. Ingham. The pair escorted Yew back to the police station, where Officer Stewart locked Yew up. Shortly after Yew was taken into the Sheriff's office, several people on the street and in adjoining buildings heard loud terrifying screams of pain emanating from the office.

The offices of the Sacramento Daily Union were right next door to the police station, and the newspaper reported the incident.

A Gross Outrage. — At dusk last evening a Chinaman was taken into the Sheriff's office, and if screams and strokes can be taken as an index, was beaten in an unmerciful manner for some ten or fifteen minutes. His cries attracted the attention of the neighbors a block off, when the windows of the office were closed. A number of citizens went to the doors of the office but found them locked. They knocked but there was no response. In a few minutes the strokes and screams were resumed. The victim seemed, from the sound, to have been gagged. He afterwards jumped through the window, and, striking on the roof of an out-building, fell to the ground. He was taken into the Sheriff's office. Sheriff Bugbey was in the room at the time. Whether any others except the Chinaman were there or not we are not advised. A large number of citizens collected around the building, and on insisting upon admission, the doors were unlocked. The Chinaman appeared to be seriously injured. Bugbey said in response to inquiries, that the man was under arrest for assault and battery.[28] - 1862 Sacramento Daily Union, Volume 23, Number 3490, 5 June 1862

The Sacramento Daily Union continued to editorialize about the incident.

The transaction was a gross outrage, and such as should not be tolerated in any civilized community. The Sheriff and his deputies are clothed by law with all the authority which the community deems it wise to entrust them with. When they arrest under legal process a miserable Chinaman, and lock themselves up out of sight to inflict torture which they would not dare administer in the presence of white witnesses, they are guilty of a cowardly and diabolical crime. If there is no law to meet such a case, the criminal code is sadly in need of amendment. After the above was written we were called upon by a Deputy Sheriff who was not present at the time of the occurrence of the affair, and one who was, together with a Chinaman who speaks English. The Deputy who was present stated that the Chinaman was not whipped and that all the noise resulted from an attempt to handcuff him. The Chinaman stated that he had seen and conversed with the Chinaman in the Sheriff's office since the affair above narrated had taken place, and that he stated that he had not been whipped. If this version of the case is correct, some fifty citizens beside ourselves were grossly deceived by the sounds which emanated from the room.[29] - 1862 Sacramento Daily Union, Volume 23, Number 3490, 5 June 1862

Deputy Ingham was charged with assault and tried later in the month. Mr. P. Coggins, while working in the offices of the Sacramento Daily Union, testified that he heard screams of a man in distress. He tried to enter the Sheriff's office, but the doors were locked. He said the torture sounded like a cane striking a man, with muffled sounds of a gagged man. Sheriff Bugbey appeared at the window, and Coggins asked why he would permit such an assault. Bugbey replied, "If you say I have whipped a Chinaman, you are a ------ liar." His reply only referred to himself, and not Deputy Ingham.

Henry Starr, who was a prominent auctioneer with an office in Sacramento, testified that Deputy Sheriff Lansing arrived and unlocked the Sheriff's office door. Bugbey came rushing forward, in shirt sleeves and panting, to prevent any of the gathered crowd from entering the office. A doctor examined Yew the next day and confirmed that many of the injuries seem to have occurred from a beating and possibly falling off a window onto the street.

Deputy Sheriff Lansing testified that he saw Yew sitting quietly in front of the stove when he entered the office, and he did not seem hurt. Then Yew got up and ran over to the window and jumped out of it. Lansing then went outside and brought Yew back into the Sheriff's office. Deputy B. B. Redding testified that Bugbey had arrested Yew for assaulting a Chinese man.

Deputy Ingham's defense was that he did not whip Yew but had only hit him once or twice while Yew was resisting Ingham putting him in leg irons and handcuffs. In addition, most of Yew's injuries resulted from him jumping out of the office window and landing on the street below.[30]

Deputy Sheriff Ingham was found guilty of assault and battery on Yew in the Sheriff's office. He was fined $40.[31] From the testimony of the officers, compared to the men who heard Yew's screams in

Benjamin Norton Bugbey

agony, it's most probable that the deputies conspired to spin a tale that mitigated any excessive force or torture on the part of Deputy Ingham and Bugbey's involvement. Bugbey received no punishment for his culpability in the assault on Chew Yew, other than possibly a blemish on his reputation.

The Sheriff's office was able to collect $1,488 for the police tax and $1,486 for the foreign miner's license from Chinese immigrants in June of 1862.[32] The police tax was found to be unconstitutional by the State Supreme Court in September of 1862.[33]

Sheriff's Sales

If Sacramento County or city residents were not able to pay their tax bills or had judgments against them for unpaid debts, it was the Sheriff's duty to sell their properties on the steps of the courthouse to the highest bidder. Since Bugbey had lost his farm out by Salisbury Station to a Sheriff's Sale, he was familiar with the procedures. If the property was not a lot or structure, there were times when Bugbey had to auction off the property on site. In one instance he had to supervise the auction of plant material. He advertised a Sheriff's Sale for the collection of choice and valuable plants and shrubs, consisting of camellias, orange trees, roses, geraniums, lilies, verbenas, heliotropes, fuchsias, and cacti from Smith's Gardens.[34]

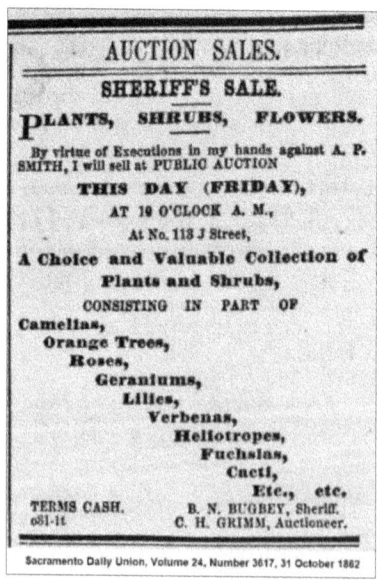

Figure 4: 1862 - Sheriff's Sale announcement for the auction of plant material in Sacramento. CDNC

The demise of Smith's Garden was the result of an unpaid loan for the business and property rent. Even though Bugbey was just following court orders, he was named as a defendant in a lawsuit to stop the sale of plant material.[35]

Nonetheless, the sale went forward, much to the delight of buyers of the trees and plants. The Sacramento Daily Union reported the Sheriff's Sale was a success. Titled "Cheap Shade Trees For Sale," the newspaper noted that the sale at 6th and K Streets of elm, linden, and locust trees had been brisk. The Union editorialized, "The readiness of our citizens to buy and plant shade trees indicates a commendable determination to improve and beautify their homesteads."[36] Bugbey helped accelerate the elm tree canopy for which Sacramento would become known, and he gained insight into the sale of agricultural products--knowledge he would use in the future.

The State Supreme Court weighed in on the matter of Bugbey's Sheriff's Sale of trees in its decision on Robinson vs Russel, in which the mortgager of the Smith's Garden property claimed the plants could be used to satisfy the delinquent mortgage. The court found that Bugbey did not overstep his authority, because he oversaw the removal of plant material from Smith's Gardens to satisfy a judgment.[37] The removable of the plant material did not diminish the value of the land on which a mortgage had been secured, the court ruled.

Social Affairs

Bugbey loved plants and growing them. He grew a variety of different raisin and wine grapes, along with orange and fig trees, at his Natoma Vineyard. He reveled in his farm produce from land he cultivated in Sutter County and displayed at the State Fair. After he made Sacramento City his permanent home in the 1880s, he planted a variety of different trees, shrubs and flowers. He donated all of his yucca flowers from his Sacramento property for the grand wedding event between Celia Simmons and Dwight Miller, who was the eldest son of Frank Miller of the banking firm D. O. Mills. The wedding and Bugbey's flower donation made the social news, noting that, "Mr. and Mrs. B. N. Bugbey fairly stripped their garden of its lovely yucca flowers for the occasion."[38]

When Bugbey closed up his Sacramento furniture shop and moved out to Salisbury Station to farm, he left Sacramento behind. As the Constable of Granite Township he travelled to Sacramento mainly for law enforcement business. Because Bugbey lived in Folsom, he may have been one of the first commuters between that city and Sacramento on the Sacramento Valley Railroad. Now he was the

Sheriff of Sacramento County and, either by choice or recruitment, he became more involved in civic affairs and entertainment.

One of his first introductions into the political power structure of Sacramento and the state of California happened when he served on the inaugural ball committee for Governor Leland Stanford. The executive committee for the January 8, 1862, event included Charles Crocker, D. O. Mills, and J. P. Robinson. Bugbey served on the general committee along with B. F. Hastings, Mark Hopkins, James McClatchy, Judge McKune and many other business and elected people of the state.[39]

He would also work with local Sacramento dignitaries as part of the Honorary Committee for the Annual Ball to raise money for Sacramento's fire engine company No.1. Other committee members included B. F. Hastings, Leland Stanford, James McClatchy, and Judge McKune.[40]

As the nation was gripped by Civil War, Bugbey started a collection for the United States Sanitary Commission to support sick and wounded soldiers of the Union Army. This was a cause near to Bugbey's heart, as his own brother George had been severely wounded in the war. In November of 1862, the Sheriff's office donated $500 to the Sanitary Fund. Bugbey contributed $187, and all of his deputies gave lesser amounts.[41]

Bugbey was one of thousands of men who travelled to Sacramento in 1849. He and other men grew so fond of the region and opportunities they decided to call it home for the rest of their lives. One of men who made the trek from the East Coast to Sacramento was W. W. Kurtz. Kurtz, along with Bugbey, James McClatchy, Israel Luce and others, sailed from New York to Mexico, where they traveled over land to Mazatlan, then took a boat to San Francisco arriving in June 1849. Kurtz found employment at the Sacramento Daily Union and became the foreman of the composing room. He worked there until he was taken ill at the end of 1862. He died in San Francisco, where he retired to regain his health, in late January 1863.[42]

Perhaps because of Kurtz's passing, Bugbey decided to formally join the Sacramento Pioneer Association. Organized in 1854, the association's goal was to preserve the stories and history of the men who came to California before January 1, 1850. This also provided Bugbey another opportunity to network with men who were '49ers but also held prominent positions in government and business, such as Governors Bigler, Johnson, and Booth, and including men from the finance world, such as B. F. Hastings and D. O. Mills. The editors of the major Sacramento daily newspapers, J. Anthony of the Union and McClatchy of the Bee, were also members of the Pioneer Association.[43]

Bugbey was also a patron and supporter of the arts in Sacramento. He and many other men were overcome with gratitude for the extended appearance of actress Annette Ince in several different plays performed at the Metropolitan Theater. Ince who lived and acted mainly in the Bay Area, spent much of October 1863 in Sacramento performing in dramas and comedies that month. Over 50 men, including Bugbey, signed their names to a letter thanking the actress for her time and performances in Sacramento and offered her a Complementary Benefit on the date of her choosing.

To Miss Annette Ince — Madam : Hearing you are about closing your engagement in this city, we, the undersigned, having enjoyed the Intellectual treat you have afforded us in your classic representations, wish to express our admiration of your worth as a lady and talent as an actress, in a substantial manner, and beg to offer you a Complementary Benefit, to take place on any night acceptable to yourself.[44] - 1863 Sacramento Daily Union, Volume 26, Number 3935, 31 October 1863

In what would be a rare family reunion, George Bugbey, Bugbey's younger brother, visited him in Sacramento. George was one of the first men from Connecticut to be injured in the Civil War. The injury to George's shoulder left him permanently disabled even though he retained the arm.[45] By contrast, Bugbey's worst injury occurred when he was wrestling Dr. Bates in Folsom, presumably in a friendly match of machismo. Bugbey landed wrong and dislocated his ankle. He recuperated at his residence in Folsom until he could return to work full time.[46]

Law Suits

Bugbey had no training in the law, and he had no training in law enforcement beyond his years as Constable of Granite Township. California had only been a state for about 11 years when he became Sacramento County Sheriff. This meant that many of the new local and state civil laws were in a state of flux as individuals appealed adverse court decisions. There were times when Bugbey felt his actions were completely within the law, only to have a court decide otherwise.

Not only were recently passed laws called into question, the actual county boundaries had not been properly surveyed. This became an issue in 1861, when Sheriff Bugbey was on the South Fork of the American River above Mormon Island collecting the foreign miner's tax on Chinese immigrants. The miners protested paying the tax because they felt they were in El Dorado County, and Bugbey had no jurisdiction. Bugbey confiscated tools and mining equipment in lieu of the miner's tax because he was certain the Chinese immigrants were mining in Sacramento County.

Benjamin Norton Bugbey

The Chinese miners sued for $10,000 in damages. After careful consideration, Bugbey decided to settle out of court for substantially reduced damages. He must have realized that there was a high probability that the miners were in El Dorado County. The lawsuit was dismissed, which left the question of the exact boundary between Sacramento and El Dorado county in doubt even as late as 1864.[47] This area along the South Fork of the American River was not unknown to Bugbey. He had mined in the region in 1849 and would go on to purchase property a couple of years later that was slightly east of Sacramento County in the county of El Dorado.

As Sheriff, Bugbey was sued no less than 15 times over his actions concerning property he either seized or sold. He was also sued several times for his actions as Constable of Granite Township. In some of the court cases Bugbey prevailed; in others he was ordered to pay damages, and a few cases were overturned in an appellant court. Several of the cases were appealed all the way to the State Supreme Court. A couple of those cases were decided in Bugbey's favor and set judicial precedent for the 19th century in California.

Woodliff v Bugbey

In 1856 Mary Woodliff sued Bugbey over a property dispute. Mary Woodliff, who was only 16 years old at the time, took a gold watch and a chair to a repairman in Folsom. Bugbey, as Constable of Granite Township, confiscated the property. Mary sued for the value of the property. Bugbey declared he could show that Mary did not own the property in question and that it had been stolen. A. P. Catlin and C. G. W. French represented Ms. Woodliff at a small trial conducted with six jurors before the Granite Township Justice of the Peace. The jury found in favor of the defendant, B. N. Bugbey.[48]

White v Bugbey

Bugbey was ordered to seize the property of A. H. White to settle a judgment against him in 1858. White contended the property seized was exempt from the judgment. The complaint by White requested to recover $98 from Bugbey, with $80 as damages. Bugbey sold the property, a clock and half a ton of hay at auction to satisfy the judgment against White. Bugbey was represented by F. S. Mumford of Mormon Island. Hopper and Ewing attorneys represented Mr. White. The case was dismissed.[49]

Woods v Bugbey

Benjamin Norton Bugbey

In the spring of 1860, a local Sacramento company owned by Mr. O'Neill had built a large kiln to fire clay bricks. The kiln was 130 feet long, 30 feet wide and 15 feet high. In October 1861, O'Neill was in debt to Mr. Woods. O'Neill had his kiln filled with green unfired clay bricks. In order to satisfy his debt, O'Neill sold the kiln full of green brick to Woods and further agreed to proceed with the firing, at his own expense, so Woods would have a finished product to sell. Woods bought a kiln of green bricks but would get finished fired bricks that he could sell at a higher price. O'Neill fired up the kiln on November 11th, and the bricks were completely fired by November 19th.[50]

Bricks were in high demand to build fire-proof buildings. As Sacramento had seen a number of fires destroy large swaths of residential and commercial districts over the years, owners wanted to rebuild with brick if possible. There were only two firms in April 1860 who were manufacturing bricks in Sacramento. The first was Callaghan, Fox & Tansman, and the other was O'Neill's.[51]

O'Neill also owed money to a Mr. Harris, who had threatened and won a lawsuit for the recovery of the debt. Before the firing of the bricks was complete, Sheriff Bugbey attached the bricks as payment for the judgment against O'Neill to Harris. Woods did not get the kiln full of bricks to sell that he bought from O'Neill. Woods sued Sheriff Bugbey over his actions and won, based on the Statutes of Frauds. Bugbey appealed for a new trial, and that motion was denied. He then appealed to the State Supreme Court. Attorney H. H. Hartley represented Bugbey and attorney George Cadwalader the respondent. Both of these attorneys would alternately represent Bugbey in court and also represent plaintiffs against him in future court battles.

The opinion of the Court, as handed down in 1866 by Justice J. Currey, focused on the possession of the property. Even though Woods bought the kiln of clay bricks from O'Neill, he never actually took possession of them. O'Neill remained in possession of the kiln and paid for the wood and employees to complete the firing of the bricks. The judgment in favor of Harris, and subsequent attachment by Bugbey, occurred while O'Neill was in the possession of the kiln and firing of the bricks. Justice Currey wrote,

> *There was nothing done by the plaintiff [Woods] to indicate to anyone that he had any property in the kiln of bricks, notwithstanding he visited the premises five time while the bricks were in the process of burning. The fact that O'Neill finished the work of burning the kiln the day before it was attached, and informed the plaintiff the next day before the Sheriff levied that he had completed the work and told to take his property, does not, in our judgment, aid the plaintiff. O'Neill had been all the while, from the time of his contract with plaintiff, in*

the actual and open possession of the property, adding by his labor, care and skill to its value, and this, too, by an arrangement made by him with the plaintiff. After he had done his work, he gave the plaintiff notice that he had completed his part of the contract, and told him to take the property. This was the first time it was ever proposed to make a complete and final delivery of the property, which if effectuated, would have amounted to an open and visible change of possession. - Woods v Bugbey Supreme Court January 1866, Woods v Bugbey, 29 Cal. 472

The judgment denying a new trial by the lower court was reversed, awarding Bugbey, and judgment for the defendant was entered.[52]

Peterie v Bugbey and Beck

Another case that reached the State Supreme Court involved the question of witness testimony. A Mr. Stackhouse owed money to Robert Beck. Mr. Beck secured a judgment against Stackhouse for the repayment of the money. Sheriff Bugbey executed the court decision by confiscating the property that Stackhouse had bought on credit from Beck. But before the seizure occurred, Mr. G. C. Peterie claimed to have bought the property in question from Stackhouse.

Beck had a partner in his operation by the name of Mr. W. Ackley. Ackley sold his interest to Beck in the operation when he saw Stackhouse's debt had become very large, and before Bugbey seized the property from Stackhouse to satisfy the judgment against him. At the Sheriff's Sale, Beck bought the property back and sold part of the property to Ackley.

Ackley testified at the trial of Peterie v Bugbey. Peterie lost in the first court case but appealed on the grounds that Ackley could not testify in the case because he had bought from Beck a portion of the property sued for and assigned his portion of the business over to Beck. Peterie won on appeal and was awarded $1,400 plus $100 in damages. Bugbey, not wanting to pay Peterie for an action he believed to be permissible under his authority as Sheriff, appealed the ruling to the State Supreme Court.[53]

At issue was whether Ackley, who was a witness for the defense, had a vested interest in the outcome of the lawsuit brought by Peterie. The Supreme Court ruled that they could not disturb the judgment rendered by the original jury trial. Even though there was conflicting testimony in the trial by the witnesses, it was the duty of the jury to weigh the evidence presented and render a verdict. Justice C. J. Sanderson wrote, "Where the testimony is conflicting, the result mainly depends upon the credibility of the witness. Of that the jury and the Court below have an opportunity to judge, but this Court has not. Should we attempt to weigh the evidence as it is presented to us and decide between conflicting statements, the chances for the intervention of error would be increased rather than diminished."[54]

Both the Woods and Peterie State Supreme Court decisions set precedent and would go on to be cited in other courts cases for decades. Bugbey did not cry over his court defeats or crow over his victories. He probably never thought he would spend so much time in a courtroom defending himself when he immigrated to California to become a gold miner. His involvement in the judicial system eliminated any intimidation he might have had about fighting for what he thought was right. He never became an overly litigious individual, but he refused to back down when he thought he was standing on the right side of the law.

1863 McClatchy vs. Bugbey

With the opening of Union County Democratic Party nominating convention in June 1863, the country was still in a Civil War, and loyalty to the Union was a political wedge issue. Delegates from the 3rd and 4th wards had chosen to leave the convention for muddled reasons. They were urged to return to the convention because it was their duty as loyal Union men to stand by the current Republican President during the time of Civil War. The delegates who left the convention countered that they left because they felt that the defeat of the candidates they endorsed was a foregone conclusion.[55]

It was during this political drama that nominations for Sacramento County Sheriff were called. Candidates James McClatchy, John Rooney and Wyman McMitchell, along with Bugbey, were put into nomination. Bugbey stated he was an unconditional Union man. His family had fought in the war of independence, and it was widely known that his brother was gravely wounded fighting for the Union. He strongly protested that he had any secessionist leanings, as some people were accusing him of having.[56]

After Bugbey's remarks to the convention, the Secretary was asked to read a document outlining the creation of Democratic Party-leaning newspaper in California by ex-Governor Bigler. Bugbey was then questioned about his role in helping fund a newspaper called the Republican. Bugbey answered that he met Governor Bigler on the street about a year earlier and was asked by the Governor if he would pay a $25 subscription to get the newspaper started.

Many of Bugbey's acquaintances were involved with the newspaper's creation, including James Lansing and Edward Christy. Bugbey told Governor Bigler that, as long as the Republican was a good Union paper, he would have no problem supporting it. After seeing the first printing, Bugbey said he thought it a secessionist newspaper and threw it away. However, the paper continued to be delivered to the Sheriff's offices, and he had no way of preventing his deputies from reading it.[57]

There were also accusations of Bugbey employing "copperhead" deputies.[58] A copperhead was a term for Democrats who opposed the Civil War and wanted an immediate peace settlement. Republicans likened people who wanted a peace treaty with the South to a venomous copperhead snake as a way of vilifying their position. Whether this was Bugbey's position or not, he never stated. But associating with or employing copperheads was a sign of disloyalty to the Union in the eyes of the Union and Republican parties.

There was no civil service system in the Sheriff's office in the 1860s. Elected Sheriffs got to select their Under Sheriff and Deputies, who were usually their friends, neighbors, and fellow political party members. There was an implied association and loyalty to the man who hired you. This loyalty was on full display when the deputies corroborated Bugbey and Ingham's claim that they never tortured or abuse Chinese immigrant Yew. Most voters understood that whomever they elected would be hiring subordinates of their same political persuasion and ideology.

After two convention ballots, Rooney and McMitchell withdrew their names from consideration, and the race was between Bugbey and McClatchy. On the fourth ballot, McClatchy was nominated as the candidate for Sheriff's office.[59]

Bugbey was still very popular in the eastern portion of Sacramento County, being seen as a country man and not a Sacramento City insider. Some of the residents of Folsom circulated a petition expressing dissatisfaction with the nomination of McClatchy and pledging support to Bugbey.[60] There was also a movement to draft Bugbey as a candidate at the Democratic County convention to be held later in June.

Bugbey, however, was a loyal party man. He placed an ad in the Sacramento Union declining the offer to be candidate for the office of Sheriff.

> *Editor Sacramento Union— Dear Sir: In your issue of today I notice, with pride, the names of many warm friends, citizens of this county, tendering me their support in the coming election for the office of Sheriff. I am indebted to the most of them, in a great measure, for the position I now occupy, and I take this opportunity of expressing to them my sincere thanks for past favors; at this time it becomes my duty to inform them that although it would have given me a great deal of pleasure to have been their candidate for that office, yet I must decline*

Benjamin Norton Bugbey

that honor, I having been before the Union Convention when another was selected for that position. I am, therefore, not a candidate, either Independent or otherwise. Respectfully yours, B. N. BUGBEY Sacramento, June 24, 1863.[61] - Sacramento Daily Union, Volume 25, Number 3825, 25 June 1863

James McClatchy would step down from his position as editor of the Sacrament Bee, run for Sheriff and win. McClatchy would encounter many of the same bureaucratic and legal challenges that Bugbey did when he was Sheriff. It was apparent that Bugbey's support within the city of Sacramento was thin. Most of his support came from the outlying townships. Also undercutting his support was a campaign, most likely with the knowledge of McClatchy, to paint Bugbey as a Confederate sympathizer. However, Bugbey was pragmatic about the situation. The fact he and McClatchy had travelled to California together did not imply any long-term loyalty or friendship. This was politics, and politics was dirty.

Possibly taking away from the sting of losing his job as Sheriff and role as official public persona was the fact that Bugbey had started acquiring land along the South Fork of the American River in 1863[62]. While law enforcement was now in his blood, along with tax collections, farming and the desire to be a farmer remained an important part of Bugbey's life. Since he was a man of high energy, shedding the constant demands on his time of his Sheriff and tax collector responsibilities meant he could devote more time to his agricultural pursuits.

Bugbey received on-the-job training and a concentrated education in the law through his time as a Constable and Sheriff. He would lean on these experiences and lessons as he faced other challenges in his life. When life's fortune turned against him, Bugbey would return to the field of law enforcement. He would also run for Sheriff several more times, none with success.

---

[1] Sacramento Daily Union, Volume 22, Number 3358, January 1, 1862, CDNC

[2] Sacramento Daily Union, Volume 24, Number 3717, February 19, 1863, CDNC

[3] Sacramento Daily Union, Volume 24, Number 3703, February 3, 1863, CDNC

[4] Sacramento Daily Union, Volume 24, Number 3730, March 6, 1863, CDNC

[5] Sacramento Daily Union, Volume 26, Number 4028, February 18, 1864, CDNC

[6] Sacramento Daily Union, Volume 26, Number 4048, March 12, 1864, CDNC

[7] Sacramento Daily Union, Volume 27, Number 4070, 7 April 7, 1864, CDNC

[8] Sacramento Daily Union, Volume 27, Number 4093, 4 May 4, 1864, CDNC

[9] Sacramento Daily Union, Volume 27, Number 4095, May 6, 1864, CDNC

[10] Sacramento Daily Union, Volume 22, Number 3295, October 19, 1861, CDNC

[11] Sacramento Daily Union, Volume 22, Number 3296, October 21, 1861 & Sacramento Daily Union, Volume 22, Number 3302, 28 October 1861

[12] Sacramento Daily Union, Volume 24, Number 3608, October 21, 1862, CDNC

[13] Ibid.

[14] Sacramento Daily Union, Volume 22, Number 3314, November 11, 1861, CDNC

[15] Sacramento Daily Union, Volume 22, Number 3417, March 12, 1862, CDNC

[16] *Water, Our History & Our Future*, (Sacramento History Journal of the Sacramento County Historical Society, Volume VI No. 1, 2, 3, & 4, 2006).

[17] Sacramento Daily Union, Volume 23, Number 3443, April 12, 1862, CDNC

[18] Sacramento Daily Union, Volume 23, Number 3530, 22 July 22, 1862, CDNC

[19] Sacramento Daily Union, Volume 23, Number 3529, 21 July 21, 1862, CDNC

[20] Sacramento Daily Union Volume 23, Number 3531, July 23, 1862, CDNC

[21] Ibid.

[22] Sacramento Daily Union, Volume 23, Number 3541, August 4, 1862, CDNC

[23] Sacramento Daily Union, Volume 22, Number 3330, November 29, 1861 & Sacramento Daily Union, Volume 22, Number 3331, November 30, 1861, CDNC

[24] Ibid.

[25] Sacramento Daily Union, Volume 26, Number 3965, December 5, 1863, CDNC

[26] Sacramento Daily Union, Volume 24, Number 3585, September 24, 1862, CDNC

[27] Yee, Alfred, *What Happened to China Slough?*, (Golden Notes Volume 40, Number 2, Summer 1994, Sacramento County Historical Society).

[28] Sacramento Daily Union, Volume 23, Number 3490, June 5, 1862, CDNC

[29] Ibid.

[30] Sacramento Daily Union, Volume 23, Number 3511, June 28, 1862, CDNC

[31] Sacramento Daily Union, Volume 23, Number 3513, July 1, 1862, CDNC

[32] Sacramento Daily Union, Volume 23, Number 3515, July 3, 1862, CDNC

[33] Sacramento Daily Union, Volume 24, Number 3585, September 24, 1862, CDNC

[34] Sacramento Daily Union, Volume 24, Number 3617, October 31, 1862, CDNC

[35] Sacramento Daily Union, Volume 24, Number 3690, 19 January 19, 1863, CDNC

[36] Sacramento Daily Union, Volume 24, Number 3694, January 23, 1863, CDNC

[37] Sacramento Daily Union, Volume 27, Number 4078, April 16, 1864, CDNC

[38] Sacramento Daily Union, Volume 81, Number 100, June 18, 1891, CDNC

[39] Sacramento Daily Union, Volume 22, Number 3340, December 11, 1861, CDNC

[40] Sacramento Daily Union, Volume 26, Number 4009, January 27, 1864, CDNC

[41] Sacramento Daily Union, Volume 24, Number 3644, November 25, 1862, CDNC

[42] Sacramento Daily Union, Volume 24, Number 3693, January 22, 1863, CDNC

[43] Sacramento Daily Union, Volume 24, Number 3705, February 5, 1863, CDNC

[44] Sacramento Daily Union, Volume 26, Number 3935, October 31, 1863, CDNC

[45] Sacramento Daily Union, Volume 25, Number 3753, April 2, 1863, CDNC

[46] Sacramento Daily Union, Volume 22, Number 3417, March 12, 1862 & Sacramento Daily Union, Volume 22, Number 3418, March 13, 1862, CDNC

[47] Sacramento Daily Union, Volume 26, Number 4024, 13 February 13, 1864, CDNC

[48] Mary Woodliff v B. N. Bugby & Mary's Guardian v Thomas B. Woodliff, January 2, 1857, Case 614, Sacramento County Court Civil Files (1850 – 1879), Box 10. Note, plaintiff name misspelled Woodlift, on Sacramento County table of cases.

[49] A. H. White v B. N. Bugby, October 5, 1858, Case 777, Sacramento County Court Civil Case Files (1850 – 1879), Box 13.

[50] Woods v Bugbey, California State Supreme Court, 1866, (29 Cal. 472).

[51] Sacramento Daily Union, Volume 19, Number 2835, April 27, 1860, CDNC

[52] Woods v Bugbey, California State Supreme Court, 1866, (29 Cal. 472).

[53] Sacramento Daily Union, Volume 27, Number 4075, April 13, 1864, CDNC

[54] G. C. Peterie v B. N. Bugbey and Robert Beck, California State Supreme Court, 1864, (24 Cal. 419).

[55] Sacramento Daily Union, Volume 25, Number 3808, June 5,1863, CDNC

[56] Ibid.

[57] Ibid.

[58] Sacramento Daily Union, Volume 28, Number 4360, March 13, 1865, CDNC

[59] Sacramento Daily Union, Volume 25, Number 3808, June 5, 1863, CDNC

[60] Sacramento Daily Union, Volume 25, Number 3824, June 24, 1863, CDNC

[61] Sacramento Daily Union, Volume 25, Number 3825, 25 June 25, 1863, CDNC

[62] El Dorado County Deed Book H, page 165. Samuel Hardesty to B. N. Bugbey, Recorded 20 January 1863. 320 Acres, Brown's Ravine, metes and bounds description, $2,200. Note: Bugbey states in his statement for the State Fair Gold Medal (*Transactions of the California State Agricultural Society During the Years 1870 and 1871*), that he purchased the Natoma Vineyard in 1861. The transaction was formally recorded in January 1863.

Chapter 6: Natoma Vineyard Begins to Grow 1863 - 1865

Bugbey had many life interests, and chief among them was agricultural. He liked to farm, be a farmer, work hard, and grow plants. He was in the emerging field of California agriculture, where men who had come to California to strike it rich in the gold mines – and seeing a diminishing return on their labors from the mining endeavors – returned to the earth. California was a desert compared to the Eastern United States. There was a tremendous growing season in the Central Valley of California along with good soil. The limiting factor was water. Outside of dry land farming, such as winter wheat or forage crops, California's recognized potential as a salad and fruit bowl to the world would hinge on dependable irrigation during the summer months. Where water was available for summer irrigation, men such as Bugbey started experimenting will all sorts of crops.

Mining to Farming

When the '49ers arrived in California's Central Valley, it was wide open and untamed land. For all practical purposes there was no government. The federal government was in technical ownership of the land through the Treaty of Guadalupe Hidalgo with Mexico. But California was not a state, and Congress had not defined a territorial government. Vestiges of the Mexican government's system of alcaldes and the recognition of land grants were nominally accepted by the residents.

There was no one to tell these gold-seeking immigrants not to dig through the earth looking for gold, or to build a dam and water canals. Which is exactly what they did. This was, after all, California, a newly minted state as of September 1850, with virtually no communication to the owner of most of the land in the state: the federal government.

Within a few short years of arriving in California, the miners had been able to glean most of the free placer gold from the river bottom by various methods. With the easy gold taken, attention then turned to the river banks and upland slopes leading down to the river. Surely, everyone thought, there must be as much or more gold surrounding the river, in the canyon, than in the river bed. But there was just one small problem, in that gold mining required the necessary element of water to wash the dirt.

It was withering and laborious work in 100° F summer heat to move wheelbarrows and sacks of dirt down to the water's edge to be washed. Some of the dry diggings could yield $2 to $20 per day in gold. The miners would easily pay $1 day for water to wash the dirt in situ and avoid the transport to flowing river water. Because there were no steam engines around to pump the water out of the river to the new dry mining ground, the next best strategy was to put the river above the ground to be washed and let it flow down. Hence emerged the concept and vision for a water ditch above the gold mining claims.

A consortium of miners constructed a dam across the South Fork of the American River in 1854, a couple miles above the mining town of Salmon Falls in El Dorado County. Along with the diversion dam, they dug a canal or water ditch to convey the water westward, closely following the South Fork of the American River. Ostensibly, the water ditch was to service the mining claims that were washing dirt above the river. As gold mining withered because of low returns, the primary customers for the Natoma water ditch along the South Fork of the American River would be farmers and the emerging city of Folsom.

Many of the East Coast and Midwest immigrants who trekked to California in search of gold had a background in farming. With a burgeoning population and lots of demand for food, many miners returned to their agricultural roots. Farming happened where there was water in the Mediterranean desert climate of California, regardless of how poor the soil was. By the mid-1850s agriculture was developing as the second wave of major economic activity in the state.

By East Coast standards, the South Fork of the American River is little more than a large creek whose flow could drop to a trickle during the summer. The modest South Fork Dam, later to be known as the Natoma Dam, was able to divert enough water to service mining claims, many of which were turned into agricultural lands in the late 1850s.

Bugbey's first foray into farming occurred in 1854 at Salisbury Station[1], approximately 16 miles east of Sacramento. It was right along the wagon road between the two communities, and the Sacramento Valley Railroad was quickly building its line right next to it. The furniture store he had opened in Sacramento had not worked out. Fresh vegetables were in higher demand than furniture and had a larger market. Crop prices were still relatively high, as production farming was still in its infancy in the 1850s. Bugbey left the Salisbury farm experiment behind when he bought property in the new town of Folsom in 1856.

South Fork American River

Even though Bugbey, as Sheriff of Sacramento County, spent most of his time in Sacramento City, he still maintained a home in Folsom. He also visited the gold mines along the American River to collect the foreign miner's tax from Chinese immigrants. Many of his friends, such as attorney F. S. Mumford, lived in the little town of Mormon Island on the river. Bugbey learned of some property in El Dorado County that was for sale. In 1861, he purchased land along the South Fork of the American River at Brown's Ravine. Later he would add more property outside of Shingle Springs, also in El Dorado County.

Bugbey purchased the property along the South Fork of the American River from Samuel Hardesty for $2,200. The land transfer is recorded using the metes and bounds description of a piece of property where topographical features and landmarks are used to describe the property boundaries.[2]

Quit claimed unto said party of the second part [Benjamin N. Bugbey] all certain piece or parcel of land situated lying and being in the County of El Dorado and State of California situated on Brown's Ravine bounded as follows viz: commencing at a small black oak tree on the south side of the McDowell Hill Road and on the Carr and Hamilton north east line blazed on two sides, running south east along said Carr and Hamilton's line fourteen hundred and twenty (1420) yards to a pine tree blazed and marked H. B. on two sides thence north east and verses Brown's Ravine eight hundred and eighty (880) yards to a bluen oak tree blazed and marked on two sides H. B. thence north west ten hundred and sixty (1060) yards to a white oak tree blazed and marked H. B. on two sides thence south east two hundred and sixteen (216) yards to a white oak tree blazed and marked H. B. on two sides thence north west six hundred (600) yards to a white oak tree blazed and marked on two sides H. B. being a tract of land containing three hundred and twenty acres more or less together with all and singular the tenements... and appurtenances.[3] - El Dorado County Deed Book H, page 165, January 5, 1863

Not mentioned in the description was that the northern boundary of the property was the South Fork of the American River. Also not included was the Natoma Ditch, which cut across part of the property as it traveled west toward Mormon Island and the City of Folsom. The Natoma Ditch gave the property irrigation water. As the property sloped up from the river, and the ditch was at a higher elevation than parts of the property, Bugbey would be able to easily irrigate his farm below the ditch toward the river. Bugbey would name this property Natoma Vineyard.

On January 15th, 1863, Bugbey bought another piece of property from Warren Lee McEwen and George W. Buckner southwest of Shingle Springs. It also was described with metes and bounds.

Benjamin Norton Bugbey

> *...all that certain tract of land situated lying and being in said county of El Dorado State aforementioned and located on both sides of the Folsom & Placerville road about forty rods above (East of) the Duroc House and particularly described as follows viz: Commencing at the North West corner of the Ranch known as the El Dorado House Ranch. Thence southerly running above the west line of said El Dorado Ranch and the west line of Bennett's Ranch to a cross fence in the E. S. Hanchett's Ranch a one hundred and twenty seven rods more or less south of the said Folsom & Placerville road. Thence west along said fence seventeen rods more or less to the center of said E. S Hanchett's Ranch. Thence northerly keeping the center of said Hanchetts Ranch two hundred and fifty rods more or less to the Eureka Ditch. Thence Easterly thirty more rods more or less to the place of the beginning being the same identical piece of land which was conveyed to the parties of the first part herein by E. S. Hanchett on the 15th day of October 1860 by the deed of that date."[4] - El Dorado County Deed Book H, page 166, January 15, 1863

This property had two advantages. First, it was next to the Placerville and Sacramento Railroad that was then under construction from Folsom and completed in 1865.[5] This gave the property easy access for shipping the crop produced on the land. Second, there was a water ditch for irrigation on the property. Bugbey would refer to this property as the Duroc vineyard.

The original Natoma Vineyard property had approximately 327 acres, and the Duroc Ranch was close to 160 acres. This gave Bugbey 487 acres from which to begin his farming operation. He would add minor amounts to both properties in later years.

All of these land transactions were speculative, in the sense that the federal government had not surveyed the land at this date. A settler could not file a claim for preemption until the territory was officially surveyed by the federal government. The confusion of all the development on the land that had not been surveyed, from railroads, water canals, and property boundaries, would come back to haunt Bugbey and many other men.

Even though Bugbey's purchase had been recorded at the county level, it was still technically federal government land. He, and all the other farmers and ranchers, were squatters until the land was officially surveyed and they were able claim a preemption or buy it from either the federal or state government. This technical point of legal ownership or clear title to the land did not impede men like Bugbey from moving forward with development plans. This was California.

Benjamin Norton Bugbey

Natoma Vineyard Topography, Soil

The Natoma Vineyard along the South Fork of the American River was not prized agricultural land, but it did have water from the recently constructed Natoma ditch. Both the Natoma Vineyard and the Duroc Ranch had some grape vine plantings when Bugbey acquired the properties. Bugbey started experimenting with crops that would grow in relatively poor soil, with a hot climate and minimal water. He evolved from a California mining pioneer to a California agricultural pioneer. The motivation, grit, and determination of Bugbey's agricultural pursuits were not a surprise. He, like many other men who made the arduous trek to California in 1849, possessed a hunger for adventure and optimism that they would succeed, even at the most foreign occupation of which they might avail themselves.

The soil along the South Fork of the American in El Dorado County is not the deep loamy soil that will sustain shallow rooted vegetable crops on a large scale. It is subsistence soil at best. No farmer would look at the landscape between the river and the rolling mound of foothills to the south as some sort of Eden begging to be planted with crops. The bench land above the river is not alluvial loam soil. The soil is thin in many spots, tends to be heavy with sand along with granite rock, cobble, and slate. There is no water holding capacity to speak of as it relates to shallow-rooted vegetable or grain crops. They will wither with the onset of the first 90° F day in June, long before harvest.

For all the challenges the land presented Bugbey, it also possessed some advantages. First was the presence of the Natoma water ditch that cut through his property. There was also a small, intermittent spring on the property, indicating that subterranean water flowed from the higher elevations down toward the river. The Natoma ditch was not lined with any concrete. It was dug into the porous soils of the area. The Natoma ditch, like all unlined water canals, allowed water to seep into the soil. Estimates of water loss due to seepage along the unlined North Fork Ditch, on the North Fork of the American River, were as high as 30 percent in the 1910s.[6] It was evident to everyone who could see that the green vegetation growing right below the ditch, in the middle of August, in 100 degree plus temperatures, when all of the other grasses had long withered away into straw, meant that the water ditch was allowing a substantial amount of water to seep into the soil and travel downhill. Fortunately for Bugbey, most of the Natoma Vineyard was below the Natoma Ditch.

The second advantage of the Natoma Vineyard was its north-facing orientation on the slope of low foothills. The northern exposure helped ameliorate the intense sunshine during summer months, which tends to scorch most south-facing landscapes. This helped conserve the moisture that was seeping from the Natomas ditch and flowing through the soil down toward the river.

Bugbey's land was not conducive to growing vegetable crops. There were too many rocks in the soil to run a plow through effectively. What did grow naturally on the land were trees and shrubs that could tap into the moisture held deep in the soil during the summer months. Another plant common and native is the California wild grape (vitis californica) which can tolerate the very dry central valley environment. While the California wild grape with its sour but edible berry was not a crop that could be marketed, certainly other grapes and vines might be successful in California.

Relative to fruit or nut trees that might also be good candidates for the land along the South Fork of the American River, grapes need minimal irrigation and start bearing fruit within just a couple of years of being planted. It might take five or more years before a fruit or nut tree would yield enough fruit to make the endeavor economically viable. Through economic and environmental considerations, Bugbey, like many other men, started planting grapevines throughout the California foothills.

Grapes were the clear winner when it came to yields, considering all the environmental factors. While fresh table grapes would command a high price in the market, there was a limited window when you can ship them to market. It was always tricky to work with perishable items because one railcar-load of grapes stuck on the tracks could go bad in a short period of time. The question was how to preserve the crop to give it a longer shelf and market life. Converting the grapes to raisins was the answer.

Natoma Vineyard

With absolutely no background in viticulture, Bugbey would become adept at managing a vineyard and learn the art of propagating vines from cuttings from existing grape plants. His thirst for learning would allow him to step into the world of wine, brandy, and champagne production. His early success and ambition would then help him become a leading authority on viticulture in California. But first, he had to master curing grapes into raisins.

One of the first challenges for Bugbey was to figure out which grape variety would produce a decent table grape. Then would this table grape make a good raisin without being leathery and tough to eat, with large seeds, after being dried? He also had to figure out the best way to dry the grapes, since mold and mildew could be a problem even in California's dry climate. Finally, if Bugbey was to take the next step and produce a commodity of higher value, he had to learn how to construct a winery and compile all the necessary equipment to bottle wine. A lot of information was already published in the field of raisins and winemaking. But not all of the printed information was relevant to the California climate. There were already men in the region making both raisins and wine that Bugbey could observe. But it is a significant leap from paper drawings and observations to a constructed reality.

Fortunately, another of Bugbey's great interests was in mechanics. He was fascinated with the design and construction of different mechanical operations. He was not an engineer, but he loved to figure out how things work. He might have made a good blacksmith if he had been so inclined. Here again, California with all its potential did not have an abundance of engineering talent residing on college campuses or manufacturing facilities. If you wanted to construct an implement to solve a problem on the farm, you had to do it yourself. This was a task that Bugbey eagerly accepted. He was on his way to becoming a vineyardist, raisin producer, and eventually a vintner.

The Natoma Vineyard was about six miles from Bugbey's house in Folsom. He could grab a stage to Mormon Island, approximately four miles away, and walk to the vineyard or ride one of his horses to the farm. Duroc Ranch was more than 15 miles to the east from Folsom. As far as real estate goes, the Natoma Vineyard was idyllic. The property sloped up a hill from the South Fork of the American River. Across the river, you had views of Negro Hill and the foothills to the north. Bugbey could build a house on a hill, with great views, high above the floodplain of the river.

By September of 1863, Bugbey was able to deliver a complimentary box of table grapes from the Natoma Vineyard to the Sacramento Daily Union, whose building was next door to the Sheriff's office. The harvested table grapes so soon after Bugbey's purchase of the property indicates that some grapevines were already planted and bearing fruit when he acquired the land.

The Sacramento Daily Union published the first of many glowing mentions of Bugbey's Fehir Sagos table grapes, which were white, thin skinned, and said to be of a luscious flavor. They noted how the grape would make a good raisin and how it should be extensively cultivated.[7]

Eighteen sixty-three was also the year that Bugbey started entering his products in the State Agricultural Society's Annual Fair. His raisin exhibit, comprising 25 pounds of raisins, was awarded a premium for dried fruit display. He also debuted his emerging wine-making skills and received a premium for 2-year-old red wine and a premium for exhibition of wines from foreign grapes by one grower.[8]

Benjamin Norton Bugbey

Bugbey Vineyardist & Promoter

Music concerts were an important form of entertainment in Sacramento. In March 1864, Bugbey was one of the sponsors of a music concert performed by the Philharmonic Society to raise funds for the Sanitary Fund. Other prominent men lending their name to the benefit concert were Judge Lorenzo Sawyer, Judge J. H. McKune, James McClatchy, and former Governor Leland Stanford. Also noted as supporting the vocal and promenade concert was B. B. Redding, who had been one of Bugbey's Deputies and had also been named as a Commissioner on the Swamp and Overflow Lands Commission. Bugbey saw how people enjoyed the music at these musical concerts. It would plant the seed of an idea for his own form of musical marketing in the future.[9]

By the spring of 1864 Bugbey could devote most of his energies to the Natoma Vineyard, as he was no longer Sheriff of Sacramento County. He began to throw himself into being a vineyardist, vintner, and promoter of mechanical arts. In addition to his entries at the State Fair, he also participated in the Mechanics' Fair, organized by the Mechanics' Institute in San Francisco. While the connection between raisins and mechanics isn't readily apparent, the structures and methods surrounding the curing of grapes into raisins are most important. Although the process was relatively simple technologically, Bugbey had to devise the drying racks and protective coverings to dehydrate the grapes after harvest. He also had to contend with the birds and rodents that wanted to munch on his curing raisins.

His favorable press attention and involvement in local organizations also garnered him visits from different newspapers and journals to see his Natoma Vineyard operation. A contributor for the California Farmer and Journal of Useful Sciences took a tour of Bugbey's farm in 1864. The journal reported how Bugbey cured his raisins.

He makes a frame work, near the vineyard, over which he places laths, making a wicker-work frame, on this he lays straw paper. The grapes must be thoroughly ripe, they are gathered and laid on this paper, in ten days they are turned over, they will then flatten and the work is done. The frames are protected from birds, bees, etc., by musketo bars. After they are thus cured they are packed in large boxes between layers of paper for a brief time, then finally packed and sent to market.[10] – California Farmer and Journal of Useful Sciences, 1864

At the time of the farm tour the Natoma Vineyard had 32,000 vines and Bugbey's Duroc vineyard, two miles west of Shingle Springs, had 17,000 vines[11]. Bugbey's large-scale curing operation

Benjamin Norton Bugbey

allowed him to produce 6,000 pounds of raisins from his 1864 harvest.[12] The yearly raisin imports into California was approximately 50,000 boxes, with the average box costing $5. The raisin imports into the Eastern United States from foreign countries were even more expensive.[13] This meant there was a healthy East Coast market for raisins from California. For any California raisin producer, $5 per box was a good return on investment. This also prompted Bugbey to propagate 40,000 cuttings of his Fiher Sagos vines and expand his operations to sell his vines to other aspiring viticulturists.[14]

The Sacramento Daily Union also reported on Bugbey's raisin exhibition at the fair of the Mechanics' Institute in San Francisco. They noted that Bugbey was continuing to experiment with different grape varietals for raisins and his overall success was a positive sign for agriculture in the foothills of California.[15]

Part of Bugbey's strategy for promoting his agricultural products was through the use of free samples. Specifically, he started sending out samples to local newspapers and regional publications. He had a knack for self-promotion and marketing. Over the years he would nurture all of his newspaper contacts to get free press mentions about his operation and products. He wasn't only promoting himself, but the overall potential of California agriculture.[16]

Bugbey was bullish on California's vineyard potential. He was studying all aspects of vineyard horticulture. By the early 1860s he learned how to propagate new vines from his existing stock. In 1864 he started advertising grape vines and cuttings for sale.[17] The grape vines were one year old and had established a root system. The cuttings were simply grape canes that had been cut after the leaves fell off in the autumn. When properly stored over the winter, they would begin to push out roots at the nodes on the cane.

> # CHOICE GRAPE VINES
> ## AND CUTTINGS FOR SALE.
>
> ### FIFTY THOUSAND FIHER ZAGOS
>
> GRAPE CUTTINGS, the best and only practical Raisin Grape in the State. For sale at THIRTY DOLLARS per thousand.
>
> #### 10,000 One-year-old Rooted Vines,
> AT SIXTY DOLLARS PER THOUSAND.
>
> Also, Cuttings of the following Choice Varieties of Table and Wine Grapes, at $20 per thousand, to wit:
> White Muscat of Alexandria, Royal Muscadine, Black Prince, White Riesling, Black Hamburg, Flame-colored Tokay, White Malaga, White Tokay, Black Zenfindol, White Sweetwater, Red Frontignon, White Nice, Verdelho, Red Frontignac, White Frontignac, Beni Carlo, Red Burgundy, Medoc Trolinger. etc., etc
>
> Raisins made from the FIHER ZAGOS GRAPE have been awarded the premium whenever contested at any Fair in this State.
>
> All orders promptly attended to when accompanied with Gold Coin, and Roots and Cuttings securely packed and forwarded through Wells, Fargo & Co.'s Express, or as directed. Address all orders to
> B. N. BUGBEY,
> Proprietor of the Natoma and Duroc Vineyards,
> Folsom, Cal.
>
> P. S.—The Fiher Zagos is a also luscious Table Grape, and excellent for White Wine and Champagne. [d19-1m

Sacramento Daily Union, Volume 28, Number 4289, 20 December 1864

Figure 5: 1864 - Choice grape vine cuttings advertisement for Bugbey's Fiher Zagos varietal. CDNC

For $30, a farmer could get a thousand of Bugbey's increasingly famous Fiher Zagos grape cuttings. For $60, a farmer could purchase the young grapevine with roots and a higher potential of survival after being planted. As advertised, all orders had to be paid for in gold coin. Bugbey would then securely pack and ship the vines or cuttings through Wells, Fargo & Co.'s Express.[18] In addition to his raisins, white wine, and champagne Fiher Zagos, aspiring vinyardists could also buy cuttings from varieties such as White Muscat of Alexandria, Royal Muscadine, Black Prince, White Riesling, Black Hamburg, Flame-colored Tokay, White Malaga, White Tokay, Black Zinfindel, White Sweetwater, Red Frontignon, White Nice, Verdelho, Red Frontignac, White Frontignac, Beni Carlo, Red Burgundy, Medoc Trollinger, and more.[19]

Bugbey's advertisement proudly mentioned that his grapes had been awarded premiums at the State Fair. Either by design or accident, Bugbey was establishing himself as an expert in all things viticulture in the state of California.

Bugbey was also planting fruit trees at his Natoma property. As a testament to his agricultural expertise, he sent to the Sacramento Daily Union a branch from his orange tree bearing five mature oranges in January 1865[20]. Fig trees were also being planted. Bugbey entered several drums of dried figs at the next State Fair.[21]

Sacramento was the beneficiary of Bugbey's produce. The store of Church & Clark on Front Street proudly displayed and sold Bugbey's raisins.[22] The general conclusion was that the locally produced raisins were equal to or better than the imported Mediterranean varieties at the same price. There was simmering local pride that California was relying less on imported goods and producing commodities and specialty crops that were better in quality than the imported items. People were eagerly anticipating the time, in the not-too-distant future, when California would be exporting more agricultural bounty, both domestically and internationally.

Since the occasional gift basket of grapes or raisins to newspapers had generated free press for those items, Bugbey started sending out cases of wine to local newspapers as well. The newsroom at the Sacramento Daily Union must have been quite excited to receive a couple of cases of complimentary wine, consisting of ten different varieties grown, fermented, and bottled at the Natoma Vineyard in 1865. The only caveat of the generous news article was the mention that "Age alone is wanting to make them a favorite beverage for experienced wine drinkers."[23] And it probably was a fair assessment, since the wines were of a recent vintage.

Perhaps because of the generous wine offering, the newspaper sent up a correspondent to inspect and report on the Natoma Vineyard.

Bugbey's vineyard at this place comprises 44 acres, containing 32,000 vines, principally - foreign and domestic varieties, all of which will bear the coming season. The vineyard is located in a little hollow or depression of land, very much in form resembling a butcher's tray. It is sheltered from all strong winds except that from the northwest, which but seldom blows. Through the middle of the vineyard runs a small stream of spring-water, while around the south and east sides runs the ditch of the Natoma Water and Mining Company, which is used three times a year in May and June for irrigating purposes.

The soil, which contains considerable stone, is composed of the debris of rotten granite quartz and slate, the latter rock in many cases cropping out of the ground. The soil varies in depth from six inches to three feet upon a substratum of decomposed slate rock, into the vertical; fissures of which the roots of the vines penetrate and derive warmth. The vines are of seventy-two varieties, the larger number of one kind being the Fiher Sagos, a variety of white grape from which Bugbey makes his raisins. By some parties this grape is claimed to be the white Malaga, with a Hungarian name— but the fruit of white Malaga, which grows in the same vineyard of which a large number of vines are in bearing, contradicts such an assumption. The Fiher Sagos is a prolific bearer, with very large, bunches of translucent, oblong-shaped fruit, while the white Malaga is a scanty bearer, with straggling, bunches of round berries. No candid person can see the two vines growing side by side and claim that they are of one variety

From the Fiher Sagos, Bugbey has, this season, made about; 10,000, pounds of raisins, besides making a large quantity of wine— they being a most excellent wine grape, also a table grape, but too tender to bear rough transportation. The process of making raisins is simply to pluck the grapes when they begin to shrivel, and place them upon scaffolding in the open air and sun, turning the bunches twice during the curing. About twenty days is consumed in this way when the bunches are put in about sixty or eighty pound boxes and pressed between boards, in layers, they sweating slightly during the process. After exposing them to the air for a short time, to evaporate the remaining moisture and become cool, the raisins are packed in boxes ready for sale.

In wine making Bugbey lets the grapes shrivel somewhat before plucking, as he thinks the wine is thereby made of better quality, although of less quantity. He has made about 8,000 gallons of wine this season, a part of which is fermented in the pulp and skins in large redwood vats containing 1,000 gallons each, and a part is made by pressing out the juice and fermenting that in the vats separate from the skin and pulp. Bugbey will probably make 1,000 gallons of cognac brandy this fall, using the second growth or late grapes exclusively for that purpose. His wine cellar and fermenting room are on the south side of the vineyard, the cellar part being built into the hill. The cellar walls and roof are composed entirely of the slatestone found on the spot; the cellar is 18 feet wide by 54 feet long, the room being 18 feet high in the clear, the walls two feet thick, the floor laid in cement, the door of heavy iron thus making it fireproof and insuring an equal temperature at all seasons of the year. The fermenting house on top is 22 feet wide by 54 feet long. In the cellar there are two casks of redwood of 1,400 gallons each, and one oak cask of 1,010 gallons, besides many smaller ones.

Some idea may be had of the climate of the vineyard from the fact that an orange tree growing in the open air bears a fine crop of fruit which matures in February. A gigantic specimen of the prickly pear, a semi-tropical plant, is in the vineyard, and bore a most plentiful crop of fruit this year. Experience having taught Bugbey the

Benjamin Norton Bugbey

inadvisability of growing a great number of varieties of grapes for wine purposes, he intends reducing the number to twelve of the best; as soon as new vines ; can come into bearing in their place.

Another vineyard of Bugbey's is located at Duroc, about two miles from Shingle Springs, El Dorado County. It consists of twenty acres, containing 15,500 vines, all of which, except 4,000, are of foreign varieties. Hundreds of similar vineyards maybe found all through the Sierras, from the foothills up to 2,800 to 3,000 feet elevation.[24]

In just a few short years after leaving the elected position of Sacramento County Sheriff, Bugbey had re-invented himself from lawman to vineyardist. He wasn't just a farmer; he was applying mechanical arts to construct a multi-faceted vineyard operation from raisins to wine. It was apparent to all who visited his Natoma Vineyard that he was not simply growing grapes; he was growing an industry.

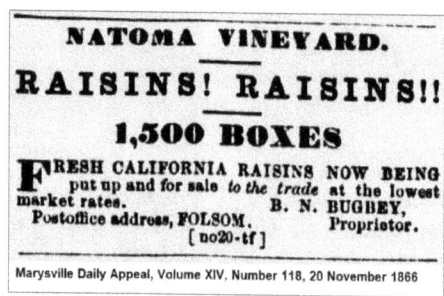

Figure 6: 1866 - Natoma Vineyard Raisins advertised in the Marysville Daily Appeal. CDNC

He had become thoughtful in his approach to expanding his operations, making sure that all his endeavors yielded a return on investment. A large part of his success at the fairs, from his exhibits to young wines, could be attributed to his attention to the details. Bugbey truly wanted to produce a good product, which meant devising structures and operations that resulted in good products for the consumer.

Political Party Civil War

The blossoming of the Natoma Vineyard did not diminish Bugbey's penchant for politics. The epic battle for the soul of the United States ended on June 22nd, 1865. With the end of the Civil War the Union Democrat Party had lost its unifying purpose, which was to support a whole United States. Even though Bugbey was spending most of his time in El Dorado County, and even had a house at the

Natoma Vineyard, he retained his residence in Folsom so he could participate in Sacramento County politics.

As one civil war had concluded, a new civil war broke out for the control of the Union Democrat Party in Sacramento. The Union Democrats had assembled in the California Assembly chambers on July 25th, 1865, to start their convention. As the delegates gathered in the Assembly chambers, the Low or Short Hair delegates were on one side of the room and the anti-Low or Long Hairs occupied the other side. The convention had barely begun to nominate convention officers when accusations that the voice votes of the Short Hairs were being ignored.[25]

In an attempt to stop W. H. Barton from being elected convention Secretary on a voice vote and taking his seat, the opposing Short Hairs intercepted him on his way up to the front of the chambers. The convention quickly devolved into a brawl. Solid hickory canes were used by both sides to beat one another. Spittoons filled with their fluid contents flew across the room like "bomb-shells on a battle-field," reported the Sacramento Daily Union. Inkstands from the Assembly desks were thrown by the warring convention delegates. Pistols were used as clubs. Chairs were broken and the pieces used to club the opposing faction. Several men were seriously injured in the melee.[26]

In the end, the Long Hair Union Democrats left the battlefield of the Assembly chambers and retired to the Turn-Verein Hall, where they would commence with their own convention.[27]

The Low Union Democrat Party convention continued the next day in the Assembly chambers and was opened by P. J. Hopper as chairman, who was also editor of the Folsom Telegraph. While there were differences on policy between the Short Hairs or Low Union Democrats and the Long Hairs in Sacramento County[28], a larger issue was the difference between rural county delegates and Sacramento City delegates. With some exceptions, the Short Hair Union Democrat delegates represented the more rural communities such as Brighton, Folsom, and Mormon Island.

One of the big issues for the Short Hair Union Democrats was a national currency and the repeal of the Specific Contract Law in California. The Union had gone off the gold standard in order to finance the Civil War. California was vigorously opposed to any monetary system not backed by gold or other precious metal. The prevailing rational was that printed federal currency, greenbacks, would lead to unregulated inflation as the government printed money with no precious metal backing.[29]

As Sheriff, Bugbey at one point refused to accept United States legal tender notes for the payment of criminal fines.[30] He, like many other businesses, specified in advertisements that payment was to be in gold only. The Specific Contract Act of 1863 specified that private contracts could stipulate how a debt was to be repaid. For instance, it could specify only gold, or that greenbacks and silver could be used to repay the debt.[31][32][33][34]

While the Specific Contract Act applied to state and local contracts, the federal government and other businesses paid for services in greenbacks. This meant that no matter how hard California tried to use only gold for its monetary system, local governments and businesses were still forced to accept paper money. This would become an issue for Bugbey: He was selling his wines outside of California and being paid in greenbacks instead of gold—but his debtors were demanding gold.

Bugbey was nominated for Sheriff at the Short Hair Union County convention, along with John Foley, Thomas McConnell and John Rooney. Bugbey withdrew his name from consideration, and the nomination went to John Rooney.[35] The current Sheriff, James McClatchy, was nominated by the Long Hair Democrats at their convention at the Turn Verein Hall.

John Rooney would withdraw from the race for Sheriff and throw his support to McClatchy in September. A competing candidate, James Lansing, had been put forth by another faction of the Union Democrat Party.[36] Lansing went on to win the election for Sheriff. Bugbey showed his support for Lansing by being listed as one of the sureties for the $100,000 bond that the elected Sheriff had to produce before being sworn into office. Bugbey committed to $10,000 for Lansing's bond.[37] Bugbey's support for Lansing would be used against him in future political dramas.

The political fight for the Union Democrat Party would create deep divisions in the community. Bugbey closed out 1865 as an honorary committee member for a grand ball to raise funds for a new Masonic Hall. The fundraiser was held at the Agricultural Pavilion on December 13, 1865. Other men on the committee for the Masonic Hall fundraiser included Judge Lorenzo Sawyer, B. B. Redding, H. H. Hartley, and Judge J. H. McKune. The ticket price was a hefty $5, and tickets could be purchased at R. Dale's and L. K. Hammer's music stores.[38] Politics aside, Bugbey was still maintaining his involvement in Sacramento civic affairs.

---

[1] *A Volume of Memoirs and Genealogy of Representative Citizens of Northern California Including Biographies of Many of Those Who Have Passed Away*, (Chicago Standard Genealogical Publishing Company 1901).

[2] El Dorado County Deed Book H, page 165. Note: Bugbey states in his statement for the State Fair Gold Medal (Transactions of the California State Agricultural Society During the Years 1870 and 1871), that he purchased the Natoma Vineyard in 1861. The transaction was formally recorded in January 1863.

[3] Ibid.

[4] El Dorado County Deed Book H, page 166

[5] Sioli, Paolo, *Historical Souvenir of El Dorado County, California*, (Paolo Sioli, Publisher, Oakland, CA, 1883).

[6] Pitzer, Gary, *150 Years of Water: The History of the San Juan Water District,* (Water Education Foundation, 2004).

[7] Sacramento Daily Union, Volume 26, Number 3904, September 26, 1863, CDNC

[8] California Farmer and Journal of Useful Sciences, Volume 20, Number 9, October 7, 1863, CDNC

[9] Sacramento Daily Union, Volume 27, Number 4056, March 22, 1864, CDNC

[10] California Farmer and Journal of Useful Sciences, Volume 22, Number 16, November 11, 1864, CDNC

[11] Ibid.

[12] Sacramento Daily Union, Volume 28, Number 4219, September 28, 1864, CDNC

[13] Ibid.

[14] Ibid.

[15] Ibid.

[16] California Farmer and Journal of Useful Sciences, Volume 22, Number 11, October 7, 1864, CDNC

[17] Sacramento Daily Union, Volume 28, Number 4289, December 20, 1864, CDNC

[18] Ibid.

[19] Ibid.

[20] Sacramento Daily Union, Volume 28, Number 4306, January 9, 1865, CDNC

[21] Daily Alta California, Volume 17, Number 5678, September 22, 1865, CDNC

[22] Sacramento Daily Union, Volume 30, Number 4562, November 4, 1865, CDNC

[23] Sacramento Daily Union, Volume 30, Number 4584, November 30, 1865, CDNC

[24] Sacramento Daily Union, Volume 30, Number 4586, December 2, 1865, CDNC

[25] Sacramento Daily Union, Volume 29, Number 4475, July 26, 1865, CDNC

[26] Ibid.

[27] Ibid.

[28] Sacramento Daily Union, Volume 29, Number 4476, July 27, 1865, CDNC

[29] Barbeau, Daniel, *Pacific Rebels: California's Monetary Secession During the Civil War*, (Grove City College, December 16, 2013).

[30] Sacramento Daily Union, Volume 28, Number 4300, January 2, 1865, CDNC

[31] Barbeau, Daniel, *Pacific Rebels: California's Monetary Secession During the Civil War*, (Grove City College, December 16, 2013).

[32] Daily Alta California, Volume 16, Number 5265, August 2, 1864, *The Specific Contract Law and Loyalty*. CDNC

[33] Moses, Bernard, et. al., *Legal Tender Notes in California*, (The Quarterly Journal of

Economics, Vol. 7, No. 1 (Oct., 1892), pp 1 – 25, Oxford University Press).

[34] Fankhauser, William C., *A Financial History of California, Public Revenues, Debts, and Expenditures, 1872 Collapse of Mining Stocks*, pp 101 - 408, (University of California Publications in Economics, Vol. 3, No. 2, November 13, 1913).

[35] Sacramento Daily Union, Volume 29, Number 4476, July 27, 1865, CDNC

[36] Sacramento Daily Union, Volume 29, Number 4510, September 5, 1865, CDNC

[37] Sacramento Daily Union, Volume 30, Number 4587, December 4, 1865, CDNC

[38] Sacramento Daily Union, Volume 30, Number 4567, 10 November 10, 1865, CDNC

Chapter 7: Natoma Expansion, Scandals, Tragedy 1866 - 1869

Land Speculator

While Bugbey was expanding his vineyard and wine making operations, he was also doing a little land speculation outside of the Folsom and El Dorado County areas. In 1862, when Bugbey was Sheriff, he bought the west quarter lot at 5th and K streets in Sacramento from Daniel Sizer[1] and Eli Mayo[2]. Daniel Sizer had also come over with Bugbey from the East Coast in 1849.[3] The lot was in the same block where he had his furniture store 10 years earlier. He invested $800 to buy the lot and then sold it in 1865 for $350 to J. E. Parker.[4]

In April of 1866, Bugbey bought 162 acres from the Joseph L. Folsom Estate in the land grant Rancho Rio de Los Americanos. The subdivision was known as Norris 162.13 A.[5] The deed notes that the land was in the southern part of Rancho, as depicted on an 1865 map drawn by F. J. Arnold. The physical boundaries were given as:

Beginning at a point from which an oak tree 42 inches in diameter marked "B.T.F." bears south 72 ¾ East 2.9 chains, running thence South 89 ½ West 59.77 chains, thence North 1 ½ East 27.87 chains, thence East 58.25 chains, thence South 1 ½ East 27.10 chains to the place of the beginning.[6] - Sacramento County Deed book document 18660604, pages 269, 270, 28 May 1866.

The Rancho Rio de Los Americanos boundaries on the 1866 patent map begin with the western boundary at an oak tree on the American River. It is unclear from the deed if that oak tree and the one marked B.T.F are one and the same. In a confirming deed entry,[7] many of the subdivisions listed as being sold in 1866 refer to the buyer's name as the subdivision. For instance, the sale of 82 acres to F. Routier is listed as the Routier 82.46 a.

Bugbey obviously had bought a subdivision of land that was originally recognized for Norris. But was this the same Samuel Norris who acquired the Mexican land grant Rancho Del Paso and Rancho San Juan in 1850? Samuel Norris decided to establish Norristown on the south side of the American River, east of Sacramento, and not on his property.[8] The town never took off, reverted to farm land, and was referred to as Norris' Ranch by 1858.[9]

In 1866, the state Agricultural Commissioners were touring California, looking for a suitable location for an agricultural, mining, and mechanical arts college. The commissioners visited Norristown, described as being four miles from the city of Sacramento.[10] The commissioners decided to select a site in Berkeley and merge with the existing College of California in 1868.[11]

Bugbey was close to the Agricultural Commissioners from his work promoting California vineyards and entries at the State Fair. He may have known that the commissioners were going to be looking at land along the American River. Whether the land Bugbey bought was located near Norristown or another location is not clear. He may have just been speculating on land with the hopes that the agricultural college would be located nearby. Bugbey had no interest in land in that area since he left the farm at Salisbury Station. All of his efforts in agriculture focused on his El Dorado County properties.

The subdivisions being sold by the Folsom Estate came with financing. To purchase property the buyer had to have 25 percent of the price as a down payment, and the remaining balance was due in 12 months at 10 percent interest.[12] Bugbey bought the Norris subdivision for $3 per acre for approximately $486. He sold the property to Samuel Dowden in July 1867 fifteen months after he bought it for $300.[13]

California Vineyard Expansions, Impending Glut

Grapes, raisins, and wine looked like a good bet to California farmers, and the acreage devoted to vineyards increased steadily through the mid-1860s. The downside for the viticulture industry was that few of these farmers had any knowledge or experience with growing grapes. Early statistics pointed to a future grape glut. One estimate was that California would have 10 to 15 million grape-bearing vines in production for 1866.[14] Bugbey's Natoma Vineyard operation in 1865 had 44 acres with 32,000 vines. He produced approximately 10,000 pounds of raisins, 8,000 gallons of wine, and 1,000 gallons of cognac brandy in 1865.[15]

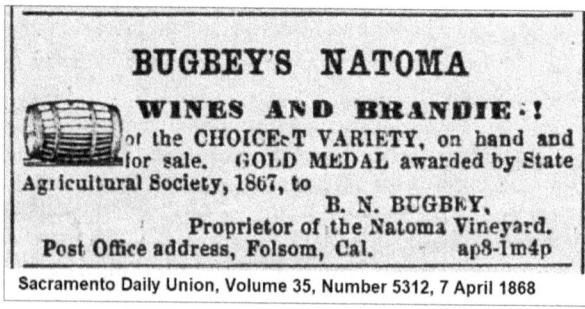

Figure 7: 1868 - Bugbey's Natoma wine and brandy advertisement. CDNC

The drum beat to plant vineyards continued even in the face of over planting and the possibility of overproduction. Economic studies were promoting a move away from purchasing recently surveyed government land at $1.25 per acre for gold and copper mining and instead planting the land in vineyards. The analysis showed a higher rate of return based on an expected grape yield and price per ton over the same capital being invested into hard rock mining. A detailed return on investment analysis estimated the cost of planting 30 acres of land ($1.25 per acre) over a six-year period to be $10,000. At the end of year six, making 28,000 gallons of wine would produce gross revenue of $32,000 per year. After subtracting production costs, the vineyard owner would net $13,000 per year.[16] A review of the analysis highlighted men such as Bugbey who had taken old mining property and were making an excellent return on their investment with vineyards to produce raisins, wine, and brandy.[17]

As the Daily Alta California pointed out in May 1866, the placer mines in the foothills had been exhausted, and the men occupying that land had turned their attention to agriculture. Based on a rough estimate of 2 million grape vines bearing fruit in Sierra foothill counties, it was estimated that 150,000 gallons of wine would be made in 1866.[18]

Later in 1866, the Sacramento Daily Union noted that with an estimated 25 million grape vines coming into full production within a couple years, leading to increasing amounts of wine being produced, there was little organized activity to increase the wine market beyond California.[19]

A strange apathy seems to possess the great mass of the wine growers of California, who, while generally aware that the prosperity of the wine interest is soon to be dependent on an export demand, yet take no measures, however simple, to stimulate or introduce the sale of their wines in foreign markets? At the present time there are at least twenty-five million vines and cuttings planted in this State, the whole of which will be in full bearing in five years, and will produce a quantity of wine far in excess of the domestic demand for the entire Pacific Coast. Many of the producers already complain that wine is being made in advance of the trade demand, and this state of things promises to increase until the wine growing interest is seriously damaged, unless exportation to foreign ports relieves the market."[20] - 1866 Sacramento Daily Union, Volume 31, Number 4804, 21 August 1866

In a small marketing effort to develop a wine market outside of California, Bugbey sent four cases of assorted wines to the International Exposition held in Paris, France. He also continued to send samples of his raisins and wines to regional newspapers[21] and back to the Department of Agriculture in Washington D. C.[22]

Bugbey must have been overjoyed when he received an order from champagne producer Louis Duvau for an assortment of his wine to be sent to France.[23] The European order must have greatly boosted Bugbey's confidence in his winery enterprise. In April of 1868, he had expanded his operation to boost the production of sparkling wine or champagne. He also hired a superintendent, with experience working for a German producer of sparkling wine, to manage his operations. The new employee had recently come to the United States from Europe, so Bugbey now had some European experience for crafting his wines.[24]

Who could deny that, within a few short years of turning his full attention to his vineyard operations, Bugbey had built a substantial operation, from raisins to wines, all on his land? His success and experience did not go unnoticed. Bugbey was invited to sit on three standing committees of the State Agricultural Society, investigating and reporting on advancement of the wine spirit industry.

On Cultivation of the Grape and Pruning the Vine, he served with I. N. Hoag of Yolo; Robert Chalmers of El Dorado; Geo. West of Stockton; B. D. Wilson of Los Angeles; J. E. Snyder of Sonoma; J. E. Nickerson of Lincoln; G. N. Swezy of Marysville; L. J. Rose of Los Angeles, and Dr. J. Strentzel of Contra Costa.

On Wine Making and Clarification of Wine, he met with A. Haraszthy of San Francisco; Craig of Sonoma; Geo. Gozinger of San Francisco; Matthew Keller of Los Angeles; B. D. Wilson of Los Angeles; Robert Chalmers, of Coloma; J. E. Nickerson of Lincoln; Geo. West of Stockton; J. Strentzel of Martinez; Jacob Nought of Sacramento, and A. Eberhardt of San Francisco.

On Manufacture of Brandy from the Grape, his fellow members were General Nagle of San Jose; Geo. Johnston of Sacramento; L. J. Rose of Los Angeles; Robert Chalmers of Coloma; O. W. Craig of Sonoma; and Chas. King of St. Helena.[25]

Through his promotion of California viticulture, Bugbey emerges as the one of the leading voices for California agriculture. He views it almost as his mission or destiny to be an agricultural ambassador for California. In December of 1865, he forwards samples of his Kona variety oranges and samples of his raisins to the Commissioner of Agriculture in Washington, D.C., as evidence of what California can produce. The new gold is California agriculture, in Bugbey's vision.[26]

At the 13th annual State Fair, he took premiums for his white and red wines, plus awards for best exhibition of grapes and wine.[27] In 1866 the Natoma Vineyard produced 200 tons of grapes with an estimate of producing 15,000 gallons of wine, 3,000 gallons of brandy, and 1,000 boxes of raisins.[28] By the end of the year, Bugbey had planted 76 acres of his property in grapevines and was employing 17 men to tend the vineyard and produce the wine.[29]

Bugbey's vineyards had become his sole source of income, and he was doing pretty well. He had a house in Folsom, another house within the Natoma Vineyard, plus a fairly impressive home on a hill that overlooked the vineyard and the South Fork of the American River.

In 1867 Bugbey expanded his nursery operation and started advertising 100,000 grape cuttings for sale. Instead of trying to handle all of the orders himself, he enlisted three other agents from San Francisco, Stockton, and Marysville to market his nursery stock. But he also had competition, as other vineyardists started to advertise grape cuttings from their farms as well.[30]

Mediocre California Wine

In an effort to add national validity to what California thought were wines rivalling the best European products, numerous vineyards from throughout the state sent samples of their soil and best wines to the United States Agricultural Department back in Washington, D.C. The results did not provide confirmation that California was producing superior wines. The report concluded:

The Committee are of the opinion that many of the samples submitted did not fairly represent the vineyards from which they were obtained, either because of very defective corking or because of the wine being bottled too soon after fermentation, or from other defective handling. Whatever may be the cause, it seemed unjust to pronounce any opinion upon the merits of wines which were plainly unfit for drinking. For this reason, the Committee do not express any other opinion (than just remarked) upon a great majority of the samples submitted to them.[31] - Sacramento Daily Union, Volume 33, Number 5049, 3 June 1867

The soil analysis from Bugbey's vineyard also indicated the soil was marginal at best. The report noted the shallow soil comprised of clay slate with a depth from zero to four feet.

[T]he soil of Bugbey is a soil of indifferent quality as regards constitution, and not capable of being benefited much by the slate rock on which it rests...[32] - Sacramento Daily Union, Volume 33, Number 5049, 3 June 1867

Benjamin Norton Bugbey

After reading the soil analysis the local newspaper reported, "That it would be called poor soil; yet it produces the finest grapes."[33] However, a later report from State Agricultural Society's standing committee on Cultivation of the Grape and Pruning of the Vine in 1872 stated that the sort of soils prevalent at the Natoma Vineyard were just fine for grapes.

No vineyard should be planted on the rich alluvial soil of our river bottoms with the expectation of producing good wine, nor are the small valleys in the foothills as favorable for this purpose as the less fertile soil of the surrounding elevations. A subsoil of broken decomposed lime or sandstone, slate or granite, with evidences of volcanic debris, is undoubtedly the best. The vast quantities of red lands of the second elevation from our river bottoms, and extending back to the foothills in all portions of the State, are well adapted to the growth of the grape for the table, for raisins, and for wines and brandies, but for the light table wines a more elevated location is deemed preferable.[34] - Transactions of the California State Agricultural Society During the Years 1870 and 1871, Sacramento: T.A. Springe, State Printer, 1872

Contradicting recommendations for soil were as common as the different cultural practices a vineyard manager might employ. Every farmer did things a little differently, sometimes yielding the same results. Bugbey generally preferred planting grape cuttings when expanding his vineyard as opposed to planting a cutting that had rooted in a separate nursery after a year. He didn't want to transplant the rooted vine, whereas some farmers preferred the transplant. This was highlighted in a report from the State Agricultural Society's standing committee, Cultivation of the Grape and Pruning of the Vine.

There seems to be a considerable difference of opinion and practice between the different members of your committee, as to whether it is the better plan to plant cuttings in the vineyard, where they will not again be disturbed by transplanting, or to plant them in beds, for rooting, to be lifted carefully at one year of age and transplanted permanently in the vineyard. Messrs. Snyder, Bugbey, and Swezy practice the former course, with some exceptions; while Messrs. Chalmers and Nickerson practice the latter, and urge strong reasons for it. Bugbey takes the precaution to plant two cuttings in each hole, to insure a growing vine, placing the bottoms in opposite sides of the hole, so as not to interfere with the roots of the one while lifting the other the following Spring, in case both grow.[35] - Transactions of the California State Agricultural Society During the Years 1870 and 1871, Sacramento: T.A. Springe, State Printer, 1872

Benjamin Norton Bugbey

Soil analysis aside, some of Bugbey's wines did rate a mention within the California State Agricultural Society report for years 1870 and 1871, if only to note potential and not necessarily quality.

Of the red wines, the red Traminer (Bugbey 1863) the red Verdelho (Bugbey 1865), and the Muscatel (Perkins, Stern & Co.) are worthy of mention rather as giving promise for the future than as realizing the proper qualities of a sweet wine.[36] - Transactions of the California State Agricultural Society During the Years 1870 and 1871, Sacramento: T.A. Springe, State Printer, 1872

If the less than sterling report on California soils or the wine being produced gave Bugbey or any other California vintner a moment of pause, it was short-lived. That the vintners had gone to the trouble of submitting soil and wine samples demonstrated how serious they were taking their agricultural enterprises. They all knew that a government report would not determine their destiny. As long as they were selling product and earning money, the California winemakers would continue growing grapes.

Mechanics' Institute

California was taking note of Bugbey's involvement in the development of a fully integrated winery. With the exception of the wine casks used for fermenting wine, everything else had to be designed, acquired and built locally for the processing of tons of grapes, crushing, fermentation and, finally, bottling. A winery is a manufacturing plant. A certain amount of mechanical familiarity was needed to construct such a facility.

One of the early promoters of the art of mechanization was the Mechanics' Institute in San Francisco. In addition to organizing an annual mechanics fair to display the latest mechanical applications and the resulting products, the Mechanics' Institute maintained a library so men could learn from others who had committed their designs in a print format. They also became involved in promoting California ingenuity and its potential.

In 1867 the Mechanics' Institute held a contest offering a $1,000 premium for best essay on "Resources of California and Best Method of Developing the Same." One half of the cash award to the winner and the balance from the first proceeds from the sale of the successful work, which was to be published by the Mechanics' Institute. All the essays were to be reviewed and voted upon by an esteemed panel of judges, one of whom was B. N. Bugbey.[37] Sadly, all the essays were destroyed in the 1906 San Francisco earthquake and resulting fire.

Bugbey was not the only grower of grapes along the American River. Directly to the west of him were Henry Mette's and Andrew Tray's vineyards. Another gentleman engaged in viticulture at Beal's Bar was Lazarus Seffer, a native of Austria. In 1867 Bugbey and A. P. Catlin, one of the original organizers of the Natoma Water and Mining Company, sponsored Lazarus Seffer to become a naturalized citizen of the United States.[38]

Fire At The Winery

As generous as Bugbey was with his time in helping out fellow farmers, it appears there were some people that either did not like him or possibly his success. On the evening of July 17, 1867, Bugbey's winery was set ablaze. One of the wine cellars caught fire, and 12,000 gallons of wine and brandy were destroyed. The estimated loss was between $8,000 and $9,000. Bugbey did have fire insurance, but it was still a setback for his operations.[39]

So convinced was he that the fire was not an accident, Bugbey took out an advertisement offering a $500 reward for the arrest and conviction of the person responsible for the arson attack.[40]

> **$500 REWARD.—I WILL PAY** the above reward for the arrest and conviction of the person or persons who burned my Storehouse and Wine at Natoma Vineyard on the night of the 17th of July, 1867.
> a16-1mlp   B. N. BUGBEY.

Sacramento Daily Union, Volume 33, Number 5128, 4 September 1867

Figure 8: 1867 - $500 Reward offered by Bugbey for the arrest and conviction of the arsonist who set fire to his wine storeroom. CDNC

Bugbey had arrested many men during his tenure as Granite Township Constable and as Sacramento County Sheriff. He even had to oversee the execution of two murderers while Sheriff. There was no shortage of people who may have wanted to harm him or derail his success. Another irritant to some men was Bugbey's employment of Chinese immigrants at his vineyard, where he employed as many as 25 Chinese laborers. In discussing labor relations, he pointed out that Chinese were considered competent, trustworthy, and faithful.[41] But there was growing anger and resentment in the community and in the state against men like Bugbey who employed Chinese immigrants. This anti-Chinese fervor would glow even brighter in the 1880s.

On September 2, 1867, Benjamin Norton Bugbey woke to his 40th birthday. He was a leading authority on viticulture and winemaking in California. Apart from the arson at this wine cellar, his business was good. He was friend or acquaintance to many of the leading men in California politics and business. He was campaigning to be elected Sacramento County Sheriff, again. While some political drama swirled around him, he had achieved more in the 18 years since he came to California than most men would attain in a life time.

Even with fire damage at the Natoma vineyard, Bugbey was able to enter his grapes, raisins, and wine at the 14th State Fair. He walked away with first premium of $3 for his Tokay grapes, best display of raisin, $15, and awards for best claret wine and brandy made from grapes, two years old.[42] Later in the year Bugbey would be awarded a Gold Medal from the State Agricultural Society for his exhibition and promotion of raisins from his vineyard.[43] The gold medal would be featured in an 1868 advertisement for Bugbey's Natoma Wine and Brandie, which failed to mention the award was for raisins, not wine or spirits.[44]

He had also managed to rebuild parts of his winery operation by the fall harvest and crush with an ability of producing over 12,000 gallons of wine in 1867.[45]

But if it was not fire ravaging Bugbey's business; it was the unpredictable autumn weather. An intense rainstorm hit the Central Valley in early October.[46] Bugbey's workers had just picked the Fiher Zagos grapes and prepared them to dehydrate into raisins in the normally warm California sun. The unexpected rain, cool weather, and high humidity destroyed the prospects of curing the grapes into raisins. Bugbey quickly gathered as much of the harvest as possible and started producing brandy with them.[47]

This marked a soft turning point for the Natoma Vineyards. Bugbey's wine production was increasing along with orders both domestic and foreign. In future years he would turn more of his capital and energy toward making wine and spirits and less to table grapes and raisins.

Bigler Assessor Appointment

In the winter of 1867, Bugbey was greeted with the news that he had been nominated by the President of the United States as California's Fourth District Internal Revenue Assessor. This was a surprise to Bugbey, because he had never sought the position and had not talked to any elected official about the job opening. Within a few short weeks, the presidential nomination, which had to be confirmed by the Senate, would turn into a vitriolic political drama centered on Bugbey's loyalty to the Union.

One of the jobs of an assessor in an internal revenue district was to calculate the taxes for the excise laws of the United States government. This meant visiting property and assessing what activities and inventory were subject to federal taxes such as those on wine and brandy. Bugbey was assessed $145.35 for inventory worth $4,844.30 in 1863.[48] In 1864 he spent a couple months working as an auctioneer, for which he was assessed $3.33.[49] He was assessed $10 for being a manufacturer of alcohol spirits and an additional $50 for 1,000 gallons of wine in 1864.[50] The assessor for each of these levies was John Avery.

Bugbey was a very good candidate for the assessor position. He had spent several years collecting taxes as Sheriff of Sacramento County, and he had also paid federal revenue taxes through business operations. Unfortunately, as the political brawl between the Long Hair and Short Hair Union Democrats demonstrated in 1865, national and local politics were much divided at the time, and all nominations by President Johnson were heavily scrutinized by the Senate.

When Abraham Lincoln ran for a second term for president as a Republican, he selected Andrew Johnson, a Democrat, as his Vice President, to broaden his base and display national unity. Andrew Johnson was a Southern Democrat who supported the Union but not necessarily full equality for former slaves. When Lincoln was assassinated, Johnson became president on April 15th, 1865. He was still viewed as a Southern Democrat by the Republican majority Congress. Johnson did not do himself any favors with the Republicans by opposing the Fourteenth Amendment to the constitution, which gave citizenship to former slaves.

Former Democratic California Governor John Bigler had failed to win a seat in Congress and was effectively out of work. In 1866 he had his brother, William Bigler, former Pennsylvania Governor and Senator, lobby President Johnson to appoint him as California's Fourth District Internal Revenue Assessor for the federal government, pushing out John Avery who had served since 1863.[51] The fact that John Bigler was a Democrat who supported slavery and was now being nominated to a federal job did not go over very well with California's Union Republican Senator John Conness.

Senator Conness decided to halt the confirmation of Bigler to the assessor position. In December 1866, Bigler wrote to the Senator to plead his case for confirmation.[52]

Bigler argued that while Senator Conness may find his appointment distasteful, John Avery's removal was welcomed by many in the Fourth District, including the city of Sacramento. Avery refused to turn over his internal revenue records to Bigler when he assumed the office before his Senate confirmation. Bigler blamed all difficulties

Benjamin Norton Bugbey

with performing the duties of assessor on the lack of cooperation of the previous assessor and assistant assessors.[53]

Bigler also countered the notion that he would only appoint rebel sympathizers. He maintained that all the applicants for assistant assessors were true friends of the Union. There was considerable pressure on Senator Conness to stop the appointment because California Governor Low, Controller Oulton, and Attorney General McCullough were lobbying him to squash the confirmation of Bigler.[54]

Senator Conness replied to Bigler's letter in late January of 1867, after the Senate had already rejected Bigler's confirmation. In his reply, Conness recounted how President Johnson told him that it was Bigler's brother who recommended him for the job. He ridiculed Bigler, a former Governor of California, for being no friend of the Union and a person who lacked the capacity to understand the importance of great political issues, namely the institution of slavery.[55]

Shortly after Senator Conness replied to Bigler's letter, he advised President Johnson to nominate Bugbey for the position of assessor. Conness knew Bugbey because he also had mined for gold on the South Fork of the American River when he came to California and was originally, like Bugbey, a member of the Democrat Party. Unfortunately, Senator Conness must not have been in touch with the politics of Sacramento County before he persuaded Johnson to nominate Bugbey. Just as there was a coordinated effort to sink the Bigler nomination, local Union Democrats and Republicans worked to scuttle Bugbey's confirmation.

One of the first darts thrown at Bugbey was his support of Democrat J. C. Goods for District Attorney and James Lansing for Sheriff in the prior election.[56]

The Sacramento Bee went after Bugbey in an editorial for being little better than a Bigler appointment.

The bully has not yet been subdued, but repeated chastisements are having their effect upon his promises, which, like all his kind, he makes only to be broken whenever opportunity offers. But Congress is the master of the situation, and if the President's race is not nearly run his power is fast falling to zero. He has professed of late to have some respect for the Senate, but he has an awkward way of showing it. It was but the other day that one of his appointees for this coast, ex-Governor John Bigler, who was nominated to the Assessorship of the Fourth California District at the special importunity of his brother, William Bigler, of Pennsylvania, was rejected by the Senate on political grounds. And now, the President, persisting in his wrong-doing, adds farther insult to the Senate by naming for that same place, B. N. Bugbey, who works and votes with John Bigler, and who therefore, on political grounds, is equally

Benjamin Norton Bugbey

obnoxious to the Union people of California. We understand that Bugbey's name was sent to the President by Hon. John Conness, and that to him belongs the glory.[57]A7 - Marysville Daily Appeal, Number 44, 21 February 1867

Bugbey was irked at the vitriol of the attacks against him. He felt his honesty with his voting record was being held against him in absence of the facts. He replied to the Sacramento Bee, and in particular to James McClatchy, in an open letter in the Sacramento Daily Union.

To the Public.— McClatchy, Editor and one of the Proprietors of the Bee, attempts to rob me of my reputation as a Union man. For those who know us both no reply to his slander is necessary. But, for the information of strangers, I will give a plain statement of facts. Since the formation of the Union party I have been a member of it and voted for its nominees. In 1863 I was a candidate before the Union Convention of this county for Sheriff; so was McClatchy. To prevent my nomination McClatchy's friends bolted the Convention, and returned only when they had secured my defeat and his nomination. I voted and worked for him and he was elected, although he fell some seven hundred votes behind the balance of the Union ticket. In 1865 we were both candidates again before the Union County Convention, when he and his friends, fearing they could not control the Convention, bolted the Union party and called a Bolters' Convention at Turn Verein Hall. I was not nominated for Sheriff, but Rooney, a Union man was. Prior to the day of election Rooney, the Union candidate for Sheriff, withdrew; as also Taylor, the Union candidate for District Attorney. On the day of election, there being for these two offices no regular Union candidates, I voted for Lansing and Goods, in preference to two bolters from the Union party, who had received nominations outside of the Union organization. I have no apologies for this course. I thought I was right, then; I think so still. I would do it again, and have no regrets for it, except that by it I was instrumental in feeding McClatchy, by aiding to give the Bee the Sheriff's and District Attorney's printing, which that paper now has.

The telegraphic dispatches to the press say the President has nominated B. N. Bugbey or J. C. Buckbee to the place of Federal Assessor in this district. If this means me, this is all I know about it. I have not sought the office, either by personal application, petition or letter. I have no reason to expect it from the President. I have been a member of the Union League from the time of its organization. I was President of the First Union Club at Folsom, organized when the rebellion broke out. I went on the bond of the State for arms to be distributed to loyal men to prevent an uprising of Secessionists in the

Benjamin Norton Bugbey

section of the country where I live. I was Sheriff of this county for two years and five months directly after the breaking out of the rebellion, during McClellan's blundering, when Secessionists hoped to involve this State in the war; and Government agents and officers of the Union League, if it were necessary— which it is not — can certify as to the exercise of the power which the law gave me to preserve peace and maintain the ascendancy of the Government. It would not become me to speak of labors and aid to the Sanitary Commission and Freedmen's Bureau during the war, or that I was an Abolitionist before the Emancipation Proclamation. I have consistently supported a radical Congress as against the President's policy, and if the dispatch of appointment has reference to me, I still support Congress as against the President. I would not give up my principles for this or any other place. Having said this much, permit me to add that, to people who know me and are familiar with our local political quarrels, the course of the proprietors of the Bee in permitting McClatchy to vent his private revenges for the defeat of his re-election to the office of Sheriff in the columns of that paper, is hardly consistent with dignified journalism. I wish further to add that to be called disloyal or published as a Copperhead is, in my opinion, as great an insult as to be branded as a liar or to have my face publicly slapped, and I shall hereafter act in accordance with this view of the case. B. N. BUGBEY.[58] - Sacramento Daily Union, Volume 32, Number 4964, 25 February 1867

The Sacramento Bee went on to connect Bugbey to the unpopular President Johnson in a follow up editorial. They accused Senator Conness of not knowing the true B. N. Bugbey.

"There was much speculation in town as to who were Bugbey's indorsers [sic] for a Federal appointment. The friends of that gentleman exercised themselves industriously upon the states repeating the tales that he was recommended by Senator Cole and indorsed [sic] by Senator Conness. Having no faith in that version, and being desirous of ascertaining the facts, a party here sent a dispatch to Washington saying, "Telegraph me the name of Bugbey's indorsers [sic]." To that the answer came yesterday, "Bugbey appointed by the President for Conness alone—not yet confirmed." This, then, settles the matter as to who his indorsers [sic] are, but certainly we did not expect to find Senator Conness among, for he was supposed to have known how false Bugbey has been to freedom and to the Union party. In this, however, it is just possible he may have been deceived, as some others professed to be, but how, it is difficult to imagine. And if granting for argument's sake, he believed Bugbey to be true to the Union party, how did he prevail on the President to send his name to the Senate? The President is in the habit of appointing his friends, and unless he had

*some, knowledge of Bugbey's recreancy to the Union party, it is not likely that he would name him for the place.*⁵⁹ - Marysville Daily Appeal, Number 48, 26 February 1867

Bugbey did have his supporters in the region. The Folsom Telegraph published how Bugbey's appointment was welcomed news.

*The appointment of B. N. Bugbey as Assessor of the Fourth District is received by the Union Party, and in fact, all parties, with feelings of gratification. The merchants and business men of Sacramento City and of Folsom are exceedingly pleased, for they know from the experience they have had when Bugbey was Sheriff of this county, that the business of that department of the Government in this district will be conducted with energy and in a business-like manner. Everybody about here knows that B. N. Bugbey is a Radical, sustains Congress, and has not had the least hesitation in making his opinions known; and they further know that he is now doing, and has for years past done as much to develop the productive resources of California as any man in it; that he invests his means in enterprises of lasting benefit to the State, instead of sinking his dollars in an old stocking and hiding it in a rat hole. We have received several communications upon this subject, but want of space lets them out.*⁶⁰ - Daily Alta California, Volume 19, Number 7094, 27 February 1867

The political pressure from the people like James McClatchy, editor of the Sacramento Bee, and other politicians was too much for Senator Conness to sustain. He withdrew his support for Bugbey and allowed President Johnson to nominate Maj. T. J. Blakeney to the assessor position in early March.⁶¹

What was evident from this political episode in Bugbey's life was that he was loyal first to his affiliated political party. It was only after his party's chosen candidate for Sheriff, Rooney, withdrew from the race that he had to make an alternate choice. He felt he could not vote for McClatchy because he was part of the group that split from the Union Democrats to create the Long Hair faction. There may have been other considerations for Bugbey to avoid a McClatchy vote, such as the accusations McClatchy made about Bugbey after McClatchy had taken over the office of Sheriff from Bugbey.

Bugbey supported McClatchy when he lost the Union Democrat Party nomination for Sheriff to him. It's possible that Bugbey's endorsement of James Lansing for Sheriff cost McClatchy the office that year, as Bugbey was popular in the eastern part of Sacramento County. Lansing was Bugbey's Under Sheriff; he knew Lansing and worked with him even if they were not in the same political party. Bugbey could have been more diplomatic in how he couched his support of Lansing, who was seen somewhat as a Southern sympathizer. But Bugbey had not demonstrated any political ambition beyond local politics. If being brutally honest about his positions cost Bugbey the opportunity to move up the political ladder, he considered it to be no cost at all, as his integrity with the local populace was more important.

For a few weeks in 1867, Bugbey was a political pawn in a larger national political drama involving President Johnson and a Republican Congress. His feud with James McClatchy was laid out in the open. This was unfortunate, because McClatchy and Bugbey had more in common in terms of political philosophy than separated them.

The political hardball of negative editorials did not deter Bugbey from continuing to participate in politics. In May of 1867, he was back as a delegate to the Short Hair Union County Convention in Sacramento.[62] The Union Party was still split into two camps, the Long Hairs and the Short Hairs after the previous brawl in 1865.

Bugbey was nominated to represent the Short Hair Union Party for Sacramento County Sheriff at their 1867 convention.[63] As the Natoma Vineyard and his winery were taking up most of his time, he did not campaign very hard for the position. One of the resolutions that set the Short Hairs apart from other political parties was a call for a shorter work day and a mechanics lien law.

Resolved. That we pledge our members of the Legislature to the enactment of a judicious law regulating the hours of labor and reducing the same from ten to eight hours per day, of a lien law which shall protect the mechanic and laborer, and ask them to memorialize Congress to provide means against the importation of coolies held as slaves in their own country and worked here as slaves for the benefit of those who own them.[64] - Daily Alta California, Volume 19, Number 6285, 30 May 1867

Bugbey was an employer, and he contracted with mechanics and craftsmen at his Natoma Vineyard. The party platform calling for reduced hours of labor and a lien law to protect mechanics and laborers went against the interests of most businessmen. The lien law, now known as a mechanic's lien in California, allows a contractor or supplier of material or services to place a lien against the property being improved. If the property owner fails to pay, contractors who have filed a mechanics lien have a variety of options to be paid for their services from foreclosure on the property to a recorded lien encumbering the property. Because Bugbey was involved with the Mechanics' Institute of San Francisco, it follows that he would want laws to protect men and women who were contracted to construct equipment or perform services from not being paid for their services.

Like any other party member, Bugbey didn't always personally support all the resolutions of his political party. But Bugbey could have easily found another political home in the fractured post-Civil War politics gripping the country. That Bugbey stayed with the Short Hair faction of the Union Democrats indicates that he was comfortable with the social and business positions that the Short Hairs were advocating at the time.

Registry Fraud

Before the 1867 political campaigns could begin in earnest, Bugbey was tripped up by another political scandal. As the political parties jockeyed for position to get their candidates and agendas elected to local office, some people were not above cheating to gain an advantage. In every political party, there seems to have been an overzealous party operative that attempts to break the rules for the good of the party.

The city of Sacramento had experienced voter fraud in the general election of 1865.[65] With a relatively small electorate, approximately 5,500 eligible voters in Sacramento County[66], even a few votes could provide a win. The small margins were even more important because the split of the Union Party into the Long Hairs and Short Hairs added another political faction to the mix.

In 1866 California passed the Registry Act that sought to create a list of all eligible voters. California counties were responsible for creating the list of registered voters, and it became known as the Great Registry. There were strict rules for adding names to the Great Registry. The collection of names was handled by the Sacramento County Assessor's office in coordination with local officials and appointed party representatives in each of the Townships. Bugbey was a clerk on the Board of Registry for Granite Township. Ed Christy[67], one of Bugbey's former Sheriff deputies, was a judge for the registry, and J. S. Mumford, an attorney from Mormon Island, was a Deputy Assessor for the county.[68]

In late July 1867, after a day of recording names on the Great Registry in Granite Township, Deputy Assessor Grove L. Johnson received a list of 61 voters to be included on the voter registration roll.[69] Johnson handed the list to E. D. Shirland in the County Clerk's office to be copied on to the Great Registry. Shirland, who had spent the day in Folsom registering voters did not recognize any of the people listed as being residents.[70]

A. P. Catlin, a resident of Folsom, attorney, and one of the officers of the Natoma Water Canal and Mining Company, examined the list and did not recognize any of the names as being local residents he knew.[71] The initial explanation was that the names had come from

Deputy Assessor J. S. Mumford's book, but none of the names were found in Mumford's book of voters he had registered.[72] The list was then distributed to the local political parties, Democrats, Long Hair Union, and Short Hair Union, and none of those men could recognize any of the names as residents of Granite Township.[73]

Grove L. Johnson, in addition to his duties as a Deputy Assessor, was also running for Sacramento County Auditor on the Union Short Hair party ticket[74], the same ticket to which Bugbey had been nominated for Sheriff.[75] Johnson was relatively new to Sacramento, having only arrived in 1865. He quickly aligned himself with the Short Hair faction of the Union Party. Johnson was described as, "In appearance he was youthful; as a speaker he was flippant, if not fluent."[76] The impression was that Johnson was trying to ingratiate himself upon the political powers in office to be appointed to positions to earn money. To that end, he was appointed as a Deputy Assessor and as clerk of the Swamp Lands Board.[77]

Shortly after the news broke that the 61 names of voters were potentially fraudulent, Assessor Ryan called upon Johnson to make a full explanation. Johnson suddenly found himself ill with fever and was not able to explain how he acquired the list for another five days. Johnson did write a letter to the Sacramento Daily Union in which he described receiving the list of names from the Post Office and assumed they came from Mumford.[78]

Several days after it was reported that Johnson had submitted the fraudulent names, he requested Bugbey and Christy to meet him at his home in Sacramento. They arrived late at night. Johnson recounted to Bugbey how he received the list from the Post Office and handed it off to the Clerk's office. Johnson also felt that he would shortly be arrested for fraud and asked if Bugbey would go on his bond to keep him out of jail. Bugbey said "[He] would go on his bond to the last grape vine [he] owned."[79] Also in the house that evening was Johnson's little son, Hiram, who had been born in September. Bugbey would meet Hiram in court several decades later. Hiram Johnson would go on to be elected Governor and U. S. Senator from California.

Grove Johnson's delay in clarifying the facts of the names and his late-night meeting with Bugbey and Christy were not seen as the actions of an innocent man. Johnson was arrested on July 26 on a complaint of E. D. Shirland, County Clerk.[80]

On August 2nd, testimony was taken before Judge Foote from several people involved in the case including Bugbey.[81] Judge Foote decided to hold Johnson over to answer to the Grand Jury.[82] Johnson resigned his positions at the county and withdrew from the race for County Auditor.[83][84] In mid-November the Grand Jury deemed there was insufficient evidence to justify an indictment of fraud against Grove L. Johnson.[85]

Benjamin Norton Bugbey

The Great Registry fraud did nothing to enhance the reputation of the Short Hair Union Party. At Grove's hearing, one of the witnesses, Jesse Couch, testified that he heard that certain people wanted to implicate Bugbey in the fraud because he would be able to get out of any charges the easiest.[86] The Short Hairs were being called tricksters, and the Union men of Sacramento County were tired of being Grove Johnsonized.[87]

Campaign Trail

Bugbey kept on the campaign trail, attending rallies and meeting some opposition to his residency. At a campaign meeting in Slough House, he had to convince people that even though his much celebrated Natoma Vineyard, where he had a house, was in El Dorado County, he considered himself a resident of Sacramento County.[88]

There were three candidates for Sacramento County Sheriff in 1867: E. F. White, the Union Long Hair nominee; Bugbey, the Union Short Hair Nominee; and Hugh M. La Rue of the Democrat Party.[89] A rumor had been floated that Bugbey was going to withdraw from the race under some sort of secret trade between the Short Hairs and the Democrats. Bugbey sent a letter to the editor of the Sacramento Daily Union denouncing such an agreement to help La Rue win.[90] He stated, "There has been no trade made, and I have no knowledge that one has been attempted. I am a candidate for Sheriff, nominated by the Union party; I expect to be a candidate until the polls are closed on the day of election. I believe I will be elected, and I solicit the votes of the citizens of Sacramento County that I may be."[91]

The Sacramento Daily Union observed that Bugbey's supporters were primarily in the eastern part of the county in Granite Township. Outside of Folsom and Mormon Island, his supporters were "…like angels' visits, few and far between."[92]

The newspaper understood the electorate, and Bugbey lost by a wide margin. La Rue was the victor, with more than 1,776 votes; White received 1,768, and Bugbey garnered only 743 votes.[93]

Like the true political animal that he was, Bugbey shrugged off the Sheriff's defeat and continued on in politics. He was elected as an alternate to the Union Party national convention in Chicago to support Ulysses S. Grant.[94] But by August 1868 he had formally become a Republican.[95]

Even though the National Union Party was fading away, Bugbey still maintained a loose association of Union Party loyalists under the Natoma Grant and Colfax Club. This political club to support the election of Ulysses S. Grant and running mate Schuyler Colfax Jr. met in the town of Mormon Island.[96] Near the end of October, the club held a big rally for Grant, with the Sacramento Daily Union noting, "If

Mormon Island ever did make an effort to do something worthy of her fair and loyal renown, surely this night was her best. The Plaza and all the cross streets were thronged with crowds of rejoicing people from the workshop, farm and mine."[97] A new liberty pole was raised in the plaza, and a 40-foot American flag donated by Bugbey was affixed to the top of the pole and fluttered in the wind.[98] Many of Bugbey's friends were in attendance, including C. G. W. French and B. C. Quigley.[99]

Shortly before election day, the town of Folsom was the scene of a big Union rally for Grant and Colfax. Bugbey was the Chief Marshall for the event, greeting over 600 people who had travelled in nine cars on the Sacramento Valley Railroad from Sacramento to

Figure 9: 1869 - Raisins, cuttings, wines, and brandy advertisement for Natoma Vineyard in California Farmer and Journal of Useful Sciences. CDNC

Folsom for the meeting. The Sacramento men were joined by another 400 residents from the surrounding townships to parade through the streets of Folsom. Many of Bugbey's local pals. such as P. J. Hopper, E. D. Shirland, and Philip Yeager, attended the rally that lasted until midnight.[100]

Natoma Vineyard Visitors

Later in 1868 Bugbey was appointed as an Agricultural Statistical Reporter for Sacramento County with the power to appoint three assistants. John Bidwell, who had recently left congress and had extensive farming operations in the Chico area, made the recommendation. Bidwell was not an enthusiastic supporter of alcoholic beverages. In the 1880s he became very involved in the Temperance Movement and the Prohibition Party. But Bidwell must have felt Bugbey's knowledge and overall contribution to agricultural sciences put him in a good position to lead the agricultural statistical reporting unit.[101]

Bugbey continued to win awards for his wines and brandy. He took several premiums at the 15th Annual State Fair for best two-year-old brandy, superior wine three years old made from Italian and Burgundy grapes, and as usual, best exhibit of wine from foreign grapes.[102] He also picked up a gold medal for best white wine at the 1868 Mechanics' Industrial Fair, along with a diploma for his raisins.[103]

The Natoma Vineyard had gained considerable notoriety throughout the state. It was becoming a destination for tourists and travelers to see where the famous Bugbey's wines were fermented and bottled. One visitor was a woman correspondent for the San Jose Mercury News, who wrote about her experience and impression of the Natoma Vineyard.

Figure 10: 1869 - Natoma Vineyard, Residence of B. N. Bugbey, photographed by J. A. Todd of Sacramento. Natoma Vineyard, Residence of B. N. Bugbey, photographer J. A Todd, Sacramento, Natoma vineyard views, Calif. photographed by J.A. Todd, BANC PIC 1905.01574--A.

Without a visit to Bugbey's vineyard my trip would have been very incomplete. I am happy to say I have not been guilty of this sin of omission. It requires some little nerve in a woman to visit a rancho that is famous for its tricks upon travelers. I believe, in fact, it is boasted that no one ever left the grounds after a second visit — sober. It is darkly rumored that the ex-Sheriff regards it a personal slight to his gold medal brands, and the numberless lighter varieties of wine and brandies with which he refreshes his guests, if the said guests display a sufficient control of "mind over matter" to be able to reach their vehicles without assistance, after taking leave.[104] - Sacramento Daily Union, Volume 36, Number 5593, 1 March 1869

Another visitor to the Natoma Vineyards also commented on Bugbey's generous hospitality. In a letter to the Placer Herald, the visitor recounted how he visited the area on the South Fork of the American River and found luxuriant growth of vineyards dotting the country along with happy homes. He and his travelling companions spent time at the Natoma Vineyard wine cellar, where they were welcomed by Bugbey.[105]

Figure 11: 1869 - Bugbey's new home in center of photograph with vineyard employees, Bugbey, and two women. Natoma Vineyard, Residence of B. N. Bugbey, photographer J. A Todd, Sacramento, Natoma vineyard views, Calif. photographed by J.A. Todd, BANC PIC 1905.01574--A.

We found Mr. Bugbey to be one of the most generous, jolly warm hearted men we ever met in any part of the country. He received us with such words as, "here my good fellow, take a little of this, it's

Benjamin Norton Bugbey

two years old; try this, it is four years old; take a drop of the third, it is six months old, and after drinking it you can have your lives insured for half price.[106] - Placer Herald, March 12, 1870, Folsom Correspondence, March 6th, 1870

The visitors toured the Natoma Vineyards' numerous buildings, including one building containing fourteen 1,000-gallon wine casks, a two-story structure filled with wine casks containing 400 gallons each, an engine house, and a cooper shop, where all the repairs were made. Bugbey also called their attention to a pond fed by an artesian well on the property, which had been stocked with gold fish.[107]

The portrait painted by visitors of Bugbey at the Natoma Vineyard is one of an affable proprietor enthusiastically greeting his guests in a most friendly and neighborly manner, introducing his visitors to the variety of wines and spirits he produced. He was proud of the Natoma Vineyard. He was a happy man with a sense of humor. The quip about drinking his wines and brandies was borne of the belief that liquor had medicinal properties. Bugbey actually sold his wines and brandies to the county hospital, where they were dispensed as medicine to the ill.

Even though more vineyards were being planted around him,[108] partially because of his success, Bugbey pushed forward with expanding his operations. In the spring of 1869, more wine casks arrived from San Francisco into the port at Sacramento. There were 48 wine pipes, 9 tierces, and 15 eighth-casks.[109] The wine pipes were long wooden barrels with tapered ends that held approximately 125 gallons of wine each. Tierces and eighth-casks were smaller. The tierce held approximately 42 gallons of wine.

An Unfortunate Accident

April along the American River is beautiful. The grass is green, oak trees are pushing out new leaves, the buckeyes are blooming, the birds are singing, and usually the wind is blowing. The Bugbey's, Benjamin and Mary Jane, spent a lot of time at the home they had built overlooking the Natoma Vineyard. In order to catch a stagecoach into Folsom, the two had to walk or ride along a dirt road about two miles to the west from their Natoma Vineyard home into the town of Mormon Island. On this particular day of April 26, 1869, Mary Jane was riding on a horse side-saddle, and Benjamin and a young girl in their care were walking along with them.[110]

With the wind blowing on this April morning, Mary Jane was leaning forward talking to the horse, as one often does to calm the animal down. Somehow Mary Jane fell to the side of the horse with the wire at the base of her skirt getting wrapped around the pommel or saddle horn. Mary Jane had virtually pulled herself up on top of the horse, when a gust of wind blew her shawl across the horse's eyes, startling it and causing it to flee. She again lost her balance and fell backwards. She was prevented from completely falling off the horse because the wire in her skirt was still wrapped around the pommel.[111]

Mary Jane cried out for her husband, "Oh Ben! Ben!" By this time, she was off the horse and being dragged behind it because wire had not yet broken. Either as she was hanging from the horse, or after she was being drug, her head hit one of the many granite rocks sticking out of the ground along the road. She was drug behind the horse for almost 125 yards before the hoop wire finally broke, and Benjamin was able to race to her side. He knelt beside her, lifted her up, cradled her in his arms, and watched her slowly pass away.[112]

Bugbey's Masonic brothers, Natoma Lodge, No. 64, F. and A. M., published their condolences in the Folsom Weekly Telegraph and Sacramento Daily Union.

Whereas, Our beloved brother, B N. Bugbey, has been deeply afflicted by the sudden and distressful death of his dearly loved wife; therefore. Resolved, That we stand, hand clasped in hand and heart beating to heart, with him in his hours of great sadness and sorrow; that by deeds mere than words we would make him feel the warmth and depth of our sympathy; and we rejoice that we can, in her absence cherish the memory of the many virtues and graces of our departed sister, and add to the good in our own characters and lives by following her example of domestic goodness and love. Resolved, That a copy of these Resolutions, under seal of this Lodge, be given to brother Bugbey, and that they be published in the Folsom Weekly Telegraph and the Sacramento Union, B. C. Quigley Committee Chairman[113] - Sacramento Daily Union, Volume 37, Number 5666, 25 May 1869

There is little documentation of the life of Mary Jane Bugbey before her tragic death. There was one small mention of her in the Sacramento Daily Union for her entry of a crocheted tidy being entered into the 15th Annual State Fair in 1868.[114] The first mention of her in any California documents was when she was listed as a debtor, along with Bugbey and Houghtaling, on the Sheriff's deed of sale for the Salisbury Farm property in 1856.[115]

On the 1860 census, Bugbey's age is listed as 33 and his wife, M. J.'s, as 23. Her place of birth is listed as Connecticut, the same as Bugbey's.[116] The grave marker for Bugbey in the Historic Sacramento Cemetery also includes Mary Jane's death date, April 26th, 1869, at 33 years of age. The age of her death in 1869 corresponds to her age listed on the census form from 1860. This would place her date of birth sometime in 1836 or 1837.

Benjamin Norton Bugbey

Figure 12: Mary Jane Bugbey grave marker on the Bugbey obelisk monument in the Historic Sacramento Cemetery. Author's collection.

After Mary Jane's death, she was buried in Folsom Cemetery. Sometime after Bugbey bought a burial plot in the Sacramento City Cemetery in 1891,[117] he had her remains disinterred from the Folsom and moved to the new resting place.[118]

---

[1] Sacramento County Deed Book 18621212, pages 398 and 399

[2] Sacramento County Deed Book 18620322, pages 179 and 180

[3] Haskins, C. W., *The Argonauts of California, Being The Reminiscences of Scenes and Incidents that Occurred in California in early mining days by a Pioneer.* (Fords, Howard & Hulbert, New York, 1890).

[4] Sacramento County Deed Book 18651013, pages 39, 40, 41

[5] Sacramento County Deed Book 18660604, pages 269, 270

[6] Sacramento County Deed Book 18660604, pages 269, 270

[7] Sacramento County Deed Book 18660512, pages 179 – 184

[8] Placer Times, Volume 1, Number 42, March 2, 1850, CDNC

[9] Sacramento Daily Union, Volume 15, Number 2240, June 1, 1858, CDNC

[10] Sacramento Daily Union, Volume 32, Number 4860, October 25, 1866, CDNC

[11] https://en.wikipedia.org/wiki/College_of_California

[12] Sacramento County Deed Book 18660512, pages 179 - 184

[13] Sacramento County Deed Book 186707729, pages 194 and 195

[14] Sacramento Daily Union, Volume 30, Number 4586, December 2, 1865, CDNC

15 Ibid.

16 Daily Alta California, Volume 18, Number 6101, November 24, 1866, CDNC

17 Sacramento Daily Union, Volume 32, Number 4902, December 13, 1866, CDNC

18 Daily Alta California, Volume 18, Number 5901, May 7, 1866, CDNC

19 Sacramento Daily Union, Volume 31, Number 4804, August 21, 1866, CDNC

20 Ibid.

21 Daily Alta California, Volume 18, Number 7003, November 26, 1866, CDNC

22 Sacramento Daily Union, Volume 32, Number 4902, December 13, 1866, CDNC

23 Sacramento Daily Union, Volume 34, Number 5150, September 30, 1867, CDNC

24 Sonoma Democrat, Number 29, April 25, 1868, CDNC

25 *Transactions of the California State Agricultural Society During the Years 1870 and 1871*, (T. A. Springer, State Printer, Sacramento, 1872).

26 Santa Cruz Weekly Sentinel, Volume 10, Number 26, December 2, 1865, CDNC

27 Sacramento Daily Union, Volume 31, Number 4822, September 11, 1866, CDNC

28 Red Bluff Independent, Number 18, October 31, 1866, CDNC

29 Sacramento Daily Union, Volume 32, Number 4913, December 31, 1866, CDNC

30 Sacramento Daily Union, Volume 32, Number 4920, January 4, 1867, CDNC

31 Sacramento Daily Union, Volume 33, Number 5049, June 3, 1867, CDNC

32 Ibid.

33 Sacramento Daily Union, Volume 34, Number 5239, 13 January 13, 1868, CDNC

34 *Transactions of the California State Agricultural Society During the Years 1870 and 1871*, (T. A. Springer, State Printer, Sacramento, 1872).

35 Ibid.

36 Ibid.

37 Daily Alta California, Volume 19, Number 6299, June 13, 1867, CDNC

38 Sacramento Daily Union, Volume 33, Number 5068, June 25, 1867, CDNC

39 Sacramento Daily Union, Volume 33, Number 5089, July 20, 1867, CDNC

40 Sacramento Daily Union, Volume 33, Number 5117, August 22, 1867, CDNC

41 California Farmer and Journal of Useful Sciences, Volume 34, Number 6, August 18, 1870, CDNC

42 Sacramento Daily Union, Volume 33, Number 5134, September 11, 1867, CDNC

43 Sacramento Daily Union, Volume 34, Number 5179, November 2, 1867, CDNC

44 Ibid.

45 Sacramento Daily Union, Volume 34, Number 5144, September 23, 1867, CDNC

46 Daily Alta California, Volume 19, Number 6418, October 11, 1867, CDNC

[47] Sacramento Daily Union, Volume 34, Number 5161, October 12, 1867, CDNC

[48] 1863 U.S. Excise Tax, California, Division 1, District 4, Assessor John Avery, B. N. Bugbey $145.35

[49] 1864 U.S. Excise Tax, California, Division 1, District 4, Assessor John Avery, B. N. Bugbey, Folsom, Auctioneer (2 months) $3.33

[50] 1864 U.S. Excise Tax, California, Division 3, District 4, Assessor John Avery, B. N. Bugbey, Salmon Falls, Manufacturer, 1,000 gallons wine, $60.00 y

[51] *The Federal Cases Comprising Cases Argued and Determined in the Circuit and District Courts of the United States*, Book 24, Case No. 14078 – Case No. 14691, (West Publishing Co, St. Paul,1896).

[52] Sacramento Daily Union, Volume 32, Number 4967, February 28, 1867, CDNC

[53] Ibid.

[54] Ibid.

[55] Ibid.

[56] Sacramento Daily Union, Volume 32, Number 4961, February 21, 1867, CDNC

[57] Marysville Daily Appeal, Number 44, February 21, 1867, CDNC

[58] Sacramento Daily Union, Volume 32, Number 4964, February 25, 1867, CDNC

[59] Marysville Daily Appeal, Number 48, February 26, 1867, CDNC

[60] Daily Alta California, Volume 19, Number 7094, February 27, 1867, CDNC

[61] Marysville Daily Appeal, Number 55, March 6, 1867, CDNC

[62] Sacramento Daily Union, Volume 33, Number 5039, May 22, 1867, CDNC

[63] Sacramento Daily Union, Volume 33, Number 5045, May 29, 1867, CDNC

[64] Daily Alta California, Volume 19, Number 6285, May 30, 1867, CDNC

[65] Sacramento Daily Union, Volume 33, Number 5089, July 20, 1867, CDNC

[66] Sacramento Daily Union, Volume 33, Number 5105, August 8, 1867, CDNC

[67] Sacramento Daily Union, Volume 33, Number 5089, July 20, 1867, CDNC

[68] Ibid.

[69] Ibid.

[70] Ibid.

[71] Ibid.

[72] Ibid.

[73] Ibid.

[74] Ibid.

[75] Sacramento Daily Union, Volume 33, Number 5045, May 29, 1867, CDNC

[76] Sacramento Daily Union, Volume 33, Number 5091, July 23, 1867, CDNC

[77] Ibid.

Benjamin Norton Bugbey

[78] Sacramento Daily Union, Volume 33, Number 5090, July 22, 1867, CDNC

[79] Sacramento Daily Union, Volume 33, Number 6001, August 3, 1867, CDNC

[80] Sacramento Daily Union, Volume 33, Number 5095, July 27, 1867, CDNC

[81] Sacramento Daily Union, Volume 33, Number 6001, August 3, 1867, CDNC

[82] Ibid.

[83] Sacramento Daily Union, Volume 33, Number 5094, July 26, 1867, CDNC

[84] Sacramento Daily Union, Volume 33, Number 5116, August 21, 1867, CDNC

[85] Sacramento Daily Union, Volume 34, Number 5194, November 20, 1867, CDNC

[86] Sacramento Daily Union, Volume 33, Number 6001, August 3, 1867, CDNC

[87] Sacramento Daily Union, Volume 32, Number 6000, August 2, 1867, CDNC

[88] Sacramento Daily Union, Volume 33, Number 5121, August 27, 1867, CDNC

[89] Sacramento Daily Union, Volume 33, Number 5127, September 3, 1867, CDNC

[90] Sacramento Daily Union, Volume 33, Number 5125, August 31, 1867, CDNC

[91] Sacramento Daily Union, Volume 33, Number 5125, August 31, 1867, CDNC

[92] Sacramento Daily Union, Volume 33, Number 5127, September 3, 1867, CDNC

[93] Sacramento Daily Union, Volume 32, Number 5132, September 9, 1867, CDNC

[94] Sacramento Daily Union, Volume 35, Number 5308, April 2, 1868, CDNC

[95] Sacramento Daily Union, Volume 35, Number 5417, August 6, 1868, CDNC

[96] Sacramento Daily Union, Volume 35, Number 5433, August 25, 1868, CDNC

[97] Sacramento Daily Union, Volume 36, Number 5489, October 29, 1868, CDNC

[98] Ibid.

[99] Ibid.

[100] Sacramento Daily Union, Volume 36, Number 5492, November 2, 1868, CDNC

[101] Sacramento Daily Union, Volume 35, Number 5366, June 8, 1868, CDNC

[102] Sacramento Daily Union, Volume 36, Number 5460, September 25, 1868, CDNC

[103] Daily Alta California, Volume 20, Number 6766, September 22, 1868, CDNC

[104] Sacramento Daily Union, Volume 36, Number 5593, March 1, 1869, CDNC

[105] Placer Herald, March 12, 1870, Folsom Correspondence, March 6, 1870. Folsom Historical Society Museum Archive

[106] Ibid.

[107] Ibid.

[108] Sacramento Daily Union, Volume 36, Number 5587, February 22, 1869, CDNC

[109] Sacramento Daily Union, Volume 36, Number 5598, March 6, 1869, CDNC

[110] 1869 Sacramento Daily Union, Volume 37, Number 5642, April 27, 1869, CDNC

[111] Sacramento Daily Union, Volume 37, Number 5647, May 3, 1869, CDNC

[112] Ibid.

[113] Sacramento Daily Union, Volume 37, Number 5666, May 25, 1869, CDNC

[114] Sacramento Daily Union, Volume 36, Number 5460, September 25, 1868, CDNC

[115] Sacramento County Deed Book 18571218, pages 148 and 149

[116] 1860 United States Federal Census, California, Sacramento, Granite Township, p. 237, B. N. Bugb(e)y, Age 33, Birth Conn., M. J. Bugb(e)y, Age 23.

[117] Sacramento County Deed Book 18911215, page 445

[118] Chapter Note: Many references have pointed to Mary Jane being born on August 10, 1834, to Samuel and Jane Wells. But that would make her 37 at the time of death, not 33. In addition, the Mary Jane Wells born in 1834 married a Hiram Perkins on December 2, 1852, with the parents listed as Samuel and Jane Wells.* This December wedding was several months after B. N. Bugbey had left the region to return to California. Mary Jane Wells' age at the time of marriage to Hiram Perkins is listed as 18, and her birth place is listed as Manchester. The age means she would have been born in approximately 1834. Census records indicate that Hiram Perkins and Mary Jane resided in Wells, Maine, for the rest of their married lives. There is no documentation to suggest that Hiram and Mary Jane were ever divorced or travelled to California.

Bugbey could have married a Mary Jane Wells from Connecticut, his home state, when he returned to the family home in late 1851. This would have put Mary Jane between 15 and 16 years old.

*Massachusetts, Marriage Records, 1840 – 1915, Gloucester

Benjamin Norton Bugbey

Chapter 8: Wine, Brandy, Champagne, Music 1869 - 1872

How does a man regain his footing after losing an indispensable partner and wife? On U.S Census data of that time, the occupation of the wife was often listed as "keeping house." The maintenance of the home, meal preparation, and other domestic duties was a full-time job. Bugbey was a busy man. If he was not managing the vineyard, overseeing the production of spirits, constructing more production facilities, attending meetings of the various philanthropic organizations he belonged to, or participating in local political party meetings, he was spending innumerous hours on the road just travelling between all his different functions.

Martinette McGlashan

At a minimum, Bugbey needed a housekeeper and cook. We can also assume that he wanted female companionship, if for nothing more than a little conversation between meeting his business and social obligations. Less than four months after the death of Mary Jane, at the age of 43, Bugbey remarried on August 23, 1869.[1]

His new wife was 26 years old and the daughter of Peter McGlashan.[2] The McGlashans had moved west after Martinette's mother died in 1849.[3] They settled in Sonoma County, where Martinette's older sister had married and was living in Healdsburg[4]. In 1868 Peter was living in Sacramento County in Lee Township near Daylor's ranch, adjacent to the Cosumnes River.[5] Martinette's sister Adelia had married George Washington Balis, who was farming in the area and keeping a boarding house.[6]

It's unknown how Bugbey became acquainted with Peter McGlashan. It is possible that Peter had been working in the vineyards in Sonoma County and perhaps worked for Bugbey. Later in 1870, Bugbey would sell part of his Duroc vineyard land to George Balis, who in turn sold it to Peter McGlashan.

Regardless of how they met, Bugbey was once again married. His new bride was now married to a prominent vineyard owner and wine producer. Martinette "Nettie" McGlashan was like Bugbey, in that she wanted more out of life. She would go on to earn her teaching credential and become a school principal. But at this busy period in Bugbey's life, the main focus was on keeping house and attending to Benjamin.

If Bugbey spent much grieving over his deceased wife or reveling in his new marriage, it was not reflected in reports of his business and social life at the time. The one area of his life that he curtailed was running for public office. At the 1869 Union Republican County Convention, he was again asked to run for Sheriff. James McClatchy made a motion that all the candidates come forward and pay their $5 assessment and give a short speech.

Bugbey paid his $5 and then declined the nomination. He said that he had heard that no man who had been Sheriff could ever get nominated again. So far this had proven correct in his case and with McClatchy. He noted how most of his attention was focused on his vineyard and thanked the convention for honoring him with such a nomination.[7]

Period of Expansion

Figure 13: 1870 - Illustration of B. N. Bugbey from the sheet music for "Bugbey's Champagne Galop". John Hopkins, The Lester S. Levy Sheet Music Collection.

Bugbey was expanding his storage capacity for the thousands of bottles of wine, brandy, and sparkling wine he was producing. In November 1869 Charles and Frank Wheeler sold Bugbey a lot in Folsom, next to Coner's Flouring Mill on Wool Street.[8] The mill was a three-story brick building that ceased operations in 1868. The third floor of the building, which fronted Sutter Street and was at a higher elevation, was rented as a meeting space for local organizations. Bugbey used the bottom floors as a wine cellar[9].

Bugbey knew some of the best marketing was done by personal testimonies and recommendations. It was even better if the recommendation came from a noted politician or influential businessman. In July of 1869, Bugbey sent three barrels of his red wine back east on the newly finished Transcontinental Railroad. One barrel went to the President of the United States, another to California Senator Conness, and the third to C. P. Huntington, Vice President of the Central Pacific Railroad. While it is not known how the men favored the Natoma Vineyard wine, the shipment did garner a story in the local newspaper.[10]

Freight costs were an issue at one of the first meetings of the newly formed Fruit Growers Association held in San Francisco in July 1869. The railroad companies were charging $100 per ton to ship fruit to Chicago. Grapes were averaging $0.10 per pound. Agricultural producers were beginning to get a taste of the monopolistic pricing practices the railroad companies were employing. Bugbey was part of the organizing force behind the Fruit Growers Association and was selected as Vice President in the summer of 1869.[11]

Later in the summer Bugbey hosted Benjamin P. Avery, founder of the Marysville Appeal, who was then an editor of the Evening Bulletin out of San Francisco. Avery, who was a prolific and descriptive writer of the California landscape, was observing the changes to the region from all the new agricultural endeavors. After a tour of the Natoma vineyards, the two Benjamins rode up to the new Japanese immigrant colony south of Coloma on Gold Hill. The Wakamatsu Tea and Silk Farm Colony were planting mulberry trees to provide food for their silk worms.[12]

No sooner was Bugbey getting settled in with his new wife when he was struck again by fire in October 1869. This time it was purely by accident from a neighbor whose brush fire got out of control. While the vineyard was not touched, Bugbey's prized house on the hill overlooking the ranch was destroyed. Completed in 1868 at a cost of $30,000, house and furniture were insured for only $21,000.[13]

Bugbey would not rebuild the home, but he did keep expanding his winery. In the same month that his house burned, Bugbey started the expansion of his operation with another wine cellar 22 feet wide, 160 feet long, and two stories tall.[14]

Bugbey enjoyed fruit trees. He had oranges and figs at the Natoma vineyard. In the beginning of 1870, he planted several rows of eastern chestnut trees. The hope was to get a harvest in approximately three years.[15]

Benjamin Norton Bugbey

Figure 14: 1870 - Bugbey's Natoma wines, brandies, and champagne advertisement. CDNC

It is never easy to discern the personality of a historical figure in its fullness. Fortunately, there are little crumbs of interest that display Bugbey's nature and humor. He was enjoying the relative celebrity of being an outspoken and engaged vintner. But he also did not take himself so seriously that he couldn't have fun with visitors to his vineyard or the marketing of his wines.

The California Farmer and Journal of Useful Sciences noted how Bugbey had labeled some of his sparkling wines.

Syebgub or Private Cuvee de Amotan

The label for his champagne stated "Syebgub or Private Cuvee de Amotan". The translations are Bugbey's and Natoma spelled backwards. The label was a subtle acknowledgement that French sparkling wines, or champagne, still enjoyed the perception that they were superior to the emerging California product. So, if you could not taste exactly like a French champagne, Bugbey felt he could at least sound like one. This no doubt must have given him a chuckle while introducing his Syebgub Cuvee De Amotan to the person with no French language skills and a wry inside joke to those who knew the sparkling wine market.[16] The article also noted that by May 1870 several thousand gallons of wine were now being stored at the flouring mill he bought in Folsom[17].

Fiher Zagos Questioned

For all of Bugbey's vineyard management skills and mechanic ingenuity at constructing a winery, he wasn't a pomologist. He had identified a grape varietal for raisin and wine production, Fiher Zagos, whose provenance was suspect. At least it was to other men who had studied viticulture. In 1870 people started questioning whether Bugbey's Fiher Zagos was the appropriate variety, and if it was, the actual suitability it had for raisin and wine production.

The California Farmer and Journal of Useful Sciences republished a stinging rebuke of the Bugbey grape by a Utah pomologist.

This, so called grape [Fiher Zagos] that for several years caused such a stir among viticulturists in California under the auspices of Mr. Bugbey and others, has finally gone the way of thousands of other Humbugs. In the first place, there is no authority that any grape by that name exists anywhere only in the imagination of a few who have made that grape a specialty. The real name of the grape is "White Romain," which we have imported from the east, and fruited, and find it identical, both in vine and fruit.[18]

The Journal added:

The fruit of this vine when fully ripe, is very delicate and nice for table use, but will make neither good wine nor a suitable raisin. The worst point it has is its disposition to crack and rot, a difficulty we have not been able to find a cure for. For the last five years we have known the grape and have not found it to justify the hopes entertained for it in one case in twenty. — We would therefore advise our readers to plant it sparingly for there are many varieties obtainable far superior, which have not this great fault.[19] - California Farmer and Journal of Useful Sciences, Volume 33, Number 20, 2 June 1870

Another vineyard owner also wrote to concur with the Utah pomologist's assessment of the Fiher Zagos grape. He asserted that the Fiher Zagos would not make a good raisin, and it was locally known as White Malmsey. He contended that the only grape that would make a good raisin was the White Muscat de Alexandre.[20]

The California Farmer and Journal of Useful Science was diplomatic in its response. After all, Bugbey was a loyal advertiser in their publication for his grape cuttings and wines. They noted that since

Benjamin Norton Bugbey

the Fiher Zagos introduction at the first State Agricultural Society Fair in Sacramento, they reported that the actual name was White Malaga, the same variety which comes from the eastern United States. The journal parted ways with the pomologist and wrote, "When grown in proper soil and rightly cultivated here in red land, or our decomposed quartz, it makes large clusters and fine raisins..." They opted not to comment on the value of the grape as a foundation for superior wine.[21]

Perhaps Bugbey realized that his wines were the best amongst a mediocre lot that were being produced in California at the time. The United States Agricultural Department when analyzing wines sent from California noted the number of samples that had spoiled due to improper handling or corking. Bugbey may simply have been better at bottling his wines than other producers, to such a degree that Bugbey's mediocre wines were still superior to a bottle of spoiled wine from Napa.

Products of the vine whose qualities are influenced less by soil, climate, and ageing are those which are distilled or produced for relatively quick consumption. Consumers of sparkling wine were less apt to be finnicky about a product's sensory elements than a connoisseur of fine wines. Champagne, or sparkling wine, was a festive alcoholic beverage and not subject to professorial criticisms about the type of grape varietal used or its suitability. Bugbey had received enough mediocre reviews of his wines to realize he needed to shift markets. Instead of trying to please wine critics, he decided to move into fermented and distilled products that commanded similar prices without the headaches of snooty wine drinkers.

Hugo Yanke-Mansfeldt

In 1864 a young man by the name of Hugo Yanke settled in Sacramento. He would become the principal pianist and organist at the Congregational Church on Sixth Street. Yanke was born in Prussia, commonly referred to as Germany in U. S. documentation in 1844. His family lived in Bromberg, near the Polish border,[22] and immigrated to New York in 1860.

The family was of modest means. While his father concentrated on being a tailor, Hugo picked up work as a clerk. This allowed him enough money to buy some sheet music to continue playing the piano, a skill he had begun to cultivate before the family left Germany. Once Hugo had mastered the music he had bought, he started giving piano lessons to his siblings and other children in the neighborhood.[23]

In 1863 Hugo, with a friend, had the opportunity to accompany a piano on a ship bound for California. At the age of 19 and with little money, he embarked on a five-week voyage at sea and land.

Benjamin Norton Bugbey

He arrived in San Francisco in February 1864 and immediately went to M. Gray's music store.[24]

At Gray's music store, he learned that a piano teacher in Sacramento was permanently leaving, and the city would be a good place for him to teach piano. The next day he traveled to Sacramento and introduced himself at Dales Music Store. There, Hugo learned that the Congregational Church was installing a new pipe pedal organ and needed an organist. Even though he had never played an organ, he interviewed for the organist position, concealing his lack of knowledge about playing an organ, and was hired for the job.

In his autobiography, Hugo Yanke-Mansfeldt discusses his anxiety about accepting the organist position. Not only had he no experience playing a pedal pipe organ, he soon learned that he was expected to perform a solo piece for a big concert celebrating the new organ. To make matters worse, the organ had not even been installed so he could not practice on it.[25]

Hugo rushed down to the music store and was able to buy a book on how to play an organ. He practiced the pieces on a piano, but that was no replication for playing the organ because he also had to push the pedals with his feet on the organ to fill the air bladders that drove the compressed air over the tubes to make the musical notes.[26]

On the day of the concert he managed to get in one hour of practice while another organist from San Francisco, who was also performing that evening, watched him play. Hugo was to play the final piece of music that evening, while the visiting San Francisco organist played before him. He sat stunned as the San Francisco organist began to play the musical piece Hugo had been practicing. As a testament to Hugo Yanke-Mansfeldt's musical genius, the 20-year-old strode to the organ, sat down, and calmly improvised for five minutes.[27] No one in the audience could tell that Hugo was literally playing by the seat of his pants.

Yanke's musical career blossomed in Sacramento. In addition to his duties at the Congregational Church, he worked with the Philharmonic Society, and began teaching students in piano, choral, and individual singing lessons. In 1864 he married Annie Sanderson in Sacramento, also a musician, who would perform with him on occasion.[28] Until he moved to Marysville in 1870 to open up a singing school[29], Yanke was either performing in concerts or organizing his own concerts that were staged at the Congregational Church, Metropolitan Theater, Agricultural Pavilion, and the Good Templars' Hall in Folsom. He was also able to recruit musical talent from the San Francisco area to perform in his concerts in Sacramento. The concerts were usually a mix of classical, contemporary, and patriotic music and songs.

Benjamin Norton Bugbey

At the young age of 26, while he was building his musical career, Hugo decided to change his name. The correct translation of his family's last name was Jahnke. As Hugo noted in his autobiography, they found the name was mispronounced in New York, because people could not soften the J in the pronunciation, so they changed it to Yanke. Unfortunately, this was further mispronounced as Yankee, as in Yankee Doodle Dandy.[30]

When Hugo landed in California, he was told the state leaned toward the Confederacy. He was also informed that Sacramento was a town that favored the Democratic Party, which as the Civil War was finally coming to an end, was aligned with the southern Confederacy. However, being called Yankee, with its northern connotations, was not his primary reason for changing his last name.

As the principle organist for the Congregational Church, organizing concerts, and instructing numerous students in piano, Hugo Yanke was a familiar face travelling around Sacramento. Since his father's primary trade was as a tailor, he inherited the disposition of always being professionally dressed in a suit when he travelled on horseback to teach his pupils.

Hugo recounts the story in his autobiography, "But the real reason for my changing my name was this…Sacramento was then only a city of 20,000 inhabitants. As I was prominent, musically, many knew me. I used to ride horses back to give my lessons, and as nearly every street boy knew me by sight, they used to yell after me the well-known lines: Yankee Doodle[31] [went to town, a riding on a pony, stuck a feather in his cap, and called it macaroni.]

The thought of Hugo's children being taunted by mean spirited children when they went to school was too much for him. When he moved to Marysville in 1871, he petitioned his name to be changed to Mansfeldt.[32] Hugo selected Mansfeldt because as he explained, "…at that time all the great pianists came from Germany." In hindsight, many decades later, Hugo still believed he made the correct choice to change his name as, "I know that my two boys escaped many unpleasant incidents by changing of the name."[33]

Musical Marketing

Musical concerts were a staple of entertainment in most towns in the 1860s, and Sacramento was no exception. Bugbey attended musical concerts and helped organize many for fundraisers and celebrations for the various social organizations he belonged to.

Before Hugo changed his last name to Mansfeldt, he was performing in Sacramento and Folsom as Hugo L. Yanke. Bugbey had most likely attended concerts where Yanke performed. He had probably also heard *Gungl's Railroad Galop* composed for the completion of the Transcontinental Railroad and performed at the 1869 Mechanics' Industrial Fair[34]. There was also the music *Railroad Kings Galop* where the images of men who organized different railroad lines were illustrated[35]. What better way to immortalize yourself and market your product than having a piece of music composed to promote and compliment the consumption of champagne?

Yanke accepted a commission from Bugbey to compose the *Bugbey's Champagne Galop*, with a patriotic release date of July 4, 1870. On the cover of the sheet music for the galop, surrounding the center illustration of Bugbey, is a wreath of grapevines with tendrils meeting at the top. On the right side of the Bugbey portrait is a champagne flute, overflowing like a volcanic eruption. To the left is a bottle of champagne blasting out its cork similar to a 4th of July firework or cannon.

Figure 15: 1870 – "Bugbey's Champagne Galop" sheet music cover. John Hopkins, The Lester S. Levy Sheet Music Collection.

A galop is a spirited piece of music with a beat similar to the running gait of a horse or railroad train. It is fun to listen to, but not necessarily suited for more staid celebrations. For more sophisticated events, Bugbey had Yanke compose the *Bugbey's Champagne Waltz*, which was published in 1871. Instead of the 2/4 timing of the Bugbey galop, the champagne waltz was written in a ¾ tempo.

On September 16, 1870, Yanke performed Bugbey's Champagne Galop at the Agricultural Pavilion at the 17th Annual State Fair. The Pavilion was constructed in 1859 by the City and County of Sacramento. It stood at the corner of 6th and M streets to accommodate the fairs of the State Agricultural Society[36]. On that September evening, Bugbey's Champagne Galop was paired with classical pieces such as selections from Trancredi by Rossini, Overture to Fra Diavolo by Auber, Cavatina from Lucrezia Borgia by Donizetti, music from Ernani by Verdi, and the Railroad Galop[37].

As was standard marketing practice for Bugbey, he sent out bottles or champagne along with the musical score of the galop to various newspapers. The Daily Alta wrote,

The champagne is very musical, and the music very champagne; and both together may be appropriately classed among the few things which make life endurable, and lighten the burden of daily cares. It is hard to say, whether the wine or the music is most [more] enjoyable- in fact, they both bubble and sparkle together; and are both delicious.[38] - Daily Alta California, Volume 22, Number 7419, 14 July 1870

Whether it was intentional or not, the cover of the sheet music noted it was composed for and dedicated to B. N. Bugbey, Esq., of Folsom, leading readers to assume that Hugo Yanke was so raptured by Bugbey's champagne as to cause him to write a whole musical score in honor of it. The Sacramento Daily Union bought into the ruse by commenting,

We are not versed in music, but the reputation of Bugbey's Sparkling Champagne is established, as one might well suppose when it has inspired a composer to render it immortal by setting it to music and sending it down sparkling and foaming to posterity.[39] - Sacramento Daily Union, Volume 39, Number 6018, 13 July 1870

Hugo Yanke was a talented young man living in Sacramento. He eventually found his way to the Bay Area to teach music and perform. In 1884 he returned to Europe to study with Franz Liszt at Weimar.[40] He returned to California after two years of study and gained notoriety as a concert pianist, instructor, and authority on musical technique.[41]

At the same State Fair where the Bugbey's Champagne Galop was played, the vintner won awards for best white wine, best sparkling wine two-years old, and, as usual, best exhibit of wines from a foreign grape.[42]

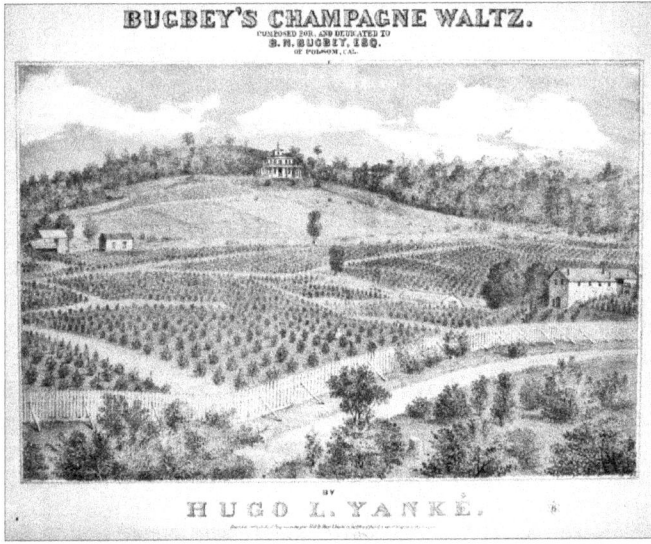

Figure 16: 1871 - "Bugbey's Champagne Waltz" sheet music cover. Note the similarities to J. A. Todd's photograph of the Natoma Vineyard from 1869. The Lester S. Levy Sheet Music Collection.

Natoma Vineyard & Winery Detailed

While Bugbey claimed he spared no expense in modernizing and expanding his operations, this was California in the 1870s. People had to be resourceful, and that meant re-purposing items for new uses. A large fire consumed the Granite Flour Mill on the north side of the American River, not far from the Natoma Vineyard, in 1867. The mill had been rebuilt after the 1862 floods that had virtually washed it away. The January fire closed the mill for good.[43] However, the stone buildings, hollowed out by fire, still stood. Bugbey bought the remains and carted them the short distance over to his vineyard. He then used them to construct a warehouse, 75 feet by 125 feet to store his inventory.[44]

In August of 1870, Bugbey purchased twenty large wooden tanks from the Central Pacific Railroad. The tanks had originally been constructed to hold drinking water for the men working on the railroad crossing the alkali flat of Nevada. Bugbey's design was to use them as fermenting vats for the manufacture for his brandy.[45]

Bugbey had every reason to be proud of his success, vineyard, and winery. He was an excellent spokesperson for the emerging wine industry in California. He also had a talent for writing and a desire to document the facts. He collaborated with a correspondent from California Farmer and Journal of Useful Sciences to provide a detailed and complimentary overview of the Natoma vineyard operations, in the publication's August 18, 1870, edition.

The Estate of which the Natoma Vineyard forms a part, is 480 acres of which there are now 125 acres in Vineyards, 88 acres are in full bearing. The crop this year surpassing all other years in quantity and quality, the crop upon these vines being much greater than most vineyards, and superior to any we know of in our state, and we can say with truth we have never seen the equal in this or any other part of the world.

There are 37 acres also of vines not in bearing, being newly planted. The collection of choice grapes in this Vineyard has no superior in our State, for in addition to the Mission Grape, generally grown the leading kinds are in the order named, rank in their quality as bearers, and also in the quantity grown.

White Malaga—this year bearing enormously, the vines being literally a mass of Grapes—the vines will give from 40 to 75 lbs each, a most remarkable crop.

The Red Tramina— also an immense crop, a mass of rich compact clusters The Zinfendal, the Verdelho, the Alicant, the Pino, and the Reisling, (Johanisburg) have all a splendid heavy crop each, and all these varieties Mr. Bugbey finds will make superior wine.

There are also Chasselas of Foutanbleau, Muscadine, Black Malaga, Hamburg, Black Malvasia, White and Grey Reisling, Sweetwater, and Black Prince, all for wine, together with Flaming Tokay, White Tokay, Cannon Hall Muscat, White St Peters, Hamburg, Rose of Peru, White Nice, and Palestine, for the table.

Although each and all these table grapes are excellent for wine, and when we shall remember that these choicest of Foreign Grapes are here in open culture on the hill sides in our dry climate, and where the thermometer has actually run up as high as 118°, and yet in this Vineyard there are thousands of clusters and well shouldered bunches of 2 1/2, 3, and even 4 lbs. each—is it not right for us to say that this showing has no superior?

This Vineyard made in the year 1868, forty thousand Gallons of Wine, the present year, 1870, it is estimated that the crop will give fully One Hundred and Twenty-Five Thousand Gallons, and of the most superior quality too —besides 8,000 Gallons of the very best Brandy.

That some estimate may be formed of the work done and now in preparation for this great harvest. We can state in addition to the

Benjamin Norton Bugbey

long range of buildings and cellars, of many hundred feet, there are now being erected in the most substantial manner, of stone and brick, wine houses of the most approved form and style some 200 feet long, 40 feet wide and 30 feet high—two stories—no cost being spared to have them the best that genius, talent and skill can produce.

The standing casks now in process of being made ready for present harvest are as follows: 69 standing casks of 800 gallons each; 20 tanks of 1000 Gallons each; 20 tanks additional ordered made, equivalent to about 110,000 Gallons. It is indeed most interesting to note the order, system and purity in and around all the buildings.

In the manufacture of the wines at this Vineyard the greatest care is paid to the preparation and the purity of the casks —the buildings being light, airy and warm, the casks are more exposed to light and heat, therefore are of the best kind, and purely sweet and perfect.

The greatest care is paid to the manufacture of these wines, and the reward for this care has been the high name already attained both at home and abroad, for the Wines of the Natoma Vineyard, or as is said, the "Bugbey Wine."

The varieties of wine made are Port, Sherry, Chambertin, Red and White wines, and Hock.— These all rank high, and are quickly saleable at good prices, and the Brandy being of extra quality is esteemed superior to much of the imported French Brandy.

The Brandy made here is by the new process of distillation, known as the "Johnstons" new process, by which the fusel oil is entirely extracted, rendering the Brandy pure and of superior quality and of greatly increased value. This process is now attracting great attention, the Proprietor, Mr. Bugbey being the first Wine and Brandy Distiller who has introduced this process into practice, yet at great cost.

Natoma Vineyard is 5 miles from Folsom, the average number of men employed through the year is 25—during harvest and Wine making 40 hands are employed, of which for gathering Grape etc., some 25 Chinamen are employed, who are considered competent, trustworthy and faithful.

Mr. Bugbey is also owner of the "Duroc Vineyard," which is 14 miles from Folsom—"Duroc" contains 200 acres of which grounds only 20 acres are now bearing vines, and principally the same variety of Grapes—the prospect being the same for this year.

Both, these vineyards are to be steadily increased in their acres of Vines, just as the merits of the Grapes are fully tested for making the best of Wines, as the proprietor is determined that none but pure and valuable Wines shall ever go from his Vineyards.

When it shall be remembered that for the foundation thus laid for these Vineyards nearly a Quarter of a Million of Dollars bas been expended, all will perceive, California is bound to be the Vineyard of

Benjamin Norton Bugbey

*the world.*⁴⁶ - California Farmer and Journal of Useful Sciences, Volume 34, Number 6, 18 August 1870.

Any mention of the Fiher Zagos grape variety, whose identity had been questioned by so many others in the viticulture field, has been excised from the vineyard description. Instead, the grape varietal White Malaga is highlighted as the big grape producer. The article notes how, despite the 100° F plus summer temperatures, the vines are producing large clusters of berries. The article also relates Bugbey's belief that wine is best fermented and aged in warm, airy cellars, as opposed to those dark, cool, high-humidity caves over in Napa or Sonoma.

The mention of a warm environment for fermenting and ageing wine was included to counter the growing sentiment that cool dark cellars are best. Vintners in Napa and Sonoma counties, using caves with cool temperatures and high humidity, were producing excellent wines. Because of the quality of the wines being produced in the Napa and Sonoma regions, The California Farmer and Journal of Useful Sciences was beginning to change their recommendation away from Bugbey's method of warm and airy fermenting process.⁴⁷

Big Investment

Also noteworthy in the 1870 story on the Natoma Vineyard is the disclosure that a capital investment of over $250,000 had been poured into the vineyard and winery operations. Bugbey was also investing in new equipment for brandy distillation. The Johnston method accelerated the removal of fusel oil⁴⁸ that can impart bitterness to the brandy, which is normally broken down by ageing the product. Hence, high-quality brandies were usually aged for 10 to 20 years before being released for sale. The reduced time it took to create product with the new Johnston distillation process meant that Bugbey could get his brandy to market sooner.

In the summer of 1870, Bugbey shipped 10 railcar-loads, or 20,000 gallons, of wine back east. He also decided to travel back east to promote his wines, visit with his family, and introduce them to his new wife.⁴⁹

His good friends at the Journal heaped praise on Bugbey in advance of his return to Connecticut.

*Mr. Bugbey has been a most indefatigable worker as a vineyardist, converting the waste and dreary places of the mountain and valley into a garden, where the new wines gush like a river. After an absence of twenty years from his native home, he returns to greet his kindred and friends, he goes bearing with the honorable evidence of his labor and untiring industry of which he can be justly proud.*⁵⁰ -

Benjamin Norton Bugbey

California Farmer and Journal of Useful Sciences, Volume 34, Number 7, 25 August 1870

Even the railroad companies were helping promote Bugbey. In the marketing publication "Lands of the Central Pacific Railroad," the railroad notes how Bugbey is cultivating a new industry of the raisin grape on a piece of land purchased from railroad near Folsom. Bugbey purchased 120 acres from the Central Pacific Railroad in 1870.[51] The property was south, and adjacent to, the Natoma Vineyard in section 21 of Township 10 North, Range 8 East. He also purchased 40 acres from CPRR at the same time at the Duroc Vineyard, section 11, Township 9 North, Range 9 East.[52] The land transactions were facilitated by E. H. Miller, Jr. for the CPRR and signed by Leland Stanford.

On his trip back east in Boston, Bugbey learned of how inferior wines were being marketed as California varieties and was inspired to expose the imposters. Along the way he picked up orders for more of his wines, brandy, and sparkling wine.[53] In December of 1870, he shipped four more rail cars of wine back east.[54] Bugbey was even able to secure the first United States shipment of wine to Shanghai, China.[55] Early in 1871, Bugbey sent 150 cases of champagne and 20 eighth-casks of brandy to Nathaniel Perkins in Manchester, N. H.[56]

Bugbey had his marketing machine in high gear and was making sales. The future looked bright. It was time to invest further in the Natoma Vineyard operations and other distillery prospects.

The Big Brandy Gamble

Bugbey was producing his brandy with a new still invented by George Johnston of Sacramento. Several men, including Bugbey, thought this new patented process was so superior and offered such a high rate of return on any investment that they formed a business association to raise $75,000 in capital to build a Sacramento distillery using the method.[57]

Shortly after the association meeting, Bugbey hosted an event at the Natoma vineyard so that interested investors and the press could witness the Johnston still in operation. The party of spectators left on the 6:15 SVRR train for Folsom. It was a gloomy, wet and cold March morning. After breakfast in Folsom, the men boarded carriages for the one-hour ride out to the Natoma Vineyard.

George Johnston was waiting for the party at the Natoma vineyard and had prepared the fire under the boilers and charged one of the tubs of wine. A reporter for the Sacramento Daily Union gave the following description:

So much has already been said concerning the still by the press of the city and State, that it is unnecessary on this occasion to give a lengthy description of its appearance. Suffice it, that it is of copper, and it consists of a column of six chambers, reaching to a height of 12 or 18 feet. The lower chamber is about four feet in diameter and three feet in height; the other five chambers are, say two feet in diameter and about two feet in height. In each chamber is a coil of pipe, connected from chamber to chamber, leading from the top of the column to the bottom, and designed to be used in regulating the temperature of the still by means of stream of cold water passing through it. The exact temperature is ascertained by means of a thermometer set in the top of the column.

Two wooden vats, strongly bound, each having a capacity of 800 gallons, act as the feeders of the still, with which they are connected in such a manner that while one is being used the other can be cleansed and re-charged. To facilitate the cleansing, each has a gate near the bottom, through which the contents are sluiced out.

One of these feeding vats being charged, either with pumace [sic for pomace], grapes or wine—whatever material is intended to be used— steam is let on from the boiler, the pressure averaging about two pounds. As the temperature increases the vapor from the vat passes into the lower chamber of the still, and rises from one chamber to another and to the top, from whence it is led to a worm in a tank nearby for condensation. The still operates upon the simple principle that the fusel oil will vaporize at a lesser temperature than the acetic ether, and that, in turn, at a lesser temperature than the alcoholic spirit.

In the experiment yesterday the fusel oil was drawn off at about 160 degrees. To maintain this heat sufficiently long to allow of the oil being thoroughly removed, a man is stationed at the top of the column to watch the thermometer. If he finds the heat increasing, he has recourse to a valve rod at hand, by means of which he is able to let a greater or less quantity of cold water into the coil of pipe, as the necessity of the moment may demand. It being ascertained by the usual tests that the fusel oil has come off, the temperature is increased to about 170 degrees until the acetic ether is also disposed of (being saved for redistillation), and then, the heat being still further increased to about 177 degrees, the pure brandy, thoroughly distilled and rectified, is produced.[58] - Sacramento Daily Union, Volume 41, Number 7133, 24 March 1871

The demonstration produced brandy of 84 per cent proof. The Johnston still was compared to another still at the winery patterned after the French method of brandy distillation constructed by William Schmidt of Folsom. The reporter noted the size of Bugbey's operation along with his tremendous investment in the property, even after suffering heavy losses due to fires in years past. For the return trip, Bugbey hired a special train to carry the men back to Sacramento.[59]

The value proposition of the Johnston still was getting a drinkable product from still to table within months instead of years. Bugbey was selling three-month-old brandy using, what must have been for Bugbey, this glorious mechanical invention. He even garnered some positive press from the Sacramento Bee, in light of his past feuds with Editor James McClatchy. Bugbey was excited about the Johnston distillation process for brandy and wanted to share his experience with the Sacramento Bee. Of course, Bugbey was also an investor in the Johnston still.

Regardless, he reported that he was able to produce 50 gallons of drinkable brandy from one ton of grapes. Grapes at that time were selling for between $20 and $25 per ton. Bugbey calculated his net cost to produce one gallon of brandy using the Johnston process at $3. Further, he was able to sell each gallon of finished product at $5 legal tender or $4.50 in gold coin.[60]

At this time California's preferred monetary system was gold coins. Legal tender, or greenbacks printed by the U. S. government, were discounted. The East Coast, a market into which Bugbey was selling, used primarily greenbacks to pay for goods and services. In California, not only was gold coin the preferred payment method, it was also stipulated into contracts and mortgages that the debt would be repaid in gold coin. The net effect to California producers selling into the East Coast market, or any market where they were reimbursed with greenbacks, meant gross revenue on sales was discounted when converted into gold coin.

Sacramento Philanthropy

That Bugbey would actually set foot in the offices of McClatchy's Sacramento Bee after their bitter political feuds of the past is rather remarkable. But now both men belonged to the Union Republican Party and could find common ground, with shared political and social beliefs. At the beginning of 1871, James McClatchy was helping organize a social ball to raise money for the Howard Benevolent Association at the new county hospital. Bugbey was on the Finance Committee representing Folsom, along with P. J. Hopper. Former Sacramento County Sheriff James Lansing, a friend of Bugbey's, was also on the Supper Committee.[61]

The Howard Benevolent Association or Howard Association, was first organized in Virginia in 1855 during a yellow fever epidemic. The association raised money to pay for the hospital care of those afflicted by the disease[62]. Sacramento's Howard Benevolent

Association was chartered in 1857.[63] Their mission was to raise money to pay for medical care at the County Hospital for those who were too poor to pay for it. The Sacramento Howard Benevolent Association had a goal of collecting $1 per month from every Sacramento City resident. Association by-laws prohibited discussion of any religious or political topics at any of the meetings of the directors,[64] a rule that probably helped men from different political backgrounds, as Bugbey and McClatchy were, participate in the organization.[65]

The winter of 1870 and 1871 was particularly difficult for the residents of Sacramento, as many had become ill and had to seek health care at the county hospital. To raise extra money to pay for the health care services of those who could not afford them, the Howards organized a fundraising dinner party at the Agricultural Pavillion.[66] The event comprised of music and supper raised several hundred dollars for the Howard's benevolent fund that evening.[67]

Natoma Water & Mining Company

The spring of 1871 may have been the high-water mark for Bugbey's wine and spirits business. However, no one could predict the numerous little financial challenges Bugbey would face in the future. At age 44, Bugbey appeared to have struck the new California gold with his Natoma Vineyard. He was even beating back large corporations from encroaching on his property.

In March 1871 Bugbey prevailed against the Natoma Water and Mining Company, which had wanted to condemn part of his Natoma Vineyard for the construction of new flume for their water ditch. Three commissioners were appointed by a District Court Judge in Placerville to assess the damages Bugbey would suffer by ceding the property to the Natoma Water and Mining Company.[68]

The commissioners took testimony over 20 days and visited the Natoma Vineyard.[69] Bugbey testified that he had between 86,000 and 90,000 grapevines in production. He expected the vineyard to produce between 500 and 800 tons of grapes that he valued at $50 per ton[70]. This was greater than the statewide average of $25 per ton. Bugbey mentioned the grapes from his Duroc vineyard operations were valued at $25 per ton, after freight costs to the Natoma Vineyard to be processed.[71]

After reviewing the testimony, the three commissioners awarded Bugbey $19,000 for the loss of production as a result of the Natoma Water and Mining Company's new flume on his property.[72] This worked out to approximately $2,000 per acre.[73] Unfortunately, the action by the Natoma Water and Mining Company would not go away. They would continue to dispute the judgment and insist that they had a legitimate right to Bugbey's land because they were there first.

Benjamin Norton Bugbey

Bugbey's finances, along with an estimated per-acre value of $2,000 in grape vines, had been so widely reported in the newspapers and journals that it spurred other landowners to plant even more grapevines. The reporting also produced an offer from a California liquor importing house to purchase a half interest in the Natoma Vineyard for $100,000. Bugbey declined the offer.[74] Just a year before, Bugbey had taken out a mortgage on the Natoma Vineyard from Sacramento Savings Bank for approximately $15,000.[75] Even though the Pacific Rural Press was complaining that savings banks were not lending to agricultural pursuits,[76] Bugbey was able to get a loan to expand his operations.

In 1871 Bugbey was just gearing up to accelerate his wine, sparking wine and brandy production. He had exclusive rights to use the new Johnston still in El Dorado County to produce and bring drinkable brandy to the market in under a year. He saw his future as being very bubbly and very bright.

Fire & Politics

Unfortunately for Bugby, the brightness of his future was dimmed by the light of a fire. In May 1871 fire struck downtown Folsom. It started at the store of Smith, Campbell & Jolly and burnt down to the basement.[77] Bugbey was using the bottom floor of the building he owned to store inventory. The building at the corner of Wool Street was close to the Sacramento Valley Railroad Depot. The origin of the fire remained a mystery, but Bugbey's loss was heavy. It was estimated that he lost $85,000 in the form of the building, wine and brandy inventory, plus furniture. Bugbey only had $29,000 in fire insurance on the property and contents.[78]

Unlike the previous fire of the wine cellar at the Natoma Vineyard, Bugbey did not offer a reward for the arrest and conviction of the arsonist. That may have been the prudent course of action, because the rumor amongst Folsom residents was that Bugbey set the fire.

Shortly after the fire, Nathaniel Knight wrote to his brother Ambrose. Nathaniel described a terrible fire that consumed several buildings leaving downtown Folsom with a wound that would take several years to heal. He went on to express his opinion of the fire noting, "Now I believe all this calamity is the work of an incendiary, a high muck a muck of a free & accepted mason." Bugbey just happened to be a Mason.[79]

In a letter dated July 2, 1871 to Ambrose, Nathaniel does not hesitate to identify the suspected arsonist.

...I believe the prevailing opinion is that B. N. Bugb[e]y set fire to his wine house to get the insurance as he was hard pressed for money at the time. His insurance was twenty-nine thousand and his wine house worth about five thousand and his wine perhaps ten thousand, that would leave him 14 thousand neat cash, a pretty little purse for burning 75 or a hundred thousand worth for his neighbors, but they were all heavily insured..."[80]

Bugbey was never charged for arson in relation to the fire that destroyed his wine cellar and several other buildings in Folsom in the spring of 1871.

By June Bugbey was preparing to rebuild the wine cellars he lost to fire.[81] In an ironic occurrence, just a few weeks before the fire, Bugbey was appointed to the advisory board of the Craftsmen's Life Insurance Company of New York for their California division.[82] Perhaps it was his past experience with fire loss that garnered the appointment.

Not content with just running a burgeoning vinicultural empire and reconstructing buildings destroyed by fire, Bugbey took another stab at being nominated for the office of Sheriff under the Republican Party.[83] In June at the nominating convention, Mike Bryte garnered 51 votes, Heilbron captured 32, and Bugbey could only muster 14 votes.[84]

Not deterred by failing to receive the party's nod for Sheriff, Bugbey remained active in county politics and was appointed to the Republican County Central Committee.[85] One of the resolutions of the Sacramento County Republicans that must have pleased Bugbey was a declaration of uncompromising opposition to the granting of railroad subsidies to corporations or individuals.[86] One of the issues was that the railroads received subsidies and were beginning to charge monopolistic freight rates. Brandy producers such as Bugbey were also levied a per-gallon tax on brandy spirit produced.[87]

New Folsom Home, C. T. H. Palmer

In July 1871 Bugbey sold a Folsom lot to a Chinese man by the name of Mum Sing.[88] Described as the east half of Lot 3 in Block 19, the site fronted Leidesdorff Street and was just west of the Sacramento Valley Railroad Depot.[89] Bugbey had bought the lot in 1862 from Gilbert Cole for $500. He sold it to Sing for $450.[90] It was no secret that Bugbey employed Chinese men to work in his vineyard.[91] But it may have been disconcerting to some Folsom residents that Bugbey had sold property to a Chinese man at a time when sentiment against Chinese immigrants in California was on the rise. There was no explanation as to why Bugbey made the sale to Mum Sing, whether it was for a business or residence. Regardless, Bugbey may have just needed to raise cash for his next move.

With fire destroying Bugbey's Natoma Vineyard house on the hill, he decided to buy a large house in Folsom. In August 1871 be bought the former residence of Charles Theodore Hart Palmer,[92] who was moving to the Bay area after a long and profitable career in the Folsom region. Like Bugbey, C. T. H. Palmer came to California in 1849. Like Bugbey, he tried his hand at mining until he found other pursuits that were not as arduous and paid better money. Palmer's career in financial transactions began to take root when he became an express agent in Ophir, west of Auburn, California. In 1854 he established a Wells Fargo branch at Rattlesnake Bar. He would continue to move south, down the North Fork of the American, opening offices at Dotan's Bar and Carrolton, until he moved to Folsom in 1856.[93]

By 1860 C. T. H. Palmer was operating the Granite Banking House, managing an assay office, and handling express packages for Wells, Fargo & Co. In 1859 Palmer constructed an iconic fireproof building, with the street-facing wall made of granite blocks.[94] After the Central Pacific Railroad Company had completed much of its line up to Auburn, Folsom began to decline as a hub of commerce.

Palmer's wife had moved to Oakland, California, for health reasons. With the decline of gold mining in Folsom, which in turn reduced the necessity of having a banking house to assay gold dust and convert it into Wells Fargo & Co. checks, Palmer decided to move to the Bay Area permanently in 1870.[95] Bugbey purchased Palmer's fine home on the corner of Bridge and Figueroa Streets (lots 7 and 8 in Block 53) in Folsom for $1,650 in August of 1871.[96] The $1,650 purchase would seem modest for a man in Bugbey's financial situation as a successful vintner. Yet he apparently needed the financial assistance of Ann Johns, J. W. Speyer, and J. M. Philip to complete the purchase.[97] Was this real estate loan, in addition to the sale to Mum Sing, an indication that Bugbey was having cash flow problems?

Bugbey would make a curious Folsom lot purchase in September 1871: He purchased the eastern half of Lot 11 in Block 9, along Leidesdorff and Reading Streets from R. W. Murphey for $100.[98] Back in 1857, Bugbey had executed a quitclaim deed on lots 10 and 11 to Murphy, along with other lots in blocks 40 and 44, for $4,000.[99] Underneath these lots, as the bluff sloped down to the river, Bugbey and others had tunneled drift mines. Was Bugbey trying to generate some revenue from gold mining? He did generate some money when he sold the eastern-northern section of lot 10 in block 9 for $1,000 to Charles Nuttall and Stephen Addison in August 1872.[100]

Despite everything that Bugbey had going on in his life, including managing a winery, marketing, and real estate transactions, he still found time to exhibit at the 1871 State Fair. Bugbey's entries, those that weren't destroyed by the Folsom fire, were still winning awards. He received a premium for his white sparkling wine, best exhibit of wines, and best and greatest varieties of wine grapes.[101] There were no awards for his raisins, but he may not have entered any in 1871, as he was devoting most of this crop to wine and spirits. However, Bugbey acknowledged the profitability of raisins. Were it not for most of his capital, and loans, being directed at the production of wine and brandy, he explained to the Pacific Rural Press, he would expand his raisin production.[102] In short, Bugbey had placed all his money on the profitability of wine, sparkling wine, and a lot of capital for the Johnston still, for the production of brandy.

By the end of 1871, Bugbey had produced 70,000 gallons of wine.[103] The Pacific Rural Press noted that the prodigious amount of wine was made without irrigation.[104] Bugbey was still in litigation with the Natoma Water and Mining Company over the construction of the flume on his property. While Bugbey may not have bought any water from the Natoma Ditch, there was enough seepage below the earth-lined canal to provide plenty of irrigation water for wine grapes.

California State Fair Gold Medal Statements

The California State Agricultural Society broke up their entries and exhibits into different departments. The Fifth Department, in which Bugbey exhibited, was made up of Brandies, Wines, Butter, Honey, and Preserved Pickles. Premiums were awarded to the best products. There could be several winners of the highest premium in a category. For example, Bugbey received a $10 premium at the 1870 State Fair for his white wine, one year old. George West of Stockton and Orleans Hill Vinicultural Society in Sacramento also received $10 premiums for their wines in the same category.[105]

Figure 17: 1871 - Full page advertisement in the Sacramento directory for Bugbey's Natoma Vineyard products featuring images of Gold Medal awards. Located through Ancestry.com

After the State Fair concluded, entrants in each department could submit a statement as to why their overall exhibits should be awarded the Gold Medal for the year. For 1870 Bugbey submitted a short, three-paragraph statement for his wines. His main argument that he should receive the Gold Medal was that he had the largest exhibit of wines and brandies produced from foreign varieties of grapes.[106] His second argument was less about the quality of his items but rather his investment and advocacy for wine production in California.

> *...thereby showing conclusively the capacity of our soil and climate to produce successfully the finer wines of France, Germany, Spain, and other wine countries of Europe. The result has been affected through great care and expense, extending over a period of nearly ten years, and is destined to have an important and favorable influence in competing with the finer varieties of wines which have heretofore been imported from Europe. The undersigned claims that he has produced as fine qualities of wines from different varieties of grapes used as can be had – age and other circumstances considered – anywhere, and that the result thus attained he has made the common property of all other viniculturists in the State. Benj. N. Bugbey.*[107] - Transactions of the California State Agricultural Society During The Years 1870 and 1871, Sacramento. T. A. Springer, State Printer, 1872

The State Agricultural Society committee agreed with Bugbey and awarded him the Gold Medal for wines and brandies. Awards were important for marketing purposes, and Bugbey proudly announced his several Gold Medals in advertisements for his wine, brandies, and sparkling wines.[108]

The agricultural items comprising the different State Agricultural Society State departments were changed for the 1871 State Fair. Wines were now judged in the Sixth Department, along with grains, garden seeds, flowers, and fruits. Silk, its production and the goods made from it was in the Third Department. However, the Agricultural Society erroneously included silk in the same category as exhibits for wines and brandies. The committee reviewing entries for Gold Medals even acknowledged its embarrassment for what the members characterized as, "...the imperfect classification of the different exhibits."

The underlying logic was that wine, brandy, and products made of silk were manufactured from agricultural products and were not standalone commodities such as wheat, corn, flowers, or fruit. One of the elements for receiving a Gold Medal was the practical value of the agricultural entry to the State. For the Fifth Department, Gold Medal statements from J. R. Nickerson of Lincoln and the Orleans Hill Vinicultural Society argued that both their previous awards and extensive investments into their vineyards showed they should receive the award.

It was Bugbey, in his statement, that specifically made the case that the wine industry was more important to California than the

Benjamin Norton Bugbey

budding silk industry. At the 1871 State Fair, he had his largest number of entries, exhibiting 29 different wines, brandy, and champagne, plus displays of grapes and raisins. But there was a new and growing industry in California: silk production. At the San Francisco Mechanics' Fair earlier in the year, the California Silk Factory had taken a gold medal for its raw, spool and twisted silk produced on a farm. There was also considerable promotion of silk production in California. In addition, people enjoyed seeing the silk worms on display, munching on mulberry leaves, and spinning their little cocoons.

Bugbey could sense the mood at the State Fair and at the Agricultural Society had shifted. Silk was the interesting commodity of the year. His 1871 statement was no less than a treatise of several pages in length, questioning the economic worth of the silk industry to California, along with a history of his accomplishments and contributions to the wine and vine industry in California.

His arguments were carefully crafted. Bugbey praised the potential of the silk industry and acknowledged that California is perfectly suited for the production of mulberry trees to feed the little silk worms. But he noted that the silk industry and production were in their infancy and had not contributed to California like the wine industry had.

Hence, the successful development of these new industries in our State will bring into use and make valuable millions of acres of a class of land that can in no other way be rendered of but little value. To the exhibitors of these particular classes in this department, then, the need of merit will doubtless be awarded, and while I would concede great merits to the pioneers and exhibitors in the silk industry, yet I think it will be admitted that sufficient has not been accomplished in silk culture to entitle the industry to rank before that of the cultivation of the vine and the manufacture of its products.

The benefits to the State from silk culture are mostly in anticipation, while those from vine culture and wine manufacture are in a fair state of realization. This advanced stage of the latter has been brought about by the foresight, enterprise, and perseverance of a few individuals[109]. - Transactions of the California State Agricultural Society During the Years 1870 and 1871, Sacramento: T.A. Springer, State Printer, 1872

In his argument, Bugbey noted that viticulture and winemaking were once dubious experiments and not guaranteed of success in the state. Advocates for the nascent California wine industry had to work hard to convince people that the state's wines were equal or superior to European imports. He then went on to argue that he should be awarded the gold medal based in part on his pioneering and experimental vineyard, plus his tireless promotion of the wine industry.

> *During this entire time I have been constantly and carefully carrying on experiments, the object of which has been to determine: first, the varieties of grapes best adapted for making superior wines of the different kinds in California, and second, the best mode of treating those wines in this climate to secure the best results from any given variety.*
>
> *For the double purpose of assisting my own judgment as to the success with which these experiments were being attended, and to establish a reputation and market for California wines in general, and my own in particular, I have taken a great deal of pains and spent a great deal of money in placing them on exhibition and competition with the wines of other producers at our own Mechanics' and State Fairs, and also exhibited them at the Universal Exhibition at Paris in eighteen hundred and sixty-seven.[110]* - Transactions of the California State Agricultural Society During the Years 1870 and 1871, Sacramento: T.A. Springe, State Printer, 1872

Bugbey then enumerates his 35 different awards from 1863 to 1871 for raisins, wine, sparkling wine, brandy, exhibits of grapes and wine. Further, he reports that he also is at the forefront of brandy production, with the construction of the first Johnston still.

> *In eighteen hundred and sixty-eight my attention was called to an improved still for the manufacture of brandy, patented by Johnston. Having satisfied myself that it was a good improvement, I built and set to work the first working still ever made under the patent. The venture proved a good to myself, and the introduction and general use of this still cannot fail to be of immense benefit to the vine interest and to the State. "Whatever that benefit may be, it gives me no small degree of satisfaction that through my patronage as a vine grower it was first introduced and proved of value. By the use of this still the operator can by one operation clear the brandy of the fusil oil and acetic ether and retain all the natural aroma. The same quantity of grapes or other fruits will make twenty per cent more spirits than by the old process, with twenty-five per cent less expense.[111]* - Transactions of the California State Agricultural Society During the Years 1870 and 1871, Sacramento: T.A. Springer, State Printer, 1872

He even lamented the monetary loss on his first attempts to produce sparkling wine. His experiments with producing champagne in 1868 cost him $12,000. The next year, he claimed, he was able to produce a drinkable product.

Benjamin Norton Bugbey

Bugbey's overall argument was that he should receive the gold medal for all that he had done for the vine and wine industry along with all his tremendous sacrifices. He noted his awards at the Mechanics' Institute Fair and how he had his California wines distributed across the country, from St. Louis, Missouri to Buffalo, New York.

In terms of specificity and stating the case for being awarded a gold medal at the State Fair, Bugbey's statement was one of the most detailed and lengthy.[112] (Bugbey's full statement is reprinted in the endnote section). Unfortunately, the State Agricultural Society awarded the Gold Medal to Edward Muller of Nevada City for exhibition of the silk business. The society's explanation was that they decided to give the Gold Medal to the industry that needed the most encouragement.[113]

Vine Growers' Association

For many California vintners, the Fruit Growers' Association that had been established was not meeting their needs. Wine production was exploding in California. The gallons of wine produced had doubled in just a couple of seasons:

- 1868 1.88 million gallons
- 1869 2.64 million gallons
- 1870 3.80 million gallons
- 1871 estimated 5.70 million gallons

The average wholesale price for wine was $0.30 to $0.50 per gallon, and California land devoted to grapevines had blossomed to 20 million acres.[114]

In 1872 vintners decided to organize a vine growers' association. A group of California vintners assembled in Sacramento in early February 1872 to launch the organization.[115] B. D. Wilson of Los Angeles was elected president. A. Schell and Bugbey were elected vice presidents of the new organization, called the Vine Growers' and Wine and Brandy Manufacturers' Association.[116] Bugbey was part of the committee for establishing a permanent organization, along with A. Schell of Stanislaus County, George Applegate, J. R. Nickerson, and T. R. Chamberlain of Placer County, C. J. Carpenter of El Dorado County, A. Eberhardt of San Francisco, George Johnston of Sacramento, I. N. Hoag of Yolo County, J. H. Cooper of Santa Barbara County, and William Caldwell of Sonoma County.[117]

Bugbey would also serve on committees reporting on the association constitution and bylaws, cultivation of the grape and pruning, and on the making and clarification of wine. The most pressing issue for Bugbey was not the cultivation of grape vines, but reduction of the federal tax on brandy. He proposed a committee to immediately work on drafting a memorandum to be sent to Congress to reduce the onerous tax. He entreated his fellow delegates, "I suppose the idea of appointing this committee is that they shall, in the name of this convention and the grape-growers of the State of California, petition our Legislature to join with us in a memorial to Congress, praying that the revenue on brandy made from the grape exclusively be reduced. I do not think there is any possibility of our urging the matter too strongly. Prompt action is required in this case. The other committees can report at their leisure. But this is a matter that won't bear delay, but must be attended to immediately."[118]

There was not a great urgency among Bugbey's fellow members to tackle a federal taxation issue. The matter was directed to a committee for further study.

The Vine Growers' meeting was held in Sacramento, which was on a short train and buggy ride out to Bugbey's Natoma Vineyard. Before the vine growers' convention commenced, Bugbey held a large party to dedicate one of the huge wine vats that he had constructed. It was capable of holding 50,000 gallons of wine and made for a suitable dance floor as well. Guests were invited to dance inside the wine vats. The wooden vats were lit up and Bugbey hired musicians to play dancing tunes[119], which must have included *Bugbey's Champagne Galop* and *Bugbey's Champagne Waltz*.

The Vine Growers' Association would continue to meet almost on a monthly basis. Except for George Johnston's discussion on fusel oil being driven off at different temperatures in the manufacture of brandy,[120] most of the reports and discussion were drawn from growers' experience. For example, one topic was whether grapes farthest from the main stalk were less sweet. Bugbey said he had never detected a difference.[121] Another discussion centered on J. R. Nickerson's assessment that the White Malaga made a good wine grape and would not crack or mildew. Bugbey confirmed Nickerson's experience and only added that his White Malaga grapes would crack after a rainstorm.[122]

Lobbying for Land Relief

At the time the vine growers were meeting, the California State Assembly was considering a bill to change how water canal companies must compensate landowners for constructing flumes across their land. One of the provisions of AB 269 was that the condemnation of land by a water canal company for the construction of a flume must adhere to the same procedures as land condemnations by the railroad companies. Specifically, the water canal company would have to deposit a sufficient amount of money into an account to cover any damages to the property owner. Once this was done, the work could move forward.[123]

Bugbey had been awarded $19,000 by the El Dorado District Court for the loss of property resulting from the construction of the Natoma Water and Mining Company flume across Brown's Ravine. Several years after the court decision, he was still waiting to be compensated. Bugbey complained to his local elected officials about how the bill might further delay his receipt of the awarded monetary compensation from the Natoma Water and Mining Company.[124]

The political lines were clearly drawn between assemblymen who favored the canal companies and their ability to expand operations and fellow assembly members who favored property owners and their rights to be compensated in a timely manner. Assemblyman Day summarized the effect of California's existing law as the water canal companies' ability to keep condemnation compensation locked up in litigation until finally adjudicated by the Supreme Court.[125]

And that is exactly what was happening to Bugbey. The Natoma Water and Mining Company was appealing the decision to award Bugbey compensation for the property they condemned for their water flume. Many of the water ditches constructed in California after the onset of the gold rush occurred before any land surveys were taken. In most instances, the water ditch was in place before the federal government recognized a settler's claim to the land through the Public Lands Survey System.

In April of 1872, AB 781 was introduced and summarized as an act for the relief and protection of agricultural interests in El Dorado County. The focus of the bill was to force water ditch companies, who had the power to condemn property, to keep and repair crossings over the ditch at their own expense. One of the provisions of the bill was that if an award for the condemnation of property was not paid in 12 months, the water ditch company would forfeit all rights to the property.[126]

Assemblyman French noted that the forfeiture provision was directly aimed at the Natoma Water and Mining Company's dispute with Bugbey and was meant to affect a case pending in court. French argued, "Mr. Bugbey bought out somebody else's place. A short time ago a dispute arose between Mr. Bugbey and the ditch company owing to some pipes or water, resulting in a case in court, which had now got into the Supreme Court."[127] The Assembly would pass an amended version stipulating that the provisions of the bill would not apply to any water ditch that was in operation 10 years prior to the passage of the act.[128] Bugbey's attempt to settle the Natoma Water and Mining Company litigation outside of the court had failed.

Assemblyman French was a landowner in Sacramento County, a friend to and fellow Mason of Bugbey. It must have stung Bugbey that a longtime friend would not support his cause against the much larger Natoma Water and Mining Company.

Death of Peter McGlashan

In the spring of 1872, Peter McGlashan, the father of Bugbey's second wife, Nettie, died on April 18th. Before he died, on April 17th, he recorded his Last Will and Testament. To his eldest daughter Elizabeth, who was living in Healdsburg, Sonoma County, he left all his property in Sonoma County.[129] To Martinette "Nettie" Bugbey, he bequeathed the land he had acquired in El Dorado County.[130] This property was most of the Duroc vineyard that Bugbey had bought in 1863 and delineated under the metes and bounds system of property description.[131]

After the government land surveys were completed, mapping California—excluding Mexican and Spanish land grants—into Townships and Ranges based on the Public Land Survey System, Bugbey sold 40 acres of the Duroc vineyard property near Shingle Springs to George Balis for $60.[132] George Balis was the son-in-law of Peter McGlashan and married to Peter's daughter Adelia.

On June 22, 1870, George Balis bought 160 acres from the Central Pacific Railroad company for $200.[133] This was also land that encompassed the Duroc vineyard. Four days later he sold the land he bought from the CPRR and Bugbey to Peter McGlashan, a total of 200 acres, for $60.[134] The next month, on July 26, Peter McGlashan gifted all 200 acres to his daughter Nettie.[135]

By 1870 Bugbey had already been involved in protracted litigation with the Natoma Water and Mining Company over his Natoma Vineyard property. Consolidating the Duroc vineyard property through Peter McGlashan and ultimately to his wife Nettie may have been his way of protecting that property under his control without his outright ownership of it. The bequeath of the property to Nettie was duplicative of his prior gift that was duly recorded.

Economic Changes

As 1872 progressed, Bugbey remained active in politics and chairman of the Sacramento County Republican Party.[136] He presided over a large meeting in front of the Orleans Hotel in Sacramento to ratify the nominations for the Philadelphia Convention to support President Grant.[137] Also active in the Republican Party at the county that year were old friends and past foes such as James McClatchy, George Cadwalader, A. P. Catlin, and A. Heilbron.

The spirits produced by the Natoma Vineyard weren't sold just for their taste; they were also sold to the Sacramento County Hospital. Alcohol had its medicinal value in the 1870s. Bugbey was selling his wines and brandy to the county hospital as stimulants. His monthly sales ranged from $87 up to $238 every month. A management audit stated that most of the wine and brandies used for stimulants came almost exclusively from the Natoma Vineyard. The supply of stimulants to the patients, the audit concluded, appeared to be exceedingly liberal.[138]

At that 1872 State Fair, the California Vine Growers and Wine and Brandy Manufacturers' Association awarded Bugbey a premium for his 1869 grape brandy and for his red burgundy vintage 1871.[139] But ten of his other entries garnered no premiums or awards.[140] He did exhibit Japanese chestnuts that he was growing at the Natoma Vineyard, for which he was awarded a special recommendation. He also displayed a model of George Johnston's brandy still at the fair.[141]

Through the first nine months of 1872, California wineries had shipped more than 749,000 gallons of wine through San Francisco, either by rail or steam ship. Many wineries were having record production years. Gerke Wines in Tehama was estimated to produce 125,000 gallons of wine and a similar amount for G. Groezinger of Yountville. Plus, many of these wineries had a like amount of previous vintages in storage.[142]

Bugbey's Natoma Vineyard was 125 acres, similar in size to G. Groezinger's, but Bugbey was only producing between 70,000 and 80,000 gallons of wine.[143] While wholesale wine prices were holding steady at about $0.50 per gallon, brandy was hovering between $1.25 and $1.50 per gallon before federal excise taxes. Bugbey had earlier estimated that each gallon of brandy he produced with the Johnston still would sell for $3 per gallon.[144]

Railroad freight rates were upwards of $2.70 per hundred pounds for shipping back to the East Coast. That was if the wine or brandy was shipped in a wooden container. The winery had to add on an additional dollar to the rates if the product was in bottles. A 750 milliliter bottle of wine could weigh as much as three pounds. This meant California wine producers would have to add as much as 10 cents per bottle of wine to ship it back east. While the shipping cost was much lower per gallon if shipped in large wooden barrels, it was still a premium that cut into the profitability.

The unfolding story in the California wine market in 1872 was that production was increasing, prices were flat, and expenses were increasing. The net revenue for some vintners was also decreasing if they sold their products into markets where they were paid in greenbacks and not gold, because federally backed paper money was discounted in California. All of this was squeezing Bugbey's cash flow

Benjamin Norton Bugbey

as he had leveraged the Natoma Vineyard to expand operations and invest in George Johnston's brandy distillery company.

---

[1] Sacramento Daily Union, Volume 37, Number 5749, August 31, 1869, CDNC

[2] 1870 United States Federal Census, California, Sacramento County, Granite Township, Bugb(e)y, Benj. N, Age 43, Occupation Wine Grower, Value of Real Estate $10,000, Value of Personal Property $20,000, Birth Conn, Martinette, Age 26, Occupation Keeping House. Other occupants at the residence include: Amasa W. Mars (m), Age 37, Occupation Carpenter, Frank Duckahl, Age 30, France, Occupation Wine Cooper, James Butler, Age 35, New York, Occupation Champagne Maker, Sing Ah (m), Age 32, China, Occupation Laborer, Chee Ah (m), Age 30, China, Occupation Laborer

[3] 1850 United States Federal Census, Wisconsin, Rock County, Town of Plymouth, Peter McGlashan

[4] 1866 California, Great Voter Registers, Sonoma County

[5] 1866 – 1898 California Voter Registers, Sacramento County & 1867, 1872 California Biological Great Book, Sacramento, Cosumnes, McGlashan, Peter, Age 63, Birth New York, Occupation Farmer.

[6] 1870 United States Federal Census, California, Sacramento County, Lee Township, Peter McGlashan, Age 65

[7] Sacramento Daily Union, Volume 37, Number 5700, July 3, 1869, CDNC

[8] Sacramento County Deed Book 18691127 pages 194 and 195 & Sacramento County Deed Book 18700129 pages 161 and 162

[9] Davis, Win. J., *An Illustrated History of Sacramento County, California*, (The Lewis Publishing Company, Chicago, 1890). page 230 "Coners' Fouring Mill was built in 1866, on the corner of Wool Street and the railroad; the mill was operated for about two years, when it was closed. The building, a three-story brick, was purchased by B. N. Bugby and used by him as a wine cellar, the third floor being rented as a hall to the societies in Folsom. The building was burned in 1871."

[10] Sacramento Daily Union, Volume 37, Number 5683, June 14, 1869, CDNC

[11] Sacramento Daily Union, Volume 37, Number 5703, July 8, 1869, CDNC

[12] Marysville Daily Appeal, Number 14, July 17, 1869, CDNC

[13] Sacramento Daily Union, Volume 38, Number 5789, October 16, 1869, CDNC

[14] Sacramento Daily Union, Volume 38, Number 5790, October 18, 1869, CDNC

[15] Sacramento Daily Union, Volume 38, Number 5886, February 7, 1870, CDNC

[16] California Farmer and Journal of Useful Sciences, Volume 33, Number 18, May 19, 1870, CDNC

[17] Ibid.

[18] California Farmer and Journal of Useful Sciences, Volume 33, Number 20, June 2, 1870, CDNC

[19] Ibid.

[20] California Farmer and Journal of Useful Sciences, Volume 33, Number 23, June 30, 1870, CDNC

[21] California Farmer and Journal of Useful Sciences, Volume 33, Number 20, June 2,

1870, CDNC

[22] Mansfeldt, Hugo, *Autobiography of Hugo Mansfeldt*, (Hugo Mansfeldt Papers, Archives Mansfeldt 1, Hargrove Music Library, U. C. Berkeley, March 1928).

[23] Ibid.

[24] Ibid.

[25] Ibid.

[26] Ibid.

[27] Ibid.

[28] Sacramento Daily Union, Volume 27, Number 4197, September 2, 1864, CDNC

[29] Marysville Daily Appeal, Number 127, December 9, 1870, CDNC

[30] Mansfeldt, Hugo, *Autobiography of Hugo Mansfeldt*, (Hugo Mansfeldt Papers, Archives Mansfeldt 1, Hargrove Music Library, U. C. Berkeley, March 1928).

[31] Ibid.

[32] Marysville Daily Appeal, Number 28, February 2, 1871, CDNC

[33] Mansfeldt, Hugo, *Autobiography of Hugo Mansfeldt*, (Hugo Mansfeldt Papers, Archives Mansfeldt 1, Hargrove Music Library, U. C. Berkeley, March 1928).

[34] Bosworth, H. H., *Gungl's Railroad Galop*, (Published by L. R. Hammer, Sacramento).

[35] Hardinge, J., *Railroad Kings Galop*, (Publisher M. D. Swisher, Philadelphia).

[36] *Sacramento City and County Directory for 1868*, by Robert E. Draper, (Sacramento, H. S. Crocker & Co., Steam Printers and Stationers, 1868).

[37] Sacramento Daily Union, Volume 39, Number 6072, September 16, 1870, CDNC

[38] Daily Alta California, Volume 22, Number 7419, July 14, 1870, CDNC

[39] Sacramento Daily Union, Volume 39, Number 6018, July 13, 1870, CDNC

[40] Mansfeldt, Hugo, *Autobiography of Hugo Mansfeldt*, (Hugo Mansfeldt Papers, Archives Mansfeldt 1, Hargrove Music Library, U. C. Berkeley, March 1928).

[41] Ibid.

[42] Sacramento Daily Union, Volume 40, Number 6073, September 19, 1870, CDNC

[43] Sacramento Daily Union, Volume 32, Number 4940, January 28, 1867, CDNC

[44] California Farmer and Journal of Useful Sciences, Volume 33, Number 18, May 19, 1870, CDNC

[45] Sacramento Daily Union, Volume 39, Number 6038, August 6, 1870, CDNC

[46] California Farmer and Journal of Useful Sciences, Volume 34, Number 6, August 18, 1870, CDNC

[47] California Farmer and Journal of Useful Sciences, Volume 32, Number 11, September 30, 1869, CDNC

[48] California Farmer and Journal of Useful Sciences, Volume 34, Number 6, August 18, 1870, CDNC

[49] California Farmer and Journal of Useful Sciences, Volume 34, Number 7, August 25, 1870, CDNC

[50] Ibid.

[51] El Dorado County Deed Book M, page 411

[52] Ibid.

[53] Sacramento Daily Union, Volume 40, Number 7039, December 5, 1870, CDNC

[54] Daily Alta California, Volume 22, Number 7579, December 21, 1870, CDNC

[55] Sacramento Daily Union, Volume 40, Number 7088, January 31, 1871, CDNC

[56] Sacramento Daily Union, Volume 40, Number 7112, February 28, 1871, CDNC

[57] Sacramento Daily Union, Volume 40, Number 7126, March 16, 1871, CDNC

[58] Sacramento Daily Union, Volume 41, Number 7133, March 24, 1871, CDNC

[59] Ibid.

[60] Marysville Daily Appeal, Number 57, March 8, 1871, CDNC

[61] Sacramento Daily Union, Volume 40, Number 7069, January 9, 1871, CDNC

[62] https://en.wikipedia.org/wiki/Howard_Association

[63] Sacramento Daily Union, Volume 14, Number 2109, December 29, 1857, CDNC

[64] Ibid.

[65] Ibid.

[66] Sacramento Daily Union, Volume 40, Number 7077, January 18, 1871, CDNC

[67] Sacramento Daily Union, Volume 40, Number 7078, January 19, 1871, CDNC

[68] Sacramento Daily Union, Volume 40, Number 7116, March 4, 1871, CDNC

[69] Pacific Rural Press, Volume 1, Number 15, April 15, 1871, CDNC

[70] Ibid.

[71] Ibid.

[72] Ibid.

[73] Pacific Rural Press, Volume 1, Number 17, April 29, 1871, CDNC

[74] Red Bluff Independent, Number 44, April 27, 1871, CDNC

[75] El County Deed Book M Page 410

[76] Pacific Rural Press, Volume 1, Number 17, April 29, 1871, CDNC

[77] Sacramento Daily Union, Volume 41, Number 7171, May 8, 1871, CDNC

[78] Ibid.

[79] Nathaniel Knight letter to Ambrose Knight, May 6, 1871, Folsom, CA. (Bancroft Library Call Number MSS 98/22 C).

[80] Nathaniel Knight letter to Ambrose Knight, July 2, 1871, Folsom, CA. (Bancroft Library Call Number MSS 98/22 C).

Benjamin Norton Bugbey

81 Sacramento Daily Union, Volume 41, Number 7201, June 12, 1871, CDNC

82 Daily Alta California, Volume 23, Number 7719, May 11, 1871, CDNC

83 Sacramento Daily Union, Volume 41, Number 7193, June 2, 1871, CDNC

84 Sacramento Daily Union, Volume 41, Number 7204, June 15, 1871, CDNC

85 Sacramento Daily Union, Volume 41, Number 7217, June 30, 1871, CDNC

86 Sacramento Daily Union, Volume 41, Number 7204, June 15, 1871, CDNC

87 Sacramento Daily Union, Volume 42, Number 7401, February 2, 1872, CDNC

88 Sacramento Daily Union, Volume 41, Number 7229, July 15, 1871, CDNC

89 Sacramento County Deed Book18620915 pages 93 and 94

90 Sacramento County Deed Book18710712 pages 525 and 526

91 California Farmer and Journal of Useful Sciences, Volume 34, Number 6, August 18, 1870, CDNC

92 Sacramento Daily Union, Volume 41, Number 7260, August 21, 1871, CDNC

93 Livingston, Robert, *Charles T. H. Palmer: Pioneer Entrepreneur of Folsom*, (Golden Notes, Vol. 37, Number 3, Fall, Sacramento County Historical Society, 1991).

94 Ibid.

95 Ibid.

96 Sacramento County Deed Book 18710807 pages 18, 19, and 20

97 . Sacramento County Deed Book 1874116, page 13

98 Sacramento County Deed Book 18710918 pages 211 and 212.

99 Sacramento County Deed Book 18570202, page 104

100 Sacramento County Deed Book 18720810, pages 496 and 497

101 Sacramento Daily Union, Volume 42, Number 7286, September 20, 1871, CDNC

102 Pacific Rural Press, Volume 2, Number 26, December 30, 1871, CDNC

103 Ibid.

104 Ibid.

105 *Transactions of the California State Agricultural Society During the Years 1870 and 1871*, (T. A. Springer, State Printer, Sacramento, 1872).

106 Ibid.

107 Ibid.

108 1871 Sacramento County Directory, Advertisement, Bugbey's Natoma Wines, Brandies and Champagnes.

109 *Transactions of the California State Agricultural Society During the Years 1870 and 1871*, (T. A. Springer, State Printer, Sacramento, 1872).

110 Ibid.

111 Ibid.

[112] *Transactions of the California State Agricultural Society During the Years 1870 and 1871*, (T. A. Springer, State Printer, Sacramento, 1872). "Fifth Department, Grape and Wine Culture." Statement of B. N. Bugbey, of Folsom; To the Committee on Gold Medals for eighteen hundred and seventy-one:

Gentlemen: Having been an exhibitor in the fifth department of the late State Fair, and believing myself justly entitled to the gold medal for the most meritorious exhibition in that department, I accept your invitation to place before you in writing the grounds upon which I base that belief. In this department were exhibited the following agricultural products:

First — The products of silk culture — cocoons, raw and reeled silks, eggs, etc.

Second — The various kinds of grains and their products, as wheat, barley, oats, corn, etc. Third — The products of the dairy, as butter, cheese, etc.

Fourth — All kinds of vegetables and roots.

Fifth — Flowers and all floral displays.

Sixth — The products of the vineyard — wine, brandies, etc.

I suppose that the first question to be decided is, as to which of these several divisions or classes is entitled to the greatest merit, or in other words, which is working the greatest benefit to the State by developing her peculiar resources and material advantages. What are the peculiar resources and natural material advantages of California, considered with reference particularly to the production of the articles above enumerated?

That California is a great grain raising State there is no longer any question. Her plains, her swamp lands, and even her foothills, high up among the mountains, have all been proven by experience to be among the best grain producing sections of the world, when properly and skill fully cultivated. But that same, experience has also demonstrated the fact that constant and exclusive cultivation of grain impoverishes the soil and must eventually work a great injury to the State. Again, nearly all the other States and Territories of the Union are well adapted to grain raising, and we cannot therefore look to them for a market for our surplus products of grains, nor are we any way sure of a continuous foreign market at remunerative prices.

As to vegetables and flowers, while we can excel in the production of these also, by their very nature we cannot to any extent become exporters, and by their production cannot expect therefore to make money as a State, or do more than to save it to the extent of the value of the home consumption.

The same may be said of the productions of the dairy. With this exception, however, that while we have a country well adapted to this industry, we are still, to our shame, importers of its products to a very great extent. This industry should be encouraged and fostered in every way possible, but not with any view to make our State to any extent an exporter of its products, for the same sources which now supply our wants, over and above our own production, will undoubtedly continue to supply themselves.

As to silk and wine, our State has undoubtedly not only peculiar, but as relates to any other State or Territory within the Union, almost exclusive advantages. We have a climate and soil well adapted to the prosecution of both of these valuable industries, and in their productions, as before intimated, we have not only no rivals within the Union, but the people of all the other States are consumers, and will be glad to become our best customers. Not only this, but we may reasonably entertain the belief that the markets of the world cannot be over supplied with either, of these products, hence we may anticipate great benefits from their successful cultivation here.

Again, the production of silk and wine does not exhaust, but rather fosters the fertility of

Benjamin Norton Bugbey

the soil, and the longer any particular piece of land is devoted to their production the better are the realized results. Then, too, the vine and the mulberry tree flourish and do best in the foothills, on land which is the least value for most other agricultural products, and which would be of very expensive cultivation for such products. Hence, the successful development of these new industries in our State will bring into use and make valuable millions of acres of a class of land that can in no other way be rendered of but little value. To the exhibitors of these particular classes in this department then the need of merit will doubtless be awarded, and while I would concede great merits to the pioneers and exhibitors in the silk industry, yet I think it will be admitted that sufficient has not been accomplished in silk culture to entitle the industry to rank before that of the cultivation of the vine and the manufacture of its products.

The benefits to the State from silk culture are mostly in anticipation, while those from vine culture and wine manufacture are in a fair state of realization. This advanced stage of the latter has been brought about by the foresight, enterprise, and perseverance of a few individuals.

The whole enterprise from the beginning was a doubtful experiment. First, it had to be proved that the grapes could be grown and the wine made. Second, a long established and deep seated taste for foreign wines had to be changed, and a taste for homemade wines cultivated and established before a market could be found for the home production. This taste for foreign wines was backed by a strong prejudice in their favor, and this prejudice had also to be removed. This has been a work of no small magnitude, and none but those personally and directly interested in it can realize the difficulties and discouragements the pioneers in the business have had to meet and overcome. That they have boldly met and overcome most of the obstacles to success, I have no doubt the committee will concede, entitles the industry they have established to the highest position of merit in the department. If this position be granted then I ask the committee briefly to review the part your humble servant has acted in the accomplishment of this work.

In eighteen hundred and sixty-one, I purchased a piece of land in Salmon Falls Township,- El Dorado County, upon which were then planted eight acres of vines. I gave to this place the name of "Natoma Vineyard," and since that time my best energies and all the capital I could command have been devoted to the industry. I have now one hundred and fifty-seven acres in vines, and for a number of years past I have made from grapes grown by myself, on my own land, on an average of from fifty thousand to sixty thousand gallons of wine per annum. Last year my product was sixty-six thousand gallons. During this entire time I have been constantly and carefully carrying on experiments, the object of which has been to determine: first, the varieties of grapes best adapted for making superior wines of the different kinds in California, and second, the best mode of treating those wines in this climate to secure the best results from any given variety.

For the double purpose of assisting my own judgment as to the success with which these experiments were being attended, and to establish a reputation and market for California wines in general, and my own in particular, I have taken a great deal of pains and spent a great deal of money in placing them on exhibition and competition with the wines of other producers at our own Mechanics' and State Fairs, and also exhibited them at the Universal Exhibition at Paris in eighteen hundred and sixty-seven.

As an evidence of the high approval with which my wines have uniformly met since eighteen hundred and sixty-three, I beg to refer the committee to the following certificate of the Secretary of that society: Rooms California State Board of Agriculture, Sacramento, December 31st, 1870.

I hereby certify that the following premiums have been awarded by the California State Agricultural Society to B. N. Bugbey, Esq., of Folsom, Sacramento County, State of California:

Benjamin Norton Bugbey

List of Premiums by Article and Date from 1863 to 1870

1863: Best red wine, two years old and over- First

1863: Second best red wine, one year old and over- Second

1865: Best one variety of grapes- First

1866: Best wine, one year old, from foreign grapes- First

1866: Best white wine, one year old- Special

1866: Best red wine, one year old- Special

1866: Best exhibit of wines from foreign grapes- First

1866: Best exhibit of wines from native grapes- First

1866: Best brandy, one year old- First

1866: Best twenty-four pounds of raisins- First

1867: Best claret wine from foreign grapes- First

1867: Best exhibit of wines from foreign grapes- First

1867: Best grape brandy, two years old- First

1867: Best wines from Calalyac, Johannisberg, Reisling, and Orleans grapes- Special

1867: Best one variety Tokay grapes- First

1867: Best twenty-four pounds of raisins- First

1867: Best exhibition in the Fifth Department- Gold Medal

1868: Best exhibition of foreign grapes- First

1868: Best one variety grapes for dessert or table use- First

1868: Best twenty-four pounds of raisins- First

1868: Superior wine, three years old, from Italian and Burgundy grapes- First

1868: Wines from Malaga and Muscat grapes- First

1868: Wines from Black Malaga grapes- First

1868: Best exhibit of wines from foreign grapes- First

1868: Best brandy, two years old- First

1868: Best exhibition in Fourth Department- Gold Medal

1870: Best still white wine, one year old- First

1870: Muscatelle wine- Special Diploma

1870: Black Prince wine- Special Diploma

1870: Best sparkling wine, two years old- First

1870: Best exhibit of wine from foreign grapes- First

1870: Best exhibition in the Fifth Department- Gold Medal

Robert Beck, Secretary

Benjamin Norton Bugbey

32 entries.

23 First Place Premiums for raisins, wine, brandy and exhibits

1 Second Place Premium for best red wine one year old

5 Special mentions for wines

3 Gold Medals for best exhibitions

This year [1871] I was awarded by the State Society:

For best sparkling wine" First premium.

For best exhibition of wine: First premium.

For best and greatest variety of wine grapes: First premium.

It is proper here to say, that by a very unfortunate mistake in the entry of my wines this year, the age of the different kinds was not marked on the bottles, and as a consequence they were excluded from competition with the wines of the same age and kinds exhibited by other parties.

Some members of your committee having served on the Wine Committee will be able to explain more fully the cause and effect of this mistake. Suffice it to say it was no fault of mine, and I would not have had it occurred for one thousand dollars. In all my exhibitions at the Mechanics' Institute my wines have been equally well and highly appreciated, having been awarded a number of premiums over all other competitors, and this year the gold medal in the class in which they were exhibited. They also received high commendation from the jury of the Universal Exhibition of Paris. In addition to having secured a large trade in our own State, I have agencies for the sale of my wines, champagnes, and brandies in Chicago, Buffalo, Albany (New York), New York City, Philadelphia, Washington (District Columbia), Hart ford (Connecticut), Worcester, Springfield, and Boston (Massachusetts), Manchester (New Hampshire), Little Pock (Arkansas), St. Louis (Missouri), Council Bluffs; and previous to the disastrous fire at Folsom the past season, which destroyed a large portion of my stock, I was sending forward to all of these agencies large quantities to supply a rapidly increasing demand. As will be seen by reference to my exhibition this year I also manufacture wine brandy, in order more fully to economize the product of my vineyard.

Brandy

I commenced the manufacture of brandy in eighteen hundred and sixty-three, and have since that time averaged about four thousand gallons per annum. My product for eighteen hundred and seventy- one was eight thousand gallons. In eighteen hundred and sixty-eight my attention was called to an improved still for the manufacture of brandy, patented by Johnston. Having satisfied myself that it was a good improvement, I built and set to work the first working still ever made under the patent. The venture proved a good to myself, and the introduction and general use of this still cannot fail to be of immense benefit to the vine interest and to the State. "Whatever that benefit may be, it gives me no small degree of satisfaction that through my patronage as a vine grower it was first introduced and proved of value. By the use of this still the operator can by one operation clear the brandy of the fusil oil and acetic ether and retain all the natural aroma. The same quantity of grapes or other fruits will make twenty per cent more spirits than by the old process, with twenty-five per cent less expense.

Champagne

I commenced the manufacture of champagne in eighteen hundred and sixty-eight. By my first year's experiments in this business my losses were not less than twelve thousand

Benjamin Norton Bugbey

dollars. My next year's operations were more successful, and though the experience was dearly bought I am now able to produce a good article of champagne with the same certainty that I can produce from a good article of a good variety of grapes a good article of still wine. My average product of champagne since- eighteen hundred and sixty-eight has been about four thousand eight hundred cases or dozens per annum. This class of wine being so much more expensive than still wines, it will be seen that their manufacture and sale at home or shipment abroad brings a proportional greater benefit to the State and its industries than the manufacture of still wines.

In this class of wines I have no competition among the exhibitors and claimants of the gold medal, and this fact alone, I submit, should be sufficient to decide the question of merit and the medal.

Raisins

I also exhibited samples of raisins produced by me. Very soon after engaging in the cultivation of a vineyard I determined to learn by personal experience whether a good article of raisins could not be made in California. My experiments were crowned with perfect success. I succeeded in proving that California is capable of not only supplying the one hundred and eighty thousand dollars worth of raisins annually imported, but if her people were disposed to engage in the business with energy and spirit, they could soon supply the entire demand for the whole United States. The annual importation of the United States is valued at about one million two hundred thousand dollars. The success of my efforts proves conclusively that we have a soil and climate in the western slope of the Sierra Nevada Mountains most eminently adapted to the successful and profitable prosecution of this industry. All we want to secure this entire trade and this large amount of money annually is a proper degree of enterprise, perseverance, and cheap and reliable labor. If there is any merit in having been the pioneer in an industry promising such vast resulting advantages to our State, then I am entitled to that merit, and I have no doubt the committee will award it to me. I have made and marketed some ten thousand boxes of raisins in this State, receiving for them the highest market price. The only reason why I have not made this a principal branch of my business is, that my wine, champagne, and brandy manufactures, and the cultivation and extension of my vineyard, have taken all my time. Were I relieved from the care of these departments, I should engage immediately in the cultivation and manufacture of raisins.

The following is a list of the articles exhibited by me at the State Fair of eighteen hundred and seventy-one:

One dozen bottles of Muscatel wine, vintage of 1869;

One dozen bottles of White Frontingnac wine, vintage of 1869;

One dozen bottles of Gray Eeisling wine, vintage of 1869;

One dozen bottles of Black Prince wine, vintage of 1869;

One dozen bottles of Alaconte wine, vintage of 1869;

One dozen bottles of Traurina wine, vintage of 1869;

One dozen bottles of White Eeisling wine, vintage of 1869;

One dozen bottles of Johannisberg wine, vintage of 1869;

One dozen bottles of White Malaga wine, vintage of 1869;

One dozen bottles of Verdelho wine, vintage of 1869;

One dozen bottles of White Nice wine, vintage of 1869;

Benjamin Norton Bugbey

One dozen bottles of Pedro Exomenus wine, vintage of 1869;

One dozen bottles of Orleans wine, vintage of 1869;

One dozen bottles of White St. Peter's wine*, vintage of 1869;

One dozen bottles of Royal Muscatine wine, vintage of 1869;

One dozen bottles of Chambertin wine, vintage of 1869;

One dozen bottles of Zinfindel wine, vintage of 1869;

One dozen bottles of Port wine, vintage of 1869;

One dozen bottles of Sparkling Muscatel wine, vintage of 1869;

One dozen bottles of Champagne wine, vintage of 1869;

One dozen bottles of brandy, vintage of 1868;

One dozen bottles of brandy, vintage of 1869;

One dozen bottles of Alacante wine, vintage of 1868;

One dozen bottles of Reisling wine, vintage of 1868;

One dozen bottles of Camberton wine, vintage of 1868

One dozen bottles of Muscatel brandy, vintage of 1868

One dozen bottles of Muscatel brandy, vintage of 1869

One dozen bottles of Catalyn wine, vintage of 1867;

One dozen bottles of Alacante wine, vintage of 1868.

Grapes

Pedro Zomenes, Malaga Muscatella, Pineaux, Black Hamburg, Isa bella, Chasselas de Fouslambleu, Blue Malvasia, Flaming Tokay, Ca tawba, Fih Zagos, Orleans, Johannesberg Eeisling, Grizzly Frontigon, Black Zinfindel, Eed Traurina, Pride of Paris, Cerian, White Palestine, White Muscat of Alexandria, Queen of Nice, Alicante.

Raisins

Twenty-five pounds of raisins.

All of which I respectfully submit, trusting your committee will award the medal to the most meritorious, exhibition, whether that falls to me or not.

Yours, etc., B. N. BUGBEY.

[113] *Transactions of the California State Agricultural Society During the Years 1870 and 1871*, (T. A. Springer, State Printer, Sacramento, 1872).

[114] Sacramento Daily Union, Volume 43, Number 7446, March 26, 1872, CDNC

[115] Sacramento Daily Union, Volume 42, Number 7401, February 2, 1872, CDNC

[116] Ibid.

[117] Sacramento Daily Union, Volume 42, Number 7400, February 1, 1872, CDNC

[118] Sacramento Daily Union, Volume 42, Number 7401, February 2, 1872, CDNC

[119] Pacific Rural Press, Volume 3, Number 5, February 3, 1872, CDNC

[120] Sacramento Daily Union, Volume 42, Number 7418, February 22, 1872, CDNC

[121] Ibid.

[122] Ibid.

[123] Sacramento Daily Union, Volume 42, Number 7427, March 4, 1872, CDNC

[124] Ibid.

[125] Ibid.

[126] Sacramento Daily Union, Volume 43, Number 7451, April 1, 1872, CDNC

[127] Ibid.

[128] Ibid.

[129] California, Wills and Probate Records, 1850 – 1953, Peter McGlashan, Sacramento, Wills, Vol A – C, 1857 – 1883.

[130] Ibid.

[131] El Dorado County Deed Book H, Page 166

[132] El Dorado County Deed Book M, pages 422 – 425

[133] Ibid.

[134] Ibid.

[135] El Dorado County Deed Book Q, pager 144 – 146

[136] Sacramento Daily Union, Volume 43, Number 6654, July 31, 1872, CDNC

[137] Sacramento Daily Union, Volume 43, Number 6656, August 2, 1872, CDNC

[138] Sacramento Daily Union, Volume 44, Number 6866, April 5, 1873, CDNC

[139] Sacramento Daily Union, Volume 44, Number 6802, January 21, 1873, CDNC

[140] Sacramento Daily Union, Volume 44, Number 6699, September 21, 1872, CDNC

[141] Ibid.

[142] California Farmer and Journal of Useful Sciences, Volume 38, Number 21, December 19, 1872, CDNC

[143] Pacific Rural Press, Volume 2, Number 26, December 30, 1871, CDNC

[144] Marysville Daily Appeal, Number 57, March 8, 1871, CDNC

Chapter 9: Public Land Survey System & The Natoma Canal

By the 1850s California had begun to be surveyed, mapped, and sliced up into neatly packaged units by the U.S. government, so the new immigrants could lay claim to the land they had been squatting on. There was no regard for any pre-historic claims of indigenous Native Americans on the lands. The initial grid system for mapping government-owned land in the west was originally put forth by Thomas Jefferson in 1784. The Land Ordinance of 1785 specified how the grid system was to operate and established the Public Land Survey System.

Public Land Survey System

Under the Public Land Survey System, territory was mapped out in a grid system of townships. A township was a square area, with the sides being six miles in length. The township square was further subdivided into 36 square sections, each with sides one mile in length. One township encompassed 36 square miles of land. The final map indicated each section in sequential order for identification.

The point of reference for the townships was a base meridian, usually one of the tallest mountains in the region. In Northern California, Mount Diablo is a base meridian for townships in the Sacramento region. townships could either be north of Mount Diablo or south of it. The second township north of Mount Diablo would start at the beginning of the seventh mile, the first six miles being the first township.

To indicate the east or west location of the township from the base meridian, the Public Land Survey System assigned a range. The second east range, similar to the second township, would begin at the seventh mile east of the Mount Diablo base meridian marker. Maps were then created that referenced the township and range. For example, Township 10 North, Range 8 East, Mount Diablo Base Meridian, would specify a particular map whose location could be described as the area 60 miles north of Mt. Diablo and 48 miles to the east.

When it came to specifying property ownership, the description was done in fractions of one of the 36 sections in the township. Each section, one mile by one mile square, contained 640 acres. A quarter section was 160 acres. For example, Mr. Smith may have been granted a land patent on the northwest quarter of Section 4 of Township 7 North, Range 5 East, Mount Diablo Base Meridian. This would be 160 acres under Mr. Smith's ownership and would be easily identifiable on the map.

The Government Land Office, the entity in charge of issuing land patents during the 19th century, would denote ownership of land by specifying the fractions and relative orientation of land by directional indicators. The patents could be broken up into small areas and were similarly indicated with the directional nomenclature. Mr. Smith may have sold the south half of the northeast quarter of his northwest quarter of section 4. That would be listed as S1/2, NE ¼, NW ¼, Section 4, Township 7 North, Range 5 East and it would equate to 20 acres of land.

Land Patent & Preemption

A land patent is essentially a grant by either the federal or state government conferring clear legal title to the property to the person or business who applied for it. If the settler had been living on the land before the official Government Land Office plats or maps were created under the Public Land Survey System, he or she could file a preemption claim under the Preemption Act of 1841. Preemption was the process of asserting a right-of-first-refusal to buy the land before it was offered to anyone else. A couple of conditions of preemption were that the settler must be living on the land and making improvements to the property, such as building a home, mining the land, or farming the property. If the claimant met all the conditions for preemption, he or she could buy up to 160 acres at $1.25 per acre and receive a land patent.

Section 16 State Property

When a California pioneer such as Bugbey decided he liked a plot of land and started to improve it with farm fields, barn or house, he had no way of knowing where the land might fall within the future township survey. Within a township, sections 16 and 36 were set aside for the respective state as either a location to build schools or to sell the land in order to raise money to build a public school. Bugbey's Natoma Vineyard that he purchased in 1863, before the maps were drawn, was in Section 16 of Township 10 North, Range 8 East, Mount Diablo Base Meridian.

In 1853 Congress passed additional legislation authorizing the President to establish Government Land Offices in California and to begin the surveying process. Section 6 of the act specified how settlers were to claim a preemption for the purposes of claiming title to the land.

Sec. 6. And be it further enacted, That all public lands in the State of California, whether surveyed or unsurveyed, with the exception of sections sixteen and thirty-six, which shall be and hereby are granted to the State for the purposes of public schools in each township, and with the exception lands appropriated under the authority of this act, or reserved by competent authority, and excepting also the lands claimed under any foreign grant or title and mineral lands, shall be subject to the preemption laws of fourth September, eighteen hundred and forty-one, with all the exceptions, conditions, and limitations therein, except as in herein otherwise provided, and shall, after the plats thereof are returned to the office of the register, be offered for sale, after six months' public notice in the State of the time and place of sale, under the laws, rules and regulations now governing such sales, or such as may be hereafter prescribed; Provided, that where unsurvey lands are claimed by preemption, the usual notice of such claim shall be filed within three months after the return of the plats of surveys to the land offices, and proof and payment shall be made prior to the day appointed...[1]

The salient point in this section is that a settler, who had improved the land with a dwelling or with agricultural practices, had three months after the survey plats, or maps, were returned to the Government Land Office to claim their preemption. In other words, if the settler wanted to prevent the land from being claimed by another individual, he or she had to provide proof they were occupying or using the land in order to preempt another claim to the property.

Section 7 of the act added further clarification for settlements in sections 16 and 36 reserved for California public schools.

Sec. 7. And be it further enacted, That where any settlement, by the erection of a dwelling-house or cultivation of any portion of the land, shall be made upon the sixteenth and thirty-six sections, before the same shall be surveyed, or where such section may be reserved for public uses or taken by private claims, other land shall be selected by the proper authorities of the State in lieu thereof,...[2]

Natoma Vineyard Section 16

Virtually all of Bugbey's Natoma Vineyard and winery operations were in section 16. That meant that if he didn't file a preemption within three months after the land plats were entered at the Government Land Office in Sacramento, the land would become the sole property of the State of California.

The survey of the Township 10 North, Range 8 East, located in El Dorado County, was completed on May 19th, 1866, and deposited with the United States Land Office in Sacramento on June 16th, 1866. Many of the land surveys to the west of El Dorado County were completed in the mid-1850s. These earlier land plats or maps show very little development other than some roads, fence lines and the occasional town. The Civil War slowed the progress of completing the land surveys.

By the time the survey crew came along in 1866 to create the township maps in El Dorado County, there were considerable improvements throughout the area. The final 1866 map of Township 10 North, Range 8 East prominently notes the B. N. Bugbey Wine Distillery, B. N. Bugbey Old House, and the B. N. Bugbey New House

Figure 18: 1866 - Government Land Office map, Section 16, T10N, R8E, noting B. N. Bugbey's Wine Distillation, Old House, and New House, along with the Natoma Ditch.

on the map. It also depicts the Natoma Water and Mining Company's ditch, winding around the Bugbey wine distillery as it mirrored the South Fork of the American River in a southwest direction.

Before the final surveys were adopted, Bugbey was inquiring about buying land adjacent to his Natoma Vineyard that had been granted to the Central Pacific Railroad (CPRR). This just happened to be the location of his prominent house on a hill overlooking the Natoma Vineyard, immortalized on the cover of the sheet music for the *Bugbey's Champagne Waltz*. In response to a letter from Bugbey, the Land Agent for the CPRR outlined how the railroad would dispose of their granted land. The railroad had been granted all odd number sections of land within twenty miles on each side of the railroad line as another form of inducement or reimbursement for constructing the Transcontinental Railroad. The CPRR was going to sell its land for $2.50 per acre. The land agent for the CPRR responding to Bugbey's letter in 1865 was B. B. Redding, a former deputy of Bugbey when he was the Sheriff of Sacramento County.[3]

Water Ditch Provision

Many of California's water ditches were constructed and put into operation in the 1850s. There was little regard for who owned the land or who might own it in the future. The water ditches were seen as an indispensable improvement for the continued mining of gold. Unlike settlers who had improved the land they were working and could claim a preemption, constructed water canals, flumes and ditches could not. That was, until Congress passed another act recognizing water ditches, which it did on July 26, 1866.

Section 9. And be it further enacted, That whenever, by priority of possession, rights to the use of water for mining, agriculture, manufacturing, or other purposes, have vested and accrued, and the same are recognized and acknowledged by the local customs, laws, and the decisions of courts, the possessors and owners of such vested rights shall be maintained and protected in the same; and the right of way for the construction of ditches and canals for the purposes of the aforesaid is hereby acknowledged and confirmed: Provided, however, that whenever, after the passage of this act, any person or persons shall, in the construction of any ditch or canal, injure or damage the possession of any settler on the public domain, the party committing the injury or damage shall be liable to the party injured for such injury or damage.[4]

Bugbey Preemption & Acquisitions

The Natoma Water and Mining Company sued Bugbey, claiming under the July 26th Congressional Act acknowledging the rights of water ditches over the public lands that they should be able to lay claim to the property. Bugbey, for his part, did not file a preemption for his property in section 16, which was designated for the State of California. If he had done so, the State of California would have sought to acquire the same acreage of land in another section where no preemption had been filed.

It's not clear why Bugbey did not file a preemption. He was clearly entitled to it, since he had obviously improved the property with vineyards, wine cellars, and a home. Perhaps Bugbey thought that, by putting in a preemption claim, he would be declaring his primary residence to be El Dorado County. He was too invested in Sacramento County business and politics to lose his Folsom residency.

Stroup Agreement

Benjamin Norton Bugbey

Another reason why Bugbey may not have filed a preemption was that he agreed to purchase the land from the State of California. Bugbey had made an agreement with his neighbor, L. T. Stroup, who was also in section 16. Mr. Stroup shared the southwest quarter of section 16 with Bugbey. A picket fence divided their claims. When the Government Land Office survey plat of their township was released, Bugbey and Stroup entered into an agreement. On July 24th, 1866, they agreed to the following contract written up by Bugbey.

Whereas, the said B. N. Bugbey seeks to obtain a title from the State of California to that tract of land described as follows, to wit: The south-west quarter of Section 16, Township 10, Range eight east, Mount Diablo meridian; now then, the said B. N. Bugbey undertakes and agrees, as soon as he shall acquire a title to said land from the State, to make and execute to said Stroup a good and sufficient deed to all of that portion of said quarter section lying on the north side of a certain picket-fence, now used and known as a line fence between the said Bugbey and Stroup, on the northerly side of an exact range of said fence from the west line or west boundary of said quarter-section, to the east line or boundary of said quarter-section, at the same price per acre and on the same terms that said Bugbey shall have paid to the State of California for said lands; and the said L. T. Stroup covenants and agrees that he will, in like manner, convey to said Bugbey all of that portion of the north-west quarter of said Section 16, being south or on the southerly side of said fence and range above described, on the same terms as provided above, touching the conveyance of the said Bugbey; and it is hereby further agreed, that the refusal of one to comply with this agreement that does [not] release the other; but each may be proceeded against and compelled by law to make good this contract.[5]

California State Purchase

As agreed, Bugbey bought the land from the State of California in 1867. He received a land patent from the State of California for 280 acres for the southeast quarter, the east half of the southwest quarter, and the northwest quarter of the southwest quarter, all in Section 16 of Township 10 North, Range 8 East, Mount Diablo Base Meridian.[6] In 1869 he purchased another 40 acres from the state, described as the southwest quarter of the southwest quarter of section 16 in the same township.[7]

CPRR Land Purchases

Benjamin Norton Bugbey

In 1870 Bugbey would purchase 160 acres from the Central Pacific Railroad that had been granted to them as part of the construction of the Transcontinental Railroad. Bugbey acquired 120 acres in section 21 of Township 10 North, Range 8 East. This parcel was adjacent to section 16 and above the Natoma Vineyard. Part of this land is where Bugbey's house on the hill was built. The other 40 acres was in Township 9 North, Range 9 East, section 11, which was where his Duroc vineyard was located.[8]

Bugbey would turn around and sell the 40 acres at Duroc vineyard to George Balis,[9] who, in turn sold it to Peter McGlashan.[10] Peter, father of Bugbey's second wife, Nettie, then gifted that parcel to Nettie in the same year.[11]

Henry Mette Land Swap

Bugbey's next-door neighbor was Henry Mette, who had a vineyard. The Natoma Ditch ran through each of their properties in Section 16 above the South Fork of the American River. The water ditch created an obstacle for each farmer to get to the other side of the ditch to work his property. In 1868 Bugbey and Mette swapped triangular portions of land on either side of the Natoma Ditch.[12][13] The parcels Bugbey acquired from Mette would always be excepted from any land descriptions when he was acquiring a mortgage on his Natoma Vineyard property.

Brown's Ravine Flume

Brown's Ravine and its accompanying seasonal creek ran through Bugbey's property in Section 16. The Natoma Ditch also went through Section 16 and had to travel across the ravine. In order to maintain the proper slope for the water to move west in the Natoma Ditch, the water canal had to travel up Brown's Ravine and then back down it. A flume across Brown's Ravine would considerably shorten the ditch and elevate the canal above the creek, which, during high rainfall events, could wash out the canal.

The Natoma Water and Mining Company did build a flume across Brown's Ravine. The timbers to support the flume destroyed part of Bugbey's vineyard and also prevented him from easy access to the land on the opposite side of the elevated flume structure. The Natoma Water and Mining Company claimed they were on the land first and did not have to compensate Bugbey for his loss of property. Bugbey contended he was the legal owner of the land, documented by his purchase of the land from the State of California.

By 1870 the Natoma Water and Mining Company was more than just a water ditch company. It was supplying water to the town of Folsom, it had acquired large portions of the Leidesdorff Land Grant (Rancho Rio de Los Americanos) for other business ventures, and it had fought and won many lawsuits brought against it. The company had become a large and diversified corporation and had the resources to fight for what was in its best interest.

NWM Co. v Bugbey

Of all the court cases that Bugbey was involved in, none probably touched his soul more than the fight over his beloved Natoma Vineyard. It was probably also this long, drawn-out court fight that influenced a shift in his worldview. In his later years, Bugbey would denounce the undue influence and monopolization of the land that he believed rightfully belonged to the settler.

Genesis of Natoma Ditch

The South Fork of the American River, with a few exceptions, flows along steep banks and hills. If the gold-bearing stretch of the river is not hemmed in by tall mountains, it has cut into the landscape created by ancient debris flows brought down from the mountains above, creating riverbanks 20 to 40 feet high. The focus of the early '49ers was to mine the placer gold resting on the bedrock over which the river flowed. By 1851 there were already significant stretches of the river that had been completely mined of the relatively easily obtainable placer gold dust and flakes.

The miners then turned their attention to the riverbanks. The problem was getting water to the dry diggings to wash it and separate the gold from the dirt and rocks. Since mechanized pumps with steam engines for power weren't really feasible because of logistics and cost, gravity-fed water was the next option. But that meant there had to be a water source above the claim the miner was digging through. Hence, the idea of running a water ditch above the river to supply water to the miners down the hill was born.

By 1851 the planning had begun to put a dam on the South Fork of the American River two miles above the mining town of Salmon Falls at Rocky Bar. The vision was to dig a ditch following the contours of the hillside and deliver water to mining and agricultural regions of McDowell Hill, Red Banks, Mormon Island, Willow Springs, Rhodes Diggings, Prairie Diggings, Alder Creek, Negro Bar, Texas Hill, Mississippi Bar, and Pennsylvania Flat. This endeavor was incorporated on July 1853 as the Natoma Water and Mining Company.

The men behind the new water canal were A. P. Catlin, D. A. Hamilton, G. W. Colby, Lucien B. Brooks, Thomas B. Williams, E. N. Strout, and James H. Henry.[14]

The first dam on the river was later improved in 1868. The second iteration measured 298 feet long, 16 feet high, with a 25-foot base. The construction material was stone and mortar with coping planks 3" x 12" x 14' spiked to three parallel timbers 10" x 12" with 8" boat spikes. The timbers were bolted to the bedrock of the river and rockwork with 1" bolts. The square face stones of the dam had 11/4" x 14' long iron rods extending through the centers and wedged into the bedrock. The face of the dam had a 22 ½ ° slope.[15]

The main ditch was a trapezoid with an 8-foot base, 5-foot sides and usually had a water depth of 4 feet. The south side of the canal, along the river canyon, used the natural earth and stone. In many places where the slope of the hill was too steep, a rock retaining wall was built out of local stones to support the canal's side wall. When finished, the Natoma main ditch was 95,600 feet in length and had a capacity of 60 cubic feet per second.[16]

The Natoma ditch, like most earthen water canals of the time, could not always be dug into a hillside. The ditch had to pass over ravines and creeks. In these places a wooden flume, equivalent in capacity to the earthen canal, was constructed to carry the water over the area. As the Natoma ditch had to be rebuilt after the numerous flooding events from the river and creeks, additional flumes were added to secure the canal and shorten its travel distance around ravines and creeks.[17]

One of the areas that was a problem for the water ditch was at Brown's Ravine, where the ditch was prone to wash out during high water flows down the creek. The water ditch also had to make a long detour up the ravine and then back down in order to maintain its gentle slope to keep the water flowing at a predictable rate. In 1870 the Natoma Water and Mining Company decided to build a wooden flume across Brown's Ravine to reduce washouts from high creek flow and shorten its length.

The wooden flume needed to be large enough to carry the same flow of water as the earthen canal. Because the flume was elevated, until it reconnected with the ditch on the other side of the ravine, the supporting lumber would mean the overall land required to construct the flume was larger in area than just a water ditch.

The new flume would traverse over Brown's Ravine and across the land being farmed by Bugbey. To accommodate the construction of the flume, Bugbey would lose land currently being farmed and future expansion, as the tall wooden flume made it difficult to reach the area on the other side. The flume was essentially a tall fence separating two pieces of land that Bugbey was farming.

Benjamin Norton Bugbey

Bugbey Protests Condemnation

Bugbey protested the taking of his property. The Natoma Water and Mining Company brought suit in El Dorado County District Court to condemn a portion of Bugbey's vineyard in order that the flume could run across it. To ascertain the value of the land to be condemned, three commissioners were appointed to appraise the damages Bugbey would sustain from the loss of the property. In March 1871 the commission concluded that Bugbey should be awarded $19,000.[18]

The damages award was based on Bugbey's own estimates and that of surrounding vineyard owners. At the time, Bugbey estimated he had 86,000 to 90,000 vines bearing fruit on his property, yielding 500 to 800 tons of grapes. At $50 per ton wholesale price, the grape production was worth on the magnitude of $25,000 to $40,000 per year. The commissioners visited Bugbey's vineyard, heard all the testimony, and even though there was some disagreement on the value, determined Bugbey's vineyard property was worth $2,000 per acre.[19]

Bugbey Wins First Round

In May of 1871, an El Dorado County judge confirmed the award of damages to Bugbey from the Natoma Water and Mining Company's condemnation of Bugbey's property to build their flume. And thus began years more of litigation between vineyard owner and the water company. The Natoma Water and Mining Company then questioned if Bugbey was even the legitimate owner of the land to begin with.

In 1872 Bugbey used his influence to get a state bill introduced that would force ditch companies to pay assessed damages to landowners for the construction of flumes within 12 months. Assembly Bill 269 was an amendment to an act to authorize the incorporation of canal companies and to provide for the construction of canals and ditches, approved April 2nd, 1870. The amendment was to make the canal law mirror similar law pertaining to the railroads, in that if land was condemned for new canals or flumes, the water canal company had to have sufficient resources to meet the damages assessed without undue litigation between the parties. As was the case between Bugbey and the Natoma Water and Mining Company.[20]

Assembly member C. G. W. French opposed any amendments that would force water ditch companies from paying damages in a timely fashion. His arguments were that most of the water ditches had been there long before the property owners. French even noted that the amendment to the water canal company law was brought forth as a result of pending litigation between Bugbey and the Natoma Water and

Mining Company. French suggested amending the legislation so that any water canal ditch in existence within 10 years previous to the law would be exempt. That amendment was not passed.[21]

The strong support for the rights of the water canal companies by French did not go unnoticed. He would be one of the attorneys to represent the Natoma Water and Mining Company in its fight with Bugbey in 1873. French was an old friend of Bugbey's, a local Folsom attorney that Bugbey had used, and they both belonged to the same political party. It must have been a disappointment to Bugbey that a pioneer like French would side with corporate interests over those of an original pioneer and settler.

Bugbey Sues NWM Co.

After the Natoma Water and Mining Company refused to pay the damages to his property already legally awarded to him, Bugbey sued the Natoma Water and Mining Company again in February of 1873 in El Dorado County 11th District Court. On the 24th of February, Bugbey and his attorneys, George Williams and G. J. Carpenter, entered Judge Adams' court to face off against the Natoma Water and Mining Company lawyers C. G. W. French and George Blanchard. Both parties waived their rights to a jury trial instead casting their fates to the jurisprudence of Judge Adams.[22]

Bugbey Wins Second Round

Both sides presented witnesses and other documents in court. After two days of testimony, the case was submitted to Judge Adams. On April 8th, Judge Adams rendered his verdict for Bugbey. The Judge awarded Bugbey the entire length and width of the Natoma Ditch that crossed his property through Section 16. Bugbey also sought to claim the property that the ditch traversed over in Section 21, which he had bought from the Central Pacific Railroad, but the Judge denied that claim.[23]

Judge Adams based his decision on several facts relating to the ownership of the land. First was that Section 16 passed to the State of California in May of 1866 when the Surveyor-General filed the survey plat with the Government Land Office.[24] Next, contrary to the arguments of the Natoma Company, the federal government had no power to impair the title to the State of California.[25] The congressional act of July 26, 1866, *An Act granting the Right of Way to Ditch and Canal Owners over the Public Lands, and for other Purposes*, was passed two months after the state had taken title to the land. Judge Adams concluded, "That at the date of passage of the act of Congress of July 26th, 1866, the General Government had no title to the lands sued for in said section 16,..."[26]

Finally, Bugbey had secured a patent from the State of California for the property in dispute on April 22, 1867. The Natoma Company never attempted to purchase the land from the state.[27] Judge Adams awarded the property to Bugbey, plus $59 in monthly rents and profits from the ditch retroactively from April 16th, 1868.[28]

Unfortunately, this was the beginning of a long legal battle. The Natoma Company would continue to appeal the decision all the way to the U.S. Supreme Court. While Bugbey was certainly grateful to his attorney for prevailing in the action against the water company, by the spring of 1873, money was getting tight for Bugbey. On the day they won the lawsuit, he assigned the property awarded him, along with past and future rents, to his attorney G. J. Carpenter—likely as payment for legal bills due.[29]

Bugbey was not the first landowner to fight against a water company over eminent domain proceedings and fair compensation for his property, and he wouldn't be the last. He believed in settler's rights and that local individual land ownership was the foundation of prosperity in the United States.

---

[1] *An Act to extend Preemption Rights to certain Lands therein mention.*, Chap. CXLIII, March 3, 1853, (Thirty-Second Congress. Session II., Chapters 143, 144, 145).

[2] Ibid.

[3] 1865 Sacramento Daily Union, Volume 29, Number 4378, April 3, 1865, CDNC

[4] *An Act granting the Right of Way to Ditch and Canal Owners over the Public Lands, and for other Purposes.* Chapter CCLXII, July 26, 1866 (Thirty-Ninth Congress. Session I, Chapter 262, 263).

[5] Baggett, W. T., editor, *Pacific Coast Law Journal, Containing All The Decisions of the Supreme Court of California, And the Important Decisions of the U.S. Circuit and U.S. District Courts for the District of California, and of the U.S. Supreme Court and Higher Courts of other States.* (Volume XI, February 24, 1883 to August 1883, San Francisco: Pacific Coast Law Printing and Publishing Co. Publishers, 1883).

[6] El Dorado County Deed Book L, Page 556

[7] El Dorado County Deed Book N, Page 36

[8] El Dorado County Deed Book M, page 411

[9] El Dorado County Deed Book M, page 422

[10] El Dorado County Deed Book M, page 423

[11] El Dorado County Deed Book Q, page 144

[12] El Dorado County Deed Book M, page 40

[13] El Dorado County Deed Book M, page 615

[14] Natoma Water and Mining Company Articles of Incorporation. (State of California, Department of State, California State Archives, March 28, 1922).

[15] 1880 Report on History and Facilities of the Natoma Water and Mining Company, (California State Archives, Public Utilities Application No. 6975, January 2, 1923, F3725:7098-7101a)

[16] Ibid.

[17] Ibid.

[18] Sacramento Daily Union, Volume 40, Number 7116, March 4, 1871, CDNC

[19] Pacific Rural Press, Volume 1, Number 15, April 15, 1871, CDNC

[20] Sacramento Daily Union, Volume 42, Number 7427, March 4, 1872, CDNC

[21] Sacramento Daily Union, Volume 43, Number 7451, April 1, 1872, CDNC

[22] B. N. Bugbey v Natoma Water and Mining Company, In the District Court 11th Judicial District of California, (El Dorado County District Court Judgment Book E, 1873, pages 223 and 224, El Dorado County Historical Society Museum)

[23] Ibid.

[24] Sacramento Daily Union, Volume 45, Number 6891, May 5, 1873, CDNC

[25] Ibid.

[26] Ibid.

[27] Ibid.

[28] Ibid.

[29] El Dorado County Deed Book T, page 545

Chapter 10: Natoma Vineyard 1873 – 1876

The year 1873 was a quiet one for Bugbey in terms of being a public figure to promote the viniculture industry, and by extension, wines, brandies, and sparkling wine in California. Even though he had won a judgment against the Natoma Water and Mining Company, the national economy and the marketplace was changing. Bugbey was beginning to feel the pinch of a marketplace flooded with wine from new vineyards, depressing prices and sales.

Natoma Vineyard Mortgage

Shortly after receiving his land patent for the Natoma Vineyard property from the State of California, Bugbey mortgaged it. In August of 1868, he borrowed $15,000 from Sacramento Savings Bank.[1] In June of 1870, he paid off Sacramento Savings Bank and mortgaged the property again, for $15,000 to the Pacific Mutual Life Insurance Company.[2] By 1872 Bugbey's cash flow must have been diminishing, because he deeded the rights to the produce from the Natoma Vineyard to E. A. James and Thomas Goosey for $2,500.[3] James and Goosey were former employees of Bugbey's at the Natoma Vineyard.[4]

The $2,500 for the production rights gave Bugbey important cash to continue paying other creditors and living expenses. It also appears that he still retained all the inventory that was produced prior to the transfer to James and Goosey. This allowed him a modest income stream from sales from the existing inventory.

Folsom Property Sales and Transfers

After Bugbey bought the C. T. H. Palmer house in 1871, his finances took a turn for the worse. In order to raise cash, he sold one of his pieces of property in Folsom. What made this property special was that it had the entrance to a drift mine on it. Block 9 of the Town of Folsom was situated above Negro Bar on the American River. Bugbey had worked a drift mine under what would become Block 40 back in the early 1850s. Miners would dig a horizontal shaft into the side of hill overlooking Negro Bar and tunnel into the hillside in a southeast direction. They would cart out the rocks and earth, then wash the dirt to capture any placer gold.

Bugbey first bought lot 10 in Block 9 from D. R. Bigelow in 1856 for $190.[5] He subsequently sold it to R. W. Murphy through a quitclaim deed in 1857.[6] This sale also included 10 other lots in Blocks 40 and 44 for a total of $4,000.[7] In 1871 Bugbey bought a portion of lots in Block 9 from R. W. Murphy for $100.[8] Less than a year later, he sold the same property to Charles Nuttall & Stephen Addison for $1,000.[9]

The relatively high prices for some of these sales indicates that it was not only the property being sold, but also perhaps the access to the tunnels under Folsom for goldmining purposes. The drift mine that Bugbey and others worked was documented during the construction of the City of Folsom's parking garage structure. Jacobson Helgoth Consultants mapped the location of a mining tunnel that began north of Leidesdorff Street, west of Decatur Street, and extended all the way southeast to Sutter Street. The entrance and location of the drift mine corresponds closely to lot 10 of Block 9 of the original map for the town grid of Folsom.

Bugbey must have sensed that because of his worsening cash position and the growing risk of losing his other Folsom properties, he had to protect these assets from potential creditors. In February 1872 Bugbey sold lots 3, 4, 5, 6, 7, and 8 in Block 40 of Folsom to Nettie Bugbey's brother, Charles McGlashan, for $1.[10]

In February 1873, at the same time Bugbey was filing a lawsuit against the Natoma Water and Mining Company, his wife Nettie sold part of the Duroc vineyard property she had been bequeathed by her late father Peter McGlashan in 1872. She sold approximately 30 acres to David Bennett for $350.[11]

Slow Demise of Natoma Vineyards

There appears to be no single one event that pushed Bugbey and the Natoma Vineyard into financial insolvency. Rather, there seems to be several factors that developed and then aligned to strangle his cash flow. One important factor seems to be Bugbey's hubris in regard to the management of his vineyard and winemaking operation.

Unlike the Gold Rush where placer mining along the river eventually dried up, Bugbey did not think California's wine production versus consumption would become so out of balance. Consumption was increasing modestly while production was doubling the supply, depressing prices. He may have been so blinded by his promotion of California vineyards and wine production that he could not see the impending oversupply of wine in the marketplace.

To his credit, he did diversify over the years. He began with raisins, then added wine, and eventually brandy and sparkling wine to the list of items he was producing. Along the way he also sold thousands of grape cuttings and rooted vines. He made a revealing statement in 1871 that the profits from raisins were so good that he could naturally see focusing on that product alone, were it not for the fact that so much of his capital had been devoted to wine, brandy, and sparkling wine production.

By his own estimate, Bugbey had invested over $250,000 into the Natoma Vineyard and its accompanying wine and liquor production. This suggests that he was plowing his profits back into the business. Except for Bugbey's house on the hill at the Natoma Vineyard, he and Nettie did not live a lavish lifestyle. Instead of spending his profits on luxury goods, fancy homes and travel, Bugbey kept investing in his operations. One of those investments was in the Johnston brandy distillation machine at the Natoma Vineyard operation. He also invested in George Johnston's business to build the stills for other brandy producers. Both of these investments were significant conversions of cash into machines or shares of stock. Unfortunately, the capital expenditures were not producing the expected return on investment or cash dividends he needed.

Bugbey's vocal insistence that the Vine Growers' and Wine and Brandy Manufacturers' Association lobby Congress to reduce or eliminate the brandy excise tax may also have been an indication he felt his production costs were too high, making his brandy, produced with the Johnston still, too expensive for the market. Regardless, Bugbey had invested money in the Johnston business that was not generating cash flow for his business. He needed the cash flow because he had borrowed heavily against the Natoma Vineyard property.

Beyond Bugbey's control were the several fires that ravaged his business. His fire insurance policies covered some of the costs, but it seems he was under-insured in many instances. While he could rebuild structures and facilities, he could not replace his inventory that was lost. It was the inventory of wine, brandy, and sparkling wine that he needed to convert into cash to pay creditors.

He was also a victim of his own success. As a successful vineyard owner and vintner, Bugbey was considered to be a role model that other farmers should follow. And they did. Vineyard plantings increased dramatically during the years that Bugbey was in production. While the extra grape production lowered the cost per ton for the grapes used for winemaking, the extra wine on the market prevented retail prices from rising. Bugbey's cost of production was increasing because of all his investments in expanding wine cellars and new brandy stills, but the price per gallon of wine or brandy was not inflating.

Even though he had developed markets in the Midwest and on the East Coast, railroad freight costs kept increasing. The added freight cost was making common table wine too expensive when shipping was added onto the wholesale price. Consequently, Bugbey had to market more of his products in an increasingly crowded California marketplace.

National Monetary Policy

There were national economic events that would also place additional strain on Bugbey's operation. First, the Coinage Act of 1873 placed the nation on a gold standard by severely limiting silver coins in circulation and available to pay debts. The act stopped the production of silver dollars except for silver trade dollars for use in foreign markets. The impact of the contraction of the monetary supply hurt businesses on the West Coast more because that was where most of the silver and gold production was.[12]

A second financial hit to Bugbey's cash flow was the Panic of 1873. The economy after the Civil War had been expanding as investment returned and rebuilt U.S. manufacturing. Unfortunately, excessive speculation, especially in railroads, led to the collapse of the major banking establishment of Jay Cooke & Company back east. Some economists also cite the demonetization of silver in the Coinage Act of 1873 as contributing to the financial panic and crisis of the year.[13] Finally, after the financial panic struck, the United States drifted into the Long Depression of 1873.[14]

The net effect of demonetizing silver, the Panic of 1873, and the subsequent economic depression was to reduce the demand for discretionary purchases on items such as wine, sparkling wine, and brandy. Unlike many farmers, who could just pull back and weather the financial storm, Bugbey had a mortgage debt to pay. In addition, the previous fires at his wine cellars at the Natoma Vineyard in Folsom decreased his stock of product that he could convert into cash.

Republican Politics

Bugbey was struggling to pay his bills, but life went on. At the June 1873 County Republican Convention Bugbey stepped down as chairman of the County Central Committee. Supporters of Governor Booth were threatening to bolt from the local Republican Party. The County Republican Party consented to changes from the Booth faction, but the compromise was not enough to satisfy them.[15] Bugbey made the decision that he could no longer serve on the Central Committee.[16]

At the convention, Bugbey supported Moses Drew for Sheriff, who lost to A. Heilbron. Heilbron would go on to win the position in the general election. Bugbey was nominated for Tax Collector, but lost to Simms, even though the Sheriff was still considered the ex-officio tax collector in Sacramento County. Bugbey was also nominated as a delegate to the Republican Party State Convention.[17] Four items that the County Republican Convention endorsed that appealed to Bugbey were more state regulation over railroad freight rates, that all government employees receive salaries in a national currency (greenbacks instead of gold coin), that growing crops should be exempt from taxation, and finally, that land held in public domain should be kept for settlers under the homestead and preemption laws and not gifted or sold to corporations.[18]

One resolution that probably made not only Bugbey, but many other Republicans uneasy at the time, was the declaration that immigration of Chinese into California was a growing evil.[19] Bugbey had employed Chinese labor and had even sold property to Mum Sing, a Chinese man. But there was a rising tide of political sentiment against the Chinese in California at the time. In order to gain votes, it was easier to side against the Chinese rather than to carefully consider their value to many different industries, such as agriculture in California.

Mortgage Default

At the same time as the County Republican Convention was underway, Bugbey's mortgage company, Pacific Mutual Life Insurance Company of California, was filing a lawsuit against him for over $30,000. The public got another glimpse of Bugbey's money problems when C. T. H. Palmer filed for foreclosure on the house he had sold Bugbey in Folsom just two years earlier.[20] Sacramento County Sheriff Mike Bryte sold the C. T. H. Palmer house in Folsom back to Palmer for $1,365.75. Listed as persons in default of the mortgage to Palmer were B. N. Bugbey, Ann Johns, J. W. Speyer and J. M. Philip.[21]

The Sheriff's Sale of his home must have been a terrible blow to Bugbey, as he had already turned over the operation of the Natoma Vineyard, and now was in eminent danger of losing his house and famed winery operation. However, it appears Nettie Bugbey's family may have come to the rescue of the couple in their precarious living situation. Eight months after the Bugbey's Palmer house at Bridge and Figueroa Streets had been sold at the Sheriff's Sale, Nettie was able to buy the property back from C. T. H. Palmer for $2,000. This purchase also included several lots in Block 53 besides the primary residence on lots 7 and 8.[22]

Natoma Vineyard Mortgage Default

In May of 1874, Judge Adams rendered his verdict of foreclosure on the Natoma Vineyard property in favor of Pacific Mutual Life Insurance Company, for a total amount of $30,940.45.[23] Bugbey's property had been appraised at only $22,000 by the State Board of Equalization in 1872.[24] The judgment against Bugbey specified that the property was to be sold at a Sheriff's Sale and payment was to be in gold coin.[25]

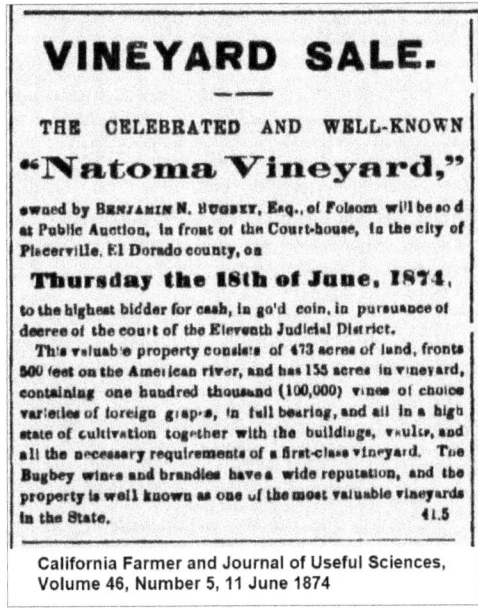

Figure 19: 1874 - Natoma Vineyard Sheriff's Sale advertisement. CDNC

Included as a defendant in the lawsuit brought by Pacific Mutual Life, in addition to Bugbey and his wife Martinette, was Ann Johns. Ann Johns was also listed as a mortgagor on the C. T. H. Palmer property that went into default. As early as March 1872, Ann Johns filed a lawsuit against Bugbey.[26] Bugbey must have taken out a loan from Ann, sometimes listed as Anna Johns, and she was listed on the mortgage papers with Pacific Mutual Life Insurance.

In 1870 Ann Johns and her husband were living with their son John Johns is the township of Salmon Falls in El Dorado County.[27] Ann Johns was born in Cornwall, England, in about 1805.[28] After her husband, Zachariah, died she moved in with Elizabeth Noyes,[29] whose husband owned property across from Mormon Island on the north side of the South Fork of the American River.[30] Ann Johns died in 1881, and her remains were reinterred in the Mormon Island Relocation Cemetery.[31]

It's not clear how Bugbey knew Ann and Zachariah Johns. Regardless, she either invested in the Natoma Vineyard or lent her name as security, thereby having her name placed on the mortgage documents with Pacific Mutual Life Insurance Company. She also helped Benjamin and Nettie Bugbey to purchase the C. T. H. Palmer

House. It is unfortunate that at the age of approximately 70 years old, her loans or investments with Bugbey evaporated.

Natoma Vineyard Public Auction

Because it was evident that Bugbey at the time could not come up with the amount of gold needed to settle the past due mortgage on the Natoma Vineyard, it was ordered sold at public auction by the El Dorado County Sheriff. This was the very sort of public auction that Bugbey, as Sheriff of Sacramento County, had overseen so many times in the early 1860s. The only exception afforded Bugbey was that he was able to keep 7 acres of land in Section 16.[32]

By June of 1874, the celebrated Natoma Vineyard was being offered for sale by the El Dorado County Sheriff. The newspaper advertisement stated,

This valuable property consists of 473 acres of land, fronts 500 feet on the American river, and has 155 acres in vineyard, containing one hundred thousand (100,000) choice varieties of foreign grapes, in full bearing, and all in a high state of cultivation, together with the buildings, vaults, and all the necessary requirements of a first-class vineyard. The Bugbey wines and brandies have a wide reputation, and the property is well known as one of the most valuable vineyards in the State[33]. - Sacramento Daily Union, Volume 47, Number 7232, 9 June 1874

The high bidder for the property was the Pacific Mutual Life Insurance Company of California for $32,600.[34]

The Sheriff's Sale was appealed, and the California State Supreme Court overturned the lower court's decision in December 1875[35]. They explicitly gave directions to the El Dorado County District Court to set aside all sales under the decree wherein the plaintiff, Pacific Mutual Life Insurance Company, was the purchaser.

The Supreme Court ruling ordering a new trial in the Natoma Vineyard mortgage default was but a brief respite for Bugbey. While it bought him a little extra time, it only delayed the inevitable. The lawsuit would once again be tried in El Dorado County in 1877. The same verdict was reached with a different judge, but the award had increased to $32,110 to Pacific Mutual Life with the added $1,000 for attorney's fees.[36]

More Debt Lawsuits

By the middle of the 1870s Bugbey was juggling various law suits for unpaid debts and loans. The bills were mounting and his inventory of wine, brandy, and sparkling wine were gone. While the lawsuit from the life insurance company was being re-litigated, Bugbey got served with another lawsuit. This time Bugbey had gotten into debt with S. W. Griffith who he had hired as a Deputy when Bugbey was Sheriff of Sacramento County in 1861.[37] Whether it was out of guilt or embarrassment, Bugbey never showed up in court to even contest the complaint by Griffith. On November 10th, 1876, judgment went to Griffith by default an was awarded $12,055.21.[38]

Strong v Bugbey, November 1874

With very little cash on hand to pay attorney's fees, Bugbey would resort to representing himself falling back on his knowledge of the law. In 1873 he purchased some alfalfa seed from a Sacramento city seed dealer. A series of communication errors resulted in the bill not being paid, and Bugbey was sued for the recovery of $106.50 for the seed by W. R. Strong. McKune and Welty represented W. R. Strong.

Bugbey lost the lawsuit and then appealed the judgment. He was not disputing that he owed the money. Bugbey's grounds for appeal was that the summons he received were issued to an alias and not his actual name. As he said in his notice of appeal, "This appeal is taken on questions of law alone."

But he had to display to the court that the appeal just wasn't a delaying tactic. Bugbey's good friend and future Sheriff of Sacramento County, Moses Drew, would be his surety or guarantee of payment to W. R. Strong & Co. if the appeal failed. Bugbey then wrote the appeal in his own hand.

Bugbey's statement of appeal was filed before Justice of the Peace John Eoff in Granite Township.

Be it remembered that the complaint in this case was filed in said court on the 5th day of November, 1873 and summons issued thereon, which said summons was never returned to court. An alias and a second alias were also issued and never returned. Not served on the 31st of October 1874 a third alias was issued and returned served on the same day, which third alias was made returnable November 3rd 1874.

The paper delivered to the defendant as a copy of summons and the only notification he had was and is the paper hereunder annexed marked "Exhibit A".

There was no other service of summons on defendant.

Judgement was rendered by default.

On the 3rd day of November 1874 and now come the defendant and asks that this statement or bill of exceptions be signed, settled and made a part of the record in this cause.
B. N. Bugbey, Defendant[39]

Bugbey had to wait until the next year to see if his gamble of wiggling out of the judgment on a legal technicality would work. But on February 15, 1875, the judgment was reversed, and W. R. Strong was ordered to pay $7 for clerk fees and transcript costs.

Not to be deterred by his fiscal misfortune, and putting on a brave face, Bugbey entered numerous selections of his wines and brandies in the 1874 State Fair. He received premiums for best 1870 brandy, best white wine, best red wine, and best California sherry.[40] Since he was no longer producing wine, having consigned that to previous employees, his inventory must have been dwindling down. If nothing else, entering what little product he had in a State Fair competition was cheap advertising.

Folsom Property Ordered Sold

Any celebration of his awards at the State Fair were short-lived, as Bugbey was set to lose more property in Folsom. In 1873 Morris, Speyer & Company sued Bugbey for damages of $430. Morris, Speyer & Company was an importer and consignment company in San Francisco that also handled insurance.[41] One of the principals in Morris, Speyer and Company was J. M Philip.[42] Speyer and Philip had assisted Bugbey in purchasing the C. T. H. Palmer house in Folsom. In December of 1874, Morris, Speyer & Company won a judgment against Bugbey. Bugbey's lots in Folsom (lots 7, 8, 9, 10, 11, 12, 13, 14, 15 and 16, in Block 53) and they were to be sold at auction by Sacramento County Sheriff H. M. La Rue on January 16, 1875.[43]

By the spring of 1875, with the collapse of his business and losing much of his real estate, Bugbey left California for Nevada. Ostensibly he was looking for new lumber and mining opportunities.[44] More than likely, he was spending time with Nettie's brother, Charles McGlashan, who lived in Truckee. Bugbey's trip out of state allowed him to escape the glare of failure from his business empire and the hounding of creditors to whom he owed money.

Duroc Vineyard Sold

The last of unencumbered property that Bugbey could sell to raise cash was the land Peter McGlashan bequeathed to his wife Nettie.

In April 1875 Nettie Bugbey sold the remainder of the property that encompassed the Duroc vineyard near Shingle Springs to Thomas Wallace for $3,600.[45]

American Water and Mining Company

Sometime in 1875, Bugbey grasped at the idea of creating his own water and mining company. Bugbey, along with his attorneys G. J. Carpenter and George C. Williams, incorporated the American Water and Mining Company with corporate offices in San Francisco.[46] The water company may have been little more than a ruse and shell company to protect Bugbey's property. He had appealed the foreclosure of the Natoma Vineyard based on the fact that the Pacific Mutual Life Insurance Company of California was the high bidder in the Sheriff's Sale of the property. While the appeal was in the court system, Bugbey sold the property to the American Water and Mining Company for $1 in July 1875.[47]

By October 1875, while the Sheriff's Sale of the Natoma Vineyard was being appealed, Bugbey was able to acquire part of the Natoma Vineyard for winemaking operations. In 1872 Bugbey had sold the rights to the operation and production of the Natoma Vineyard to James and Goosey. They sold those rights back to Nettie Bugbey for $1 in 1875.[48] The Folsom Telegraph reported that the grape crop at Bugbey's vineyard looked promising for 1875. The newspaper commented that it was happy to see he was getting his business affairs in order and would soon be engaging in wine making again.[49]

The return of the operations to the Bugbey family for the low price of $1 may also have been a recognition that there was little profit in wine making. The costs of producing, marketing, and shipping the product had not decreased. It seemed to be the Bugbey persona that helped sell the wines, brandy, and sparkling wine. With zero capital, Bugbey wasn't really in a position to keep the winery or brandy distillation in operation—not with his huge debt.

Eucalyptus Tree Experiment

By 1876 the Bugbey family seemed to have weathered the worst of the financial and economic storms that had ravaged their lives. Nettie Bugbey was awarded her teaching credential in February 1876.[50] In addition to tending the vineyard, Bugbey started selling eucalyptus and lime trees.[51] He advertised that he had 30,000 eucalyptus trees in heights from 3 to 8 feet for prices between $10 and $40 per hundred. He also was selling 5,000 lime trees for $3 to $6 per dozen.[52]

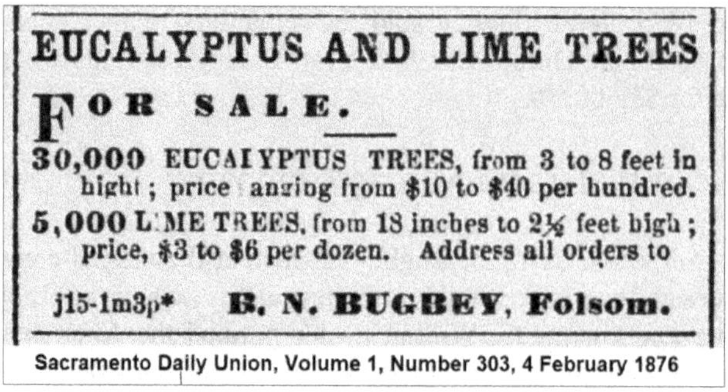

> **EUCALYPTUS AND LIME TREES**
>
> **FOR SALE.**
>
> 30,000 EUCALYPTUS TREES, from 3 to 8 feet in hight; price ranging from $10 to $40 per hundred.
> 5,000 LIME TREES, from 18 inches to 2½ feet high; price, $3 to $6 per dozen. Address all orders to
>
> j15-1m3p* **B. N. BUGBEY, Folsom.**

Sacramento Daily Union, Volume 1, Number 303, 4 February 1876

Figure 20: 1876 - Eucalyptus and lime trees advertisement by Bugbey. CDNC

He was not growing the trees on his property but may have been importing them. Eucalyptus trees were promoted as a fast-growing hardwood that was perfectly suited for California's climate, which was similar to that of Australia, their native habitat. In the summer of 1875, Bugbey and his wife Nettie traveled to Southern California.[53] If Bugbey had not read about Ellwood Cooper and his promotion of the eucalyptus tree in Santa Barbara, he might have encountered the farmer and college president while in Southern California.

Ellwood Cooper had settled in Santa Barbara in 1870 and started experimenting with all sorts of crops on his farm.[54] By 1873 he had 1,000 English walnuts, 5,000 olive trees, 6,000 grapevines, and 6,000 blue gum eucalyptus trees planted, plus a variety of other fruit trees and grain crops on his Ellwood Ranch.[55] Cooper was being held up as the example of how to create a forest of trees for shade and profit by planting the eucalyptus tree.[56] Another element of credibility was that he was the president of the Santa Barbara College boarding school.[57]

Ellwood Cooper was a man Bugbey could admire. Cooper had a big ranch with all sorts of trees and had become a noted expert in the field of eucalyptus trees and horticulture. Another connection between the two was education: Cooper served as president of Santa Barbara College; Nettie Bugbey had just gained her teaching credential.

It's not known if Bugbey ever met with Ellwood Cooper. But he most certainly had read about him and his work in agriculture and forestry. It would not be surprising if Ellwood Cooper, who was also from the East Coast and just two years younger than Bugbey, would be an influence on Bugbey's decision to dive into selling eucalyptus trees.

Life for the Bugbey's was getting back to a semblance of normality. Nettie, who was 17 years younger than her husband, was able to make time for friends closer to her own age. At a large picnic held at the popular Natoma Grove, Nettie took second place in a target shooting competition sponsored by the Sacramento Light Artillery company.⁵⁸ In July of 1876, Nettie was in place as a teacher and principal of the Folsom elementary school.⁵⁹ Her teaching salary was most vital to paying the living expenses for the Bugbey's. In an attempt to augment the family income, Nettie sold a couple of lots to Augustus Cobwell for $200 from the property she was able to regain from Palmer.⁶⁰

---

[1] El Dorado County Deed Book L, Page 558

[2] El Dorado County Deed Book M, Page 409

[3] El Dorado County Deed Book O, Page 11

[4] Lee, Catherine Paik, *The Geography of Viticulture in Amador, El Dorado, and Calaveras Counties: Studies of History, Tourism, and Regional Identity*, (Thesis, University of California, Davis, 2001)

[5] Sacramento County Deed Book 18710918, pages 210 and 211

[6] Sacramento County Deed Book 18570202, page 104

[7] Ibid.

[8] Sacramento County Deed Book 18710918, pages 210 and 211

[9] Sacramento County Deed Book 18720810, pages 496 and 497

[10] Sacramento County Deed Book 18721126, page 254

[11] El Dorado County Deed Book O, page 283

[12] https://en.wikipedia.org/wiki/Coinage_Act_of_1873

[13] https://en.wikipedia.org/wiki/Panic_of_1873

[14] https://en.wikipedia.org/wiki/Long_Depression

[15] Sacramento Daily Union, Volume 45, Number 6923, June 11, 1873, CDNC

[16] Ibid.

[17] Ibid.

[18] Ibid.

[19] Ibid.

[20] Sacramento Daily Union, Volume 45, Number 6969, August 5, 1873, CDNC

[21] Sacramento County Deed Book 1874116, pages 13 – 15

[22] Sacramento Count Deed Book 18741116, page 15

[23] The Pacific Mutual Life Insurance Company of California v B. N. Bugbey, Martinette Bugbey, and Ann Johns, In the District Court 11th Judicial District Court, (El Dorado County Judgement Book E, 1874, page 237, El Dorado County Historical Society Museum).

[24] Sacramento Daily Union, Volume 44, Number 6830, February 22, 1873, CDNC

[25] The Pacific Mutual Life Insurance Company of California v B. N. Bugbey, Martinette Bugbey, and Ann Johns, In the District Court 11th Judicial District Court, (El Dorado County Judgement Book E, 1874, page 237, El Dorado County Historical Society

Museum).

[26] Sacramento Daily Union, Volume 42, Number 7428, March 5, 1872, CDNC

[27] 1870 Federal Census California, El Dorado, Salmon Falls

[28] 1880 Federal Census California, El Dorado, Salmon Falls, 053

[29] Map of the County of El Dorado, California: compiled from the official records and surveys, (Library of Congress https://www.loc.gov/maps/?q=el+dorado)

[30] Mormon Island Relocation Cemetery (http://www.usgwtombstones.org/california/californ.html)

[31] Ibid.

[32] The Pacific Mutual Life Insurance Company of California v B. N. Bugbey, Martinette Bugbey, and Ann Johns, In the District Court 11th Judicial District Court, (El Dorado County Judgement Book E, 1874, page 237, El Dorado County Historical Society Museum).

[33] Sacramento Daily Union, Volume 47, Number 7232, June 9, 1874, CDNC

[34] Marysville Daily Appeal, Number 147, June 21, 1874, CDNC

[35] Daily Alta California, Volume 27, Number 9389, December 18, 1875, CDNC

[36] The Pacific Mutual Life Insurance Company of California v B. N. Bugbey, Martinette Bugbey, and Ann Johns, In the District Court 11th Judicial District Court, (El Dorado County Judgement Book E, 1877, page 295, El Dorado County Historical Society Museum).

[37] Sacramento Daily Union, Volume 22, Number 3285, October 8, 1861, CDNC

[38] S. W. Griffith v B. N. Bugbey, In the District Court of the 11th Judicial District, November 10, 1876. (El Dorado County Judgment Book E, 1876, page 289, El Dorado County Historical Society Museum).

[39] W. R. Strong and Company v B. N. Bugbey, Sacramento County Court, 1875, (Civil Case Files 1850 – 1879, Case 3125 or 3126, Box 46)

[40] Sacramento Daily Union, Volume 47, Number 7329, September 30, 1874, CDNC

[41] Daily Alta California, Volume 23, Number 7734, May 26, 1871, CDNC

[42] Daily Alta California, Volume 22, Number 7229, January 5, 1870, CDNC

[43] Sacramento Daily Union, Volume 48, Number 7398, December 19, 1874, CDNC

[44] Sacramento Daily Union, Volume 1, Number 42, April 10, 1875, CDNC

[45] El Dorado County Deed Book Q, page 200

[46] Sacramento Daily Union, Volume 1, Number 116, July 8, 1875, CDNC

[47] El Dorado County Deed Book S, page 287

[48] El Dorado County Deed Book S, page 21

[49] Pacific Rural Press, Volume 10, Number 17, October 23, 1875, CDNC

[50] Sacramento Daily Union, Volume 1, Number 300, February 1, 1876, CDNC

[51] Sacramento Daily Union, Volume 1, Number 303, February 4, 1876, CDNC

52 Ibid.

53 Daily Alta California, Volume 27, Number 9253, August 4, 1875, CDNC

54 Santos, Robert, *The Eucalyptus of California, Seeds of Good or Evil?* (California State University Press, 1997

55 Santa Barbara Weekly Press, Volume V, Number 13, September 27, 1873, CDNC

56 Santa Barbara Weekly Press, Volume VI, Number 30, January 23, 1875, CDNC

57 Ibid.

58 Sacramento Daily Union, Volume 2, Number 63, May 4, 1876, CDNC

59 Sacramento Daily Union, Volume 2, Number 116, July 7, 1876, CDNC

60 Sacramento County Deed Book 18761010, page 410

Chapter 11: Bugbey Crash & Return 1877 – 1879

With the dawn of 1877, Bugbey was out of money and out of resources. He and Nettie were living on her income as a school teacher.[1] But he still had outstanding debts he could not pay. On March 2, 1877, Bugbey filed for bankruptcy.[2] His liabilities were listed as $21,025. Bugbey still maintained he had assets of 493 acres of land, but the land was not available to him because of pending litigation.[3]

In somewhat of an odd political play, Bugbey was hoping to be nominated for County Treasurer by the Sacramento County Republican Party. In July 1877, he even took out an advertisement in the Sacramento Daily Union to announce his interest in the office.[4] Considering Bugbey could not pay his bills and had just declared bankruptcy, it defies logic that anyone would vote for him to be the County Treasurer. Bugbey was most likely looking for any sort of work that would earn him an income. He was not nominated as treasurer for the Republican ticket.

When Bugbey was rebuffed by his Republican Party, he was no longer moored to any of the pillars that supported his life and identity: law enforcement, farmer, vintner, or political operative. He had failed at business and politics. The celebrated B. N. Bugbey of the famed Natoma Vineyards, who had musical scores composed to honor himself and his sparkling wine, winner of State Fair Gold Medals, was now dependent on his wife. Bugbey was in a hole that he could not climb out of, psychologically or financially.

The Crash, Attempted Murder

As he approached his 50th birthday, the man who used to produce the alcohol now turned to alcohol for solace. He also turned on Nettie. He became abusive towards her.[5] It just wasn't the alcohol that was impairing Bugbey's mind; he was having a mental breakdown. He was having difficulty keeping track of people and places. He was having episodic mood swings, and with each new instance of his mental fog, Bugbey would become more violent.[6]

In early September 1877, Nettie had retreated to Truckee, to the home of her brother, Charles McGlashan. Bugbey, in a drunken stupor and mental collapse, assumed his wife had left him or escaped her home confinement. This enraged Bugbey. He not only had lost control of his life, but also of his wife. He proceeded to destroy everything in their house, from the piano to the furniture.[7] Bugbey's "insane frenzy," as described by the local newspaper, triggered an arrest warrant for his destructive behavior.[8]

Constable William Krimble found a drunken and belligerent Bugbey at the home he was destroying. But Bugbey was not going to be arrested by anyone. In a manner consistent with respect for a fellow former law enforcement officer, Constable Krimble tried to serve the arrest warrant papers. Bugbey grabbed the papers and drew his pistol, pointing it at Krimble, who quickly moved to the side. The inebriated Bugbey got off one shot, which grazed Krimble's head.[9]

Krimble started to wrestle with Bugbey to take his gun away, but not before Bugbey fired the pistol two more times. Krimble then struck Bugbey with his own pistol to subdue him and secured him with cuffs. Krimble was able to escort Bugbey to appear before Justice Anderson for a bail hearing. But Bugbey continued in his frenzied state of agitation, again becoming violent. Bugbey was remanded to custody in the local jail, as he was determined to be unfit to be released.[10]

When Bugbey was able to attend his court hearing, represented by W. C. Crossette and O. C. Lewis, he admitted he was still confused and could not go on with the examination.[11] Contrary to newspaper reports, Bugbey claimed he never abused his wife, and she had not been in Folsom for several days. Nettie confirmed that she was not in Folsom on the day of his raging frenzy. Regardless, Bugbey admitted the entire episode was his fault.[12]

On the charge of the attempted murder of Constable Krimbal, Bugbey's case was quickly brought to trial. He was found not guilty in a jury trial in late October of 1877.[13]

At the height of Bugbey's mental collapse, a child was born. Nettie's sister Adelia, who was married to George Balis, had moved to Red Bluff, California, and had given birth to a son in September 1877. Possibly not knowing the state of Bugbey's erratic behavior, or in spite of it, George and Adelia named their son Benjamin Bugbey Balis.[14] This would be the only child to be named after B. N. Bugbey, as he never had any children of his own.

Exile To San Francisco

Bugbey's bankruptcy petition was being heard in the San Francisco District Court of the United States. Since he had to appear in San Francisco, and no one was welcoming him home to the house he had torn up in Folsom, Bugbey moved to San Francisco.[15] He was able to find employment as something of a watchman or security guard at the U. S. mint in San Francisco.[16]

In November, Bugbey was duly declared bankrupt.[17] He was finally finished. He had lost everything, including his wife. He had exiled himself to San Francisco, far from the Sacramento Valley landscape he loved. He had to have wondered if there was life remaining for a pioneer who was 50 years old and bankrupt.

Bugbey decided life was not over. It was not in his character to retreat until he was absolutely out of options. As Constable and Sheriff, he had visited the scenes of suicide of men just like himself: miners who were broke, miserable, and saw no options other than suicide. As a younger man, Bugbey had bounced back after failures in the furniture retail business and farming.

Bugbey also recognized the role alcohol had played, not only in his financial failure, but in his personal life. While living in San Francisco, he started attending Gospel-Temperance Union meetings. In December of 1877, he announced he had taken a pledge of sobriety.[18]

U.S. Supreme Court Victory

At the same time Bugbey was getting sober, he received word that the U.S. Supreme Court would hear his case against the Natoma Water and Mining Company.[19] This had to be a small glimmer of light in an otherwise very dark period for Bugbey. Shortly after the New Year, the U.S. Supreme Court rendered its decision in favor of Bugbey.[20]

Chief Justice Waite delivered the opinion for the court, echoing the ruling of the El Dorado County District Court in 1873. The crucial point was that the act of July 26, 1866, granting rights to land over which a water ditch traversed, became law after Bugbey had purchased the Natoma Vineyard land from the State of California. Chief Justice Waite wrote,

Here the company does not claim under settler's title, but seeks by means of it to defeat that of the State, and thus leave the land in a condition to be operated upon by the act of July 26. The settler, however, was under no obligation to assert his claim, and he having abandoned it, the title of the State became absolute as of May 19, 1866, when the surveys were completed. The case stands, therefore, as if at that date the United States had parted with all interest in and control over the property. As the act of July 26 was not passed until after that time, it follows that it could not operate upon this land in favor of the company. - Water and Mining Company v. Bugbey, United States Supreme Court.[21,22]

While Bugbey must have been ecstatic over the vindication of his position, he most certainly did not toast the decision with a glass of sparkling wine. He had triumphed over a large corporation, but the victory must have been hollow compared to the significant losses he had sustained.

On the day the Sacramento Daily Union reported on Bugbey's U. S. Supreme Court victory, they also published the delinquent tax list in the newspaper.[23] Not only was Bugbey delinquent on his property taxes, his good friend and current Sheriff of Sacramento County, Moses Drew, noticed he would have to sell Bugbey's Folsom properties to the highest bidder on February 23, 1878.[24]

Emma Bugbey

Nettie's brother, Charles McGlashan, had helped protect the properties in Folsom at Sutter and Burnett Streets in 1872 by taking title to the lots for a nominal sum of money. But he obviously wasn't going to pay the property taxes, now that Nettie had decided to separate from Bugbey and ultimately get a divorce. Nettie was able to buy back the properties on Bridge and Figueroa Streets in Folsom from C. T. H. Palmer. In December 1877, while Bugbey had retired to San Francisco to get sober and deal with his bankruptcy, Nettie sold the property at Bridge and Figueroa Streets, lots 5 – 16 in Block 53, to Emma Bugbey, who was Benjamin's niece.[25]

Later in December 1877, Emma would sell the same property back to Benjamin.[26] Both transactions were for $2,000, so Emma was not out any money. It was essentially a transfer of cash to Nettie, who had repurchased the property from C. T. H. Palmer for $2,000. Where all the money came from to initially re-purchase the Palmer house and then have Emma Bugbey buy the property from Nettie is unclear. There is scant documentation about Emma Bugbey and her direct relationship to Bugbey. It is doubtful that a young unmarried woman who had travelled from the East Coast would have $2,000 laying around. It is only speculation that Bugbey himself somehow scraped up the money, or had a hidden stash some place, that he provided Emma to purchase the property from Nettie. The net result was that the property was back in B. N. Bugbey's name.

Rev. Elias W. Wible

Bugbey had not been an overly religious man in terms of allotting his time to raise money for his local church or other religious causes. With his world collapsing around him, and imbibing massive quantities of alcohol to numb the pain, one might have expected Bugbey to at least investigate a religious faith as a means of finding some guidance, as many do in those circumstances. Bugbey had been raised in the Methodist Episcopal Church, as his father was a part-time minister for the protestant denomination back in Connecticut. There was not an actual Methodist Episcopal Church in Folsom, but there was a pastor of the faith ministering to a small community of adherents in the area.

Benjamin Norton Bugbey

Elias A. Wible was licensed to preach in the Methodist Episcopal Church in 1858 and came out to California with his family in 1859. Reverend Wible was the same age as Bugbey and was born back east in Pennsylvania. By the time Rev. Wible was stationed in the eastern Sacramento area, he had been preaching and setting up congregations all over Northern California. His first appointment was in Pilot Hill in 1859 and then on to Georgetown, Forrest Hill, Yankee Jims, Copperopolis, Sonora, Livermore, and Red Bluff.[27]

In 1877 Rev. Wible and his large family--his wife, Sarah, and six children--relocated to Sacramento.[28,29] Wible's task was to minister to the eastern portion of Sacramento County including Folsom. This included lots of travel with a horse and carriage and the inevitable mechanical failure of the carriage's axle. On Rev. Wible's long rides to meet with parishioners, he envisioned an improvement to the carriage to reduce maintenance and failures: an improved carriage axle.[30] At some point while Bugbey was attending one of Rev. Wible's church services, the two obviously had a discussion about the new axle design.

Wible Axle Promoter

Bugbey loved mechanical inventions. In addition to Rev. Wible's spiritual guidance to Bugbey, they talked of mechanics, axles, spindles, improvements, patents, and finally, promotion. Even though Bugbey had a job at the U. S. Mint in San Francisco, it was apparent that he wanted to get back to Sacramento. The Sacramento-Folsom area was home, even if it was also the site of his most spectacular personal and financial failures. The revolutionary new axle design appeared to be a reinvention of the carriage… and a reinvention of Bugbey's career. The next step was to use Bugbey's marketing skills to promote the new axle design. Bugbey arranged for a demonstration of Rev. Wible's novel improvement to the running gear for carriages. The public was invited to see Wible's unique, and soon to be patented, hub and axle design, at Stanley's Stables at K and 10th Streets, on November 16, 1878.[31] It was no surprise that the announcement in the Sacramento Daily Union for the demonstration of Wible's invention noted that Bugbey had been appointed the representing agent.[32]

Nettie Divorces Benjamin

As Bugbey was working to generate income in the Sacramento region by promoting the Wible invention, Nettie decided that their marriage was over. She filed for divorce in January 1879.[33] In order to allow Bugbey to move back to Folsom, she moved in with her brother Charles McGlashan in Santa Cruz.[34] Charles McGlashan had moved down to the Bay Area from Truckee to work on his book on the Donner Party, which he announced in 1878.

McGlashan had taken over the local Truckee Republican newspaper in 1876. He immediately became fascinated with the Donner Party catastrophe of 1846-47. With a team of locals, he did a crude archeological survey of the cabin sites east of Donner Lake and turned up a whetstone that belonged to James Reed of the party. McGlashan communicated incessantly with the survivors of the Donner Party to gain their trust so they would participate in his book. He was successful and traveled down to the Bay Area to interview many of the survivors.[35] McGlashan's *History of the Donner Party, A Tragedy of the Sierra*, was one of the first comprehensive treatments of the tale of the immigrants' ordeal. He had hundreds of letters from survivors and oral interviews. It's possible that his sister Nettie helped him on the project.

As a school teacher, Nettie was able to apply her occupation in the Santa Cruz area and board with her brother and his family. Her divorce from Bugbey was finalized in late February of 1879. As part of the divorce settlement, Bugbey was to pay Nettie $1,000,[36] and she released title in the Folsom property back to him.[37] So ended Bugbey's second marriage.

Bugbey was never able to reclaim the property he originally purchased in Folsom in 1856. He had sold this property (Lots 3 – 8, Block 40, bounded by Burnett, Figueroa, Forrest, and Sutter Streets) to Nettie's brother, Charles McGlashan, for $1. After Bugbey's little incident during which he tried to kill the Constable of Granite Township, and with divorce from his sister seemingly imminent, Charles McGlashan in 1878 granted the property to Sarah Moore, who in turn granted it to M. M. Sheldon.[38]

Invitation to Execution

Bugbey was back in circulation in Sacramento. Moses Drew, one of Bugbey's closest and lifelong friends, had been elected Sheriff of Sacramento County. Sheriff Drew knew that Bugbey had overseen the executions of two men by hanging and enlisted his old friend for guidance on his watch. Troy Dye, the Public Administrator for Sacramento County, along with his accomplice, Anderson, shot and killed Aaron Tullis in his Grand Island orchard on August 2nd, 1878. Sheriff Drew worked the case over several weeks, arresting Dye and Anderson. The motive for murder was that as Public Administrator, Dye could make extra money from the estates of deceased individuals when it went through probate because he could be appointed executor of the estate. Aaron Tullis was supposedly wealthy and had no relatives in the immediate area. Dye and Anderson were found guilty in April and sentenced to death.[39]

At the invitation of Sheriff Drew, Bugbey assisted with the hanging of both men. Bugbey strapped down the arms and legs of the men to be hanged on the May afternoon. When Dye began vomiting during a reading from Dye's spiritual advisor, Mr. MacEwen, Bugbey took command and begged MacEwen to shorten the reading, as Dye continued to spew the contents of his stomach onto himself and the scaffolding. Order was somewhat restored, and both men were hanged.[40]

It was only 18 months earlier that Bugbey had been on the wrong side of the law. A few inches nearer the head of Constable Krimble, whom he shot, and Bugbey might have been facing a murder charge and execution. But on this spring day in 1879, Bugbey was assistant executioner. Regardless of Bugbey's past, it was apparent that Sheriff Moses Drew saw Bugbey as a trusted ex-law enforcement officer. So trusted in fact, that Drew would hire Bugbey as one of his deputies later in the year.

Bugbey was on the road to redemption in Sacramento County. He was also back to politics, being elected as a delegate to the Republican State Convention.[41] One of the resolutions at the Republican State Convention was that the concentration of corporate land ownership was not healthy.

> *That an independent and intelligent agricultural population is the chief element of a nation's strength and prosperity, and it should be the policy of the State and general government to encourage the acquisition of lands in small holdings for actual use, and to discourage the monopoly by individuals or corporations in large bodies.*[42] - Sacramento Daily Union, Volume 8, Number 88, 19 June 1879

After Bugbey's fight with the Natoma Water and Mining Company, he could testify to the power and ability of large corporations to harass small landowners. Bugbey was also getting back to his good nature and humor. He entertained the Republicans at the convention with light-hearted nominations meant to take the edge off of a long day of speeches and votes.[43]

Folsom Lamblett Murder

A gruesome murder took place in Folsom in August of 1879 that thrust Bugbey back into the law enforcement spotlight. Only this time it was Deputy Sheriff Bugbey who was tasked with investigating the Lamblett murder. Francois "Frank" Lamblett had immigrated with his wife to California and became a naturalized citizen in 1865. He opened up a barber shop in Folsom.[44] On a hot Friday evening, he left the barber shop and went home to his house in Folsom. Frank Lamblett claimed he was awakened about 12:30 a.m. by the sound of his wife, Rosella, being assaulted. He was stabbed twice and jumped out of a back window at the instructions of his wife, who, he claims, was in the throes of being stabbed to death. When he was able to summon help and return to his house, Mrs. Lamblett had been brutally stabbed and slashed with a knife and died shortly thereafter.[45]

Since Bugbey lived in Folsom, Sheriff Drew had Bugbey gather evidence and information about the murder. Bugbey worked with Granite Township Constable Krimble,[46] whom Bugbey had tried to shoot two years earlier while he was in an alcohol-fueled frenzy of delirium and depression. Bugbey knew all the people in Folsom. The Lamblett's daughter, Eugenia, was married to Henry Mette.[47] Henry Mette's vineyard was next to Bugbey's Natoma Vineyard and they had swapped adjoining land parcels in 1868.[48]

Bugbey interviewed Frank Lamblett on the details of the murder, which focused on two suspects other than Lamblett.[49] Several days after the murder, Lamblett attempted suicide at his home by cutting his own throat. Bugbey was able to arrive shortly after the incident and applied pressure to the wound until the doctor could stitch up the cut.[50] In a statement printed in the Sacramento Daily Union, Bugbey opined, "Thus far no clue has been found which throws any light upon the murder. A great deal of speculation is going on among people. About half the people, without any positive evidence, accuse Lamblett of committing the crime, but I have not sufficient evidence to cause me to think anything of the kind."[51]

Not everyone was keen on the fact that Bugbey, a friend of Lamblett, was involved in the case. Rumors flew that Bugbey had refused to serve an arrest warrant for Lamblett and had vowed to stand by his friend. The San Francisco Chronicle published some statements from Folsom residents that were not favorable to Bugbey.[52] In an attempt to correct the record of events, District Attorney George Blanchard, a friend of Bugbey's, posted a statement in the Sacramento Daily Union on September 29, 1879.[53] Blanchard acknowledged that there was a feeling of distrust about Bugbey among Folsom residents. However, Blanchard could find no fault with how Lamblett was being watched by Bugbey or any deficiency with how the murder investigation was being handled.

Frank Lamblett was ultimately charged with the murder of his wife. At trial, Lamblett was defended by Henry Edgerton, W. C. Crossette and A. P. Catlin.[54] Bugbey testified that he arrested Lamblett but denied ever saying he would not serve an arrest warrant or stating that he would stand by Lamblett in the affair. Bugbey admitted he never thought Lamblett was guilty but said that he tried to prosecute the investigation in a fair and impartial manner.[55] In March 1880, Frank Lamblett was acquitted of the charge of murder against his wife.[56]

Even with his duties investigating the Lamblett murder, Bugbey found time, as he always seemed to do, to exhibit Rev. Wible's patented wagon axle at the 1879 State Fair.[57] He was able to lobby the State Agricultural Board, persuading them to award a diploma of merit to Wible's invention.[58]

Julia Wible Courtship

Before Bugbey became consumed with the Lamblett murder, he hosted the wedding of Richard H. Moore and Mattie M. Clark at his home in Folsom. The presiding clergy was the Reverend Wible.[59] With Bugbey's divorce from Nettie finalized earlier that year, he was free to find a new spouse. He did not have to look too far or for too long: On December 17, 1879, he married Julia Florinda Wible, the 25-year-old daughter of Rev. E. A. Wible.[60]

The last three years had been a wild ride for Bugbey. He exacerbated his problems by consuming too much alcohol in an attempt to obscure the realities of the collapse of his personal finances and business. One biographer used the term indefatigable to describe Bugbey when discussing his promotion of the winemaking industry in California. But the term could be as aptly applied to his approach to his entire life thus far. What was the wellspring of hope that sustained Bugbey in those darkest days? He had certainly been humbled, helpless to stop the collapse of his beloved Natoma Vineyard. One could say he was an opportunist, in the best sense of the word. When an opportunity presented itself, Bugbey tried his best to accommodate it and utilize it.

His return to Sacramento from exile in San Francisco was aided by his many longtime friends, such as Moses Drew. His support network did not come from his associates in the vineyard industry. Most of those who still believed in him and supported him were acquaintances from the Republican Party in Sacramento County—the one exception being the Rev. E. A. Wible. Bugbey was able to demonstrate to Wible that he truly had turned away from alcohol and was able to lead a sober life. This contributed to Wible's blessing of the marriage between Bugbey and Wible's daughter Julia.

---

[1] Sacramento Daily Union, Volume 3, Number 52, April 24, 1877, CDNC

[2] Sacramento Daily Union, Volume 3, Number 8, March 2, 1877, CDNC

[3] Ibid.

[4] Sacramento Daily Union, Volume 3, Number 122, July 19, 1877, CDNC

[5] Sacramento Daily Union, Volume 3, Number 161, September 3, 1877, CDNC

[6] Sacramento Daily Union, Volume 3, Number 162, September 4, 1877, CDNC

[7] Sacramento Daily Union, Volume 3, Number 161, September 3, 1877, CDNC

[8] Ibid.

[9] Ibid.

[10] Ibid.

[11] Sacramento Daily Union, Volume 3, Number 162, September 4, 1877, CDNC

[12] Ibid.

[13] Sacramento Daily Union, Volume 3, Number 214, October 24, 1877, CDNC

[14] 1880 U. S. Federal Census for Benjamin Balis, California, Tehama, Red Bluff, 140.

[15] 1878 San Francisco Directory, Bugbey, B. N., watchman U.S. Mint, dwelling 413 Fifth

[16] Ibid.

[17] Sacramento Daily Union, Volume 3, Number 227, November 8, 1877, CDNC

[18] Sacramento Daily Union, Volume 3, Number 255, December 11, 1877, CDNC

[19] Ibid.

[20] Sacramento Daily Union, Volume 3, Number 279, January 8, 1878, CDNC

[21] Water & Mining Co. v Bugbey, (U.S. Supreme Court, October 1877)

[22] Sacramento Daily Union, Volume 7, Number 80, May 22, 1878, CDNC

[23] Sacramento Daily Union, Volume 3, Number 301, February 2, 1878, CDNC

[24] Ibid.

[25] Sacramento County Deed Book 18771226, page 510

[26] Sacramento County Deed Book 18780215, page 35

[27] Anthony, Charles Volney, *Fifty Years of Methodism, A History of the Methodist Episcopal Church, Within the Bounds of the California Annual Conference From 1847 to 1897*, (Methodist Book Concern, 1901)

[28] 1880 U.S. Federal Census, California, Sacramento, Brighton

[29] 1879 California Voter Registers, Sacramento County

[30] Sacramento Daily Union, Volume 7, Number 228, November 16, 1878, CDNC

[31] Ibid.

[32] Ibid.

[33] Sacramento Daily Union, Volume 7, Number 283, January 25, 1879, CDNC

[34] 1880 U.S. Federal Census, California, Santa Cruz, McGlashan

[35] McGlashan, Charles F., *History of the Donner Party, A Tragedy of the Sierra*, forward 1940 by George Hinkle and Bliss McGlashan Hinkle, (Stanford University Press, 1968).

[36] Sacramento County Deed Book 18810203, page 144

[37] Sacramento Daily Union, Volume 7, Number 310, February 27, 1879, CDNC

Benjamin Norton Bugbey

[38] Sacramento County Deed Book 18820524, pages 243 and 244

[39] Sacramento Daily Union, Volume 8, May 30, 1879, CDNC

[40] Ibid.

[41] Sacramento Daily Union, Volume 8, Number 83, June 12, 1879, CDNC

[42] Sacramento Daily Union, Volume 8, Number 88, June 19, 1879, CDNC

[43] Ibid.

[44] 1874 California Voter Registers, Sacramento, Granite Township

[45] Sacramento Daily Union, Volume 8, Number 137, August 18, 1879, CDNC

[46] Ibid.

[47] 1870 and 1880 U.S. Federal Census, California, El Dorado, Salmon Falls, and 1900 Find A Grave Index

[48] El Dorado County Deed Book M, pages 40 and 615

[49] Sacramento Daily Union, Volume 8, Number 137, August 18, 1879, CDNC

[50] Sacramento Daily Union, Volume 8, Number 139, August 20, 1879, CDNC

[51] Ibid.

[52] Sacramento Daily Union, Volume 8, Number 173, September 29, 1879, CDNC

[53] Ibid.

[54] Sacramento Daily Union, Volume 11, Number 14, March 9, 1880, CDNC

[55] Ibid.

[56] Sacramento Daily Union, Volume 11, Number 18, March 13, 1880, CDNC

[57] Sacramento Daily Union, Volume 8, Number 157, September 10, 1879, CDNC

[58] Pacific Rural Press, Volume 18, Number 18, November 1, 1879, CDNC

[59] Sacramento Daily Union, Volume 8, Number 50, May 1, 1879, CDNC

[60] Sacramento Daily Union, Volume 8, Number 340, December 17, 1879, CDNC

Chapter 12: The Reinvention of Benjamin Bugbey, 1880 – 1885

A new decade, a new marriage, a new lease on life for Bugbey. At 52 years of age, Bugbey found himself reinventing his life in 1880. He was on his third marriage, had a new job as a Sheriff's Deputy, and had no money. In the succeeding years, he would search for his new Natoma Vineyard. As he did in his early pioneer days in Sacramento, managing a hotel, opening a furniture store, and farming at Salisbury Station, Bugbey would cycle through other opportunities, trying to find that elusive enterprise that would put him back on top, as the Natoma Vineyard had propelled him to prominence in the 1860s.

Bugbey would leverage his people skills, marketing knowledge, and knack for promotion with each new venture. He would demonstrate his commitment and tenacity with each new project he would undertake. He was not a quitter. If anything, he had learned to let failure and disappointment roll off of his back. He would also become more philosophical about life, while keeping his sense of humor.

New Family Saves Folsom Property

Even though Bugbey had regained control of his Folsom property (Lots 5 -16 in Block 53, bounded by Mormon, Bridge, Figueroa, and Coloma Streets) with the assistance of his niece Emma Bugbey, he still owed delinquent property taxes on the land and homes. Sheriff Moses Drew facilitated the sale of the property for delinquent property taxes to Evarilla Wood for $33.91.[1]

Evarilla Wood, who was living in Brighton near Sacramento, was the aunt of Julia Wible Bugbey.[2] After purchasing Bugbey's remaining Folsom property at the Sheriff's Sale, Evarilla then gifted the property to Julia Bugbey. She specifically stated in the deed grant that the property was to be held separately by Julia and "…free from the management and control of her said husband,…"[3] It's not known if the stipulation that the property not be treated as common property between husband and wife was a result of Evarilla's concern about Bugbey's character or a way to shield the property from seizure due to his past debts and bankruptcy.

With the election of Adolf Heilbron as Sheriff of Sacramento County[4], Bugbey was out of a job as a Deputy Sheriff.[5] Released of the constraints of a daily law enforcement job, Bugbey focused on other income pursuits.

One of Bugbey's favorite events every year was the State Fair. Not only was he able to connect with a variety of people throughout California, he always enjoyed exhibiting his latest venture. At the 1880

State Fair, Bugbey exhibited Rev. Wible's self-lubricating vehicle axle that he had been promoting. To compensate Bugbey for his marketing efforts, his new father-in-law, Rev. Wible, made him a part owner in the patented invention.[6] Bugbey also exhibited Wible's latest engineering efforts in the form of a drawbridge concept. Instead of a centerpiece rotating horizontally to allow boat traffic, the new design had the bridge dividing in the center and both parts lifting up vertically.[7]

Bugbey had his spirits buoyed by a surprise write-in candidacy for the Justice of the Peace in Granite Township. While Bugbey only received 20 write-in votes to first-place finisher George A. Knote's 69, it demonstrated that Bugbey still had his supporters. Bugbey was grateful for the show of support and humorously thanked his supporters in a note to the Sacramento Daily Union.

I notice in your issue of today that I received twenty votes for Justice of the Peace. I was not aware of the fact before, and now perceive the necessity of reading the news more than ever before. As I was not a candidate for the high and honorable position, I desire through your columns to return my hearty thanks to the few friends who perpetrated the joke.[8] - Sacramento Daily Union, Volume 12, Number 70, 11 November 1880

One of the last pieces of property Bugbey owned in Folsom connected to the Natoma Vineyard business was lost in 1881. Bugbey had purchased the Coner Flouring Mill in Folsom and converted most of it to storage for his wines, brandy, and champagne. It was destroyed by fire in 1871. All that remained was a pile of brick rubble. Bugbey was either unable or uninterested in paying the property taxes on the property, so it was sold at a Sheriff's Sale.[9]

Butter Cooler

Bugbey was back exhibiting at the State Fair in 1881, but not with the Wible axle or drawbridge. Bugbey was enthralled with a new and unique household utensil: the butter cooler. In typical Bugbey fashion, he was able to get the local newspapers to actually write about what was alternately called a refrigerator for butter.[10]

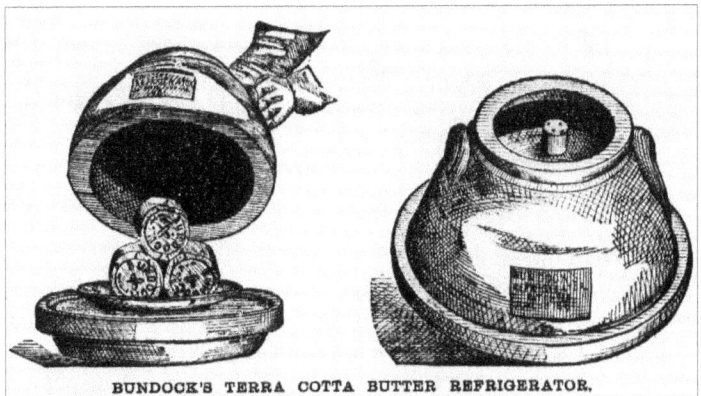

Figure 21: Bundock's terra cotta butter refrigerator that Bugbey was representing in the 1880s. CDNC

In 1880 Sacramento Pottery was owned by Henry Bundock, manufacturing a variety of terra cotta earthenware.[11] Terra cotta, before it is glazed and fired to make it impervious to liquids, will absorb water. If the surrounding air is sufficiently dry and warm enough, water will evaporate from the terra cotta keeping the container and its contents slightly cooler. Either Henry Bundock or one of his family members involved in the pottery company applied the evaporative cooling potential of terra cotta and designed a two-piece container for butter.

Both the bottom base and the upper cover were hollow and could be filled with water. The butter, which sat on a tray on the bottom of the cooler, covered with the top portion, was kept cool by the constant evaporation of the water.[12] Sacramento, with its low humidity and warm summer temperatures, was an ideal location to market the butter cooler. Apparently, Bugbey's exhibit of the butter refrigerator attracted quite a bit of attention at the State Fair.[13]

Bugbey was so keen on this new invention that he started selling them. He was able to arrange for a little retail space at 3rd and J Street in Sacramento to display and sell the butter cooler.[14] He even placed ads in the Sacramento Daily Union requesting housekeepers to come and view a butter cooler in action.

1,000 Housekeepers Wanted to call at 329 J Street, near Fourth, and see the wonderful Refrigerator for keeping butter hard and sweet, without ice and in any room. One of the Refrigerators can be seen at the above place, standing in the hot sun, with butter cold and hard within – the severest test that can be made, and perfect success. Cheapest Cooler known, and no expense after purchase. Don't fail to see it in operation. B. N. Bugbey, Sole Proprietor for the United States.[15]
- Sacramento Daily Union, Volume 16, Number 19, 12 September 1882

Bugbey may have missed his calling. Perhaps he should have gone into business as a copywriter or marketing consultant, considering the way he wrote the advertisement for the butter refrigerator. With just a little bit of embellishment and exaggeration, Bugbey made a compelling pitch for the terra cotta butter cooler. While it probably did not keep the butter cold as advertised, it most likely helped retard spoilage.

What did spoil was the relationship between Bugbey and the Bundock family. One of the family members, Samuel Bundock, died in the spring of 1882. Bugbey and W. H. Hobby were appointed as appraisers for the estate.[16] Bugbey was selling the butter cooler out of Hobby's Stone and Earthenware store at 317 J Street.[17] A dispute arose between the parties, and Bugbey and Hobby ended up suing the Bundocks in 1883.[18] While the butter cooler was not Bugbey's train ride to retirement, the whole evaporative cooling concept planted a seed that would grow into another future Bugbey vision.

Slickens Debris Trial

It was also during this period that hydraulic mining was wreaking havoc on the American and Sacramento Rivers. Sacramento's fragile levee system was under siege from rising river beds from the deposits of hydraulic mining debris. The mining debris, washed down the American river from the hydraulic mines in the Sierras, was inhibiting navigation and allowing the swollen winter river to overtop Sacramento's levees. It was reported that the mining debris had raised the riverbeds of the American and Sacramento rivers 35 feet in some places.

In July 1881 California's Attorney General Hart filed a complaint in Sacramento Superior Court against the Gold Run Ditch and Mining Company for an injunction to stop the mine from discharging mine waste and tailings into the North Fork of the American River.[19]

In the absence of before-and-after pictures, or even any documented river depths prior to the initiation of hydraulic mining in the 1860s, eyewitness testimony was a central component of the state's case. Bugbey, who had mined on the American River and its related forks, was a credible eyewitness to what the river looked like in 1849 and could contrast that to the condition of the river in 1881.

In the case *The People vs. The Gold Run Ditch and Mining Company*, Sacramento was represented by Attorney General Hart, Judge A. L. Rhoades, I. S. Belcher, W. C. Belcher, and George Cadwalader. The Gold Run Ditch company was represented by Samuel Wilson, Judge W. T. Wallace, A. P. Catlin, J. K. Byrne, and A. B.

Dibble.[20] Many of these men were personal acquaintances of Bugbey and had at various times represented him or sued him in court.

A central claim of the Gold Run Ditch was that mining activity along the American River from sluice boxes, used by early goldminers such as Bugbey, was a heavy contributor to the debris in the river. Even though most mining along the banks of the American River had ceased years earlier, some miners continued to work claims with the aid of water from the North Fork Ditch and Natoma Canal.

Testimony Expert Witness Bugbey

The Slickens Debris Trial, as it was known, commenced in late November 1881. On the 18th day of the trial, Bugbey stepped into the witness box to give his eyewitness account of the changes to the American River since the onset of hydraulic mining.[21] Bugbey was questioned first by George Cadwalader about his time mining and the different mining bars. Bugbey recounted that he had been able to see Negro Bar from his home in Folsom when he had lived there from 1856 to 1869.

The bulk of Bugbey's testimony centered on the mining bars, flats and hills around Folsom. He mined in the area in 1849 and 1850. As Sheriff, he had to visit mining claims and collect the foreign miners' tax from the Chinese men. When Bugbey came to California in 1849, he described how he mined on the North Fork of the American River at Condemned Bar and Little Oregon Bar above Beal's Bar. He also worked a claim east of Negro Hill, near the confluence of the North and South Forks of the American River. He recounted how he worked at Big Gulch, also known as Ashland, and then moved over to the south side of the river to mine at Negro Bar. From there he went up the hill to run a mining tunnel under what would become Block 40 of the town of Folsom. This property, over the drift mine, would be one of his first purchases of land in Folsom.[22]

Under questioning from Cadwalader, Bugbey testified that most of the bars, flats and hills had been worked out 15 years earlier. By 1881, there were only a few Chinese men using rockers to mine for placer gold along the river. One of the exceptions to that rule was Chris Lawson's mining claim near Folsom State Prison. Bugbey had collected samples from Negro Bar of what he described as the new white quartz pebbles that were creating new bars along the American River. The white quartz debris was what was being flushed down the river from the hydraulic mining occurring at the Gold Run Ditch mining claim.[23]

Cross Examination by A. P. Catlin

The cross examination of Bugbey by Amos P. Catlin for the defense was at times contentious. Catlin was trying to get Bugbey to admit that he did not know how much of the debris from past and current mining contributed to the raising of the American River.[24] The following is from the hand written, recorded transcript of the cross examination.

Catlin: *I will ask you if these quartz pebbles about the size of those that you produced here are not readily to be found all through that section of the country on the surface of the ground where it is gravelly, on the top of the hill and in other places?*

Bugbey: *There are some places where you can find them on the top of the hill, but in regards to the bars on the river, I have been over most of the bars and have never found them in any quantity until since 1862.*

Catlin: *Are there not plenty in the natural formation on the Salt Bar Hill?*

Bugbey: *I have never examined on the Salt Bar Hill.*

Catlin: *There is considerable excavation on Salt Bar Hill?*

Bugbey: *Yes sir, considerable, but I have never examined it, I have never been back in Salt Bar Hill since they commenced working there, except on the wagon road.*

Catlin: *Is there not all through the red hills around Folsom, in the formations from the bed rock to the tip, is there not plentiful supply of those quartz pebbles?*

Bugbey: *I have never examined any of the excavations.*

Catlin: *Do you know where Chris Lawson's claim is?*

Bugbey: *I do.*

Catlin: *Do you know about the extent of it and the depth of it?*

Bugbey: *By passing I have seen quite a territory there, but I could not give the exact area.*

Catlin: *Can you not pick out of that claim a plentiful amount of those quartz pebbles like those that you have there?*

Bugbey: *I do not think you can.*

Catlin: *Why do you not think so?*

Bugbey: *Well, I was going to answer the question by saying that I have not investigated it, so that I am not qualified to give an opinion.*

Benjamin Norton Bugbey

Catlin: *In passing from the town of Folsom by that short rail road that runs to the quarries, you cross over the sluice ways, the outlet of Chris Lawson's claim, do you not?*

Bugbey: *Yes, sir.*

Catlin: *You see his tail pile running into the river, do you not?*

Bugbey: *I have seen the tailings there, yes, sir.*

Catlin: *Now then, cannot you [place] from that tail pile at any time any quantity of those quartz pebbles?*

Bugbey: *I have never seen enough [of] the tailings to be able to [be] certain. I have never noticed them sufficiently.*

Catlin: *You do not know then?*

Bugbey: *No, sir.*

Catlin: *In excavating under these claims that run along under the town of Folsom, there, the [place], where they have drifted a great deal, you have been engaged or interested in claims at that place [during] your day?*

Bugbey: *Yes, sir.*

Catlin: *Does not that material drifted out of there show a good deal of those quartz pebbles?*

Bugbey: *No, sir, not as far as my experience goes.*

Catlin: *Does it show any?*

Bugbey: *I do not think it does. You may once in a while find a white stone but very seldom.*

Catlin: *Why do you say you do not think so, and why do you say you may find them once in a while?*

Bugbey: *Well, a scattering one.*

Catlin: *Now then, you say that if the Court should go up there to Negro Bar and look at the bar, that has lots of quartz pebbles [we'd find] specimens of the appearance which that bar would present, is that your statement?*

Bugbey: *No, sir, that is not my statement.*

Catlin: *That was the way I understood it?*

Bugbey: *The surface in Negro Bar toward the stream out from the bank is strewn with stone like these on exhibition here.*

Benjamin Norton Bugbey

Catlin: *What is the general appearance of Negro Bar standing on the edge of the bar there and looking down upon it, what does its general appearance present?*

Bugbey: *The appearance of a bar.*

Catlin: *What kind of a bar? A sand bar?*

Bugbey: *Well sir, a gravel and sand and stream with pebbles.*

Catlin: *Would you see any of these pebbles standing on the bank?*

Bugbey: *With a white cast. I do not know whether you would notice it particularly so as to select them out, but you could not help noticing the white appearance that they give. I suppose that I could explain my meaning to you, so that you could understand it better, if I would say that this is not the only kind of rock there, by any means, but they are in there with other rock, and in great quantities, and different from what they were prior to 1862.*

Catlin: *Well, are not these pebbles seen with other rocks in the original bank formation upon both sides of the [river] material which is mined, is it a light sandy material or is it a hard cemented material?*

Bugbey: *Well, it varies, pretty heavy material as a general thing that is mined in the river and on the banks, some coarse sand and some of a clayey texture, a clayey character.*[25]

Bugbey discussed his drift mining days at Folsom, specifically, how the miners would separate the pay dirt from the cobblestones in the mine. Cobblestones were left behind, the dirt hauled out to be washed for placer gold. Catlin also focused on Texas Hill, which was west of Negro Bar. It had been completely sluiced away by miners, leaving only cobblestones. In questioning Bugbey, Catlin asked how Texas Hill had been reduced to a pile of cobblestones. Was it by rockers or sluices? Bugbey replied, "Well, in early days, some by long toms, in a ditch that you used to be interested in, that used to supply them with water."[26]

A. P. Catlin was one of the founders of the Natoma Water and Mining Company that supplied water to the Texas Hill area for mining. Bugbey casually slipped in this reference to highlight Catlin's responsibility for any debris in the river that was now causing problems. Earlier in the cross-examination, Catlin had grilled Bugbey on his current occupation.

Catlin: *What is your occupation now?*

Benjamin Norton Bugbey

Bugbey: *I am now introducing a patent right, I am living at Folsom, however engaged in a small degree in fruit raising.*

Catlin: *Fruit raising and introducing a patent right?*

Bugbey: *Yes sir, introducing a refrigerator.*

Catlin: *Any other occupation?*

Bugbey: *No sir, I have been handling other articles, but that is my occupation now.*

Catlin: *What has been your occupation for the last several years?*

Bugbey: *I have been engaged in fruit raising in Folsom, until within a year I have been engaged in canvassing for the refrigerator that I spoke of and for books.*

Catlin: *Well, what has been your occupation say, for the last 12 years?*

Bugbey: *Up to within from year I have been engaged (indecipherable), the previous 4 1/2 years was engaged in the vineyard business in winemaking and vinicultural business.*

Catlin: *You were engaged a good many years in winemaking, viticulture at a point where the gravel-fill[ed] mines were above Mormon Island on the South Fork?*

Bugbey: *Yes, sir.*

Catlin: *Bugbey's vineyard?*

Bugbey: *Yes, sir.*[27]

While Catlin's line of questioning was to establish that Bugbey was not an expert on the matter of mining in the last 12 years, Bugbey may have taken the questions as a subtle jab at his financial and personal misfortunes. Bugbey and Catlin had known each other for more than 25 years. They both seemed to be sparing with one another in the best possible professional terms. Bugbey would have more interactions with Catlin in the years to come.

Bugbey's Almond Orchard

Free from his employment as a deputy sheriff, Bugbey returned to one of his favorite occupations as farmer. In the spring of 1881, the Folsom Telegraph noted how Bugbey's almond orchard was in full bloom, resembling a sea of popcorn.[28] Unfortunately, a late frost that year killed many of the blossoms, and only a partial crop was expected.[29] It is unknown how Bugbey came by the almond orchard, if he was renting the land or had taken over the management of an existing orchard.

The property may have been along the American River below Folsom. It was reported in January 1880 that Bugbey had unearthed the vertebrae of a whale in an area known as Tutt's Bar.[30] The find was associated with a mining claim that Bugbey may have been working six miles below Folsom.[31] The vertebrae was forwarded to the Academy of Sciences.[32]

One of the occupations Bugbey mentioned in his debris trial testimony was selling books. Bugbey was a collector of books and enjoyed reading. He never had a bookstore and may have sold his own personal collection to generate money. Bugbey would have had a large collection of books related to vineyards, viticulture, and winemaking. The Sacramento City Free Library reported the approval of payment to Bugbey for $26[33] and $8.50[34] in 1881. He may have been selling some of his collection to the library to generate cash.

James Lansing Murder

James Lansing, like Bugbey, was a California Pioneer. Sacramento was shocked and saddened when Lansing was murdered in 1882. In 1861 both Lansing and Bugbey were nominated as candidates for Sacramento County Sheriff in the Union Democratic Party.[35] After a withering 58 ballots, Bugbey prevailed over Lansing for the nomination.[36] Lansing, also the Secretary of the Settler's Committee, helped Bugbey secure that group's endorsement for the 1861 campaign that Bugbey won to become Sheriff.[37]

After Bugbey became Sheriff, he hired James Lansing as one of his deputies.[38] Lansing demonstrated his loyalty to Bugbey when he testified that he saw no brutality by Bugbey or other deputies in the beating of a Chinese man in the Sheriff's office in 1862.[39] In 1865, Bugbey and Lansing had aligned themselves with different Union political parties. Bugbey was not nominated to run as a candidate for the Union Democratic Party. James Lansing had secured the nomination from the Democratic Party, which was seen as being southern or rebel sympathizers. Bugbey's candidate, John Rooney, withdrew from the race, forcing Bugbey to support a candidate not associated with his political party.[40]

Bugbey ultimately decided to vote for Lansing. After Lansing won, Bugbey even committed $10,000 to Lansing's Sheriff's bond.[41] Bugbey's vote for Lansing and additional support, for a person outside of his Union Democrat Party, would be used against him in the future. When Bugbey was nominated to be an Internal Revenue Assessor, James McClatchy went after Bugbey in editorials that questioned his loyalty to the Union because of his support of Lansing.[42] McClatchy's arguments prevailed, and Bugbey's presidential nomination was withdrawn.

James Lansing served one term as Sheriff. He also served as Assessor of Sacramento County and a U. S. Marshall. He gave up the rigors of public life and law enforcement and, with his wife, opened the International Hotel on K Street between 3rd and 4th Streets in Sacramento. On April 10th, 1882, James Lansing was attending to the chores of the hotel in the back alley. He was unaware that, as he worked, a man, Raten, was attempting to kill an old foe with a pistol in front of the hotel. The shot missed the intended target and hit a passing pedestrian in the hand.[43]

Raten then fled around the block and started running down the alley. As Raten ran by, Lansing, the retired law enforcement officer, gave chase after hearing the cries to stop Raten. Raten turned toward Lansing, and, as Lansing protested "don't shoot," Raten fired the pistol, hitting Lansing in the chest.[44]

News of Lansing's being shot and his impending death spread quickly. Bugbey reached his old friend's side as he lay dying in his bed. Lansing knew he was close to death and wanted to make a statement of the facts about his being shot. He recounted how he did not know the fleeing man and was only running after him to offer assistance. Lansing stated that he was shot fewer than 15 feet away from Raten, then stumbled back to the hotel as fast as he could. Bugbey was a witness to his statement.[45]

Bugbey and Lansing had many shared interests other than law enforcement and politics. They were also members of the Order of Chosen Friends.[46] The order was founded with the mission of securing funds to pay for old age and disability benefits for its members.[47] Bugbey and Lansing were both in their 50s, and Bugbey had proven how easily it was to lose everything you had worked for in a short period of time. Bugbey was one of the pallbearers for Lansing representing the Order of Chosen Friends.[48]

Final Folsom Fire

One month after laying Lansing to rest, Bugbey was visited once again by fire. While he and Julia were at church, their home in Folsom caught fire.[49] Even though Bugbey did have some fire insurance, it wasn't enough. The cost to rebuild was beyond his means.

Bugbey's second home was the State Fair. Every September, Bugbey could be found at the Agricultural Pavilion exhibiting his latest product, invention, or produce from his latest farming adventure. In 1882 Bugbey exhibited not only the Bundock patented butter-cooler, but also a combination doorbell and burglar alarm.[50] The inventor of the doorbell-burglar alarm was John P. Odbert, a farmer and rancher in the Slough House and Brighton Townships. Bugbey knew Odbert through political affiliations, and Odbert had once served as Justice of the Peace for Lee Township.[51]

J. P. Odbert was one of the first in the area to experiment with a steam-powered plow at his vineyard in Brighton.[52] Bugbey was attracted to big machines and mechanical inventions. But in 1872, at the time the steam plow was pulverizing the earth outside of Sacramento, Bugbey was beginning the fight to save his own vineyards and in no position to experiment with the new technology at the Natoma Vineyard.

Bugbey's Railroad Refrigerator Car

Before Bugbey even launched his vineyard, he was a witness on a patent for a steam-powered railroad locomotive turntable. In 1861, Gilbert Cole, who was living in Folsom at the time, was issued a patent for powering a turntable, a circular platform that would rotate, constructed next to a locomotive roundhouse, powered with steam from the engine.[53] Instead of manually rotating the large turntable to the proper track, with the engine resting upon it, steam would be piped from the engine to supply the motive power to the cog-works.[54]

Perhaps out of necessity, the early 1880s were Bugbey's creative period. He needed to generate an income, but he also had plenty of time to think. Over the prior 25 years, he had witnessed some pretty amazing events and inventions. There were the massive water projects of the Natoma Canal and North Fork Ditch that supplied water to miners along the north and south forks of the American River. Gold mining began with picks and pans, evolved to rockers, sluice boxes, and finally to the giant monitors used for hydraulic mining and dredging machines.

He watched as the first railroad west of the Mississippi was built from Sacramento to Folsom. Then a towering bridge over the American River was constructed for the California Central Railroad in Folsom. That was followed by the Transcontinental Railroad that started in Sacramento and conquered the Sierra Nevada over Donner Summit.

Bugbey had his own pioneering construction with his Natoma Vineyard and the Johnston brandy still. He watched as Sacramento grew and California's state capitol was built with granite from his home town of Folsom.

When Bugbey arrived in Sacramento in the summer of 1849, the city was a collection of wooden buildings, outnumbered by canvass tents, that often times served the dual purpose of business by day and residence by night. He had seen men become fabulously wealthy through gold mining, mercantile businesses, and railroad investing.

Benjamin Norton Bugbey

Even though the great Gold Rush had subsided decades earlier, Bugbey was surrounded by men who were still capitalizing on the potential of the Central Valley of California.

Even at the age of 55, Bugbey didn't slow down. He couldn't slow down. He had a young wife to support, and he was still optimistic about the future and his prospects. It was just a matter of finding the next big idea, solution, or invention.

Three elements that were prominent in Bugbey's life in 1882 were his marketing of the butter cooler, the two railroads that operated out of Sacramento (CPRR and SVRR), and the sweltering heat of a Central Valley summer. It's not a stretch to conclude that those elements, combined with the entrepreneurialism prevalent in Sacramento, led Bugbey to design a refrigerated or water-cooled railroad car.

Bugbey decided to apply the evaporative cooling effect of the water-filled terra cotta butter cooler and incorporate it into a railroad freight car. In a sense, he was proposing a giant butter cooler on railroad wheels. As improbable as this may seem, Bugbey was awarded a United States Patent for his Refrigerator-Car design on January 9, 1883.[55]

Refrigerator Car
To all whom it may concern:
Be it known that. I, BENJAMIN N. BUGBEY, of Sacramento, in the county of Sacramento and State of California, have invented a new and Improved Refrigerator-Car, of which the following is a full, clear, and exact description.

My invention consists of a layer of clay, plaster-of-paris, or other porous absorbent material, located between the outer shell of boards and an inner partition, the said clay or plaster layer being provided with a system of water-courses of perforated metallic pipes, clay pipes, or otherwise-formed water channels or courses arranged for the circulation of water throughout the clay or plaster for saturating it to produce a cooling effect by evaporation; and the invention consists of the combination, with the said evaporating-layer, of an inner course or layer of charcoal, pulverized and closely packed between partitions of the sides of the car, for the destruction of unpleasant odors from the goods in transit, and in the combination, with said system of water-courses in a clay or plaster layer and the said charcoal layer, of a layer of sawdust to take up the dampness and protect the interior of the car from moisture, all as hereinafter fully described. - United States Patent No. 270,383, January 9, 1883

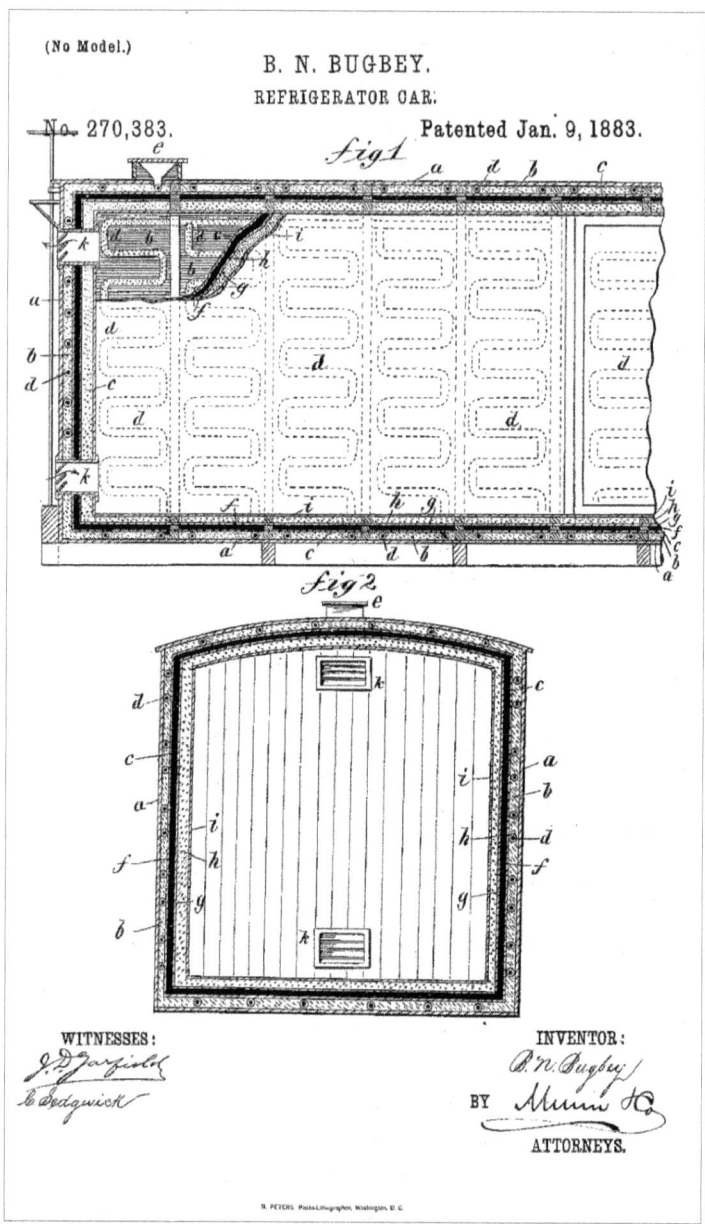

Figure 22: 1883 - Railroad freight car refrigerator illustration patented by B. N. Bugbey.

While Bugbey's description and line drawings were very detailed, there was no inclusion in the patent submission as to the cooling capacity of the design. It may not have performed any better than the currently practiced method which was to fill the box car with ice to keep the contents cool on its journey. The other issue was construction and weight. The water-filled clay liner on all sides of the box car would have added several hundred pounds, at a minimum, to the weight of the freight car. This would have reduced the number of cars that could be attached to an engine for the climb up and over Donner Summit. However, it might not have been Bugbey's intention to actually build and sell any refrigerator cars. He was most likely hoping someone would pay him for the patent rights.

Patching & Darning Tool

In the spring of 1883, Bugbey started promoting a patching and darning utensil. More specifically, he was advertising to enlist men and women to sell Bugbey's Patching and Darning tool. For the low price of only Fifty Cents, this new invention was touted as a labor saver similar to the sewing machine. Bugbey's pitch was that the initial investment in inventory on the part of a person willing to canvas the countryside would result in a good return on the investor's capital. People interested in getting in on the ground floor of this investment opportunity were encouraged to visit Bugbey's display at Hobby's Stone and Earthenware at 317 J Street, Sacramento. Hobby's was also the location where Bugbey was selling his celebrated butter cooler.[56]

Of course, at the State Fair in 1883, Bugbey displayed the darning and patching tool, butter cooler, Wible's patented lubricated axle, and the model of a new design for drawbridges, also invented by Rev. E. A. Wible.[57] For his wonderful display of unique and time-saving devices, Bugbey was awarded a diploma by the State Agricultural Committee.[58] Later in 1884, Bugbey would add an improved farm gate to the growing list of items he represented. He advertised for sales agents to represent the *Best Farm Gate In The World*.[59] Prospective consumers and agents could examine Bruce's Patented Farm Gate on display at the Seavey House on the corner of 12th and J streets in Sacramento.[60]

With the loss of his Folsom residence to fire, Bugbey and Julia were renting a home in Sacramento. Bugbey was also managing the Seavey House Hotel and was living at 614 Thirteenth Street in Sacramento.[61] This only made sense because his consumer base was located in Sacramento, along with most of his business associates.

Benjamin Norton Bugbey

Bugbey Leaves Folsom For Sacramento

By 1884 Bugbey had made the permanent move from Folsom to Sacramento. He would never again call Folsom his home. While Bugbey's heart may have been in the country, his business interests were now tied to the large metropolis of Sacramento. One of his first orders of business was to run for elected office. Bugbey announced his candidacy for the First Trustee position in the city of Sacramento in February 1884.[62] He was formally nominated at the Republican Party Sacramento City Convention in March.[63] The convention was chaired by Grove L. Johnson, who was tied to Bugbey in a voter fraud scandal in the 1860s.

Real Estate Sales

Bugbey was not successful in his attempt to become a city trustee. Nor was he successful in a later attempt in 1884 to be elected Sacramento County Clerk.[64] Bugbey may have become interested in the County Clerk position as he launched a new career path as a real estate agent. In March of 1884, he started advertising his services as a real estate agent and mortgage lender.[65] He was advertising two farms for sale, one in Placer County. In addition, he could arrange the financing in sums of $500 to $10,000.

By August of 1884, he was advertising the sale of eight different farm properties. There was the E. B. Crocker ranch in Penryn, 160 acres at Rose Springs north of Folsom, and 257 acres west of Shingle Springs, known as the old Duroc Ranch, on the railroad line that ran from Folsom to Placerville. Bugbey had owned the Duroc vineyards before he had to sell it off in pieces in the 1870s to raise cash.[66] Bugbey also reminded people in the advertisement that his past experience in agriculture meant they could rely on his assessments of the property.

All of the above property is of the choicest selections. I have had large experience in fruit and grape growing, and a general knowledge of soils, and I recommend the above as the best quality. I offer them at a bargain. For terms apply to B.N. Bugbey. 614 Thirteenth St.[67] – Sacramento Daily Union, Volume 51, Number 140, 2 August 1884

Bugbey's real estate business quickly grew to include residential property in the city of Sacramento. He was offering a one-story brick home at the corner of 3rd and S streets for $3,500. There was also a lot on S Street for $750, with the bonus that it was higher than the surrounding grade.[68]

He also listed some commercial properties. He had a grand bargain, in his words, for three different hotels in downtown Sacramento. Monthly rental receipts were $900 with a clean title. He opined that, "This is the best chance for a cash investment ever offered in Sacramento since the days of '49."[69]

Figure 23: 1886 - Real Estate advertisement in the Pacific Rural Press, listing properties that B. N. Bugbey had for sale in Northern California. CDNC

The Miracle Worker

At 57 years old, Bugbey was not without his ailments. He apparently suffered from deafness in his left ear. He not only found a cure, he found another way to get his name in the newspapers. A traveling medicine man by the name of Dr. MacLennan visited Sacramento and advertised some of the wonderful cures he had accomplished as a celebrated healer. Bugbey lent his name to be included in a testimonial of the doctor's medical prowess.

> *Mr. B. N. Bugbey, an old and well known resident of this city, and formerly sheriff of this county, living at 614 Thirteenth street, was instantly cured the other day of a long-standing case of deafness of the left ear.*[70] - Sacramento Daily Union, Volume 52, Number 52, 24 October 1884

There was no mention of the type of treatment Bugbey received from Dr. MacLennan. However, a buildup of ear wax is easily removed and restores hearing instantly. With his hearing restored, not that it was ever an impediment for Bugbey, he proudly marches with the Sacramento City Republican Third Ward Club in October 1884. He was also named a vice president of the club.[71]

As 1884 closed, it had been six years since Bugbey was forced into bankruptcy. As a solidly middle-aged man, he was able to rebuild income for him and Julia in Sacramento. He still had many friends who believed in him, even if he could not get elected to any office he ran for. He exhibited a sense of optimism in all his endeavors. He still had faith in himself. From his political and social activities, he was once again a fixture and personality in the city of Sacramento.

Since recovering from his devastating bankruptcy, Bugbey had been forced to diversify his income streams. As much as he tried to build any of the numerous business ventures he undertook, none were a solid and consistent form of income. In 1885 he added fire and life insurance to a portfolio of products he was now representing. He had left behind his focus on retail products such as the butter cooler and darning and patching contraption in favor of professional services, such as real estate, appraisals, and insurance sales. Bugbey's new service offerings meant that he needed a proper space to conduct business.

He set up an office in Mike Bryte's building on the southwest corner of 7th and J streets. In addition to the newly acquired insurance business, he continued to sell real estate and arrange mortgage loans. He was also promoting himself as a property manager who would collect rents and bills for a fair commission.[72]

Bugbey was able to pick up a few clients for his new business endeavors. In March he advertised two cottages for rent, located in the "...healthiest part of the city."[73] The adjective "healthiest" was a subtle acknowledgement that Sacramento had a sanitary sewer drainage problem. Animal and human waste was either held on site or dumped in sloughs, creating areas of foul-smelling air.[74] The miasma, or unhealthy vapors, was thought to cause all sorts of medical illnesses at the time.

Representing the Sun Insurance Company as an agent, Bugbey was successful in selling some fire insurance. A fire at 12th and G streets, behind Frank Ruhstaller's home at 13th and H streets, damaged one of Bugbey's client's homes.[75] Bugbey's experience with fire loss made him a natural agent for home insurance to protect from the financial losses of such calamities.

Mike Bryte

As Bugbey's real estate and insurance business grew, he was able to rent a real office in the Mike Bryte building as opposed to working out of his house. Mike Bryte had died in February 1882,[76] but Bugbey was an old acquaintance of his. Both men came to California in 1849. Whereas Bugbey's first attempt at farming out at Salisbury Station failed, Bryte started a dairy farm across the river from Sacramento in Yolo County and was successful. Bryte's dairy operation grew, and he was able to invest in other business opportunities, such as the Odd Fellows Bank of Savings.[77]

Mike Bryte was also a fellow Republican Party member. In 1871 he was nominated over Adolf Heilbron and Bugbey to be the party's nominee for Sheriff of Sacramento County.[78] As Sheriff of Sacramento County, Bryte had to auction off Bugbey's home in Folsom after Bugbey failed to repay the mortgage to C. T. H. Palmer.[79] Bryte was also on the State Agricultural Society Board[80] and was active at the State Fair.

After leaving the position of Sheriff, Bryte invested in the Johnston Winery and Distillery and was named president of the corporation.[81] Bugbey's was one of the first wineries to promote the patented George Johnston brandy distillation process at his Natoma Vineyards. Both Bryte and Bugbey had also been chairmen for the County Republican Central Committee.[82] The lives of both men intertwined and crossed each other's paths often in Sacramento.

With the exception of his early death at the age of 53, Mike Bryte represented to Bugbey the ascendency of a pioneer life that he aspired to. This ideal life revolved around agriculture, business and law enforcement. It was Bryte's solid dairy operation that generated the cash flow that allowed him to become involved in law enforcement, civic activities, and other Sacramento business interests. It was the demise of the Natoma Vineyards that curtailed Bugbey's preferred arc of life as agriculturist and political operative. But Bugbey continued to press forward, nurturing opportunities for income and working to once again be relevant in politics and the social affairs of Sacramento. Given his history and connection with Mike Bryte, it was a natural decision for Bugbey to set up an office in the building of a former friend.

Benjamin Norton Bugbey

Sacramento Home

In March 1885 Bugbey made it official that he would never be returning to Folsom as a permanent resident. The property in Folsom, lots 5 – 16 in Block 53, which had been deeded to his wife, Julia, was finally sold to Mancron Slayback for $1,400.[83,84] With the cash from the sale of the Folsom property, Bugbey could look to purchase a permanent home in Sacramento. He and Julia located a nice home at the corner of 23rd and N streets in Sacramento.

They purchased the property from Catherine Wright for $3,000.[85] The home purchase was a complicated set of transactions, because a friend of Bugbey's, John Parker, was also part-owner of the house.[86] Bugbey was eventually able to arrange other financing by selling his interest in the home to William Wackford of Placer County[87] and buying out Parker.[88] Bugbey was able to get a mortgage from Henry Wittenbrick to pay off Wackford in 1886.[89] The number of different owners and lenders illustrates how Bugbey, while earning enough money to pay for his daily bread, was still struggling financially.

Then a curious event occurred in June of 1885, while Bugbey was arranging financing for his new home. Bugbey was arrested for disturbing the peace by officer Farrell.[90] In July the case was dismissed.[91] Reports don't mention Bugbey being inebriated, so he probably had not fallen off the wagon. It is unclear whether Bugbey was arguing or celebrating. However, Bugbey's fortunes seemed to be on an upswing. In December of 1885, he traveled to San Francisco[92], which may have been a harbinger of new opportunities in 1886.

---

[1] Sacramento County Deed Book 18800323, page 18

[2] Sacramento County Deed Book 18810103, page 144

[3] Ibid.

[4] Sacramento Daily Union, Volume 8, Number 154, September 6, 1879, CDNC

[5] Sacramento Daily Union, Volume 11, Number 5, February 27, 1880, CDNC

[6] Sacramento Daily Union, Volume 12, Number 28, September 23, 1880, CDNC

[7] Ibid.

[8] Sacramento Daily Union, Volume 12, Number 70, November 11, 1880, CDNC

[9] Sacramento Daily Union, Volume 12, Number 144, February 5, 1881, CDNC

[10] Sacramento Daily Union, Volume 14, Number 28, September 22, 1881, CDNC

[11] Land Park News, Lance Armstrong, October 13, 2016, Valley Community Newspapers, Inc.

[12] Pacific Rural Press, Volume 23, Number 4, January 28, 1882, CDNC

13 Sacramento Daily Union, Volume 14, Number 30, September 24, 1881, CDNC

14 Sacramento Daily Union, Volume 16, Number 19, September 12, 1882, CDNC

15 Ibid.

16 Sacramento Daily Union, Volume 15, Number 72, May 16, 1882, CDNC

17 Sacramento Daily Union, Volume 17, Number 54, April 25, 1883, CDNC

18 Sacramento Daily Union, Volume 18, Number 65, November 6, 1883, CDNC

19 Sacramento Daily Union, Volume 13, Number 137, July 30, 1881, CDNC

20 Sacramento Daily Union, Volume 14, Number 75, November 16, 1881, CDNC

21 Sacramento Daily Union, Volume 14, Number 96, December 10, 1881, CDNC

22 *The People of the State of California vs The Gold Run Ditch and Mining Company, In the Superior Court of the State of California, in and for the County of Sacramento*, testimony of B. N. Bugbey, December 9th and 10th, 1881, Sacramento, Ca, California State Archives microfilm MF2:9 (46) Roll 4, Pages 4558 – 4599

23 Ibid.

24 Ibid.

25 Ibid.

26 Ibid.

27 Ibid.

28 Sacramento Daily Union, Volume 13, Number 10, March 4, 1881, CDNC

29 Pacific Rural Press, Volume 21, Number 21, May 21, 1881, CDNC

30 Sacramento Daily Union, Volume 10, Number 123, January 13, 1880, CDNC

31 Daily Alta California, Volume 32, Number 10872, January 20, 1880, CDNC

32 Sacramento Daily Union, Volume 10, Number 123, January 13, 1880, CDNC

33 Sacramento Daily Union, Volume 13, Number 117, July 7, 1881, CDNC

34 Sacramento Daily Union, Volume 14, Number 63, November 2, 1881, CDNC

35 Sacramento Daily Union, Volume 21, Number 3199, June 28, 1861, CDNC

36 Sacramento Daily Union, Volume 21, Number 3201, July 1, 1861, CDNC

37 Sacramento Daily Union, Volume 21, Number 3236, August 12, 1861, CDNC

38 Sacramento Daily Union, Volume 22, Number 3285, October 8, 1861, CDNC

39 Sacramento Daily Union, Volume 23, Number 3511, June 28, 1862, CDNC

40 Sacramento Daily Union, Volume 29, Number 4510, September 5, 1865, CDNC

41 Sacramento Daily Union, Volume 30, Number 4587, December 4, 1865, CDNC

42 Sacramento Daily Union, Volume 32, Number 4964, February 25, 1867, CDNC

43 Sacramento Daily Union, Volume 15, Number 42, April 11, 1882, CDNC

44 Ibid.

45 Ibid.

46 Sacramento Daily Union, Volume 15, Number 44, April 13, 1882, CDNC

47 https://en.wikipedia.org/wiki/Order_of_Chosen_Friends

48 Sacramento Daily Union, Volume 15, Number 44, April 13, 1882, CDNC

49 Sacramento Daily Union, Volume 15, Number 71, May 15, 1882, CDNC

50 Sacramento Daily Union, Volume 16, Number 21, September 14, 1882, CDNC

51 Sacramento Daily Union, Volume 23, Number 3574, September 11, 1862, CDNC

52 Sacramento Daily Union, Volume 43, Number 7466, April 18, 1872, CDNC

53 Sacramento Daily Union, Volume 22, Number 3337, December 7, 1861, CDNC

54 G. M. Cole Turn Table, September 17, 1861, U.S. Patent No. 33294

55 B. N. Bugbey Railroad Refrigerator Car, January 9, 1883, U.S. Patent No. 270383

56 Sacramento Daily Union, Volume 17, Number 54, April 25, 1883, CDNC

57 Pacific Rural Press, Volume 26, Number 12, September 22, 1883, CDNC

58 Ibid.

59 Sacramento Daily Union, Volume 19, Number 24, March 20, 1884, CDNC

60 Ibid.

61 Ibid.

62 Sacramento Daily Union, Volume 19, Number 7, February 29, 1884, CDNC

63 Sacramento Daily Union, Volume 19, Number 9, March 3, 1884, CDNC

64 Sacramento Daily Union, Volume 51, Number 115, July 4, 1884, CDNC

65 Sacramento Daily Union, Volume 19, Number 31, March 28, 1884, CDNC

66 Sacramento Daily Union, Volume 51, Number 140, August 2, 1884, CDNC

67 Ibid.

68 Sacramento Daily Union, Volume 51, Number 147, August 11, 1884, CDNC

69 Sacramento Daily Union, Volume 51, Number 160, August 26, 1884, CDNC

70 Sacramento Daily Union, Volume 52, Number 52, October 24, 1884, CDNC

71 Sacramento Daily Union, Volume 52, Number 55, October 28, 1884, CDNC

72 Sacramento Daily Union, Volume 52, Number 135, January 31, 1885, CDNC

73 Sacramento Daily Union, Volume 53, Number 31, March 31, 1885, CDNC

74 *Water, Our History & Our Future*, (Sacramento History Journal of the Sacramento County Historical Society, Volume VI No. 1, 2, 3, & 4, 2006).

75 Sacramento Daily Union, Volume 53, Number 137, July 31, 1885, CDNC

76 Sacramento Daily Union, Volume 14, Number 142, February 4, 1882, CDNC

77 Sacramento Daily Union, Volume 40, Number 7063, January 2, 1871, CDNC

[78] Sacramento Daily Union, Volume 41, Number 7204, June 15, 1871, CDNC

[79] Sacramento County Deed Book 1874116, pages 13 – 15

[80] Sacramento Daily Union, Volume 25, Number 3888, September 7, 1863, CDNC

[81] Sacramento Daily Union, Volume 2, Number 268, January 1, 1877, CDNC

[82] Sacramento Daily Union, Volume 3, Number 137, August 6, 1877, CDNC

[83] Sacramento Daily Union, Volume 53, Number 23, March 20, 1885, CDNC

[84] Sacramento County Deed Book 18850318, page 119

[85] Sacramento County Deed Book 18850318, page 114

[86] Ibid.

[87] Sacramento County Deed Book 18851024, page 301

[88] Sacramento County Deed Book 18851024, page 303

[89] Sacramento County Deed Book 18861109, page 219

[90] Sacramento Daily Union, Volume 53, Number 104, June 23, 1885, CDNC

[91] Sacramento Daily Union, Volume 53, Number 118, July 9, 1885, CDNC

[92] Sacramento Daily Union, Volume 54, Number 91, December 5, 1885, CDNC

Benjamin Norton Bugbey

Chapter 13: Return to Law Enforcement 1886 U.S. Commissioner

Bugbey had a variety of interests in life that he pursued and that were part of his identity. He loved politics and agriculture. He also developed a deep association and identity with law and its enforcement. He would always gravitate back to law enforcement for many reasons, not the least of which was that it provided a source of income. It was a line of work that he could slip back into when the opportunity arose, based on his past experience as Constable and Sheriff. He worked brief stints as a night watchman in San Francisco, as deputy sheriff, and as a courier who delivered prisoners to Folsom State Prison.[1]

These episodic employment opportunities were largely based on his relationships with whomever happened to be Sacramento County Sheriff at the time. If a Republican happened to be Sheriff, Bugbey might be able to pick up some side work, if not be fully employed by the department.

If one of the hallmarks of the life of a man is measured by the company he keeps, Bugbey felt most comfortable with people from law enforcement. Even though Bugbey was involved in church, civic affairs, mining, and agriculture, his closest confidants throughout his life were usually men from law enforcement and former Sheriffs. Most of Bugbey's longtime friends and acquaintances were former law enforcement officers and Sheriffs, such as James Lansing, Mike Bryte and Moses Drew. Many of these men, as Sacramento County Sheriff, had to auction off Bugbey's property or actually arrest him in the course of their professional duties.

For Bugbey, they were just doing their jobs, just as he had performed his duties when serving as Sheriff. The actual determination regarding the sale of his property or whether he had broken the law was a matter for the courts to decide. Bugbey was exonerated by the court system on numerous occasions for actions that, at the time, seemed to violate the law.

Moses Drew

One of the closest friendships Bugbey had was with former Sacramento County Sheriff Moses Drew. Drew came to California in 1851. Bugbey may have first met him when Drew was working a mining claim with A. P. Catlin at Mormon Island.[2] Catlin would go on to form the Natoma Water and Mining Company and become a judge in Sacramento. From Mormon Island, Drew mined in different locations throughout Northern California.[3]

Drew drifted back to Sacramento and opened up a saloon at 6th and K streets, noted as a gathering place for local citizens and politicians.[4] Since Bugbey was in the business of making and selling wine, brandy and sparkling wine from his Natoma Vineyards, he undoubtedly called on Drew at the saloon.

Both Bugbey and Drew were active first in the Union Party[5] and later in the Republican Party. In 1873 Bugbey supported Moses Drew's nomination for Republican Party candidate for Sacramento County Sheriff.[6] Drew was elected Sheriff in 1874. By 1877 Bugbey's personal and financial life had fallen apart. In September, under the influence of too much alcohol, Bugbey shot Constable Krimble in Folsom.[7] In October, after a jury trial, Bugbey was found not guilty of attempted murder.[8] One can't wonder if Sheriff Drew somehow influenced the proceedings, between arrest, interrogation, and the District Attorney's prosecution of Bugbey.

In 1878, at the height of Bugbey's financial collapse, Drew had to preside over an auction of Bugbey's Folsom property for delinquent property taxes.[9] Fortunately, Emma Bugbey purchased the property and deeded it back to Bugbey. In 1879 Sheriff Drew recruited Bugbey to assist him with the execution of a man convicted of murder on Grand Island.[10] Bugbey, who had once been arrested for attempted murder, stood next to Sheriff Drew on the execution scaffolding to prepare a man to be hanged for murder. Even though Bugbey had lost his winery and his marriage, and had been arrested for shooting a man, he was in the company of the current Sheriff of Sacramento County, along with former sheriff H. M. La Rue and Chief of Police E. M. Stevens. This was affirmation that, regardless of Bugbey's lost status as a businessman or transgressions of the law, he was still viewed as a lawman. This was all at the direction of Moses Drew.

Later in the year, Bugbey and Drew were selected as delegates to the Republican Party State Convention.[11] Sheriff Drew hired Bugbey to be a Deputy Sheriff, and Bugbey became the lead investigator in the Lamblett murder investigation in Folsom.[12] In February of 1880, Sheriff Drew had to execute the order to sell Bugbey's Folsom property again, this time to satisfy a judgment against Bugbey by his ex-wife, Martinette.[13] Bugbey would be saved by the aunt of his new wife, Evarilla Wood, who would buy the property and deed it to Julia Bugbey. Even through all of Bugbey's personal and financial troubles, Moses Drew had faith in Bugbey. Whenever possible, he gave Bugbey a job.

When Adolf Heilbron became Sheriff of Sacramento County, Bugbey was out of a job as a Deputy Sheriff. However, in 1881 Moses Drew became a United States Marshal, whose headquarters was in San Francisco.[14] The role of U.S. Marshals is to enforce federal laws. They work in close cooperation with the Department of Justice attorneys and federal judges. San Francisco was the seat of the United States District Court for the District of California at the time. U. S. Marshals also assist U. S. Commissioners in serving warrants and making arrests at the Commissioner's direction.

Moses Drew would leave the position of U. S. Marshall in 1885. Bugbey made a trip to San Francisco in December of 1885, at the time that Drew was leaving his U.S. Marshal position.[15] Sometime between when Bugbey traveled to San Francisco and March of 1886, he received an appointment as a United States Commissioner based in Sacramento. Given the close relationship between Moses Drew and Bugbey, it's possible Drew encouraged the court to appoint Bugbey as a U. S. Commissioner.

Commissioner Bugbey

A U.S. Commissioner position was usually less than part-time work. A typical case might involve someone not paying a federal excise tax. Bugbey had two Roseville men arrested after they were accused of not paying the federal tax on cigars that they had purchased for resale. Bugbey examined the men and their stories. Bugbey determined that it was a misunderstanding between the men and the cigar factory on I Street, and the charges were dropped.[16]

The first newspaper account of Bugbey's appointment as a U. S. Commissioner was a March 13th story about Commissioner Bugbey presiding over a case involving Chinese men being driven out of the hop fields where they were working in Nicolaus, California.[17]

Nicolaus Mob Drive Out Chinese

This appeared to be a federal case because the action against the Chinese men, who were not U. S. citizens, was a violation of a treaty between the United States and China. Commissioner Bugbey received a complaint from John Sing of Nicolaus that Thomas Baldwin, also of Nicolaus, had conspired with 15 other men to drive him and other Chinese out of their homes near the hop fields where they were working.[18] The complaint asserted that the conspiracy to drive the Chinese out of Nicolaus was an action that deprived the Chinse men of their right to equal protection under the law.

The Chinese Vice-Consul was also in attendance during John Sing's sworn testimony to Bugbey.[19] Representatives of the Chinese government had been very active in pursuing the federal government's agreement to stop the harassment of the Chinese, not only in California, but in other incidents of violence in Oregon and Washington.[20] Vice-Consul Fredrick A. Bee saw to it that Bugbey was aware that the

Benjamin Norton Bugbey

actions of the Nicolaus conspirators also violated the Burlingame Treaty of 1868 between the U.S. and China.[21] The treaty provided that Chinese in the United States would be free from persecution on account of their religious faith or worship in either country and granted certain privileges to citizens of either country residing in the other.

Anti-Chinese Movement

The backdrop for all this international drama, playing out in Bugbey's 10-by-12-foot office on the second floor of the Mike Bryte building in downtown Sacramento, was what could accurately be portrayed as mass hysteria against the Chinese on the West Coast. The racism against Chinese immigrant workers was at a full crescendo in the 1880s. Anti-Chinese sentiment was manifested in proposed expulsion legislation, boycotts, clubs and conventions. An anti-Chinese convention was held in Sacramento in March of 1886.[22] One of the tools to drive Chinese out of California was an endorsement to boycott businesses who employed Chinese labor. Bugbey was familiar with many of the men in the anti-Chinese movement. Charles McGlashan, his former brother-in-law when he was married to Martinette, was hired by the Anti-Chinese Convention to help organize against Chinese immigrants in California.[23] Grove L. Johnson, a fellow Republican, was also active in anti-Chinese groups and meetings.

Anti-Chinese clubs were being formed in small communities across California. The Marysville Anti-Chinese Association was formed in February 1886. Its mission statement was similar to other associations and clubs that were forming regionally.

The object of the Association are to maintain a permanent organization, which shall labor, in all lawful and honorable ways, to discourage and prevent the employment of Chinese labor; to organize agencies for the purpose of furnishing laborers to take the place of the Chinese, and to encourage and promote the manufacture, sale and distribution of the products of white labor, appoint and sustain permanent committees to work in conjunction with other anti-Chinese organizations, to accomplish the peaceable removal of the Chinese from our midst.[24] - Sacramento Daily Union, Volume 54, Number 151, 15 February 1886

The goal of the anti-Chinese clubs was to create such a hostile work and economic environment that the Chinese men would voluntarily leave California. While most of the anti-Chinese clubs were trying to keep their hatred of Chinese workers and desire to expel them completely from California within the boundaries of law, such fevered racist rhetoric against the Chinese was bound to push less ethical and moral men to vigilante actions. The Anti-Chinese Club at Nicolaus in Sutter County gave the Chinese working on hop ranches in the vicinity 10 days to leave the area. In mid-February, members of the Anti-Chinese club, wearing masks, descended on the hop ranches around Nicolaus and drove 46 Chinese workers off of the property and herded them to a barge on the river.[25]

The Nicolaus confrontation and intervention against Chinese men was viewed by Bugbey as a violation of the Burlingame Treaty between the United States and China, and therefore a federal issue. After hearing the complaint by John Sing and Chinese Vice-Consul Bee, Bugbey issued arrest warrants against the men who drove the Chinese out of Nicolaus on the charge of conspiracy to violate the laws and treaties of the United States.[26] U. S. Marshal Franks and Deputy Marshal Robinson then traveled to Nicolaus, where they arrested 16 men and brought them back to Sacramento.[27] Bugbey's decision to arrest the men would trigger a court action that would reach all the way to the United States Supreme Court.

Bugbey went from selling butter coolers and real estate to adjudicating violations of international treaties in a matter of months. He had also placed himself in the vortex of public discourse over whether the Chinese should be allowed to work or even remain in California. No matter how he ruled or what actions he took, he was sure to create enemies in Sacramento.

Even though his Republican Party called for limits on Chinese immigrants and had some elements of strong anti-Chinese sentiment, Bugbey did not necessarily share those opinions. He was a man who had employed Chinese labor at his Natoma Vineyard and went out of his way to describe his Chinese employees as loyal and hardworking. He had also sold real estate to the Chinese man Mum Sing in Folsom. If Bugbey did harbor racist attitudes towards the Chinese, as potentially illustrated in the beating of Chew Yew when he was Sheriff in 1862, they had evolved over time. While Bugbey was a loyal member of the Republican Party and was frequently mentioned in newspaper stories about party activities, his name never surfaces as a member of any anti-Chinese club or convention in Sacramento.

U. S. Commissioner Duties

U. S. Commissioners did not have to have legal training. In the late 1700s, their duties focused on supporting federal circuit court judges with routine functions such as taking bail. Over the decades, the duties of U. S. Commissioners expanded to take affidavits, depositions of witnesses, and the power to arrest and imprison those accused of federal crimes. After the Civil War, commissioners were expected to enforce the Civil Rights Act of 1866. U. S. Commissioners also were empowered to order the removal of any Chinese who were unlawfully residing in the United States.[28]

Most U.S. Commissioners were attorneys who were able to conduct the federal court business out of their offices. Bugbey was not an attorney and was working out of a small office on the second floor of the Mike Bryte building.[29] This necessitated attorneys, defendants, and witnesses to cram into Bugbey's small office and overflow into the hallway. Fortunately, it was spring when the Nicolaus affair occurred with pleasant Sacramento weather. There is no doubt that the temperature inside the little office and that of the attorneys would certainly spike as the case was argued. Bugbey had inserted himself into a culture war.

Shortly after the Nicolaus vigilantes had been arrested, Bugbey set a date for a preliminary hearing and subpoenaed 25 Nicolaus residents to testify to the events. The men arrested were represented by A. L. Hart and Bugbey's longtime acquaintance, Grove L. Johnson.[30]

Constitutional Questions

The central argument for the defense was that Section 5519 of the Revised Statutes of the United States of 1874, under which Bugbey had arrested the men, had been decided unconstitutional by the U. S. Supreme Court in 1882. Section 5519 gave the federal government the authority to prosecute individuals who had conspired to deprive citizens of equal protection under the law. The statute was written to support the 14th Amendment and deter violence against black Americans in the old Confederacy.[31]

The constitutionality of Section 5519[32] was tested when a group of white men from Tennessee were tried and convicted under the statute for assaulting a group of black criminal defendants in the custody of local authorities. The U.S. Supreme Court struck down Section 5519 because they determined the Constitution did not give the federal government the power to legislate against private conduct that was under the purview of a state's jurisdiction.

Section 5519, Revised Statutes of the United States:

If two or more persons in any State or Territory conspire, or go in disguise on the highway or in the premises of another, for the purpose of depriving, either directly or indirectly, any person or class of persons of the equal protection of the laws, or of equal privileges and immunities under the law; or for the purpose of preventing or hindering the constituted authorities of any State or Territory from giving or securing to all persons within such State or Territory the equal protection of the laws: each of such persons shall be punished by a fine of not less than five hundred nor more than five thousand dollars, or by imprisonment, with or without hard labor, of not less than six months nor more than six years, or by both such fine and imprisonment.

Bugbey, along with local attorney A. C. Hinkson, who was representing the Chinese, concluded that Section 5519, as it applied to the Chinese, was constitutional, because the Chinese were not U.S. citizens, and their expulsion from Nicolaus where they were working was a violation of Article VI of the Burlingame Treaty. The Nicolaus incident was not the first ejection of Chinese workers by local men. Earlier in the year, Chinese had been driven out of their homes in Seattle and Tacoma. Riots in Rock Springs, Wyoming, had killed 28 Chinese laborers.[33] Even though President Cleveland announced the federal government would work to maintain order and bring the perpetrators to justice,[34] little happened on either the federal or state level to protect the Chinese.

The violence against the Chinese was widely reported in the newspapers. Bugbey was certainly aware, not only of the other acts against the Chinese, but of the growing anti-Chinese sentiment bubbling over in local town meetings. What was also evident was that the federal government, state or local law enforcement departments were doing nothing to prevent the atrocities.

Given the current anti-Chinese political climate, why would local law enforcement attempt to intervene against local men and in favor of the Chinese? The anti-Chinese movement was strong and growing. No Sheriff or District Attorney was willing to risk his job and political future to oppose the apparent will of his constituency and voters. More than likely, many of the elected officials who could have initiated action against the Nicolaus mob held the same view as the mob: the Chinese did not belong in their communities, working on farms, or for local merchants.

The only means left to Bugbey in the pursuit of justice was to apply Section 5519 in an attempt to hold the Nicolaus mob accountable for its participants' actions. This was a pivotal moment for Bugbey. He clearly knew the federal statute under which he had the Nicolaus men arrested was declared unconstitutional. U. S. Attorney S. G. Hilborn had let it be known that he felt the case should be dismissed.[35] In essence, the local, state, and federal officials were against Bugbey's moving forward with holding the men accountable for their actions. It was only Judge Sawyer who gave Bugbey a little judicial wiggle room.

Judge Lorenzo Sawyer

Benjamin Norton Bugbey

Bugbey and Judge Lorenzo Sawyer became acquainted when Sawyer was elected as a justice to the California Supreme Court in 1863.[36] They would serve together on several local philanthropic committees in Sacramento.[37,38] As a California Supreme Court Justice, Sawyer would hear various cases pertaining to Bugbey related to his time as Sacramento County Sheriff. Judge Sawyer voted to overturn a lower court's decision and order a new trial in *J. Pettri v Bugbey & Beck* in Bugbey's favor in 1864.[39]

In 1870 Lorenzo Sawyer was confirmed as a United States circuit court judge for the Ninth Circuit in California.[40] In 1884 Judge Sawyer ruled against the North Bloomfield Gravel and Mining Company in a lawsuit focused on the tailings generated from North Bloomfield's hydraulic mining operations. His ruling effectively ended hydraulic mining in most of California, and it became known as the Sawyer Decision.[41]

Lorenzo Sawyer was now the supervising judge overseeing U. S. Commissioner Bugbey's execution of his duties. In communication from Judge Sawyer, Bugbey was informed that Section 5519 had been declared unconstitutional. However, in a telegraph to the defendant's attorneys, Hart and Johnson, Judge Sawyer deemed it improper to instruct a judicial officer [Bugbey] on what action Bugbey should take.[42] Sawyer was giving some deference to the position of a U. S. Commissioner and to Bugbey. This deference provided Bugbey just enough room to keep the case in play.

Bugbey could have dismissed the charges against the men and avoided any reprisals, either socially or professionally, for defending Chinese immigrants. But he did not dismiss the charges. The only conclusion that can be drawn is that Bugbey truly believed that, in the absence of any local or state action, the federal government had to hold these men accountable for their despicable actions against a class of people who were just trying to earn a living.

Habeas Corpus

As Commissioner, Bugbey did not get very far in his examinations of the Nicolaus men held on violation of Section 5519 before the attorneys for the defendants filed a petition for a writ of habeas corpus[43] on March 16th.[44] This triggered a hearing before Judge Sawyer to determine if the defendants' detention was lawful. Since Judge Sawyer had already communicated that Section 5519 was unconstitutional, he could only really determine that most of the men should be released on their own recognizance.[45]

On March 18th, Deputy Marshal Franks and U.S. Attorney Hilborn brought Thomas I. Baldwin, one of the Nicolaus mob who had driven out the Chinese, before Judge Sawyer. All the attorneys had agreed that Baldwin would be the individual who would represent the entire group of men before the judge. Vice-Consul Bee had retained Hall McAllister to take over representing the Chinese men.[46] McAllister argued before Judge Sawyer that Section 5519 applied to the Chinese, because they were not citizens, and the Supreme Court's decision only applied to citizens of the United States. After hearing McAllister's arguments and that of Hart for the defendants, Judge Sawyer promised to render a decision the next day on March 31.[47]

Judge Sawyer determined that Section 5519 did apply to the persecution of the Chinese at the hands of U.S. citizens. The men who had driven out the Chinese conspired to deprive them of their rights and protection under the law. He wrote,

> *If this section...is valid as to Chinese subjects residing in the United States, and embraces the acts set out in the petition and return, then the acts of all public meetings throughout the land looking to, and providing for, depriving Chinese subjects of the rights, privileges, immunities, and exemptions secured to them...by means of popularly known as 'boycotting,' or any other coercive means, no matter in what form, or through what channels applied, are criminal, and all those participating in them must be subject to the very severe penalties denounced by the statute.*[48]

However, Judge Sawyer knew that there were problems with his interpretation of the section's constitutionality. Statutes that specifically separated different classes of populations in which it applied could be found constitutional to one class, but not the other. Unfortunately, Section 5519 did not make a distinction between U.S. citizens and another class of population, such as immigrants allowed to work in the United States without citizenship.[49]

Sawyer's associate on the Circuit Court, Judge Sabin, dissented. In deference to the prior Supreme Court ruling, Sawyer included a certificate of division of opinion allowing either party to file a writ of error to trigger a U.S. Supreme Court review. In Sawyer's case record sent to the Department of Justice, he asked for a swift review by the U.S. Supreme Court. He wrote, "I can imagine no case that so urgently requires prompt action. The whole [west] coast is inflamed by active men who are organizing to perpetrate similar outrages. If there is any law making such action criminal, it ought to be authoritatively declared."[50]

U. S. Supreme Court Opinion

The U.S. Supreme Court, while acknowledging the severity of the crimes committed by the Nicolaus vigilantes, found that Section

5519 could not be applied to the Chinese, because of the way it was written, and because it did not have separate parts or distinct classes of populations. The federal government could not make laws that superseded the jurisdiction of the states.[51]

Chief Justice Waite delivered the opinion of the court in March 1887. In it he wrote,

> *The result of the decision is that there is no national law which can be invoked for the protection of the subjects of China in their right to reside and do business in this country, notwithstanding the language of the treaty with the empire…Their only protection against any forcible resistance to the execution of these stipulations in their favor is to be found in the laws of the different states. Such a result is one to be deplored.*[52]

Ultimately, Bugbey's actions in defense of the rights of Chinese laborers were not validated. But Bugbey and Judge Sawyer must have felt some solace in the fact that, even though the Supreme Court denied the constitutionality of Section 5519 as it applied to the Chinese, the justices also recognized the monumental injustices being perpetrated upon the Chinese by U. S. citizens. Possibly because of the nod by Judge Sawyer to Bugbey that the Chinese were being unfairly persecuted, Bugbey continued his pursuit of justice for the Chinese.

The Republican Party did not sympathize with Bugbey's arguments in support of the Chinese. At the Republican County Convention of 1886, which Bugbey attended, the platform called for the abrogation of the Burlingame Treaty.[53] The articles of the treaty were part of the foundation of Bugbey's argument as to why the federal government could intervene against efforts to drive Chinese workers away from their jobs. Whether or not the call to abandon the Burlingame Treaty was directed at Bugbey's efforts to use the treaty as a legal means to protect the Chinese is not clear. In any event, Bugbey had to have felt a small sting of rebuke from so many of his friends who supported the anti-Chinese platform.

Chinese Slavery Arrests

Perhaps because Bugbey had stood up to the anti-Chinese influenza infecting so many white people of the time, another complaint was brought before him. This time it was a Chinese man complaining about other Chinese in the Sacramento community. In May of 1886, Ah Wong swore out a complaint against Lee Ah Dot, a Chinese man, and Yu Gim, a Chinese woman, alleging they had purchased and imported Chinese women into Sacramento for the purposes of prostitution.[54] Wong complained that Dot and Gim were holding five women in involuntary servitude at a house on Third Street near I Street.[55]

Similar to the Nicolaus case, the unlawful actions of Dot and Gim were seen as a local law enforcement issue involving illegal confinement and prostitution. Another similarity to the Nicolaus fracas was that local Sacramento law enforcement was not necessarily aggressive in investigating such activities in the Chinese community. Commissioner Bugbey decided to take action and had Dot and Gim arrested for violating the 13th Amendment to the U.S. Constitution prohibiting slavery and Section 5377 of the Revised Statutes, providing against any colored persons being brought to the United States from a foreign country for the purposes of slavery.[56]

Of the five women identified as being held in slavery, only four could be found by the Deputy Marshal. The fifth woman was alleged to have been hidden by her captors.[57] Bugbey needed to examine the women to see if they were indeed held in bondage. One of the four women stated she was a married woman and not under the control of either Dot or Gim.[58] Because of the unusual circumstances, in which one of the women had vanished and there was potential pressure on the women to lie about their situations, Bugbey had the remaining three women, Suey Hoy, Ting Que, and Suey Ye, put under protective custody.[59] The three women went on to allege that Dot had purchased them and that they were held against their will by Gim.[60] Additionally, they had been forced into a life of prostitution and never allowed to leave the house unless accompanied by a man, to ensure they would not run away or be stolen.[61]

General John T. Carey was hired to represent Dot and Gim. Bugbey set their bail at $10,000, required white men to be their bondsmen, and stipulated that, in default of bail, he would send the defendants to jail in San Francisco pending trial in the United States Court.[62] One of the women under protective custody decided she wanted to leave. Bugbey fixed her bond to appear as a witness at $1,000, and she was released.[63] General Carey then procured writs of habeas corpus for the other two women held in protective custody.[64]

On May 23rd Commissioner Bugbey and Deputy Marshal Parker appeared before Judge Van Fleet in the habeas corpus hearing. Bugbey and Parker were represented by Judge S. S. Holl, who argued that if the women were released from protective custody they would be threatened and intimidated by their masters not to testify.[65] Bugbey testified that the women requested some sort of protection from their masters and that they were not imprisoned, but free to leave at any time from the care of a person designated to protect them.[66]

General Carey contended that Bugbey's description of the circumstances surrounding the women was no answer at all. He then went on to accuse Bugbey of entering into a conspiracy with other

Chinese to keep the women for themselves.[67] Judge Van Fleet, dismissing the surprise conspiracy theory against Bugbey, ordered the women to be brought into court for examination.[68]

Bugbey Assaulted By Defense Attorney

The court recessed so the women could be located and brought into court. It was during this interlude that General Carey began to interrogate Bugbey as to his actions in the case. Carey accused Bugbey of delaying the proceedings of Dot and Gim so he could secure passage for the women on a train to San Francisco.[69] The train trip may have been a ruse by Bugbey to keep associates of Dot and Gim from scouring the city to find the women. In reality, they had not permanently left Sacramento.

The animated discourse and subsequent altercation between the two men was reported in the Sacramento Daily Union.

Bugbey attempted to explain that his ruling was not inconsistent with his subsequent action, but Carey interrupted the statement, exclaiming: "Oh, you do not answer my question at all, and you cannot."

"I do not propose that you shall cram any statements down my throat," exclaimed Bugbey.

"And I propose to cram the facts of this case down your throat, and so far into your insides, that they will stick there for years," exclaimed General Carey.

"And I will show that you are attempting to force these women back into slavery and prostitution, in an illegal and cowardly manner," replied Bugbey.

The men were glaring at each other savagely, and the last remark of Bugbey caused Carey to let fly with his right a blow directed at the face of the Commissioner. The latter warded it off and raised his cane to strike back, when the Deputy Sheriffs interfered, and what promised to be a pugilistic encounter was prevented. The affair created considerable excitement, especially among the hundred or more Chinese present, whose jabberings filled the Court-room with a noise equal in inharmonious sounds to that of the confusion of tongues at Babel. After a moment's reflection, General Carey, regretting his act, apologized to Mr. Bugbey. The apology was accepted and the matter dropped.[70] - Sacramento Daily Union, Volume 55, Number 79, 24 May 1886

The Chinese present at the proceedings witnessed a white man being struck by another white man for defending the human rights of Chinese women.

After a short recess, the Chinese women were brought into the court room. They testified they were owned by a Chinese man and forced into prostitution. Neither wanted to return to Sacramento's Chinatown, as they were certain they would be forced to return to their old lives.[71] They stated that they would rather remain in the protective custody of Commissioner Bugbey than return to Chinatown.[72] Judge Van Fleet ruled that he was convinced that Commissioner Bugbey had not violated the rights of the women, and they were free to leave with whomever they wanted.[73] They chose to leave with Commissioner Bugbey and return to their safe house in Sacramento.[74] General Carey, on the losing side of the afternoon's proceedings, left for San Francisco to present his case to Judge Sawyer.[75]

Chinese Confidants

Bugbey had some close confidants within the Chinese community in Sacramento. One was Charley Chung, who was arrested on a vagrancy charge.[76] The police were convinced that Chung was a sentry of sorts for an illicit gambling game known as fan-tan along I Street. Chung claimed he was not a vagrant, but was gathering information for Bugbey. He also accused the arresting officer of extorting him for payment in exchange for not arresting him. The Court dismissed Chung's defense as nothing more than a diabolical lie.[77]

The organized crime elements that Bugbey was working against in the Chinese community knew of Bugbey's informants and used legal means to curtail the investigation into their activities. Charley Chung and Frank Kee had tried to extricate some of the Chinese women being held as prostitutes and move them away from Chinese community.[78] The owners of the women sought a local complaint of conspiracy against Chung and Kee for trying to remove Sing Doy from servitude.

Chung and Kee had been released from custody on their own recognizance, facilitated by supplying a bond underwritten by none other than Bugbey. At the court proceeding against Chung and Kee on conspiracy charges, attorney for the prosecution C. T. Jones argued that Bugbey, who was the bondsman for the defendants, had a conflict of interest in that he was also a U. S. Commissioner in a Chinese slavery case in which both men were involved.[79] It was further argued that Bugbey did not own enough property to act as surety for the amount of the bond.[80] However, the court determined that Bugbey was within his rights to act as a bondsman and had sufficient capital to do so.[81]

Benjamin Norton Bugbey

Bugbey's Above-Ground Railroad

Bugbey's crusade against Chinese slavery and prostitution quickly devolved into a chess match of legal maneuvers. Bugbey was not satisfied with the safety of the women he had removed from the house of prostitution managed by Dot and Gim. There was a fear that the women would be coerced into returning to Chinatown to resume their previous lives of forced prostitution. Bugbey was intent on moving the women down to San Francisco and away from their slave owners.[82] When the women's owners learned of Bugbey's intentions, they had the women subpoenaed as witnesses to the conspiracy charges against Chung and Kee.[83]

Word of the young women's impending departure from Sacramento spread quickly. Officer Sullivan was waiting at the train depot to serve the subpoena to the women. Also gathered to watch the legal confrontation were several Chinese and white men who were patrolling around the depot to make sure the women were not secretly boarded upon the train.[84] Shortly before the train was to depart, Bugbey arrived with the women and boarded the train. Officer Sullivan served the subpoena, and Bugbey accepted the service on their behalf.[85]

Bugbey announced to the officer, newspaper reporter, and others within hearing distance, that the women were being transported to the Presbyterian Mission Home in San Francisco.[86] He also added that Lee Ah Dot and Yu Gim, who were held to answer to him for violating the U. S. law prohibiting slavery, would have the complaint against them heard by a Grand Jury in San Francisco.[87] Since the young women's presence at the Grand Jury proceedings involving Dot and Gim took precedence over the local matter surrounding Chung and Kee, the women would continue on their journey to San Francisco and not stay in Sacramento.[88]

Bugbey's plan to extricate the women from Sacramento and protect them from being forced to return to their owners, was a small legal victory in a larger war. Before any Grand Jury proceedings could occur, a writ of habeas corpus was brought to the United States Circuit Court in San Francisco on behalf of Dot and Gim, held by Commissioner Bugbey. Judges Sabin and Hoffman ruled that Dot and Gim could not be held on violations of Section 5377 of the Revised Statutes with respect to slavery.[89]

Chinese are not Colored People

The ruling that released Dot and Gim had two parts. First, Section 5377[90] refers to people of color, and Chinese immigrants did not fall into that category. Second, slavery was repealed by the 13th Amendment to the Constitution; therefore, the crime of slavery no longer existed.[91] On the first point, a literal interpretation of the statute was applied. Judge Hoffman argued that Section 5377 referred only to Ethiopians or Africans for the purposes of preventing African people who had been kidnapped and transported to the United States from being held in bondage.[92] The word colored could not apply to Chinese, because there was no history of white men importing kidnapped Chinese for the purposes of slavery.[93]

Slavery Not A Federal Crime

On the second point, that slavery had been abolished and was no longer a federal crime, it was asserted that a slave in another country, once he or she sets foot on American soil, transforms into a person who is now free and can assert his or her liberty.[94] Judge Hoffman noted he had consulted with Judge Sawyer, who also concurred with his position.[95] This meant that even though the master of a slave thought he was the slave's owner, the reality was that one person could not own another person in the United States. This left bondage or forced captivity of one human being by another person to be addressed by the statutes of the state. This is assuming that the local authorities would actually arrest and prosecute a Chinese man or woman for false imprisonment or prostitution charges. It was the failure of local law enforcement to prosecute Chinese individuals for the exploitation of young Chinese women imported from China that Bugbey was fighting against.

Bugbey was not the only rational person who failed to understand the application of the law, even though he respected it. Even in the height of anti-Chinese sentiment, the Sacramento Daily Union editorialized on the non sequitur that slavery had been abolished, given the evidence of its continued existence in the city. "To 'outside barbarians' it seems strange that Chinese women can be held in servitude in this country to the extent they are. It cannot be possible that they are unaware of the law of the land, and it follows that if they are aware of their rights it is only fear of personal injury that keeps them in restraint."[96] While the newspaper denounced the actions of the Chinese, and placed the burden of demanding freedom upon women who did not speak English, they did not explicitly call out local law enforcement for its lack of diligence in eradicating the forced confinement of Chinese women for purposes of prostitution.

If one of Bugbey's objectives was to spur local law enforcement to address the human rights abuses occurring in the Chinese community, his efforts in charging Chinese people of crimes under anti-slavery statutes seemed to have little effect. A modest achievement was, at a minimum, to get the local newspapers to write about the deplorable conditions in which some Chinese women were held in Sacramento's Chinatown. Bugbey garnered a modest mention in the local press when he attempted to retrieve from Ah Dot the clothing of the women who had been transported to San Francisco, as they left with only the clothes they were wearing.[97] Bugbey was not successful in his attempt to collect their personal belongings.

Chinese Target Bugbey

While Bugbey may have had little impact on blunting the anti-Chinese sentiment swirling throughout the state and locally, his efforts to stop criminal enterprises within the Chinese community were answered with increased intimidation toward those Chinese cooperating with him. Even though Dot and Gim had been released from custody and the complaint against them dismissed, they were still without the women they owned, as Bugbey had secured their transfer to San Francisco. Rumors began to spread that Chinese fighters were to be brought up to Sacramento, and a gang war could soon break out in Sacramento's Chinatown.[98]

For their cooperation with Bugbey, it was reported that Charley Chung and Frank Kee had a bounty of at least $1,000 for their assassination on their heads.[99] Another Chinese man, Tom Lee, who happened to let it be known he was acquainted with Chung and Kee, was assaulted by half a dozen Chinese men for his suspected association with the men.[100] The elements of the Chinese community who favored the status quo underground illegal activities were now resorting to intimidation and violence to discourage any cooperation with Bugbey.

Gout You Arrested

Bugbey was not deterred in his efforts to thwart the human bondage and prostitution in Chinatown. Five months after the case against Dot and Gim was dismissed, Bugbey had Gout You arrested for keeping three females in involuntary servitude and forced prostitution.[101] Unfortunately for Bugbey, the intimidation of complainants and witnesses by fellow Chinese was escalating. A Chinese man, reportedly only a cousin of the man who filed the complaint against Gout You, visited the police stationhouse requesting protection.[102] He stated that a large crowd of angry Chinese had gathered in front of his business at 318 I Street, threatening him and urging a boycott of his business.[103]

Bugbey had to postpone hearings on several occasions because important witnesses against Gout You were absent. He also expressed his belief that the women freed from Gout You's house of prostitution were being intimidated by friends of You.[104] Bugbey then

Benjamin Norton Bugbey

ordered the United States Marshals to transfer the women to a more secure location to avoid further coercion and intimidation.[105]

The Chinese in attendance at the hearing were decidedly in support of Gout You and immediately began to protest the transfer.[106] The loud cacophony of Chinese protestations piqued the interest of numerous people in the area, creating a large group of white gawkers at the commotion in downtown Sacramento.[107] The spectacle of noise was enhanced when the women began to protest about being led to a more secure safe house. The women screamed, refused to move, and threw themselves down on the sidewalk.[108] This led the Marshals to hail a carriage, and, upon being put into the hack, one of the women broke a glass window out with her shoe.[109]

When the women finally were crammed into the carriage, it was surrounded by Chinese men continuing their vocal protests against the women being taken away. The carriage driver used his whip on the Chinese men to get them to back away, and Marshal Colla drew his pistol in another sign of the seriousness of his intent to transport the women.[110] After the fracas, Bugbey again had to postpone the hearing until the next day. It was later determined that the women were instructed to resist, lie down on the sidewalk, and subsequently break the carriage glass by Chinese men shouting instructions at them to do so.[111]

The Chinese men who made the complaint against Gout You were similarly intimidated by her followers. One man left Sacramento for San Francisco. Bugbey was able to lure him back to Sacramento and then promptly had him jailed for contempt of court.[112] The other witness was more successful at hiding his location and was not found.[113] Finally, in early December, Bugbey was able to hold a hearing at which Hong Kee and Wong Ah Fong testified that the women were held in slavery by Gout You.[114] Commissioner Bugbey concluded that there was enough evidence to sustain the charge against Gout You, and the case against her would be sent to the United States Grand Jury. Counsel for You declined to post the $3,000 bail, as they were certain to secure her release upon a habeas corpus proceeding.[115]

Bugbey knew that Gout You would be released upon a writ of habeas corpus, just as Dot and Gim had been, and the Nicolaus mob as well. The complaint of slavery against You was not materially different from the prior case six months earlier. His real intention seemed to be getting the women who had been held by Gout You out of Sacramento. He declined the request of Gout You's attorneys to introduce testimony and evidence in You's defense[116] because it might necessitate bringing the women into the courtroom and subject them to further intimidation.

After You had been remanded to custody at the jail, along with Kee and Fong for their own protection, Bugbey summoned the three women extricated from You's house of prostitution for a

Benjamin Norton Bugbey

discussion about their rights to live where they wanted. Singly, Bugbey, through an interpreter, explained her options to each of the women. They could leave Sacramento for San Francisco and live at the Presbyterian mission, where he guaranteed their safe passage, or they could return to Chinatown. At that moment in time, all the women expressed a desire to return to Chinatown.[117] This must not have been a surprise to Bugbey, as he understood the coercion and intimidation that was being directed at the women by Gout You's supporters.

Bugbey Helps Chinese Woman Escape

Bugbey's offer to help transport Chinese women held in bondage was not completely dismissed. Two days after the Chinese women had decided to return to Chinatown, Bugbey was approached by a local Chinese man, who knew of a Chinese woman held in Chinatown who wanted to escape to the Presbyterian Mission in San Francisco.[118] Bugbey, acting outside of his official U. S. Commissioner position, orchestrated a plan to spirit the woman away.[119] This was not easy, as Chinese women in these circumstances were carefully watched. This woman was allowed a short daily walk close to Chinatown every day.[120]

It was arranged that she and her Chinese male companion would walk to an area where Bugbey had a carriage waiting. Upon entering the carriage, the woman crouched near the floor so as not to be seen from the sidewalk. The rendezvous was carefully timed to be at the railroad station at the last possible moment to purchase a ticket. She was seen by local Chinese as she exited the carriage, received her ticket, and boarded the train. But by the time her captors were alerted in Chinatown, she was on the train. Bugbey entered the passenger car and explained to the other travelers that the Chinese woman was making a desperate attempt to flee from her captors in Chinatown.[121] The passengers all agreed to protect her and make sure she arrived safely in San Francisco.[122] Bugbey had telegraphed Rev. Masters at the mission in San Francisco to expect her arrival and placed with the woman a "red paper" constituting a note of introduction.[123]

Exit U.S. Commissioner

The position of U. S. Commissioner raised Bugbey's profile as a champion of Chinese immigrants who were vilified and exploited by the local white merchants and landowners. What all of his work did not do was remunerate him for his time. Bugbey was paid only $58.40 for his time adjudicating the Nicolaus vigilante and other cases in the first half of 1886.[124] He earned another $33 for all his trouble on the

Chinatown slavery cases and other items brought before him in the second half of 1886.[125]

Bugbey was not an attorney who could parlay his work as a U. S. Commissioner into legal clients. He was still selling real estate to pay the bills for him and his wife, Julia. In November of 1886, Moses Drew, who may have been instrumental in getting Bugbey the U.S. Commissioner appointment, was elected Sheriff of Sacramento.[126] Shortly after the Gout You case was coming to an inconsequential ending in December, it was announced that Bugbey's old friend and newly elected Sheriff, Moses Drew, would appoint Bugbey as Under Sheriff.[127]

The prospect of a steady paycheck as Under Sheriff was more important to Bugbey than the arduous fight against the entrenched opposition to Chinese immigrants and the federal District Court Judges who failed to see his viewpoint, that the United States Constitution guaranteed equal protection under the law to all residents living in America.

It is hard to estimate to what extent Bugbey's political philosophy toward the Chinese question was shaped or had evolved during his time as U.S. Commissioner. We know that he had no problems employing Chinese at his Natoma Vineyard and sold property to a Chinese man in Folsom. It may have occurred to Bugbey, as it apparently did not too many other white immigrants, that when he came to California, he, too, had been an immigrant, on soil only recently controlled by the United States through the Treaty of Guadalupe. His time spent mining on the American River meant that he routinely encountered not only white miners from the East Coast, like himself, but negro men, some of whom were considered slaves, along with men from countries all over the globe.

As a Gold Rush '49er, Bugbey witnessed how a man's success was measured by his work ethic, along with a little bit of luck in finding the right pocket of placer gold. Success was not determined by the color of a man's skin, religion, or ethnicity. French and German men were just as successful as black men from the south. And there was no disputing the extraordinary amount of work the Chinese sojourners displayed in working claims that had been abandoned or sold after the original claimants had scoured the easily accessible gold.

It was an indisputable fact that the overwhelming majority of men and women who populated California were, in a sense, foreigners. The Native Americans had been decimated by disease and driven onto reservations. Native Mexicans were few to begin with, and their share of the population plummeted with the enormous wave of East Coast immigration into the state.

While we don't know how Bugbey's position on Chinese immigration and the human rights afforded to Chinese immigrants in the United States may have been shifted by his time as U. S. Commissioner, his actions illustrate a man who was willing to buck prevailing anti-Chinese sentiment to take a stand. His attempts to bring justice to Chinese men driven from the hop farms in Nicolaus and then targeting Chinese immigrants who were exploiting young Chinese women were not out of character for Bugbey.

Bugbey was always vocally certain that his position was right. That's why he fought all the lawsuits brought against him and had a very good record of prevailing in those disputes.

But defending the Chinese was not personal for Bugbey, in the sense that his property was at stake. By using his position as U. S. Commissioner to focus a bright light on the hypocrisy of the current treatment of Chinese immigrants, Bugbey risked being ostracized socially and politically. However, at 59 years old, Bugbey may have felt that it was more important to stand up for his principles than to curry favor with either politicians or the voters. He probably also knew that his defense of the Chinese was quietly supported by most people. The newspapers editorialized as much, opining that no man or woman should suffer the indignities to which the Chinese were subjected. Unfortunately, in the overheated climate of racial anti-Chinese rhetoric at the time, few people were willing to openly take a position in defense of human rights.

So Bugbey left his position as U.S. Commissioner in December of 1886. As Under Sheriff he was finally back to the occupation that he felt most suited for in law enforcement.

---

[1] Sacramento Daily Union, Volume 51, Number 82, May 27, 1884, CDNC

[2] Sacramento Union, Volume 161, Number 58, October 28, 1911, CDNC

[3] Ibid.

[4] Ibid.

[5] Sacramento Daily Union, Volume 33, Number 5045, May 29, 1867, CDNC

[6] Sacramento Daily Union, Volume 45, Number 6923, June 11, 1873, CDNC

[7] Sacramento Daily Union, Volume 3, Number 161, September 3, 1877, CDNC

[8] Sacramento Daily Union, Volume 3, Number 214, October 24, 1877, CDNC

[9] Sacramento Daily Union, Volume 3, Number 301, February 2, 1878, CDNC

[10] Sacramento Daily Union, Volume 8, May 30, 1879, CDNC

[11] Daily Alta California, Volume 31, Number 10653, June 13, 1879, CDNC

[12] Sacramento Daily Union, Volume 8, Number 139, August 20, 1879, CDNC

[13] Sacramento Daily Union, Volume 10, Number 154, February 18, 1880, CDNC

[14] Sacramento Union, Volume 161, Number 58, October 28, 1911, CDNC

[15] Sacramento Daily Union, Volume 54, Number 91, December 5, 1885, CDNC

[16] Sacramento Daily Union, Volume 56, Number 94, December 9, 1886, CDNC

[17] Sacramento Daily Union, Volume 55, Number 18, March 13, 1886, CDNC

[18] McClain, Charles J., *The Chinese Struggle for Civil Rights in the 19th Century America: The Unusual Case of Baldwin v Franks*, 3 Law & Hist. Rev. 349, (Berkeley Law Scholarship Repository, Faculty Scholarship, 1985).

[19] Sacramento Daily Union, Volume 55, Number 18, March 13, 1886, CDNC

[20] McClain, Charles J., *The Chinese Struggle for Civil Rights in the 19th Century America: The Unusual Case of Baldwin v Franks*, 3 Law & Hist. Rev. 349, (Berkeley Law Scholarship Repository, Faculty Scholarship, 1985).

[21] https://en.wikipedia.org/wiki/Burlingame_Treaty

[22] Sacramento Daily Union, Volume 55, Number 19, March 15, 1886, CDNC

[23] Ibid.

[24] Sacramento Daily Union, Volume 54, Number 151, February 15, 1886, CDNC

[25] Sacramento Daily Union, Volume 54, Number 155, February 19, 1886, CDNC

[26] Sacramento Daily Union, Volume 55, Number 18, March 13, 1886, CDNC

[27] Ibid.

[28] History of U.S. Commissioners https://www.fjc.gov/history/administration/court-officers-and-staff-commissioners

[29] Sacramento Daily Union, Volume 55, Number 21, March 17, 1886, CDNC

[30] Sacramento Daily Union, Volume 55, Number 20, March 16, 1886, CDNC

[31] McClain, Charles J., *The Chinese Struggle for Civil Rights in the 19th Century America: The Unusual Case of Baldwin v Franks*, 3 Law & Hist. Rev. 349, (Berkeley Law Scholarship Repository, Faculty Scholarship, 1985).

[32] Sacramento Daily Union, Volume 55, Number 21, March 17, 1886, CDNC

[33] McClain, Charles J., *The Chinese Struggle for Civil Rights in the 19th Century America: The Unusual Case of Baldwin v Franks*, 3 Law & Hist. Rev. 349, (Berkeley Law Scholarship Repository, Faculty Scholarship, 1985).

[34] Ibid.

[35] Sacramento Daily Union, Volume 55, Number 21, March 17, 1886, CDNC

[36] https://en.wikipedia.org/wiki/Lorenzo_Sawyer

[37] Sacramento Daily Union, Volume 27, Number 4056, March 22, 1864, CDNC

[38] Sacramento Daily Union, Volume 30, Number 4567, November 10, 1865, CDNC

[39] Sacramento Daily Union, Volume 27, Number 4075, April 13, 1864, CDNC

[40] https://en.wikipedia.org/wiki/Lorenzo_Sawyer

[41] https://en.wikipedia.org/wiki/North_Bloomfield_Mining_and_Gravel_Company

[42] Sacramento Daily Union, Volume 55, Number 21, March 17, 1886, CDNC

[43] Habeas corpus (/ˈheɪbiəs ˈkɔːrpəs/; Medieval Latin meaning literally "that you have the body") is a recourse in law through which a person can report an unlawful detention or

imprisonment to a court and request that the court order the custodian of the person, usually a prison official, to bring the prisoner to court, to determine whether the detention is lawful. https://en.wikipedia.org/wiki/Habeas_corpus

[44] Sacramento Daily Union, Volume 55, Number 21, March 17, 1886, CDNC

[45] Sacramento Daily Union, Volume 55, Number 23, March 19, 1886, CDNC

[46] McClain, Charles J., *The Chinese Struggle for Civil Rights in the 19th Century America: The Unusual Case of Baldwin v Franks*, 3 Law & Hist. Rev. 349, (Berkeley Law Scholarship Repository, Faculty Scholarship, 1985).

[47] Ibid.

[48] Ibid.

[49] Ibid.

[50] Ibid.

[51] Ibid.

[52] Ibid.

[53] Sacramento Daily Union, Volume 55, Number 153, August 18, 1886, CDNC

[54] Sacramento Daily Union, Volume 55, Number 77, May 21, 1886, CDNC

[55] Ibid.

[56] Ibid.

[57] Ibid.

[58] Ibid.

[59] Ibid.

[60] Ibid.

[61] Ibid.

[62] Sacramento Daily Union, Volume 55, Number 78, May 22, 1886, CDNC

[63] Ibid.

[64] Ibid.

[65] Sacramento Daily Union, Volume 55, Number 79, May 24, 1886, CDNC

[66] Ibid.

[67] Ibid.

[68] Ibid.

[69] Ibid.

[70] Ibid.

[71] Ibid.

[72] Ibid.

[73] Ibid.

Benjamin Norton Bugbey

[74] Ibid.

[75] Ibid.

[76] Sacramento Daily Union, Volume 53, Number 137, July 31, 1885, CDNC

[77] Ibid.

[78] Sacramento Daily Union, Volume 55, Number 80, May 25, 1886, CDNC

[79] Ibid.

[80] Ibid.

[81] Ibid.

[82] Ibid.

[83] Ibid.

[84] Ibid.

[85] Ibid.

[86] Ibid.

[87] Ibid.

[88] Ibid.

[89] Sacramento Daily Union, Volume 55, Number 81, May 26, 1886, CDNC

[90] S1. Section 5377. Every person who brings within the jurisdiction of the United States, in any manner whatsoever, any negro, mulatto or person of color, from any foreign kingdom or country, or from sea, or holds, sell or otherwise disposes of any negro, mulatto, or person of color, so brought in, as a slave, or to be held to service or labor, shall be fined not more than $10,000, nor less than $1,000, one half to the use of the United States, and the other half to the use of the party who prosecutes the indictment to effect; and moreover, shall suffer imprisonment at hard labor not more than seven years nor less than three years.

[91] Sacramento Daily Union, Volume 55, Number 81, May 26, 1886, CDNC

[92] Ibid.

[93] Ibid.

[94] Ibid.

[95] Ibid.

[96] Sacramento Daily Union, Volume 56, Number 95, December 10, 1886, CDNC

[97] Sacramento Daily Union, Volume 55, Number 84, May 29, 1886, CDNC

[98] Sacramento Daily Union, Volume 55, Number 82, May 27, 1886, CDNC

[99] Sacramento Daily Union, Volume 55, Number 84, May 29, 1886, CDNC

[100] Ibid.

[101] Sacramento Daily Union, Volume 56, Number 84, November 27, 1886, CDNC

[102] Sacramento Daily Union, Volume 56, Number 87, December 1, 1886, CDNC

Benjamin Norton Bugbey

[103] Ibid.

[104] Sacramento Daily Union, Volume 56, Number 92, December 7, 1886, CDNC

[105] Ibid.

[106] Ibid.

[107] Ibid.

[108] Ibid.

[109] Ibid.

[110] Ibid.

[111] Ibid.

[112] Ibid.

[113] Ibid.

[114] Sacramento Daily Union, Volume 56, Number 93, December 8, 1886, CDNC

[115] Ibid.

[116] Ibid.

[117] Ibid.

[118] Sacramento Daily Union, Volume 56, Number 95, December 10, 1886, CDNC

[119] Ibid.

[120] Ibid.

[121] Ibid.

[122] Ibid.

[123] Ibid.

[124] *The Executive Documents of the House of Representative for the First Session of the Fiftieth Congress 1887 – '88 In Thirty Volumes.* (Washington: Government Printing Office 1889.) Moneys paid by C.N. Jordan, Treasure, during the third quarter, 1886 on account of Judiciary. B.N. Bugbey, U.S. Commissioner $58.40.

[125] *The Executive Documents of the House of Representative for the First Session of the Fiftieth Congress 1887 – '88 In Thirty Volumes.* (Washington: Government Printing Office 1889.) Moneys paid by C.N. Jordan, Treasure, during the first quarter, 1887 on account of Judiciary. B.N. Bugby, U.S. Commissioner $33.00.

[126] Sacramento Daily Union, Volume 56, Number 66, November 6, 1886, CDNC

[127] Sacramento Daily Union, Volume 56, Number 100, December 16, 1886, CDNC

Chapter 14: Back to Farming & Mining 1887 - 1892

After leaving the U. S. Commissioner position, Bugbey would enjoy six years of continuous employment in the Sacramento County Sheriff's Department and a return to both farming and mining. He would become a plainspoken, if not sarcastic, representative for the Sheriff's office and something of a wise sage. Even though he continued to be involved in the Republican Party, he grew weary of identity politics, in which unquestionable loyalty to a political party was a measure of a man's position in the organization.

Sutter County Kirkville Ranch

When Bugbey was not holding hearings as U. S. Commissioner in his little office on the second floor of the Mike Bryte Building, he was attending to his real estate business. In the summer of 1886, he advertised 11 different agricultural properties for sale.[1] Many of the farms or ranches were close to his beloved Folsom. But he also had listings in Lassen and Sutter counties. Because of his real estate knowledge, he was also called upon to be an appraiser of estates for individuals who had died.[2]

As much as Bugbey loved law enforcement, it is fair to say that he enjoyed being a farmer just much as arresting a bad guy or holding a judicial hearing. It's as if he could not restrain himself from having at least one foot in the agricultural domain. He was so impressed with one of the properties he was contracted to sell that he started farming on the land until he sold it. The property consisted of 1,007 acres located on the Sacramento River in Sutter County, at the small community of Kirkville.[3]

Probably one of the best aspects of being back into agriculture for Bugbey was the opportunity to once again hold court with an exhibit at the State Fair. Bugbey exhibited broom corn from the Kirkville farm in the 1886 State Fair.[4] Broom corn is actually sorghum. After the seed heads have been removed, the stiff stalks were used to make brooms.[5] Bugbey displayed bushels of the broom corn that were three feet in height.[6] He also exhibited a number of brooms and dust branches made from the broom corn.[7] The Pacific Rural Press, evidently impressed with the agricultural crops from the Kirkville Ranch, gently scolded Sutter County for not having a display at the fair because of the excellence of Bugbey's produce.[8] As was typical of Bugbey's agricultural exhibits, they won premiums for best bushel of yellow corn and bundles of broom corn at the State Fair.[9]

The Sutter County farm would come to be known as Bugbey's Kirkville Ranch, even though it is not certain he ever owned the property. He visited it often but left the daily operations in the hands of other men, as he was busy as Under Sheriff of Sacramento County. Even though Bugbey continued to be active in the world of agriculture, he never went back to viticulture or managing a winery. It's possible that the collapse of the Natoma Vineyard and his bankruptcy had left too much of a bitter taste for grapes on his pallet. But he also had sworn off alcohol, and perhaps the hypocrisy of a winery run by a teetotaler was too much for him to stomach.

Instead of grapes, Bugbey turned to planting grains and tree fruit on the rich soil of the Kirkville Ranch. In the spring of 1887, he began planting 15 acres of Bartlett pears on the property.[10] In addition to corn, sorghum, and the pears, Bugbey also planted squash, sweet potatoes, carrots, turnips, barley, and wheat.[11] What caught the attention at the 1887 State Fair was not only the cornucopia of produce on display from the Kirkville ranch, but the exhibit Bugbey built to display his bounty.

The Sacramento Daily Union fairly gushed at Bugbey's produce and exhibit.

All those who have witnessed the individual exhibit made by B. N. Bugbey in the Pavilion, north of the music stand, of the products of his farm, will agree that land which will successfully grow the many varieties shown in his display must be productive. Mr. Bugbey's ranch is located 26 miles above the city, on the Sacramento river, at Kirkville, Sutter county. Two miles of the farm front on the river. It is capable of growing anything that the soil of California will produce. As an evidence of that fact, we simply invite the readers' attention to Mr. Bugbey's display, which surely speaks more eloquently than the pen can. This individual exhibit, which is one of the noteworthy attractions at the Pavilion, consists of seven varieties of squashes, apples, Bartlett pears, prunes, Irish potatoes, sweet potatoes, carrots, turnips, barley, wheat, yellow corn, Egyptian corn, pop-corn, tomatoes, beets, etc. The cornstalks, of which a bunch is shown, measures fourteen feet and six inches in height. On this place wild oats grow six and one-half feet high, and blue joint five and one-half feet. Mr. Bugbey may well feel proud of his individual exhibit, for the developed condition of his farm products shown in the Exposition building are the most convincing evidence of the productiveness of the soil in that vicinity. Kirkville Landing is a part of the farm. At this place all the steamers which ply on the upper Sacramento river have a good and convenient landing for the shipment of farm products direct to tide water. The proprietor offers two hundred acres of his farm for sale. Those who may desire to purchase will do well to examine the exhibit at the Pavilion, and satisfy

Benjamin Norton Bugbey

themselves as to what the soil will produce.[12] - Sacramento Daily Union, Volume 58, Number 29, 23 September 1887

What Bugbey was not able to exhibit at the September State Fair was his pumpkins, which had not been harvested yet. In November Bugbey hauled down a 138-pound pumpkin, measuring 2 feet in diameter, and set it outside the Sheriff's office as a little autumnal decoration.[13]

At the 1888 State Fair, Bugbey's exhibit from the Kirkville Ranch was even grander. It was a massive display packed with all the various products grown on the Kirkville Ranch, from grains and vegetables to tree fruits.[14] Bugbey's produce exhibit was one of the main attractions at that year's fair.[15] The Sacramento Daily Union noted, "The large variety of fruits, vegetables and other farm and orchard products shown go to prove that Mr. Bugbey is the fortunate possessor of one of the model farms of the State."[16] The recognition from Sacramento that Bugbey was once again an agricultural success must have meant more to him than any award from the State Fair committee for the exhibit.

The display and fecundity of his farm made headlines all the way back to his home state of Connecticut. Bugbey had sent his brother George, who was a depot officer in Hartford, Connecticut, a picture of his Kirkville Ranch produce exhibit at the State Fair. The Thomasville Press reported on the photo sent to George. The report noted that Benjamin Bugbey had only been back to his home state once in the last forty years but, judging from the exhibit and farming success, had obvious reason to be satisfied with his adopted home.[17]

Of course, neglected from the brief item in the Thomasville Press was the many other successes and failures Bugbey had endured in those 40 years. The Kirkville ranch and impressive exhibit at the State Fair that garnered Bugbey notable praise were reasons for Bugbey to be very satisfied with his home in Sacramento, California. Bugbey certainly could have put his energy into other endeavors that might have made him more money, notoriety, or given him more political clout. Instead, outside of his employment in law enforcement, he focused on agriculture and marketing. Even when he was immersed in the Natoma Vineyard, it was still all about farming and marketing for Bugbey.

Pioneer Raisin Farmer Disputed

Bugbey was a stickler for setting the record straight. He was quick to the pen to dash off a letter to the editor of the daily paper to correct any reported facts or misconceptions. Time after time, he would write the Sacramento Daily Union to disavow a rumor about him, negative comments about the Sheriff's office, or put into context statements attributed to him. He was also very proud and protective of his accomplishments in life. When the Record-Union named farmer R. B. Blowers of Yolo County as "pioneer raisin-maker of California," Bugbey became apoplectic. One can only imagine the fervor in which Bugbey penned the following letter contesting the paper's attribution of "raisin pioneer" to someone other than himself.

In your issue of Tuesday, an article appears that robs me of my honest deserts. I don't like to find fault with little matters, generally, but if there is one act of development in my life of which I am jealous, it is a well-established fact, fully accredited in all the Sacramento papers, and in fact all the leading papers throughout the State twenty five years ago, that B. N. Bugbey, owner and proprietor of the Natoma and the Duroc Vineyards, was the first producer of raisins for the market in America. Booth & Co will inform you that they purchased for their trade, from me twenty-five years ago, one hundred boxes of raisins at one time. I wish to state that I first made raisins in the fall of 1862, while Sheriff of Sacramento County. The agricultural reports of the State will give you this information, and further, that the State Agricultural Society did award B. N. Bugbey of the Natoma Vineyard, a gold medal in 1863 for his exhibit of raisins, the most meritorious exhibit in the Fifth Department, etc., and again, another gold medal was awarded in 1865.

I was about eight years ahead of R. B. Blowers in the raisin business. In fact, I had quit raisin making before Blowers commenced. I shipped raisin-grape cuttings to all parts of the State, and wrote essays on raisin-making before others took hold of the enterprise.

No, all I care about the matter is this: If there is any credit attached to an old '49 pioneer, in being the pioneer grape-curer, or raisin-maker, it does not belong to R. B. Blowers, nor does Mr. Blowers claim anything of the kind. I am well acquainted with Mr. Blowers, and have visited his establishment at Woodland. I indorse Mr. Blowers as being a perfect gentleman and just the kind of a man to manage 'California on Wheels.'

I wish to say in conclusion, that I am proud of being the introducer of the raisin culture in the United States, and in America. I don't like to appear in print, but I do wish you would say in your journal that Mr. Blowers was not the 'pioneer raisin-maker of California,' but that a very humble citizen of Sacramento, who landed in Sacramento in June 1849, by the name of Bugbey, is entitled to this honor.[18] - Sacramento Daily Union, Volume 79, Number 23, 20 March 1890

Benjamin Norton Bugbey

Bugbey, from all indications, was not the first farmer to turn California grapes into raisins. But he worked hard to select a grape that would make a good raisin for the local consumer market and worked to improve the drying methods. What really set him apart from other growers, not only with raisins, but with other products such as his wine and brandies, were his marketing efforts. Bugbey was not content to just grow and cure the raisins; he went out and developed the market. This marketing skill also set him apart from other viticulturalists when it came time to push his wine, brandies, and sparkling wines into the marketplace. He was unique in that he had the ability to both grow a good agricultural commodity and promote the finished product.

Shasta County Little Nellie Mine

Sometime after the 1888 State Fair, Bugbey was either able to sell the Kirkville ranch or otherwise extricate himself from the management of the farm. As a real estate agent, Bugbey had property listings in the northern part of California and was familiar with the area. In the summer of 1888, he bought into the Little Nellie quartz mine east of Redding in Shasta County.[19] He purchased his three-quarter share of the mine for $20,000, with a $10,000 initial investment and the remainder due after one year.[20,21]

Bugbey, who had not been floating in cash since the Natoma Vineyard was foreclosed on, may have been able to raise the money from real estate transactions or the sale of the Kirkville Ranch. He certainly could not have saved $20,000 from his salary as the Under Sheriff. Regardless, Bugbey had segued from farming back into his first California occupation as miner. Obviously, at 61 years of age, Bugbey wasn't physically mining, and he still had to attend to his duties as Sacramento County Under Sheriff.

However, being a mine owner was not a foreign concept or side investment for Bugbey. In 1863, while Sheriff of Sacramento County, Bugbey invested in the Hanks Ravine Copper Mining Claim. The claim was situated one mile below the Atkinson Hotel in Salmon Falls Township.[22] The Hanks Ravine copper mine would have been just a few miles to the east, up the South Fork of the American River from Bugbey's Natoma Vineyard. In 1864 Bugbey had small stake in the Cosumnes Copper Mining Company in Amador County.[23] It doesn't appear that Bugbey ever made any money from these mining investments, but he thought the Little Nellie Mine was different.

In early August, Bugbey returned from a trip to the newly purchased Little Nellie Mine in Shasta County[24] bearing ore to be assayed.[25] He had also hired Mr. Elliott, a mining expert from Idaho, to be the mine superintendent.[26] Bugbey spread the ore out on the table in the Sheriff's office for reporters and others to examine.[27] Assays revealed the ore, from a 4-foot ledge in the mine, to contain a good amount of precious metal.[28] This led some newspapers to report that Bugbey had struck a bonanza.[29] Before any real ore-processing could take place, Bugbey had to install a mill to crush the ore. Fortunately, there was a creek nearby with at least 100 feet of fall to power the stamp machine.[30]

By October of 1888, Bugbey was shipping ore from the Little Nellie Mine to the Selby Smelting Works at Vallejo Junction.[31] Assays made by John Eitel on 5 pounds of ore showed a value of $1,297.13 of gold per ton.[32] Almost 40 years after Bugbey arrived in California seeking a golden future, he finally stumbled upon a real gold strike. By 1889 Bugbey was reporting that the Little Nellie Mine was producing decent quantities of gold bullion.[33]

In 1890 the California State Mining Bureau published its *Tenth Annual Report of the State Mineralogist*,[34] which gave an overview of the Little Nellie mine. The report noted three different tunnels, with the principle ore body above tunnel number 3. All the tunnels were timbered, and the mine was ventilated by air shafts that connected all three tunnels. The ore, the report noted, was transported to the crushing mill on a sled, at a cost of $0.50 per ton. A Dodge ore crusher pulverized the gold- and copper-bearing rock, and the gold was caught on Triumph concentrators. The works were driven by 100 miner's inches of water from a nearby creek.

The Mining Bureau's review also included information on labor at the mine. Six men were employed working the mine, and another eight worked the mill. The average mining wages were $50 per month, and that included board. Men working the ore crusher and concentrators received $35 per month and board. Gold production from the mine was estimated at $160,000 in the 1880s.[35]

Even though some newspaper accounts listed the Little Nellie as a payday for Bugbey, that doesn't seem to have been the case. As with most of Bugbey's real estate ventures after the Natoma Vineyard, he was always marketing the business at the same time he was involved with it. In 1889, no longer involved in the Kirkville Ranch, Bugbey exhibited gold and silver ore from the Little Nellie Mine at the State Fair. Bugbey had his mining Superintendent, J. M. Gleeves, bring down ore specimens for the mining exhibit for the 1892 State Fair.[36]

Insolvent Debtor

If Bugbey was searching for a buyer for his share of the Little Nellie Mine, he didn't find one at the State Fair. Since he had been in difficult financial situations before, Bugbey seems to have taken the precautionary step to be declared an insolvent debtor by the courts. In September 1893, Superior Court Judge A. P. Catlin, an old acquaintance, decreed that Bugbey was an insolvent debtor and that his home and furnishings would be exempt from any attempts to sell the property to pay his debts.[37]

Bugbey was able to get a patent on the Little Nellie land from the Government Land Office in 1894. It encompassed not only the Little Nellie Mine but other sections where mining was occurring.[38] He was then able to sell part of the property to C. W. Fielding on March 18, 1895.[39] Later in September he transferred what appears to be the rest of the property to Mountain Mines, Ltd.[40] With the last transaction, Bugbey exited the world of gold mining.

It is only speculation that the Little Nellie mine gold production tapered off in the early 1890s. Regardless of the circumstances, with the Little Nellie Mine, Bugbey clearly did not make the fabled gold strike that every '49er dreamt of. That he had to go to the lengths he did to seek court protection from creditors for his house and furnishings denotes his financially weak position. Perhaps, had he sold the gold mine earlier, when it was producing better, his investment might have paid off.

But this seemed to be a pattern with Bugbey's investments: He let go of the money-makers in favor of opportunities he felt would yield a greater return. For example, instead of investing so much money in the Johnston brandy distillery, he might have stuck to curing raisins. He even said as much in 1869. Instead of trying to return to his youthful visions of a big California gold strike, he probably should have continued farming the Kirkville Ranch property.

Under Sheriff Bugbey

At the age of 60 in 1887, Bugbey was no longer the agile crime fighter he had been back in the 1850s and 1860s, when he was Constable of Granite Township or Sheriff of Sacramento County. He was still, however, a very able administrator and a man who, as we know from his time as U. S. Commissioner, was not shy about stating and defending his actions or those of the Sheriff's Department. Because of Bugbey's experience with business and court paperwork, not to mention his friendly relations with local newspapers, Sheriff Drew seemed to leave most of the public relations and administration of the office to Under Sheriff Bugbey. So successful was Bugbey as Under Sheriff, he would retain the position under other Sheriffs through 1893. He served as Under Sheriff for Sheriff McMullen, and then Sheriff Stanley.[41]

One of Bugbey's first official acts as Under Sheriff was to preside over the property sale of the Johnston Brandy and Wine Manufacturing Company. As owner of the Natoma Vineyard, Bugbey was an early supporter and investor in George Johnston's brandy distillery. In 1871 Bugbey hosted a party of men, including George Johnston, to review the new Johnston apparatus for distilling grape brandy at the Natoma Vineyard.[42] It may have been Bugbey's investment in this new and improved method for distilling brandy that squeezed his cash resources, leading to default on his mortgage on the Natoma Vineyard.

In 1872 George Johnston opened a distillery on Front and S streets in Sacramento.[43] By 1886 the distillery had run into financial troubles and was unable to repay a loan from D. O Mills & Co. Bank.[44] To satisfy the loan, the property was auctioned off by Under Sheriff Bugbey and sold for $6,000.[45]

Earlier in 1887, the Sacramento County jail experienced an embarrassing event when T. C. Casey, held on charges of burglary from the Golden Eagle Hotel, was able to escape the jail confines. Bugbey offered a $50 reward for the capture of the escaped prisoner.[46] Casey was quickly apprehended within a few days, while trying to cross the American River near Brighton.[47]

Casey was arrested by the Sacramento City Police force and held in the county jail. A dispute arose over the furnishing of a meal to Casey's wife while Mr. Casey was incarcerated. In testimony given in defense of Mr. Casey at trial, a Mr. Connor said that Mrs. Casey was allowed to dine at the officers' table at the expense of the county.[48] While this testimony was immaterial to Casey's trial on burglary charges, it piqued Bugbey's ire over what he felt was a misrepresentation of the facts. He fired off a letter to the Sacramento Daily Union in defense of the County Jail operations.

> *Eds. Record-Union: I desire to say, in reply to the statement of W. W. Connor, a witness for the defense in the Casey burglary case, that the county has nothing to do whatever with furnishing supplies of any kind for feeding the county prisoners. The Sheriff pays for every dollar's worth of all the provisions used out of his own pocket, and the county pays the Sheriff the paltry sum of 25 cents per day each for boarding and guarding the prisoners. This includes keeping the jail clean, sweet and tidy. This Mr. Connor knew as well as I when he gave his testimony, wherein he stated "that the officers' table was supplied from the county's meat," which is not true.*
>
> *Furthermore, if Mrs. Casey ate a meal in the county jail since the 4th day of January, 1887, Mr. Connor received his share, or one-half of all that Mrs. Casey paid for her meals. She never ate there at the instance of the Sheriff.*
>
> *In writing the foregoing, I do so to correct a wrong impression created by a garbled report of the reporter of the Bee on the 12th instant. I further desire to state that from the profits of the officers' table Mr. Connor's board was reduced to the sum of $7.60 for three*

Benjamin Norton Bugbey

square meals a day for the period of three months, at which Mr. Connor says he "kicked." In making this showing I wish it understood that I know whereof I write, as all the bills are paid through me, and what I state I know of to be stated.

One thing more I desire to add for the benefit of the Bee, to show how tender the Sheriff is of fallen humanity. In addition to giving good board, he even permits Casey, the man who broke jail and is now on trial for burglarizing the Golden Eagle Hotel, to subscribe for and read the Bee, without even questioning the propriety of the privilege, and I do not suppose that the proprietors of that paper would feel kindly if this privilege were denied to any criminal who was able to buy it— not even "Basset." Respectfully, B. N. Bugbey, Under Sheriff[49] - Sacramento Daily Union, Volume 57, Number 124, 15 July 1887

Contempt of Court

Bugbey's open letter disputing the testimony given in court did not sit well with Casey's defense attorney, Grove L. Johnson. The next day in court, Johnson requested that Bugbey be held in contempt of court.[50] Judge Freer dismissed the matter of citing Under Sheriff Bugbey for contempt of court because, beyond Grove L. Johnson, no one seemed opposed to Bugbey's correction of the testimony.[51]

While Bugbey could be very direct, and somewhat sarcastic, in his communications, he was also skilled in the art of diplomacy. This served him well with the constant tug of war between the Board of Supervisors and its funding of the Sheriff's operation. One of the reasons why several elected Sheriffs kept Bugbey in the job of Under Sheriff was his ability to state the case of the Sheriff's office without becoming overly contentious.

In one instance, the Board of Supervisors called Under Sheriff Bugbey before their session to explain a bill of $26 for mattresses for the county jail.[52] After being read the "riot act," as described by the Sacramento Daily Union, Bugbey calmly explained that the Sheriff had the right to purchase the mattresses without authorization from the Board, but he did prefer to humor them by submitting requests whenever he could.[53] He apologized that he had not informed the Board in advance, as the mattresses were needed immediately.[54]

On another occasion, Supervisor Bates was incredulous that the Sheriff's office had submitted a bill for a sleeper car for a deputy transporting a prisoner on the train from Los Angeles to Sacramento.[55] Supervisor Bates refused to sign off on the invoice, protesting that the Sheriff's office was riding in luxurious accommodations. Bugbey quickly presented himself before the Board with an explanation that Deputy Sheriffs were human beings and were entitled to some comforts when traveling for business.[56] Bugbey's diplomatic response in support of the Deputy Sheriff assuaged the Board's ill-informed assessment of the situation, and the bill was approved.[57]

Judge A. P. Catlin

Issues related to expenses and funding of the Sheriff's office extended beyond the Board of Supervisors. Judge A. P. Catlin, who was noted for a short temper and being rather irascible, summoned the Sheriff to his courtroom to learn why there was no deputy to act as a court bailiff.[58] Sheriff Stanley found other business to attend to and sent Judge Catlin's old acquaintance, Bugbey, to answer to the court.

"Why is it, sir, that my court is not attended by a Sheriff?" demanded his honor, when the Under Sheriff appeared. "Well, your honor," explained Mr. Bugbey, "we have been caught in another pinch and have not men enough to do the work. Our deputies are all out on court business, though—serving subpoenas for you. The trouble is we have not enough deputies." "Go and hire some more," said the court, rather irritably. "Well, if we do that, we will have to pay them ourselves—the Supervisors won't."[59] - Sacramento Daily Union, Volume 81, Number 137, 31 July 1891

Judge Catlin was not satisfied with the answer, but accepted it. He decided to take up additional funding for the Sheriff's office with the Board of Supervisors. Sheriff Stanley also sent Bugbey to the Board of Supervisors to plead for more deputies to fulfill the tax collection duties. Bugbey was able to successfully argue that the additional deputies needed to be hired in September for the October collections cycle.[60] By a 3-to-2 vote, the Board approved two more deputies for the Sheriff's office.[61] Under Sheriff Bugbey was also the de facto tax collector and was the spokesperson for the Sheriff's office to encourage people to pay their taxes when they came due.[62]

Bugbey on Human Nature

After five years as Under Sheriff, Bugbey had settled into the role of unofficial source of information regarding Sheriff operations and also as something of a pundit, offering social commentary on the nature of people. A Sacramento Daily Union reporter hanging around the Sheriff's office was astonished when a domestic abuse victim requested a visit with her husband and abuser.[63] Bugbey admonished the woman that she was going in at her own request and risked another beating at his hands.[64] The reporter was puzzled as to why she might be assaulted while in the confines of the jail with deputies nearby.[65]

Benjamin Norton Bugbey

Bugbey explained that his comments to the woman were not in regards to the current visit, but that establishing contact, forgiveness, and normalization would result in abuse in the future. The woman's husband was serving a jail term for abuse that she had reported. Yet, like so many other victims of abuse, the women would invariably visit the abuser in jail to console them, bring them cookies and other treats.[66] Astounded at such a contradiction of behavior, the reporter asked if Bugbey had many of those types of cases.[67]

Bugbey replied, "Do we? Why, no end of them. I don't think we ever have had a case of a wife-beater here in which the beaten wife did not come prowling around here to fondle the brutal fellow and bring him nice things and long for the time when he will be liberated— so he can lick her again. Oh, women are funny people, I tell you."[68]

Republican Politics

Even with all of Bugbey's involvement in farming, mining, and duties as Under Sheriff, he remained active in Republican politics. In June of 1888, he organized a Republican Club in Sacramento's Fourth Ward.[69] Over 100 people signed up for the organization, including Bugbey's boss at the time, Sheriff Moses Drew.[70] Bugbey was later named vice president during a big bonfire rally at the corner of 7th and N streets.[71]

As the 1890 primaries started to get underway, there was division within the Republican ranks concerning support for Leland Stanford as Senator. Bugbey was again elected chairman of Precinct 3 of the Fourth Ward and opened the meeting with a humorous and sarcastic observation that the assembled men looked like a fine lot of "boodlers."[72] A boodler was a derogatory term applied to men who profited from public service without providing any benefit to the communities who elected them. At the meeting, Bugbey rallied the crowd in support of Leland Stanford and denounced any effort to peal support away from Stanford's candidacy.[73]

Bugbey was a loyal party man. He valued loyalty and tried to reciprocate as best he could. In 1889 Bugbey supported an initiative to place a $600 license on all retail liquor establishments in the city and force them to close between midnight and 5 a.m.[74] As a former alcoholic and law enforcement officer, he saw the damage liquor created in the community, from crime to domestic abuse. Nonetheless, Bugbey supported John Stevens, a fellow Republican, for City Trustee, even though Stevens refused to pledge his support to the retail liquor license initiative. Bugbey noted in his advertisement of support, "I am for John Stevens. I am ready to take the man on general principles. If we can't trust such a man, it is time to close up business."[75]

Regardless of Bugbey's high ethical standards, politics was still awash with money, booze, and moral contradictions. There were people such as Grove L. Johnson in the Republican Party who pushed anti-Chinese legislation and whose own political ambitions superseded a moral compass. It was not surprising to find Bugbey at the Citizens Nominating Convention in 1892.[76] The focus of the Citizens' Nominating movement was to nominate candidates for municipal office based on the individual's fitness for office irrespective of party affiliation.[77]

At the age of 65, 43 years after he first landed in Sacramento, Bugbey had evolved socially and politically. He found himself slightly out of the mainstream of the current political climate and power structures. He was at a minimum marginalized from the current Republican Party over his defense of the Chinese and, at worst, ostracized by some in the party for his outspoken positions. He had been a loyal Republican and supported fellow Republicans, such as John Stevens, with whom he did not necessarily agree. Bugbey's loyalty began to fade as he saw too many boodlers running for office and generally unethical campaign practices such as buying votes with free liquor. It was time for Bugbey to forge his own political path.

---

[1] Pacific Rural Press, Volume 32, Number 1, July 3, 1886, CDNC

[2] Sacramento Daily Union, Volume 55, Number 114, July 3, 1886, CDNC

[3] Pacific Rural Press, Volume 32, Number 1, July 3, 1886, CDNC

[4] Pacific Rural Press, Volume 32, Number 13, September 25, 1886, CDNC

[5] https://en.wikipedia.org/wiki/Broom

[6] Pacific Rural Press, Volume 32, Number 13, September 25, 1886, CDNC

[7] Ibid.

[8] Pacific Rural Press, Volume 32, Number 12, September 18, 1886, CDNC

[9] Pacific Rural Press, Volume 32, Number 14, October 2, 1886, CDNC

[10] Sacramento Daily Union, Volume 57, Number 33, March 31, 1887, CDNC

[11] Sacramento Daily Union, Volume 58, Number 29, September 23, 1887, CDNC

[12] Ibid.

[13] Sacramento Daily Union, Volume 58, Number 77, November 18, 1887, CDNC

[14] Sacramento Daily Union, Volume 60, Number 18, September 11, 1888, CDNC

[15] Sacramento Daily Union, Volume 60, Number 17, September 10, 1888, CDNC

[16] Sacramento Daily Union, Volume 60, Number 20, September 13, 1888, CDNC

[17] Thomasville Press, November, 1888

[18] Sacramento Daily Union, Volume 79, Number 23, March 20, 1890, CDNC

[19] Sacramento Daily Union, Volume 59, Number 136, July 31, 1888, CDNC

[20] Ibid.

[21] Sacramento Daily Union, Volume 59, Number 137, August 1, 1888, CDNC

[22] El Dorado County Deed Book H, page 286 and 288

[23] Sacramento Daily Union, Volume 27, Number 4162, July 23, 1864, CDNC

[24] *Appendix to the Journals of the Senate and Assembly of the Twenty-Ninth Session of the Legislature of the State of California, Volume V*, (Sacramento, 1891) Flat Creek District, Little Nellie Mine, page 634.

[25] Sacramento Daily Union, Volume 59, Number 140, August 4, 1888, CDNC

[26] Ibid.

[27] Sacramento Daily Union, Volume 59, Number 151, August 17, 1888, CDNC

[28] Ibid.

[29] Sacramento Daily Union, Volume 59, Number 140, August 4, 1888, CDNC

[30] Sacramento Daily Union, Volume 59, Number 151, August 17, 1888, CDNC

[31] Sacramento Daily Union, Volume 60, Number 42, October 9, 1888, CDNC

[32] Sacramento Daily Union, Volume 60, Number 64, November 3, 1888, CDNC

[33] Sacramento Daily Union, Volume 61, Number 147, August 14, 1889, CDNC

[34] *Tenth Annual Report of the State Mineralogist, 1890*, (California State Mining Bureau).

[35] State Mining Bureau, First Annual Catalog, May 9, 1890: Gold Quartz, Little Nellie Mine, Flat Creek District, Shasta County.

[36] Sacramento Daily Union, Volume 84, Number 21, September 14, 1892, CDNC

[37] Sacramento County Deed Book18931006, page 445

[38] U.S. Department of the Interior, Bureau of Land Management, General Land Office Records. Accession CACAAA 013472, Bugbey, Benjamin N, 08/01/1894, Document 24666, California, Mount Diablo Meridian, Township 33 North, Range 6 West, Sections 26, 27, 34, 35, Shasta County.

[39] *California Journal of Mines and Geology, Division of Mines*, 1947, page 130.

[40] Ibid.

[41] Sacramento Daily Union, Volume 80, Number 117, January 6, 1891, CDNC

[42] Sacramento Daily Union, Volume 41, Number 7133, March 24, 1871, CDNC

[43] Sacramento Daily Union, Volume 44, Number 6729, October 26, 1872, CDNC

[44] Ibid.

[45] Ibid.

[46] Sacramento Daily Union, Volume 57, Number 55, April 26, 1887, CDNC

[47] Sacramento Daily Union, Volume 57, Number 56, April 27, 1887, CDNC

[48] Sacramento Daily Union, Volume 57, Number 124, July 15, 1887, CDNC

[49] Ibid.

[50] Sacramento Daily Union, Volume 57, Number 125, July 16, 1887, CDNC
[51] Sacramento Daily Union, Volume 57, Number 126, July 18, 1887, CDNC
[52] Sacramento Daily Union, Volume 81, Number 88, June 4, 1891, CDNC
[53] Ibid.
[54] Ibid.
[55] Sacramento Daily Union, Volume 82, Number 118, January 7, 1892, CDNC
[56] Ibid.
[57] Ibid.
[58] Sacramento Daily Union, Volume 81, Number 137, July 31, 1891, CDNC
[59] Ibid.
[60] Sacramento Daily Union, Volume 81, Number 144, August 8, 1891, CDNC
[61] Ibid.
[62] Sacramento Daily Union, Volume 82, Number 30, September 25, 1891, CDNC
[63] Sacramento Daily Union, Volume 84, Number 34, September 29, 1892, CDNC
[64] Ibid.
[65] Ibid.
[66] Ibid.
[67] Ibid.
[68] Ibid.
[69] Sacramento Daily Union, Volume 59, Number 99, June 18, 1888, CDNC
[70] Ibid.
[71] Sacramento Daily Union, Volume 60, Number 35, October 1, 1888, CDNC
[72] Sacramento Daily Union, Volume 79, Number 123, July 17, 1890, CDNC
[73] Ibid.
[74] Sacramento Daily Union, Volume 61, Number 10, March 5, 1889, CDNC
[75] Sacramento Daily Union, Volume 61, Number 15, March 11, 1889, CDNC
[76] Sacramento Daily Union, Volume 82, Number 138, January 30, 1892, CDNC
[77] Ibid.

Chapter 15: Independent Candidate for Sheriff 1892 - 1894

For the previous five years, Bugbey had served faithfully, and by all accounts effectively, as Under Sheriff of Sacramento County. He oversaw the jail, administered the tax collections, and successfully tangled with the Board of Supervisors and judges, in addition to assisting the Sheriff in apprehending criminals. But Bugbey had grown weary of the Sacramento political establishment. His attendance at the Citizens' Nominating Convention kindled a fire in him and gave him the confidence to run, one more time, for Sheriff. Only this time, he was going to be an independent candidate.

He would make two unsuccessful runs for Sacramento County Sheriff: once in 1892, and again in 1894. In an effort to differentiate himself from the field of other candidates, Bugbey unveiled his very progressive, and some would say radical, ideas for government in 1894. His manifesto on a jubilee-style government spoke more to his California experience of fighting large corporations over his Natoma Vineyard property than it did about law enforcement.

1892 Independent Candidacy

In October 1892 Bugbey announced his independent candidacy, stating his own personal platform.

B. N. BUGBEY, Independent Candidate for Sheriff Of Sacramento County.

TO THE VOTERS OF SACRAMENTO - County—Sirs and Gentlemen: Having received the endorsement of about 1,400 electors of Sacramento County (848 of which are now on file with the County Clerk) as an independent candidate for the office of Sheriff. Having filed my petition in compliance with law, I am now before the people, and am public property open for and seeking criticism.

Politically, I am a Republican, but have swung sufficiently far around the circle as to take a step in advance, and am now in favor of electing all officers by direct vote of the people, from President to Constable, thereby overcoming the evil of ring, bossism and boodle in polities.

I am opposed to, and shall neither buy whisky or voters to secure my election. But if you elect me I shall perform the duties of the office without fear or favor. I thoroughly understand the workings of the office, which I seek for myself personally. I have no enemies to punish, but shall feel very kindly to my friends, but will show no partiality in enforcing the laws.

I am in favor of tempering justice with mercy, but strictly in favor of ferreting out and punishing criminals—both the rich and poor alike— and, if elected, shall act in the future, as in the past, for the best interest of the tax payers of the county.

With the foregoing declaration I offer myself as an independent, unpledged candidate for the office of Sheriff of Sacramento County. I realize that no man can elect himself. I therefore humbly ask your labor and your votes, and if elected will be your faithful servant. Truly yours, B. N. BUGBEY, Independent Candidate for Sheriff of Sacramento County.[1] - Sacramento Daily Union, Volume 84, Number 44, 11 October 1892

> **Down With Boss Rule, Ring Power and Boodle!**
>
> **VOTE FOR B. N. BUGBEY (thus X) FOR SHERIFF**
>
> Throw Off the Yoke! Don't Remain Bond-Slaves Under the Crack of the Party Whip any Longer! Tear Off the Collar!
>
> President Lincoln struck the shackles from the colored slaves. The late decision of the Supreme Court of the State of California has done the same for all voters.
> Truly yours,   B. N. BUGBEY.
>
> Sacramento Daily Union, Volume 84, Number 60, 29 October 1892

Figure 24: 1982 - Campaign advertisement for Bugbey's first run as an independent for Sacramento County Sheriff. CDNC

While Bugbey confesses his allegiance to Republican principles, he rebukes party political machines in calling for all offices to be elected directly by the voters, side-stepping political primaries. The call for nonpartisan elections was not new, but it ensured that Bugbey would not have the backing of any political organization during the election. He appealed to voters who were disgusted with politicians using liquor and other means to buy votes. He also alludes to a more uniform application of justice that routinely favored white wealthy individuals over others. Of course, it is a bit ironic that Bugbey, on several occasions, was the beneficiary of leniency from his law enforcement friends for his own past transgressions of the law.

No Alcohol

Because Bugbey was the Under Sheriff, with a varying schedule, his opportunity to campaign was limited. He apologized in one advertisement for not being able to socialize and visit as much as he would like.[2] Part of the routine of campaigning and visiting potential voters was in saloons. Bugbey was not courting the saloon vote and made it known to the general public. He also dispelled the notion that his independent candidacy was not a strategic and cynical ploy to help another candidate in the race. He addressed those rumors in a letter to the editor of the Sacramento Daily Union.

> It has been reported by one of my opponents, and his friends, that I am working in the interest of another candidate. I therefore take this opportunity of stating in the most positive manner, that I am working for and seeking for the election of Myself PERSONALLY for the office of Sheriff of Sacramento County. To this end I ask the support and votes of all who do not sell out for a drink of whiskey, that class I cannot expect to get, nor do I seek them.[3] - Sacramento Daily Union, Volume 84, Number 65, 4 November 1892

On the ballot, for party affiliation, Bugbey's entry was Independent, Prohibition.[4] If no one had ever read one of his political advertisements, when they read the ballot, they would know that Bugbey, famed vintner of the Natoma Vineyards, celebrated for the Bugbey champagne galop and waltz, was ardently opposed to alcohol.

Raging Against the Political Machine

Bugbey's political advertisements for his campaign were very much targeted toward Sacramento residents who may have shared his frustration with politics as usual. One headline read, "Down With Boss Rule, Ring Power and Boodle!"[5] He also evoked images of the Civil War and the emancipation of slaves. He entreated the voters to "Throw Off The Yoke! Don't Remain Bond-Slaves Under the Crack of the Party Whip Any Longer! Tear off the Collar!"[6]

The implication that the political power structure, of which he had once been a loyal member, was tantamount to a slave master, and the voters were the slaves. This rhetoric against the political party system must have gone over like the proverbial dead rat in the punch bowl for party leaders. He finished his campaign advertisement with, "President Lincoln struck the shackles from the colored slaves. The late decision of the Supreme Court of the State of California has done the same for all voters."[7] The reference to the California Supreme Court alluded to opinions and laws that were curtailing the closed-party nominating system and moving toward political primaries where all party members, rather than just a handful of party rulers, could select the nominee.

Bugbey's independent Civil War imagery did not catch fire with the majority of white voting males. Until the end, he tried to rally the sleepy voters with arguments about throwing off the tyranny of the political machines and reclaiming their rights to vote for whom they wished.

> *To All Honest Voters; I ask you to vote for B. N. BUGBEY for Sheriff, and thereby veto the selling of county offices by the ring bosses and county committees. I have no party organ to advocate my cause. I am taking a "lone hand." I ask your aid, your work and your votes. I appeal to you to come out and be freemen. Throw off the yoke of boss rule; dare to be independent and boldly stand up for the right. Don't allow your birthright to be sold from you by boodlers. I respectfully ask your votes for the office of Sheriff, and by the help of God you will floor ring power. Don't be faint-hearted; stand up and make this trial and win. Truly yours, B. N. BUGBEY, Candidate for Sheriff.*[8] - Sacramento Daily Union, Volume 84, Number 67, 7 November 1892

Old Pete The Drunk

Bugbey lost the election. He did keep his Under Sheriff position, until the newly elected Sheriff O'Neil was installed and Bugbey was replaced by Peter Rooney. While he was still a fixture at the Sheriff's office, he continued to entertain reporters. Under Sheriff Bugbey recounted his days in Folsom with one of his drinking buddies, affectionately known as Old Pete. Bugbey introduced Pete Wilson, a reformed drinker now in the service of the Salvation Army, to a Sacramento Daily Union reporter.[9]

> *"Pete and I were once what they call sports nowadays,"* continued the Under Sheriff, and he gazed fondly on the old man. *"That's when I lived in Folsom. Pete and I entered into a sort of contract once to drink up all the whisky there was in that town, and we were well aware that there was a deuced lot of it there, too, in those days. We went at it in fine style, but somehow or other it was like trying to bale the water out of a boat. We finally had to beat a retreat, but I tell you we were both pretty bad off. Then we both reformed. Neither of us have touched a drop in years. As I said before, we were 'sports' in those days. We were patted on the backs and styled as jolly good fellows —which always meant that we should set 'em up again. But now we are both cranks, Pete in particular. He's got more courage than I have to put on those duds [Salvation Army uniform], but I admire Pete just the same.*[10] - Sacramento Daily Union, Volume 84, Number 109, 26 December 1892

Even as Bugbey was on his way out, he was still a source of entertainment for the newspapers, always eager for a quip or quote as filler on a slow news day. Upon being asked about any news concerning the jail, Bugbey retorted, "You may say that the County Jail now has no less than 86 inmates—guests, you might call them, and, I assure you, our capacity for entertaining winter boarders is taxed to its utmost.'[11]

County Constable

After leaving the position as Under Sheriff, Bugbey was nominated for County Constable by one of the County Supervisors.[12] The vote did not go Bugbey's way. However, when Constable Bissel broke his ankle chasing after a chicken thief, Bugbey was appointed to look after his duties until Bissel returned to work.[13] This position entailed summoning citizens for jury duty, among other tasks.[14] The modest income from the constable position helped pay the bills. Bugbey, who requested to be declared an insolvent debtor in the autumn of 1893 to stave off creditors, was still in a cash-poor situation. The Little Nellie gold mine was not providing the income that Bugbey may have hoped for, and he was actively trying to sell his investment in the mining operation.

In an effort to raise cash, Bugbey took out an ad to sell the numerous law books he had collected over the years.[15] He advertised it as a law library, consisting of 530 volumes that included California Reports, American decisions, and a large number of standard text books.[16] He did secure an appointment, and was commissioned, as a Notary Public.[17] He also took on the occasional appraiser contract to review the estates of men and women who had died.

1894 Equal Rights Candidate for Sheriff

Without full-time employment, Bugbey had time to reflect on his failed 1892 campaign for Sheriff. One area of deficiency was not having enough time to meet and greet voters and explain his candidacy. Another element that he felt he must have overlooked was a full biography and platform that could have differentiated him from the other candidates. Sacramento was a growing town. Even though he was a Sacramento '49er and had been Under Sheriff for five years, there were vast numbers of men who really did not know who he was. However, at the age of 67, he was absolutely certain that he had the professional experience, world experience, and wisdom to make an excellent Sheriff.

With this certitude, Bugbey set out to create one of the larger collections of written campaign advertisements of any man who had run for Sheriff in Sacramento County. In October 1894 he launched his campaign with the slogan, "Equal Rights to All; Special Privileges to

None."[18] He also challenged other candidates to be measured by his record of accomplishments and platform for the office.[19] He promoted himself as a candidate with a record and encouraged voters to read his manifesto.[20] The campaign ads were accompanied with a handsome drawing of candidate Bugbey.[21]

For younger voters, or those who may have recently come to Sacramento, Bugbey wrote a succinct history of his life, noting important accomplishments.[22] Of course, he was a California Pioneer who came to California with James McClatchy, but he was also a miner, hotel operator, engaged in the mercantile business, farmer, and Constable of Granite Township who, "…cleared all off that section of the country the horde of robbers, highwaymen and burglars that infested that region."[23] Bugbey was referencing his successful operation to arrest a gang of thieves who had been preying upon residents around the town of Folsom in 1857.

He noted the men he appointed to different positions when he was elected Sheriff in 1861, including William Hoag, B.B. Redding, James Lansing, and Ed Christy. All these men went on to serve in other prominent positions in government and business.[24] Bugbey went on to document his success with the Natoma Vineyards, his numerous gold medals from the State Fair and Mechanics' Institute, along with other awards for his exhibits, wines, brandy, and raisins.[25] To remind voters that he was not some old man who had been out of the law enforcement arena, he outlined his role as Under Sheriff for Sheriffs Drew, Stanley and O'Neil.[26]

At the heart of his campaign strategy is his independence. He appeals to "…all votes of all parties, who are in favor of good government and the thorough enforcement of the law, who have the moral courage to act from their own honest conviction, independent of political bosses, boodlers and ring-managers…"[27] While he is still angry and frustrated at the power of political parties to select candidates, he has dropped the analogy that the current system makes voters slaves and they need to be emancipated by voting for an independent candidate such as himself. The implication that party loyalty was tantamount to Southern Confederacy slavery probably rubbed many voters the wrong way.

Progressive Socialist

Bugbey was not content with high-level campaign rhetoric, and he decided to add details to his introductory biography. In a postscript he adds,

I am in favor of all constitutional, civil, and religious rights and am "for the greatest good to the greatest number," therefore

opposed to monopoly. I am a friend of the progress, a friend to railroads, for we need them to build up our country, but for the good of all concerned, and to prevent continued strikes, I believe it better for the Nation that the Government own all railroad and telegraphy lines and manage them under the Civil Service Reform System. I am in favor of removing from office all Sheriffs, Constables, Policemen, Supervisors and all other officials who neglect to enforce the law at all times, and of severely punishing all who are caught stealing from the county, directly or indirectly.[28] - Sacramento Daily Union, Volume 88, Number 52, 20 October 1894

Bugbey set himself up as a politically progressive socialist when, as a candidate for Sheriff, he didn't need to reveal that level of political philosophy. He openly called for the nationalization of the railroads and telephone lines. This surely did not score him any points with the business establishment at the time. But scoring points was not what Bugbey's campaign was about. Bugbey wanted a complete revolution of the political and government system. The campaign for Sheriff was simply his platform upon which to enunciate his broader vision. This vision of government that Bugbey had been working toward for many decades was underpinned by his many experiences as a pioneer in California. At the heart of the revolution, he believed, was real land reform. He felt the current system of land distribution, which at its core was directed at settlers, had been perverted by large corporations in the form of special land grants and subsidies.

Bugbey's Manifesto of Jubilee Government

In an effort to educate the voters about his vision for a reorganization of government, Bugbey published in the Sacramento Daily Union what he referred to as his "Within Jubilee System of Government" proposal. He also called it his manifesto in campaign advertisements. The genesis for the proposal was borne of Bugbey's experience fighting for his land against the Natoma Water and Mining Company, his bankruptcy that was partially inflicted by the demonetization of silver, his work as a U.S. Commissioner defending the rights of Chinese, the consolidation of land holdings he witnessed on the part of the railroads, the poverty and injustice he saw working in law enforcement, and, finally, his religious faith and sobriety. Many of his progressive, socialist, and protectionist ideas and proposals were not unique. Several people had called attention to the monopolies and large land holdings of corporations as a cause for poverty, especially in the West.

Benjamin Norton Bugbey

Figure 25: 1894 - Illustration of B. N. Bugbey from his second run as an independent candidate for Sacramento County Sheriff. CDNC

Special Privileges to None

In 1850 the Democratic Party, in preparation for a Sacramento election for local government, published a resolution that stated, "That in Municipal, as well as State and National Governments, the laws should be framed so as to secure equal rights to all, and special privileges to none."[29] While that resolution was generally accepted, it was not always put into practice in Sacramento or California.

Benjamin Norton Bugbey

Bugbey's use of the campaign slogan of equal rights and no special privileges harken back to not only the founding of Sacramento, but the principles upon which the United States was formed. The Civil War was fought, in part, to manifest the "equality for all" notion. Bugbey had tried to apply this concept when he was a U.S. Commissioner.

When Bugbey's Natoma Vineyard was going strong, and he was in regular contact with the political and business moguls of the day, he most likely did not broach the topics of land distribution and monopolies. Bugbey had always been a big supporter of Leland Stanford, who was part of the Big 4 of the Central Pacific Railroad. By 1894 many of those people were dead, out of power, or of no consequence to Bugbey. He could speak his mind on political graft, boodlers, and the concentration of arable land in the hands of a few corporations, and suffer little consequence.

Henry George

One gentleman who was agitating over the unequal distribution of land in California was Henry George. In 1871 Henry George published a collection of essays on the failed system of land distribution in the United States, *Our Land and Land Policy*. His research and conclusions were even cited on the floor of the California Assembly, in arguments over monopolies and collusion to prevent immigrants from securing title to property.[30]

In *Our Land and Land Policy* George noted that the disproportionate amount of land available for settling was not provided to farmers, as was the original intention of Congress.

> *...that is to say, six sevenths of the land have been put into the hands of people who did not want to use it themselves, but to make a profit (that is, to extract a tax) from those who do use it. A generation hence our children will look with astonishment at the recklessness with which the public domain has been squandered. It will seem to them that we must have been mad. For certainly, our whole land policy, with here and there a gleam of common sense shooting through it, seems to have been dictated by the desire to get rid of our land as fast as possible.*[31] - Our Land and Land Policy, Speeches, Lectures and Miscellaneous Writings, Henry George, Garden City, New York, Doubleday, Page & Company, 1911

Henry George was not a product of an elite university. He was man with a simple public school education. George was born in 1839 and made his way to California in 1858. He worked, among other jobs, in the printing and newspaper business. While Bugbey was in self-imposed exile in San Francisco in 1879, George was also there, working on a tome that would encompass his entire economic, political, and social philosophy. His book, *Progress and Poverty, An Inquiry Into The Cause Of Industrial Depression And Of Increase Of Want With Increase Of Wealth, The Remedy*, was published in 1879 and helped cement his reputation as an American economic philosopher.

One of the themes of *Progress and Poverty* is that industrial advancements correlate with increased poverty. As George writes, "The 'tramp' comes with the locomotive, and almshouses and prisons are as surely the marks of 'material progress' as are costly dwellings, rich warehouses, and magnificent churches."[32] George's central premise, or the problem, was that as wealth increases, because of the business and economic structure, poverty also increased. The remedy, as stated by George, was, "To extirpate poverty, to make wages what justice commands they should be, the full earnings of the laborer, we must therefore substitute for the individual ownership of land a common ownership."[33] And to drive the point home George wrote in italics, "We must make land common property."[34]

Bugbey Articulates the Problem

In a much more condensed version of George's hypothesis that industrial advancement, coupled with unequal distribution of land, was the source of poverty, Bugbey echoes George's economic philosophy in his Jubilee remedy. First, Bugbey states the history and developments that have led to the current problems in the nation. Even though all men have been born free and equal, he writes, their inalienable rights, including the pursuit of happiness have been systematically degraded.

...thwarted by great accumulative capital and the centralization of power, brought under and controlled by the great monopolies of the day, and by the absorption of the public domain, whereby the greater portion of the arable timber and other lands of our State are owned and controlled by a few persons, monopolists and foreign capitalists, to the great deprivation and distress of the great masses of our native-born citizens, thereby inaugurating a system of "peonage" and causing a vast majority of our citizens to become bond-slaves to a few arrogant monopolists, who hold our lands in large tracts, ranging from five thousand to many hundreds of thousands of acres of our best farming lands, which prevents the thorough settling up and populating of our State, and causing the masses dependent on labor to seek employment in our over-crowded cities,...[35] - Sacramento Daily Union, Volume 88, Number 58, 27 October 1894

Benjamin Norton Bugbey

The result of a manipulated political and economic system, in Bugbey's perspective, was to force industrious citizens into poverty, just as George had observed. Bugbey continues to echo George's economic philosophy and adds a current event as well.

> ...*thereby forcing our white population, the greater part of whom were well-raised, that would otherwise be industrious and good citizens, to become houseless, homeless "tramps," and, because of poverty and hunger, induced to seek relief by organizing and joining the "Commonweal Army" of the discouraged unemployed, thus threatening the perpetuity of both our State and Nation.*[36] - Sacramento Daily Union, Volume 88, Number 58, 27 October 1894

The Commonweal Army, also known as Coxey's Army, was a protest march of unemployed workers from Ohio to Washington, D.C., in 1894, during one of the worst economic depressions the U.S. had ever suffered.[37] There were also similar marches on the West Coast that placed the blame for high unemployment at the feet of the railroad companies and monetary policies.[38] Bugbey, similar to George and other politicians of the day, also placed some blame for white poverty on foreign immigration. Instead of using the term Chinese, Bugbey highlighted Mongolians and insinuated that their presence was driving down wages.[39] As progressive as Bugbey had become, he still could not see past the racist implications of his argument and that by favoring the "white population," he was undercutting his religious foundation that all men are born free and equal.

Unfortunately, Bugbey's racist perspective was in line with many of his progressive contemporaries at the time. For the most part, Bugbey's assessment of the problem, tinged with racism, bigotry, and protectionism, that land concentrated in the hands of the monopolies was the cause of poverty, was mirrored in the writings of many other men, including Henry George. Where Bugbey diverged from the mainstream of economic populist solutions was his jubilee remedy. George's position was that land should be held in common. At a minimum, there had to be some sort of restructuring of land ownership. But how could this be achieved?

The foundation of great land wealth and concentration rested not only with generous land subsidies to railroad companies to build the Transcontinental Railroad, but with the fabrication of land titles conveyed to people and corporations from federally held land. By virtue of the Treaty of Guadalupe Hidalgo after the U.S. defeated Mexico, the federal government then controlled huge tracts of land. While the Mexican and Spanish land grants were honored, Native Americans' rights to their lands were conveniently ignored. When the Public Land Survey System was finally deployed in California, it sliced and diced up land into neat little squares. The federal government then offered the land for sale, with priority given to squatters who had made some nominal improvements to the land.

Imaginary lines drawn on a piece of paper and then codified in a land patent or title, irrespective of who might have lived on the land for hundreds of years, was the basis for wealth creation. The Natoma Vineyard, which was primarily land purchased from the State of California with an addition from the Central Pacific Railroad, made Bugbey a wealthy man for a short period. Bugbey was able to take out loans on the property to expand his operations because he held the title to the land. As we know, Bugbey could not repay a mortgage on the land and eventually went bankrupt.

Jubilee is the Remedy

The only way to untangle the contrived system of federal land distribution and its exploitation by large corporate monopolies, from Bugbey's point of view, was an equally magical proposal to apply the biblical year of jubilee.[40]

For this and many other reasons I am in favor of, and would have our legislature pass a law, declaring and making the year A.D. 1900 a year of jubilee, and every seventh year thereafter years of release, after the old Mosaic system, and would have our legislature enact such laws that would compel the great land-holders and monopolists to dispose of their vast holding to actual citizens having no land, on reasonable terms, in tracts not exceeding 320 acres of tillable, nor more than 640 acres of pasture, timber, mountain or desert lands, by providing by law that all lands be held in greater quantities than above designated by one person shall, by action of law, be confiscated to the State of the first day of said year of jubilee, or release, and by the State systematically subdivided and sold to bona fide citizens having no land, who will become actual settlers thereon, in fraction of not less than twenty acres, and in quantities not exceeding the maximum number of acres, according to character of land as above stated, on a five-year credit, at the rate of $5 per acre for tillable and $2.50 per acre for other lands, and should be forever exempt from execution, except for taxes, and should constitute and be a homestead and a continuous heritage to such purchasers and their descendants.[41]- Sacramento Daily Union, Volume 88, Number 58, 27 October 1894

The jubilee concept comes from the Leviticus in the Old Testament of the Bible.

Benjamin Norton Bugbey

> *8 You shall count off seven weeks of years, seven times seven years, so that the period of seven weeks of years gives forty-nine years. 10 And you shall hallow the fiftieth year and you shall proclaim liberty throughout the land to all its inhabitants. It shall be a jubilee for you: you shall return, every one of you, to your property and every one of you to your family.*
>
> *23 The land shall not be sold in perpetuity, for the land is mine; with me you are but aliens and tenants. 24 Throughout the land that you hold, you shall provide for the redemption of the land.*
>
> *25 If anyone of your kin falls into difficulty and sells a piece of property, then the next of kin shall come and redeem what the relative has sold. 26 If the person has no one to redeem it, but then prospers and finds sufficient means to do so, 27 the years since its sale shall be computed and the difference shall be refunded to the person to whom it was sold, and the property shall be returned. 28 But if there are not sufficient means to recover it, what was sold shall remain with the purchaser until the year of the jubilee; in the jubilee it shall be released, and the property shall be returned.*[42] -

Leviticus 23: lines 8, 10, 24 – 28, The New Oxford Annotated Bible, New Revised Standard Version

There is no evidence that any government put such a jubilee concept into practice in the Middle East. From God's mouth to Bugbey's pen, there was no reason why a jubilee concept could not be instituted in California. At least that was Bugbey's assessment of the situation. He had obviously given some critical thinking time to the concept. Bugbey was very specific about the cost of the land and the acreage limitations. Leviticus was similarly specific about the conditions of jubilee land distribution as well.

Bugbey's incarnation of a jubilee system of government land reform was crafted to reflect the existing order and land titles under the Public Land Survey System. His goal was to break up large holdings and get the land back into the hands of settlers, farmers, and ranchers. His concept was to force large holders to divest of their vast real estate holdings in order to address the question of land distribution. This is where he splintered slightly from Henry George, who advocated for common ownership of property. Bugbey did not want to give the land away for free. He recognized that settlers who had an investment in the property were more likely to use the land. Of course, investments sometimes generate mortgages or other loans.

Bugbey's next jubilee proposal spoke to indebtedness, which, from experience, could destroy a settler when economic conditions beyond his control occurred. Similar to the Biblical jubilee, Bugbey suggested a seven-year cycle, beginning after 1900, for release of all lands used as security for loans.

Benjamin Norton Bugbey

> *And all claims for the payment of money, or binding contracts, should on the first day of each year of release become void and cancelled, to the end that every citizen of the State should be free and equal, and all persons having gold, silver, or other evidences of actual wealth in excess of $250,000 per capita, over and above their just debts, the said excess should be confiscated to the State, and should form a fund to be known as a "Relief Fund," and should be used under just and proper regulations for the relief of all persons actually and unavoidably in great need of assistance, to the end that no cause for "tramps" should exist nor be tolerated in our State. All persons or corporations should have until the first day of January A.D. 1900, to arrange their affairs so as to welcome the ushering in of the first year of jubilee system: under our present system the rich are becoming richer and the poor poorer day by day.*[43] - Sacramento Daily Union, Volume 88, Number 58, 27 October 1894

The term radical may not be strong enough to characterize Bugbey's debt relief proposal. Every seven years, he wanted debts, secured by land, to be cancelled. All individual wealth would be capped at $250,000 in liquid assets. The excess wealth confiscated by the government would become a relief fund for the destitute. Not only was Bugbey proposing land redistribution, but wealth redistribution as well. However, he was emphatic that the current system was enriching the already wealthy class of Americans, while families of little property became poorer and more destitute.

James McClatchy, Bugbey's political nemesis, would have been bemused, if not shocked, at Bugbey's proposal. McClatchy, who died in 1883, was a champion of land reform and settlers' rights. At the time of the settler's revolt or riot in 1850, McClatchy had been imprisoned over his support and advocacy of settlers' rights over land speculators in Sacramento. Both McClatchy and Bugbey were previous Sacramento County sheriffs. They both had to auction off property and real estate to satisfy court judgments. Hence, if Bugbey's jubilee land debt relief proposal was enacted, many people would have been spared the agony of losing their land because economic conditions had changed preventing the repayment of mortgages.

Specific National Proposals for Change

Bugbey went on to enumerate other points of change he felt were necessary to eliminate corrupting influences in the political system and address poverty. Many of the proposals had a genesis in his own experience of losing the Natoma Vineyard but were also directed at campaign and government reform. At the national level, Bugbey was in favor of monetizing silver again and of the nationalization of railroad and telegraph lines.[44] The de-monetization of silver, which constricted the money supply, was a contributing factor to Bugbey's 1870s cash flow problems. He hoped that if the government owned communication and transportation infrastructures, labor strikes or boycotts would be avoided.

In 1894 Bugbey's electorate was comprised mainly of white men, since women could not vote. He supported women's suffrage, but with a caveat that there should be an education qualification for all voters.[45] Bugbey's radical ideas did not play well with most white men in Sacramento. Women were more likely to support his proposals of equality, debt relief, and land reform.

Another Bugbey proposal that would appeal to women was the establishment of storehouses for the storage of grains.[46] The state would pay producers 80 percent of the market value of the crop. The goal was to reduce speculation, which caused wild swings in pricing, and provide stability to the marketplace for California grains and cereals. Bugbey also stated his opposition to hydraulic mining, whose debris was a hazard to farmland along certain rivers.

Bugbey wanted to prohibit candidates from providing or buying alcohol for potential voters, and he wanted Sunday to be declared a day of rest from all work.[47] In effect, he wanted all businesses, especially saloons, to be closed on Sundays. In another proposal aimed at supporting labor, Bugbey wanted to restrict immigration for at least five years and deny entry to anyone who could not verify a good moral character.[48]

Several of Bugbey's proclamations and proposals were aimed at the entrenched political parties controlled by a handful of individuals. He supported the adoption of the Australian Ballot,[49] already in use, that provided one printed ballot to each voter to be filled out in a private voting booth. Previously to the secret balloting process, any organization could supply a ballot to a voter, greatly enhancing the organization's prospects of having their candidates prevail. Secret voting diminished the power of political parties. In addition, Bugbey wanted direct elections.[50] He thought this would severely curtail, if not abolish, political parties.

Bugbey: The Reformed Capitalist

Bugbey's jubilee system of government proposal, along with his other reforms, was a repudiation of the business and political life he had led since arriving in California. Up until 1892 and his first independent campaign for Sheriff, Bugbey had been a loyal party man. Bugbey was also the beneficiary of the federal government's land distribution system. He built a nice little winery empire on 320 acres he bought from the State of California[51] for a fraction of the revenue the land was generating. Vast tracts of land were also given to the Central Pacific Railroad as compensation for the construction of the Transcontinental Railroad. Bugbey bought 160 acres from the Central Pacific Railroad in 1870, with Leland Stanford himself signing the deed book conveying title to Bugbey.[52] Chinese immigration also supplied Bugbey with low-cost labor for his vineyard and winery. In short, before Bugbey's financial collapse, he was part of the problem that he now claimed had led to so many social ills in America, and which his jubilee system would correct.

In a 1871 statement to the state Agricultural Committee, Bugbey argued that he should be awarded a Gold Medal because of his participation in the system he now sought to dismantle.

In eighteen hundred and sixty-one, I purchased a piece of land in Salmon Falls Township, El Dorado County, upon which were then planted eight acres of vines. I gave to this place the name of "Natoma Vineyard," and since that time my best energies and all the capital I could command have been devoted to the industry. I have now one hundred and fifty-seven acres in vines, and for a number of years past I have made from grapes grown by myself, on my own land, on an average of from fifty thousand to sixty thousand gallons of wine per annum. Last year my product was sixty-six thousand gallons.[53] - Transaction of the California State Agricultural Society During The Years 1870 and 1871, Sacramento, T. A. Springer, State Printer, 1872

I think it fair to say that Bugbey would have been appalled at his own jubilee system of government if it had been pitched to him in 1871. He was able to parlay a very modest investment in land into a powerhouse of a vineyard. It is doubtful that, had Bugbey's viticulture empire grown and made him a wealthy man into the 1890s, he would have had such impetus to change the status quo of government. But his viticulture empire did crumble, and Bugbey struggled over different periods of his life thereafter to be financially sound.

Was the jubilee system of government just a product of Bugbey's sour grapes over an economic system he believed had pushed him into financial ruin?

At his core, Bugbey was a Jacksonian Democrat, who favored expanded voting privileges, more accountability in government, and a belief that the nation's prosperity depended on agrarian principles by which farmers and ranchers were given easy access to homestead federal property. Since his arrival in California, where the term 'wild west' was an understatement, Bugbey had seen small landholders and entrepreneurs pushed aside in favor of large corporations such as the Central Pacific Railroad. It was no secret that large corporations like the Natoma Water and Mining Corporation and the Central Pacific Railroad employed litigation tactics meant to wear the landowner down, forcing him to either settle a dispute or sell out entirely.

Figure 26: 1894 - Photograph of B. N. Bugbey used for newspaper illustration for is 1894 campaign. Courtesy of the El Dorado County Historical Museum.

The bitter experience of losing land and home to what was believed to be a rigged or corrupt system was not unique to Bugbey. Many men had experienced it. Unfortunately, even if many men did sympathize with Bugbey, and wanted the system to be reformed, they did not vote for him. Bugbey lost his final bid to be elected Sheriff of Sacramento County.[54]

---

[1] Sacramento Daily Union, Volume 84, Number 44, October 11, 1892, CDNC

[2] Sacramento Daily Union, Volume 84, Number 65, November 4, 1892, CDNC

[3] Ibid.

[4] Sacrament Daily Union, Volume 84, Number 55, October 24, 1892, CDNC

[5] Sacramento Daily Union, Volume 84, Number 60, October 29, 1892, CDNC

[6] Ibid.

[7] Ibid.

[8] Sacramento Daily Union, Volume 84, Number 67, November 7, 1892, CDNC

[9] Sacramento Daily Union, Volume 84, Number 109, December 26, 1892, CDNC

[10] Ibid.

[11] Sacramento Daily Union, Volume 84, Number 135, January 25, 1893, CDNC

[12] Sacramento Daily Union, Volume 85, Number 91, June 7, 1893, CDNC

[13] Sacramento Daily Union, Volume 85, Number 92, June 8, 1893, CDNC

[14] Sacramento Daily Union, Volume 85, Number 97, June 14, 1893, CDNC

[15] Sacramento Daily Union, Volume 86, Number 14, September 6, 1893, CDNC

[16] Ibid.

[17] Sacramento Daily Union, Volume 86, Number 205, December 20, 1893, CDNC

[18] Sacramento Daily Union, Volume 88, Number 52, October 20, 1894, CDNC

[19] Ibid.

[20] Ibid.

[21] Ibid.

[22] Sacramento Daily Union, Volume 88, Number 52, 20 October 1894

Bugbey Autobiography:

A CANDIDATE WITH A RECORD B. N. BUGBEY, Ex-Sheriff; Author of the Within Jubilee System of Government; Candidate for Sheriff of Sacramento County.

Equal Rights to All; Special Privileges to None.

ELECTION, NOVEMBER 6, 1894.

PLEASE READ MY MANIFESTO. I Hereby Challenge all Other Candidates for the Office of Sheriff to Compare Record and Platform.

Record of Ex-Sheriff B.N. Bugbey

NOW A CANDIDATE FOR SHERIFF OF SACRAMENTO COUNTY ON HIS OWN Platform.

He was born in the town of Stafford, State of Connecticut on the 3d day of September, 1827. His father was a Methodist Minister of no little note and a veteran of the War of 1812, at the old Serenac Bridge at Plattsburg, New York, and one of a gun squad who manned one of the small gunboats that pulled close alongside of the British fleet, under cover of that memorable dense fog that settled down on New London Harbor where the British fleet was anchored, and so peppered the enemy with their little six-pound cannonade as to drive them from the harbor. His grandfather, John, Bugbey, born A.D. 1751 in Tolland Conn., was a veteran of the Revolution, having served from the Battle of Bunker Hill to the close of the war, and died at Tolland in 1838, at the age of 87 years. His two younger brothers served in the late War of the Rebellion, the oldest of which, George H. Bugbey, was the first man wounded from the State of Connecticut and now resides in Hartford.

B. N. Bugbey. candidate for Sheriff arrived in California the 11th day of June, 1849, having chartered the schooner John Castner in company with the late James McClatchy, Isral Luce and others in New York, sailing thence to Brazo, Santiago thence through Mexico to Mazatlan, thence by bark Olympia to San Francisco.

On his arrival here he immediately engaged in mining on the North Fork of the American River five miles above Folsom. In spring of 1850 he engaged in mercantile business in company with G.W. Champion, now of Red Bluff. In 1852 he kept the Monte Christo Hotel on the Coloma road. In 1853 he commenced the furniture business on the northeast corner of Fifth and K streets, in Sacramento.

The following year he engaged in farming opposite Salisbury Station, on the American River, sixteen miles east of Sacramento. In February, 1856, he built the first frame building in the town of Folsom. In September following he was elected Constable of Granite Township, and served five years – elections having been held annually in those days. The first year after he was elected he cleared all off that section of the country of the horde of robbers, highwaymen and burglars that infested that region.

On September 5, 1861, he was elected Sheriff of Sacramento County, and took office in

Benjamin Norton Bugbey

October following, with William M. Hoag as his Under Sheriff, B.B. Redding, bookkeeper; James Lansing, George A. Putnam, S.W. Griffith, George C. Haswell, J.B. Saul, Leander Culver, John Harper, M. Conley, and Ed Christy as Deputies, all of whom have since died excepting Hoag and Christy.

When the Sanitary Commission was organized for the relief of the sick and wounded soldiers he (Bugbey) headed the list with a subscription of $500 for the Sheriff's office, which was sent East.

Bugbey planted and owned both the original Natoma and Duroc Vineyards, and was the first producer of raisins for the market in the United States. He received three gold medals from the State Fair and two gold medals from the Mechanics' Institute Fair, beside he received from time to time forty-three diplomas from the two Fairs mentioned for best and most meritorious exhibits of vineyard products, consisting of wines, brandies, champagne and raisins.

In September, 1870, he shipped five carloads of wine, brandy and champagne East at one shipment, of his own manufacture. He lost heavily by fire, having been burned out six different times, after which he served as United States Commissioner for two years; and also engaged extensively in mining in Shasta County; served as Under Sheriff under M.M. Drew and Lee Stanley, two years each; served as Under Sheriff three months under O'Neill to teach him the duties of the office, and now seeks the office of Sheriff himself, and herby appeals to all votes of all parties, who are in favor of good government and the thorough enforcement of the law, who have the moral courage to act from their own honest conviction, independent of political bosses, boodlers and ring-managers, to favor him with their vote, for which you shall have his sincere gratitude,

Respectfully, B.N. Bugbey Candidate for Sheriff of Sacramento County.

P.S. – I am in favor of all constitutional, civil, and religious rights and am "for the greatest good to the greatest number," therefore opposed to monopoly. I am a friend of the progress, a friend to railroads, for we need them to build up our country, but for the good of all concerned, and to prevent continued strikes, I believe it better for the Nation that the Government own all railroad and telegraphy lines and manage them under the Civil Service Reform System. I am in favor of removing from office all Sheriffs, Constables, Policemen, Supervisors and all other officials who neglect to enforce the law at all times, and of severely punishing all who are caught stealing from the county, directly or indirectly.

Please give me your support, and I will be your faithful servant in the future as in the past.

[23] Sacramento Daily Union, Volume 88, Number 52, October 20, 1894, CDNC

[24] Ibid.

[25] Ibid.

[26] Ibid.

[27] Ibid.

[28] Ibid.

[29] Eifler, Mark, *Gold Rush Capitalists Greed and Growth in Sacramento*, (University of New Mexico Press, 2002, 1st edition).

[30] Sacramento Daily Union, Volume 42, Number 7401, February 2, 1872, CDNC

[31] George, Henry, *Our Land and Land Policy, Speeches, Lectures and Miscellaneous Writings*, (Garden City, New York, Doubleday, Page & Company, 1911).

[32] George, Henry, *Progress and Poverty, And Inquiry Into The Cause Industrial Depression And Of Want With Increase Of Wealth, The Remedy*, (Fiftieth Anniversary Edition, Robert Schalkenbach Foundation, New York, 1935).

[33] Ibid.

[34] Ibid.

[35] Sacramento Daily Union, Volume 88, Number 58, October 27, 1894, CDNC

[36] Ibid.

[37] https://en.wikipedia.org/wiki/Coxey%27s_Army

[38] Ibid.

[39] Sacramento Daily Union, Volume 88, Number 58, October 27, 1894, CDNC

[40] Sacramento Daily Union, Volume 88, Number 58, October 27, 1894, CDNC

Declarations of B.N. Bugbey [*Jubilee system of government*]

Independent Candidate for Sheriff of Sacramento County

Having determined to place my name before the voters of Sacramento County as an Independent Candidate for the office of Sheriff, to be voted for at the general election to be held in November, A.S. 1894, it behooves me, as such candidate, to make public my public opinions and to briefly outline my platform and my pledge of faith, to which I faithfully promise to adhere:

First, realizing that Almighty God has made of one flesh all nations to dwell on the face of the earth, and that all men by right are born free and equal, and all citizens of the United States are by our Constitution guaranteed certain inalienable rights, among which are life, liberty and the peaceful pursuit of happiness. And, whereas, such rights vouchsafe to every American citizen has been, and now are, thwarted by great accumulative capital and the centralization of power, brought under and controlled by the great monopolies of the day, and by the absorption of the public domain, whereby the greater portion of the arable timber and other lands of our State are owned and controlled by a few persons, monopolists and foreign capitalists, to the great deprivation and distress of the great masses of our native-born citizens, thereby inaugurating a system of "peonage" and causing a vast majority of our citizens to become bond-slaves to a few arrogant monopolists, who hold our lands in large tracts, ranging from five thousand to many hundreds of thousands acres of our best farming lands, which prevents the thorough settling up and populating our State, and causing the masses dependent on labor to seek employment in our over-crowded cities, where Mongolians, thereby forcing our white population, the greater part of whom were well-raised, that would otherwise be industrious and good citizens, to become houseless, homeless "tramps," and, because of poverty and hunger, induced to seek relief by organizing and joining the "Commonweal Army" of the discouraged unemployed, thus threatening the perpetuity of both our State and Nation.

For this and many other reasons I am in favor of, and would have our legislature pass a law, declaring and making the year A.D. 1900 a year of jubilee, and every seventh year thereafter years of release, after the old Mosaic system, and would have our legislature enact such laws that would compel the great land-holders and monopolists to dispose of their vast holding to actual citizens having no land, on reasonable terms, in tracts not exceeding 320 acres of tillable, nor more than 640 acres of pasture, timber, mountain or desert lands, by providing by law that all lands be held in greater quantities than above designated by on person shall, by action of law, be confiscated to the State of the first day of said year of jubilee, or release, and by the State systematically subdivided and sold to bona fide citizens having no land, who will become actual settlers thereon, in fraction of not less than twenty acres, and in quantities not exceeding the maximum number of acres, according to character of land as above stated, on a five-year credit, at the rate of $5 per acre for tillable and $2.50 per acre for other lands, and should be forever exempt from execution, except for taxes, and should constitute and be a homestead and a continuous heritage to such purchasers and their descendants.

Every seventh year after A.D. 1900 should be declared a year of release and restitution of all lands held in pledge or lien as security for the payment of money should be made to the proper owner thereof.

And all claims for the payment of money, or binding contracts, should on the first day of each year of release become void and cancelled, to the end that every citizen of the State should be free and equal, and all persons having gold, silver, or other evidences of actual wealth in excess of $250,000 per capita, over and above their just debts, the said excess should be confiscated to the State, and should form a fund to be known as a "Relief Fund," and should be used under just and proper regulations for the relief of all persons actually and unavoidably in great need of assistance, to the end that no cause for "tramps" should exist nor be tolerated in our State. All person or corporations should have until the first day of January A.D. 1900, to arrange their affairs so as to welcome the ushering in of the first year of jubilee system: under our present system the rich are becoming richer and the poor poorer day by day.

Therefore, First – I am in favor of just and equal rights to all and opposed to special privileges to any.

Second – I am in favor of a strict and impartial enforcement of all laws.

Third – I am in favor of the free coinage of silver.

Fourth – I am in favor of the Government owning and managing all railroad and telegraph lines, thereby removing all cause for strike or boycott.

Fifth – I am in favor of extending the elective franchise to females, and an education qualification for all voters.

Sixth – I am in favor of passing such laws that will compel the cutting up of large land estates into small holdings and their sale to actual citizens at a low rate and on easy terms to all citizens having no land, thereby setting up, beautifying and enriching our State, and supplying labor to the unemployed.

Seventh – To prevent gambling in breadstuffs and to aid the cultivators of our State, I am in favor of the State establishing storehouses in the several counties for the storage of cereals and all imperishable products free of charge, and advancing to all actual producers thereof 80 percent, of their final full face value for the period of one year, at a rate of interest not to exceed 3 per cent, per annum.

Eighth – I am in favor of repealing the Crawford Primary Election Law, and holding all primary and general elections strictly under the Australian ballot system.

Ninth – I denounce ring and boss rule in politics as criminal and destructive alike to an honest expression of the people and to good laws and good government, which should be protected by law under the most severe penalty. I appeal to all citizens to assert their rights and stand boldly up as free men and refuse longer to wear the collar of any ring, boss or boodler in politics, and to be no longer bond-slaves to corrupt managers, thereby putting down everything that threatens the freedom and rights of American citizens. Vote for men and principle and put down corruption in office.

Tenth – I am in favor of a law prohibiting candidates treating or buying intoxicating drinks for voters during their candidacy.

Benjamin Norton Bugbey

Eleventh – I am in favor of a Sunday law and its strictest enforcement, that all may have one day in seven for rest.

Twelfth – I am in favor of protecting our farms and homes in the valley against encroachments of debris coming from hydraulic mining in the mountains, at all hazards.

Thirteenth – I am in favor of electing all political officers by direct vote of the people.

Fourteenth – I am in favor of the fee system in office, instead of the counties paying large salaries.

Fifteenth – I am in favor of restricting immigration for at least five years, and forever to all who can't establish good moral character.

Sixteenth – Hereby declaring my faith in God, the Creator and Ruler of us all, before whom I most reverently bow and adore, I appeal to all labor organizations, laborers and citizens in the State of California to investigate and carefully consider the foregoing, and if it meets your approval it will not be approved by the rich monopolists or politicians, all who are not afraid of ring power, political bosses, boodlers or the proverbial crack of the party whip, monopoly and capital, rally your friends and neighbors, consider and nominate, and in November next you will elect suitable legislators that will not sell out, but will faithfully pass such laws that will secure the inauguration of the jubilee system in January, A.D. 1900.

This is your power. Labor has a majority of nineteen to one over capital. If you will you have the power to throw off the yoke of slavery, and not only claim by have equality with capital. Five years' time with your efforts, if true to yourselves, will bring about this change without friction or injustice to any. Do not delay, but "put the ball in motion," and the result is sure. Peace and prosperity will then reign in the land, and bread and clothing in abundance shall be found in every home, and our uncultivated lands become settled and cultivated fields, orchards and vineyards, all occupied by happy families. Then all may sit beneath his own vine and fig tree, and worship God according to the dictates of his own conscience, and none shall dare molest or make afraid.

On the declarations and principles herein set forth I submit my name to the voters of Sacramento County as an Independent Candidate for the office of Sheriff, and earnestly solicit your assistance and votes, but will buy none either whiskey or money. If elected I shall perform all the duties of the office faithfully and impartially. Respectfully, B.N.Bugbey

P.S. – If the foregoing system be inaugurated political bossism and monopoly will be forever retired.

[41] Sacramento Daily Union, Volume 88, Number 58, October 27, 1894, CDNC

[42] Leviticus 23: lines 8, 10, 24 – 28, The New Oxford Annotated Bible, New Revised Standard Version

[43] Sacramento Daily Union, Volume 88, Number 58, October 27, 1894, CDNC

[44] Ibid.

[45] Ibid.

[46] Ibid.

[47] Ibid.

[48] Ibid.

[49] Ibid.

Benjamin Norton Bugbey

[50] Ibid.

[51] El Dorado County Deed Book L, page 556, and El Dorado County Deed Book N, page 36

[52] El Dorado County Deed Book M, page 411

[53] *Transactions of the California State Agricultural Society During the Years 1870 and 1871*, (T. A. Springer, State Printer, Sacramento, 1872).

[54] Sacramento Daily Union, Volume 88, Number 102, December 18, 1894, CDNC

Chapter 16: The Silver Republican Tax Collector 1898

After a humiliating defeat in his bid to be Sacramento County's Sheriff at age 67, Bugbey went into semi-retirement from politics. For a man who put so much effort into a political and economic treatise on government reform with his manifesto and jubilee system proposal, no one expected Bugbey to abandon politics altogether. The last chapter of his political life had not been written. In 1896 he resurfaced as a delegate at the Independent Republicans Convention of Sacramento County.[1]

By 1898 Bugbey was on the periphery of the mainstream Republican Party again. He was appointed to the committee to see to it that every Republican was listed on the Great Register, so they would be able to vote in the next election.[2] It was at this same meeting that Bugbey had to endure an address by ex-Congressman Grove L. Johnson, whose numerous ethical and moral lapses in judgment were well documented, and from whom Bugbey developed such disdain for party politics.[3]

Silver Republicans

Bugbey found his political muse in William Jennings Bryan, who emerged as a crusader against the Gold Standard and in favor of expanded coinage of silver currency in 1896.[4] The advocacy of monetizing silver again for U.S. circulation must have been music to Bugbey's ears, most likely a galop, and not a waltz. The only problem was that Bryan was a Democrat. But other Republicans were advocating for the monetization of silver. Bugbey was once again inspired to jump into the political scrum and aligned himself with the Silver Republicans.[5]

In August of 1898, Bugbey boarded a train with eight other Silver Republican delegates and traveled down to Los Angeles for the big convention.[6] Upon returning from Los Angeles, the Silver Republicans, a modest 40 members in all, gathered for the first-ever Silver Republican Convention in Sacramento at the Pythian Hall.[7] Moses Drew was nominated as the convention's chairman, and Bugbey seconded the nomination.[8] At the age of 71, Bugbey was back in party politics.

At this first-ever Silver Republican Convention in Sacramento, Bugbey sat on the Platform and Resolutions Committee.[9] As expected, full attention was given to remonetizing silver. The platform quoted Abraham Lincoln, who said it was a heinous crime to contract the money supply after government debt had been incurred.

The Silver Republicans wanted both gold and silver to be fully valued and equally honored as currency to pay debts.[10] They called for the coinage of silver in a 16-to-1 ratio with gold and a return to a bimetallism currency.

The Sacramento County Silver Republicans also put forth resolutions that advocated for the Nicaragua Canal, a system of storage reservoirs and canals to convey water to farms in California, the prevention of corporations from importing foreign labor and rigid enforcement of an eight-hour workday, plus pensions for disabled soldiers and sailors.[11]

Fusionists

As progressive as the Silver Republicans may have been, potentially shepherded with Bugbey's own thoughts and pen, they couldn't endorse William Jennings Bryan for President. In October of 1898, Bugbey and Drew, along with other Silver Republicans, had become Vice-Presidents of the Fusion Party.[12] As the name implies, this new political organization was a fusion of Democrats and Republicans who held similar political goals, namely remonetizing Silver.

At the Sacramento Fusion Rally of 1898, W. H. Alford, chairman of the Democratic State Central Committee, spoke about the destruction of the economy when silver was de-monetized.[13]

> *In that time two streams ran quietly side by side- not streams of water, but of gold and silver. Then the unscrupulous, in order to get control of the two streams, set about to divert one of them, and their scheme was successfully accomplished in 1873, when silver was de-monetized. Then it was that hard times began. Interest was made payable in gold, and the prices for products of the farm had dropped, and as the farmers had nothing with which to purchase the products of the factories, the latter were obliged to close down.*
>
> *The silver had been turned out of the stream of commerce, and the gold left had increased in value until the products of the country were practically valueless, and the farmer could raise no money on his growing crops or livestock, because there was no sale for them. The banker was the man who had profited by diverting the silver stream, and the farmer and the laboring man were the ones who suffered from it.*[14] - Sacramento Daily Union, Volume 96, Number 49, 9 October 1898

Alford's synopsis of the de-monetization of silver and the economic chaos that ensued was also the encapsulation of the tale of Bugbey's Natoma Vineyard collapse. While the United States'

Benjamin Norton Bugbey

adoption of a gold standard was not the only factor in Bugbey's bankruptcy, it was a federal policy decision that made a significant contribution to squeezing Bugbey's cash flow and ability to make his mortgage payment. Regardless of how much impact the de-monetization of silver really had on Bugbey's ultimate financial collapse, he attributed a significant weight to the importance of what he determined was a ruinous monetary policy for him.

Campaign for Tax Collector

Bugbey was finally hearing a validation of his grievances of federal monetary policy from both the Democratic Party and the Republican Party. This new political landscape invigorated him so much that he filed as a candidate for Sacramento County Tax Collector.[15] The only problem with his candidacy was that the Sheriff was the ex-officio Tax Collector. The elected position on the ballot was Sheriff – Tax Collector. In order to be the Tax Collector, you had to be the Sheriff.

Legal Battle to get on Ballot

However, Bugbey had a strategy and an abundance of historical knowledge to back up his claim as the only person to file a candidacy for county Tax Collector. After Bugbey filed his election papers, the County Clerk's office determined that it could not print his name on the ballot as there was not a Tax Collector office; rather tax collection fell under the Sheriff's office.[16]

In 1884 the County Board of Supervisors passed a resolution consolidating the offices of Sheriff and Tax Collector.[17] Even though the resolution was passed, the Supervisors never formally adopted an ordinance to consolidate the offices.[18] Bugbey knew this, as he was the Under Sheriff to Sheriff McMullen when the issue of consolidation was discussed in 1890.[19]

With his attorneys Holl & Dunn by his side, Bugbey petitioned the County Clerk to place his name on the ballot for office of Tax Collector and strike the words "and Tax Collector" after the names of those men running for Sheriff.[20] This was a bold legal move and one that would become contentious.

Judge Johnson agreed to hear Bugbey's petition in late October 1898, just weeks before the election. Both men running for Sheriff and Tax Collector were represented in court opposing Bugbey's petition to be listed as the sole candidate for the office of Tax Collector as a Silver Republican.[21] J. M. Morrison, Fusion candidate for Sheriff, was represented by Hiram W. Johnson.[22] Bugbey had first met little

Hiram back in 1867, when Hiram's father, Grove L. Johnson, was accused of voter fraud.

Hiram Johnson was a young attorney, working for his father Grove L. Johnson, in Sacramento. Bugbey and Hiram Johnson were acquainted with one another as adults because Hiram, as a defense attorney, came to the jail to interview individuals while Bugbey was the Under Sheriff.[23] Hiram Johnson would go on to be elected Governor of California in 1910 on a progressive platform very similar to Bugbey's manifesto proposals of 1894, sans the jubilee celebration.

Hiram Johnson

But before Hiram Johnson gained statewide notoriety for prosecuting corruption cases, he represented J. M. Morrison in his bid to stop Bugbey from running solely for the office of Tax Collector. The prime argument against Bugbey's petition to be included on the ballot only for the position of Tax Collector was that the courts did not have the jurisdiction and could not order the Board of Supervisors to direct the County Clerk to include Bugbey on the ballot.[24] Additionally, the Supreme Court had ruled that acts of consolidation of elected offices need not have an official ordinance passed by a county Board of Supervisors.[25]

Attorney Dunn, arguing on behalf of Bugbey's petition, contended the offices of Sheriff and Tax Collector were separate because they were never consolidated.[26] A point of contention was the 1877 County Government Act of the Legislature that allowed consolidation of offices. However, a later County Government Act repealed that portion of the consolidation directive and left it up to the counties to officially consolidate offices.[27] But Sacramento County never officially consolidated the offices; it only passed a resolution to do so.[28]

Bugbey Wins Legal Questions

After a day of taking oral arguments from both sides, Judge Johnson retired to consider the petition. On the following October day, the Judge ruled in favor of Bugbey's petition that the offices of Sheriff and Tax Collector were separate, and Bugbey could be a candidate solely for the Tax Collector office.[29] The Judge cited the County Government Act of 1896 that repealed the consolidation that was directed in 1874 Act of the Legislature.[30] Furthermore, the Board of Supervisor's resolution to consolidate the offices was not an ordinance and did not conform with the law.[31] Judge Johnson summed up his decision thus,

As I said before, the argument was close. If the petitioner is entitled to have his name upon the ticket, it is time it should be placed there, otherwise irreparable injury will be done which he cannot redress if the name of the office is not voted for and he is entitled to be on the ticket. If, on the other hand, he is wrong and the office of Sheriff covers the office of Tax Collector, then he has acquired nothing by being on the ticket, for the man that is elected Sheriff will be ex-officio Tax Collector.[32] - Sacramento Daily Union, Volume 96, Number 67, 27 October 1898

Bugbey Finally Wins an Election

Bugbey was allowed to have his name on the ballot as the only candidate for the office of Tax Collector. But that did not prevent other people from writing the names of other candidates they wanted to vote for. And indeed, three other candidates advertised in the Sacramento Daily Union as write-in candidates.[33] After the November election votes had been counted, Bugbey received 3,084 votes.[34] The nearest write-in candidate was W. R. Lusk with 2,034 votes.[35] Bugbey finally had a landslide victory in an election at the age of 71.

Even though Bugbey won the election, there was still more litigation to contend with. After the election had been certified and Bugbey declared the winner, he visited Sheriff Johnson's office to receive the Tax Collector books.[36] Sheriff Johnson, it was reported, gave him a derisive laugh and informed Bugbey that he would not turn over the books.[37] Bugbey was not a man to be laughed off. In early January 1899, Bugbey and his attorneys filed a petition with the Superior Court to order Sheriff Johnson to relinquish the Tax Collector books.[38]

Hiram Johnson Attempts to Derail Bugbey

Hiram Johnson and Charles T. Jones represented Sheriff Frank L. Johnson before Judge Hughes. Johnson and Jones argued that the question was not Bugbey's election to the office, but the title of the office.[39] In other words, they were still disputing the separation of the Sheriff's office from the Tax Collector position. Mr. Dunn, attorney for Bugbey, submitted that the Judge should evaluate the current petition based on all the judicial and electoral events that had already taken place.[40]

Bugbey testified that he had received a certification of election as Tax Collector from the Sacramento County Clerk's office, taken his oath, and had filed his bond.[41] But Sheriff Johnson refused to vacate the office where the tax collection books were kept so that Bugbey could perform the duties of his elected position.[42] Sheriff Johnson contended that he was in possession of the tax collecting office and that the Tax Collector and Sheriff's office were one. Therefore, he was not willing to relinquish the office, vault and safe of the tax collection books to Bugbey.[43]

Judge Hughes ruled, similar to Judge Johnson before him, that Sacramento County had not taken the proper steps to consolidate the Sheriff and Tax Collector office. There was, however, one sticking point, and that was the term "incumbent" that was woven into the laws. In one sense, because Bugbey had won the election, taken the oath, received a certificate of election, and paid his bond, he could be considered the incumbent who could rightfully fulfill the Tax Collector position.[44] Hiram Johnson argued that Bugbey was not the actual incumbent, but that the designation went to Sheriff Johnson. In addition, Johnson argued, separating the Tax Collector from the Sheriff could only be accomplished by a proceeding brought in the name of the people of the State and in the nature of a quo warranto.[45]

Upon reflection of the circumstances, Judge Hughes found Bugbey to be the incumbent.[46] With regard to the separation of the Tax Collector from the Sheriff's office, Judge Hughes noted that an Act of the Legislature in repealing the previous County Government legislation created problems because the county governments still had to pass new ordinances to comply with the new law.[47] But until that happened, it was the duty to uphold both statutes where possible. In the end, Judge Hughes decided he had to give more weight to the repeal of the consolidation.

In reaching this conclusion, the court has not been unmindful of the decisions cited by counsel for the respondent, wherein it is uniformly held that the repeal of an Act of the Legislature by implication is not favored in law, and that it is the duty of the court to uphold both statutes, if it may consistently do so. These rules have been carefully considered; yet the court finds it impossible to reconcile the provisions of the two statutes in such a manner as to give full force and effect to both, and has therefore reached the conclusion above stated — that the statute of 1874 was repealed by the subsequent Act of the Legislature passed in 1883.[48] - Sacramento Daily Union, Volume 96, Number 138, 7 January 1899

Judge Hughes decided in Bugbey's favor on all points. Hiram Johnson's arguments did not prevail. Hiram Johnson lost the court case to a 71-year-old California '49er pioneer. Bugbey could now take over the Tax Collector office and the handsome annual salary of $2,500.[49] He also collected another $1,800 for the employment of two assistant deputies. Bugbey appointed W. L. Matlock and Charles Weinrich as his assistants.[50]

Benjamin Norton Bugbey

Sheriff Blocks Bugbey

Even though Sheriff Johnson lost in court, he decided to continue making Bugbey life's difficult. Sheriff Johnson refused to let Bugbey use the Sheriff's office for tax collection purposes. He was willing to give Bugbey all the books, but no space to administer the process of collecting taxes.[51] Bugbey and his attorney visited the County Board of Supervisors meeting to press their case to force Sheriff Johnson to allow Bugbey use of the Sheriff's office.[52] A lengthy discussion ensued, with suggestions that Bugbey use the License Collector room.[53] Many people agreed that the room was too small. The imperfect resolution was to have Bugbey attempt to use the License Collector room and, if it was not sufficient, find another office to rent—and hope the Building Committee would approve the rental of a new office.[54]

Eventually, Bugbey was able to find room at the Hall of Records for his tax collection operation.[55] By early February 1899, Bugbey had reported collecting $2,765 in licenses for the month of January.[56]

Several of the Supervisors were irritated that Bugbey had prevailed in splitting the Tax Collector away from the Sheriff's office and making them look like dysfunctional managers of county policies. In addition to siding with the Sheriff over the office dispute, some Supervisors opposed to Bugbey continued to harass his operations in little ways. Supervisor Gillis challenged a bill from Bugbey for new furniture for the Tax Collector's office. In an arrogant manner Gillis contended that there was no need for the furniture and no room for it in the office.[57] Of course, Supervisor Gillis was not running the tax and license collection office; Bugbey was.

Bugbey pressed forward in his usual resourceful manner of adapting to the situation. In his advertisement to taxpayers about their unpaid taxes, he noted, "Having no place to safely keep money in my office, I daily deposit all collections with the County Treasurer, whose safe is closed with a time lock at 4:30 p.m. Therefore, I can't receive money for taxes at a later hour than stated above."[58] With the notice, Bugbey effectively took a swipe at both the Supervisors and Sheriff, while demonstrating that he was administering the Tax Collector office in unfavorable conditions. The County Board of Supervisors allowed Sheriff Johnson to keep the safe that normally would be used for tax collections. The notice Bugbey placed in the local newspaper was a gentle reminder that other elected officials were attempting to hamper the efficient and effective operation of his office and his duties as duly elected Tax Collector.

Benjamin Norton Bugbey

Splendid Showing Collecting Taxes

In June 1899, the Sacramento Daily Union headline was, "A Splendid Showing, Sacramento Has Practically No Delinquent Taxes."[59] On assessed property value of $30,000,000,[60] Bugbey collected $149,576,[61] with a delinquent balance of $248.[62] Bugbey's incredible collection rate of near 100 percent was even reported in the Los Angeles Herald.[63] It was reported that the collections might have been higher if Bugbey had not been blocked by the judicial action pre-empting the collection of tax on certain properties.[64]

Part of the uncollected tax, preempted by court action, was from an assessment on National Bank of D. O. Mills & Co. amounting to $7,734.90.[65] The Supreme Court had decided against the County Assessor regarding the disputed amount.[66] Bugbey told the Board of Supervisors that, given the adverse decision against the Assessor's Office, it would be useless to advertise and sell the property of D. O. Mills Bank for delinquent taxes.[67] The board wanted Bugbey to attempt to collect the taxes against Bugbey's advice. When Bugbey did try to collect the taxes, National Bank of D. O. Mills was successful in getting an injunction against the Tax Collector's office.[68]

The first half of 1899 had been very busy for Bugbey. He prevailed in numerous court opinions to uphold his legitimacy to hold the elected office of Tax Collector. He battled the Board of Supervisors and Sheriff, sometimes to a draw. He successfully collected almost 100 percent of the assessed taxes while being forced to share offices and having to close early to deposit tax collection receipts with the County Treasurer. In July, Bugbey and his long-time friend, Moses Drew, left for a trip to Alaska for a vacation.[69]

More Battles with Board of Supervisors

Upon returning from his Alaska trip, Bugbey once again had to approach the Board of Supervisors for the necessary equipment to do his job. Bugbey requested a vault to secure the tax collection receipts.[70] Supervisor Gillis said Bugbey could continue to use the Treasurer's vault.[71] In a sign of resignation that the Board of Supervisors would never acquiesce to helping him perform his duties in a proper fashion, Bugbey said he would just leave the request with them. Bugbey returned to the board to again request a safe for the tax collections in October.[72] The board reminded him that they had provided a night watchman with a gun to protect the treasury.[73] As he was only seeking a safe for the interest of the county, Bugbey declared he would not hold himself responsible if the office was robbed.[74]

With no help from Board of Supervisors to improve the process of residents paying their taxes, Bugbey improvised. He was working out of small room with no exterior windows. Inside, Bugbey strung a network of wires over the tax collector clerk's window for improved safety and added wire fencing to improve the flow of residents arriving to pay their taxes.[75] The Sacramento Daily Union commented that Bugbey's improvements to his snug little office were great improvements over the previous tax collection period.[76] With all the wires and fencing, Bugbey had to have been transported back to when he was curing grapes into raisins upon wire structures he had devised at the Natoma Vineyard in 1865.

After the second installment of taxes was collected through November 1899, Bugbey again outpaced collections relative to when they were handled by the Sheriff. Bugbey collected $351,205 in taxes, $94,806 more than on the spring assessment period.[77] Bugbey's tax collections efforts yielded an increase of $29,629 over the same collection period when the Sheriff was in charge.[78] It was apparent to all that a Tax Collector office separate from the Sheriff was more efficient and effective at collecting tax revenue for the county coffers than if it had been left under the Sheriff's office. If anyone on the Board of Supervisors or in the Sheriff's department ever acknowledged Bugbey's success, it was never reported, and most likely never uttered aloud.

In 1900 Bugbey attended the Silver Republican Convention in Los Angeles and was appointed to the platform committee.[79] Bugbey could lay claim to being one of the few Silver Republicans who had been elected to office. This was also Bugbey's last political convention. At 73 years old, he was beginning to slow down. Bugbey ran for a second term as Tax Collector but was thwarted by the political party system. He ran as an independent, but in 1902 men with strong political party affiliation were able to capture loyal party voters over an independent such as himself.[80]

---

[1] Sacramento Daily Union, Volume 91, Number 183, August 28, 1896, CDNC

[2] Sacramento Daily Union, Volume 95, Number 150, July 21, 1898, CDNC

[3] Ibid.

[4] https://en.wikipedia.org/wiki/William_Jennings_Bryan

[5] Sacramento Daily Union, Volume 96, Number 5, August 26, 1898, CDNC

[6] Ibid.

[7] Sacramento Daily Union, Volume 96, Number 14, September 4, 1898, CDNC

[8] Ibid.

[9] Ibid.

Benjamin Norton Bugbey

[10] Ibid.

[11] Ibid.

[12] Sacramento Daily Union, Volume 96, Number 49, October 9, 1898, CDNC

[13] Ibid.

[14] Ibid.

[15] Sacramento Daily Union, Volume 96, Number 65, October 25, 1898, CDNC

[16] Ibid.

[17] Sacramento Daily Union, Volume 2, Number 29, November 30, 1890, CDNC

[18] Ibid.

[19] Ibid.

[20] Ibid.

[21] Sacramento Daily Union, Volume 96, Number 66, October 26, 1898, CDNC

[22] Ibid.

[23] Sacramento Daily Union, Volume 2, Number 38, February 8, 1891, CDNC

[24] Sacramento Daily Union, Volume 96, Number 66, October 26, 1898, CDNC

[25] Ibid.

[26] Ibid.

[27] Ibid.

[28] Sacramento Daily Union, Volume 2, Number 29, November 30, 1890, CDNC

[29] Sacramento Daily Union, Volume 96, Number 67, October 27, 1898, CDNC

[30] Ibid.

[31] Ibid.

[32] Ibid.

[33] Sacramento Daily Union, Volume 96, Number 74, November 3, 1898, CDNC

[34] Sacramento Daily Union, Volume 96, Number 95, November 24, 1898, CDNC

[35] Ibid.

[36] San Francisco Call, Volume 85, Number 34, January 3, 1899, CDNC

[37] Ibid.

[38] Sacramento Daily Union, Volume 96, Number 135, January 4, 1899, CDNC

[39] Sacramento Daily Union, Volume 96, Number 136, January 5, 1899, CDNC

[40] Ibid.

[41] Ibid.

[42] Ibid.

[43] Ibid.

Benjamin Norton Bugbey

44 Sacramento Daily Union, Volume 96, Number 138, January 7, 1899, CDNC
45 Ibid.
46 Ibid.
47 Ibid.
48 Ibid.
49 Ibid.
50 Ibid.
51 Sacramento Daily Union, Volume 96, Number 139, January 8, 1899, CDNC
52 Ibid.
53 Ibid.
54 Ibid.
55 Sacramento Daily Union, Volume 97, Number 9, March 2, 1899, CDNC
56 Sacramento Daily Union, Volume 97, Number 8, March 1, 1899, CDNC
57 Sacramento Daily Union, Volume 97, Number 17, March 10, 1899, CDNC
58 Sacramento Daily Union, Volume 97, Number 46, April 8, 1899, CDNC
59 Sacramento Daily Union, Volume 97, Number 126, June 27, 1899, CDNC
60 Ibid.
61 Sacramento Daily Union, Volume 97, Number 127, June 28, 1899, CDNC
62 Ibid.
63 Los Angeles Herald, Number 270, June 27, 1899, CDNC
64 Sacramento Daily Union, Volume 97, Number 126, June 27, 1899, CDNC
65 Sacramento Daily Union, Volume 97, Number 19, March 12, 1899, CDNC
66 Ibid.
67 Ibid.
68 Sacramento Daily Union, Volume 97, Number 101, June 2, 1899, CDNC
69 Sacramento Daily Union, Volume 97, Number 145, July 16, 1899, CDNC
70 Sacramento Daily Union, Volume 98, Number 23, September 13, 1899, CDNC
71 Ibid.
72 Sacramento Daily Union, Volume 98, Number 64, October 24, 1899, CDNC
73 Ibid.
74 Ibid.
75 Sacramento Daily Union, Volume 98, Number 54, October 14, 1899, CDNC
76 Ibid.
77 Sacramento Daily Union, Volume 98, Number 108, December 7, 1899, CDNC

Benjamin Norton Bugbey

78 Ibid.

79 Los Angeles Herald, April 11, 1900, CDNC

80 Sacramento Union, Number 59, October 22, 1906, CDNC

Chapter 17: Retirement of a Pioneer 1902 - 1914

With his retirement from public office, Bugbey's life revolved around caring for his ailing wife, Julia, a little notary work, a few real estate transactions with Moses Drew, selling books, and attending more funerals. Because of his ground-breaking election as Tax Collector and subsequent duties, Bugbey had not faded away from the local consciousness, even at the age of 79.

The Sacramento Union profiled Bugbey in 1906 for his preference to wear a shawl to keep the winter chills away.[1] The story, accompanied by a photo of Bugbey wearing his shawl, speculated that he was probably the last person to keep the old-fashioned custom of such dress.[2] Bugbey recalled that at one time it was not unusual to see many prominent citizens walking along J or K streets wrapped in fine shawls as proud as the late Queen Victoria.[3]

Figure 27: 1906 - Profile of B. N. Bugbey as the last supporter of wearing a shawl for warmth during the winter. CDNC

60 Years A Sacramento Pioneer

In June 1909 Bugbey celebrated his arrival in Sacramento 60 years earlier.[4] It was estimated that he was one of the last remaining argonauts still in a vertical position. Judge Anderson reminisced on the early days of Sacramento and prominent citizens he had known in an article for the Sacramento Union.[5] He recounted how Bugbey shut down the Tom Bell gang around Robber's Ravine above Folsom after a fierce battle.[6] The 1857 Constable of Granite Township, Benjamin Norton Bugbey was still among the living in Sacramento in 1911.

Unfortunately, prior glory or current affection did not pay Bugbey's bills. In 1906 he petitioned the courts to either allow him to mortgage his home or sell it, as the home was exempted from being attached for debts back in 1893.[7] Bugbey needed to generate funds to pay for Julia's care.[8] The only way to do that was to sell his remaining asset, his home at 23rd and N streets. Julia had mental health challenges that would eventually lead her to be confined at the Napa State Hospital in 1910.[9,10] By 1908 Bugbey had put his home on the market.[11] He was able to sell it to G. A. Burns for $7,000.[12] He and Julia then moved to a rented house on L Street.

After Julia was permanently hospitalized for the deterioration of her mental health, Bugbey suffered another great loss with the death of his friend Moses Drew, with whom he was sharing a house at 1914 L Street, in 1911.[13,14] In the spring of 1912, at the age of 84, Bugbey took a nasty fall.[15] Initial suspicion was that he had had a stroke, but he was able to recover with no effects of a stroke.[16] Even though he was suffering from bouts of depression, Bugbey persevered.[17]

Bugbey had improved enough to have his guardian, Flora Beal, file a lawsuit over commissions he said were due him from the sale of property for his old buddy Drew.[18] Bugbey was suing the administrators of Moses Drew's estate.[19] It's not clear if the 1913 law suit was with merit, or if Bugbey was trying to find some money for his own care based on a past unfulfilled promise of a real estate commission.

Historic Sacramento Cemetery Plot

While Bugbey's current financial situation may have been precarious, he had paid in full for his final resting place. In 1891 he purchased a burial plot in the Sacramento Cemetery. For $75 he purchased the north half of lot 2039 between the cemetery alleys of Violet and Buch.[20] The title was signed over to Bugbey by W. D Comstock, at the time a City of Sacramento Board Trustee.[21] Bugbey had his first beloved wife, Mary Jane, who died in 1869, disinterred from the Folsom Cemetery and buried in the Sacramento plot.

On November 20, 1914, Benjamin Norton Bugbey, perhaps one of Sacramento's last '49er pioneers, died at his home at the age of 87.[22] He was a member of the Methodist Episcopal Church, but his services were held at the funeral home of Clark, Booth, Yardley, at 917 H Street.[23] As a member of Masons Sacramento Lodge No. 40 F. and A. M, and past master of the Natoma Lodge No. 64 in Folsom, he was given a Masonic funeral and then interned at the city cemetery, where a cast concrete obelisk bears his name.[24] Bugbey's wife, Julia, died two years after him and was buried next to him.

Figure 28: Bugbey grave marker obelisk monument in the Historic Sacramento Cemetery. The smaller headstone to the right marks the grave of his third wife Julia. Author's collection.

Benjamin Norton Bugbey came to Sacramento as a humble man with little means and left the same way.

---

[1] Sacramento Union, Number 159, January 29, 1906, CDNC

[2] Ibid.

Benjamin Norton Bugbey

[3] Ibid.

[4] Sacramento Union, Number 112, June 13, 1909, CDNC

[5] Sacramento Union, Number 40, December 10, 1911, CDNC

[6] Ibid.

[7] Sacramento Union, Number 151, July 22, 1906, CDNC

[8] Ibid.

[9] https://www.findagrave.com/memorial/128352251/julia-florinda-bugbey

[10] 1910 United States Federal Census, California, Sacramento County, District 123, Sacramento Ward 9, Bugb(e)y, Benjamin N, Age 82, 1914 L Street, Primary Louisa Dickson

[11] Sacramento Union, Number 138, January 10, 1908, CDNC

[12] Sacramento Union, Number 116, June 20, 1908, CDNC

[13] Sacramento Union, Number 60, October 30, 1911, CDNC

[14] Sacramento Union, Volume 164, Number 20, March 20, 1912, CDNC

[15] San Francisco Call, Volume 111, Number 111, March 20, 1912, CDNC

[16] Sacramento Union, Volume 164, Number 20, March 20, 1912, CDNC

[17] Ibid.

[18] Sacramento Union, Number 86, September 24, 1913, CDNC

[19] Ibid.

[20] Sacramento County Deed Book 18911215, page 620

[21] Ibid.

[22] Sacramento Union, Number 20, November 20, 1914, CDNC

[23] Ibid.

[24] Ibid.

Thoughts on Benjamin Norton Bugbey

Agriculture

A major theme throughout Bugbey's life was agriculture. Even though he did not have a background in production farming, he was drawn to a life on the land, or at least managing it. He had the farm on the American River north of Salisbury Station, Natoma Vineyard, and the Kirkville Ranch. In between the Natoma Vineyard and Kirkville, it was reported that Bugbey was tending to an almond orchard, possibly on the SVRR line.

In the case of most of Bugbey's big agricultural adventures, he always leaves the farm for what he believes are greater opportunities. He let his Salisbury Farm go so he could move to Folsom and be closer to mining operations. Bugbey converted this exit from farming into a lifelong career in law enforcement when he became the Constable of Granite Township.

In 1861, after he dispensed with the Salisbury farm, he started farming on acreage in El Dorado County with eight acres of vineyards. By this time, he was transitioning from Constable to Sheriff of Sacramento County, but the lure of farming, the earth, was too strong for Bugbey to ignore. He would nurture and improve the modest farm on the South Fork of the American River into the celebrated Natoma Vineyard.

The Natoma Vineyard became his prime focus in 1864, after he lost his nomination bid for Sheriff. And for the next several years he devoted his energies to producing table grapes, raisins, wine, and sparkling wine. He started to step away from agriculture as he became more enamored with distilled spirits of grape brandy. He mortgaged the Natoma Vineyard to expand his brandy production with the George Johnston's new distillation process for brandy.

Bugbey took a gamble and lost. He lost it all. He lost all his Natoma Vineyard property, the Duroc vineyard near Shingle Springs, many of his Folsom lots, and, ultimately, his marriage. Bugbey even said there was plenty of money in raisins, and had he not shifted his focus to distilled spirits, he would have produce more raisins. The investment in brandy distillation was not the sole reason for Bugbey's financial collapse, but it did not help.

Ten years after losing the Natoma Vineyard, Bugbey would bring the Kirkville Ranch into production and notoriety. Similar to his marketing of his raisins, fermented and distilled products at the State Fair, Bugbey built huge exhibits of the farm products being produced up in Kirkville in Sutter County. Bugbey was not getting rich off of the Kirkville farm endeavor, as he still kept his day job as Under Sheriff.

The prospect of gold in a hard rock mine in Shasta County diverted Bugbey's attention away from farming. Again, Bugbey abandons agriculture in a gamble for greater profits on the other side of the fence. While Bugbey did make some money with the Little Nellie Mine, it appears that the mining expenses quickly overtook the money generated from the gold bullion produced. Bugbey had to petition to become an insolvent debtor in 1893 to protect his house from being sold to creditors. He eventually sold the mining property in 1895.

Bugbey's failure to learn or failure to recognize a pattern in his life decisions is not unique to him. I see it in my own life and in the lives of other men.

Political Ambitions

In considering Bugbey's overall involvement in politics, his positions in the different political parties, and his candidacy for various local positions, I was surprised that he never attempted to run for a statewide or congressional office. I can understand not wanting to run for Congress, as he would have to leave California, and he was obviously in love with the Sacramento region.

But I have never been able to pinpoint why Bugbey did not run for the state legislature. After all, Sacramento was the state capitol; he would not have to move from the area to serve in the legislature. Regardless, his focus always remained on attempting to become elected the Sheriff of Sacramento County a second time. As his Republican Party would not nominate him, he ran as an independent candidate twice. It was his second candidacy that revealed his frustrations over political parties and big corporate enterprises. His manifesto of a jubilee system of government, aimed at land reform, certainly set him apart from any man running for office in Sacramento at the time.

In 1898 he successfully circumvented the established political machines and was elected Tax Collector as a Silver Republican. Victory at the polls and in the courtroom was the culmination of all his legal experience, knowledge, and patience. He then administered the Tax Collector office, albeit in a hobbled fashion, with some of the lowest delinquency rates known to Sacramento County at the time.

Bugbey never seemed to yearn for fame, but he certainly would have liked a more comfortable retirement. Even though he blamed the concentration of land holdings among corporations for many of the ills of society, he never openly laid his failures at that doorstep. He took responsibility for his successes and failures. He worked very hard to climb back out of the hole of debt after failures with the Natoma Vineyard and Little Nellie Mine.

Social Progressive

Perhaps the biggest surprise of Bugbey's life was his advocacy and action on the part of the Chinese as a U.S. Commissioner. To have white men arrested for harassing Chinese men was unheard of and unthinkable in 1886. Bugbey knew he was swimming upstream with his legal foundation of federal statutes that had been declared unconstitutional. But he pressed forward nonetheless. He played a legal, and sometimes illegal, chess game to facilitate the transfer of young Chinese women held against their wills to San Francisco, away from their Sacramento captors.

When he left the U.S. Commissioner position to become Under Sheriff, Bugbey never seemed to wade into those murky legal waters again. However, his manifesto pointedly calls for a justice system that treats all people the same. Bugbey's writings reflect a man who had obviously given much thought to the notion of liberty and equal protection under the law. Unfortunately, Bugbey was ahead of his time, even if we factor in some of his bigoted views.

Evolution

Bugbey came to California a young man, searching for gold so he could become rich. He fell in love with Folsom and the greater Sacramento region. He had plenty of opportunities to move, but he never did. As he was loyal to his political party, he was even more loyal to Sacramento.

The Natoma Vineyard provided Bugbey with a modest amount of wealth and fame. He was capitalizing on California's climate and fertile soil in a capitalist environment. He saw his fortunes crash by forces beyond his control at the local and national levels.

He witnessed an anti-Chinese hysteria develop in California. But the Chinese were just scapegoats for a variety of monetary and land policies that were depressing prices and creating poverty. Bugbey recognized that white men were over reacting to the threat of Chinese labor. Worst of all, they were treating the Chinese in a fashion that no man or woman deserved to be treated.

Bugbey evolved from a naïve capitalist to a magical-thinking socialist. He realized the government did not always have his best interests at heart when they de-monetized silver and allowed the railroads to monopolize rates and hoard land. He became a progressive socialist, some would say a communist, by his advocacy to nationalize the railroad and telephone lines. In addition, he wanted a cap on landholdings and the amount of wealth a man was allowed to own.

Neither Bugbey's advancement of viticulture in California nor his advocacy for political and land reform elevated him to the level of honorable mention for a street name or park site in either Folsom or Sacramento. His crusade for better treatment of the Chinese and his actions to protect them does bear mention as a footnote in some larger historical context.

With the understanding that no man or woman is perfect, and that we are all complicated, Bugbey's life is an interesting study of a California pioneer who just could not leave the state and Sacramento region. He tried hard to be a good and productive citizen. Sacramento shaped his life more than he shaped the city. He was married to the region. It was his identity.

Bugbey is the mirror of Sacramento in human form. He had successes and failures. When a levee broke in his personal life, he worked to repair it, just as Sacramento built and repaired levees to protect the city. He and Sacramento grew up together and evolved over time. Sometimes Sacramento has been bold and progressive, and at other periods, stubborn and recalcitrant. Bugbey was the same way.

Figure 29: Wine cellar of B. N. Bugbey's house on the hill at the Natoma Vineyard, it is above Folsom Lake and can still be viewed. Author's collection.

It was a long and eventful life that ended in 1914. When Bugbey came to Sacramento in 1849, the city was a collection of dusty streets, canvass tents for stores and homes, and a few wooden structures. By the time he died, there were cars driving up and down the street in front of his home. Bugbey had witnessed the birth of a city. He had been a part of the maturation of Sacramento, which, for a brief period of time, was a major economic hub on the west coast.

Undoubtedly, Bugbey would have mourned the loss of the remnants of his Natoma Vineyard to Folsom Lake. Overall, in reflecting upon Benjamin Norton Bugbey's life, I think he would have been impressed with the way both Folsom and Sacramento have developed in the century after his death.

Bibliography

Books, Published Documents

A Memorial and Biographical History of Northern California, Illustrated, Containing a History of this Important Section of the Pacific Coast from the Earliest Period of Its Occupancy...and Biographical Mention of Many of Its Most Eminent Pioneers and Also of Prominent Citizens of Today, (The Lewis Publishing Company, Chicago, 1891).

A Volume of Memoirs and Genealogy of Representative Citizens of Northern California Including Biographies of Many of Those Who Have Passed Away, (Chicago Standard Genealogical Publishing Company 1901).

Anthony, Charles Volney, *Fifty Years of Methodism, A History of the Methodist Episcopal Church, Within the Bounds of the California Annual Conference From 1847 to 1897*, (Methodist Book Concern, 1901)

Appendix to the Journals of the Senate and Assembly of the Twenty-Ninth Session of the Legislature of the State of California, Volume V, (Sacramento, 1891) Flat Creek District, Little Nellie Mine, page 634.

Baggett, W. T., editor, *Pacific Coast Law Journal, Containing All The Decisions of the Supreme Court of California, And the Important Decisions of the U.S. Circuit and U.S. District Courts for the District of California, and of the U.S. Supreme Court and Higher Courts of other States*. (Volume XI, February 24, 1883 to August 1883, San Francisco: Pacific Coast Law Printing and Publishing Co. Publishers, 1883).

Barbeau, Daniel, *Pacific Rebels: California's Monetary Secession During the Civil War*, (Grove City College, December 16, 2013)

California Journal of Mines and Geology, Division of Mines, 1947, page 130.

Clarke, Asa Bement, *Travels in Mexico and California: Comprising a Journal of a Tour from Brazos Santiago, through Central Mexico, by way of Monterey, Chihuahua, the Country of the Apaches, and the River Gila, to the Mining Districts of California*, (Boston: Wright & Hasty, Printers, 1852).

Davis, Win. J., *An Illustrated History of Sacramento County, California*, (The Lewis Publishing Company, Chicago, 1890).

Eifler, Mark, *Gold Rush Capitalists Greed and Growth in Sacramento*, (University of New Mexico Press, 2002, 1st edition).

Folsom Historical Society, *Images of America Folsom California*. (Arcadia Publishing 2004).

George, Henry, *Our Land and Land Policy, Speeches, Lectures and Miscellaneous Writings*, (Garden City, New York, Doubleday, Page & Company, 1911).

George, Henry, *Progress and Poverty, And Inquiry Into The Cause Industrial Depression And Of Want With Increase Of Wealth, The Remedy*, (Fiftieth Anniversary Edition, Robert Schalkenbach Foundation, New York, 1935).

Haskins, C. W., *The Argonauts of California, Being The Reminiscences of Scenes and Incidents that Occurred in California in early mining days by a Pioneer*. (Fords, Howard & Hulbert, New York, 1890).

Fankhauser, William C., *A Financial History of California, Public Revenues, Debts, and Expenditures, 1872 Collapse of Mining Stocks*, pp 101 - 408, (University of California Publications in Economics, Vol. 3, No. 2, November 13, 1913).

Grobel, Kendrick, *The First Church of Stafford, Connecticut known as "The Stafford Street Congregational Church" from its birth, 1723, to its Death, 1892*, Kendrick Grobel, Th. D. Pastor of the Congregational Church of Stafford Springs, Conn. (Published by the The Women's Council of the Congregational Church, Stafford Springs, 1942)

Lee, Catherine Paik, *The Geography of Viticulture in Amador, El Dorado, and Calaveras Counties: Studies of History, Tourism, and Regional Identity*, (Thesis, University of California, Davis, 2001)

Livingston, Robert, *Charles T. H. Palmer: Pioneer Entrepreneur of Folsom*, (Golden Notes, Vol. 37, Number 3, Fall, Sacramento County Historical Society, 1991).

McClain, Charles J., *The Chinese Struggle for Civil Rights in the 19th Century America: The Unusual Case of Baldwin v Franks*, 3 Law & Hist. Rev. 349, (Berkeley Law Scholarship Repository, Faculty Scholarship, 1985)

McGlashan, Charles F., *History of the Donner Party, A Tragedy of the Sierra*, forward 1940 by George Hinkle and Bliss McGlashan Hinkle, (Stanford University Press, 1968).

Benjamin Norton Bugbey

Mansfeldt, Hugo, *Autobiography of Hugo Mansfeldt*, (Hugo Mansfeldt Papers, Archives Mansfeldt 1, Hargrove Music Library, U. C. Berkeley, March 1928).

Minerals Yearbook, Inyo Mountains, Inyo County, California – the Inyo Marble Company Marble Quarry (Marble), United States Bureau of Mines, Geological Survey (U.S.) 1886, "Structural Materials - Pacific Coast," pp. 545. http://quarriesandbeyond.org/states/ca/quarry_photo/ca-inyo_photos_2.html

Moses, Bernard, et. al., *Legal Tender Notes in California*, (The Quarterly Journal of Economics, Vol. 7, No. 1 (Oct., 1892), pp 1 – 25, Oxford University Press).

Pitzer, Gary, *150 Years of Water: The History of the San Juan Water District*, (Water Education Foundation, 2004).

Rasmussen, Louis J., *San Francisco Ship Passenger Lists, Volume IV, June 17, 1852 to January 6, 1853*. (California State Library)

Sacramento City and County Directory for 1868, by Robert E. Draper, (Sacramento, H. S. Crocker & Co., Steam Printers and Stationers, 1868).

Santos, Robert, *The Eucalyptus of California, Seeds of Good or Evil?* (California State University Press, 1997)

Sioli, Paolo, *Historical Souvenir of El Dorado County, California*, (Paolo Sioli, Publisher, Oakland, CA, 1883).

Stapp, Cheryl Anne, *Before The Gold Rush, The Sinclairs of Rancho Del Paso 1840 – 1849*. (Cheryl Anne Stapp 2017).

State Mining Bureau, *First Annual Catalog, May 9, 1890: Gold Quartz*, Little Nellie Mine, Flat Creek District, Shasta County.

Tenth Annual Report of the State Mineralogist, 1890, (California State Mining Bureau).

The Executive Documents of the House of Representative for the First Session of the Fiftieth Congress 1887 – '88 In Thirty Volumes. (Washington: Government Printing Office 1889.) Moneys paid by C.N. Jordan, Treasure, during the third quarter, 1886 on account of Judiciary. B.N. Bugbey, U.S. Commissioner $58.40.

The Executive Documents of the House of Representative for the First Session of the Fiftieth Congress 1887 – '88 In Thirty Volumes. (Washington: Government Printing Office 1889.) Moneys paid by C.N. Jordan, Treasure, during the first quarter, 1887 on account of Judiciary. B.N. Bugby, U.S. Commissioner $33.00.

The Federal Cases Comprising Cases Argued and Determined in the Circuit and District Courts of the United States, Book 24, Case No. 14078 – Case No. 14691, (West Publishing Co, St. Paul,1896).

Transactions of the California State Agricultural Society During the Years 1870 and 1871, (T. A. Springer, State Printer, Sacramento, 1872).

Water, Our History & Our Future, (Sacramento History Journal of the Sacramento County Historical Society, Volume VI No. 1, 2, 3, & 4, 2006).

Yee, Alfred, *What Happened to China Slough?*, (Golden Notes Volume 40, Number 2, Summer 1994, Sacramento County Historical Society).

Congressional Acts

An Act to extend Preemption Rights to certain Lands therein mention., Chap. CXLIII, March 3, 1853, (Thirty-Second Congress. Session II., Chapters 143, 144, 145).

An Act granting the Right of Way to Ditch and Canal Owners over the Public Lands, and for other Purposes. Chapter CCLXII, July 26, 1866 (Thirty-Ninth Congress. Session I, Chapter 262, 263).

Court Cases

A. H. White v B. N. Bugby, October 5, 1858, Case 777, Sacramento County Court Civil Case Files (1850 – 1879), Box 13.

B. N. Bugbey v Natoma Water and Mining Company, In the District Court 11th Judicial District of California, (El Dorado County District Court Judgment Book E, 1873, pages 223 and 224, El Dorado County Historical Society Museum)

G. C. Peterie v B. N. Bugbey and Robert Beck, California State Supreme Court, 1864, (24 Cal. 419).

Mary Woodliff v B. N. Bugby & Mary's Guardian v Thomas B. Woodliff, January 2, 1857, Case 614, Sacramento County Court Civil Files (1850 – 1879), Box 10. Note, plaintiff name misspelled Woodlift, on Sacramento County table of cases.

S. W. Griffith v B. N. Bugbey, In the District Court of the 11th Judicial District, November 10, 1876. (El Dorado County Judgment Book E, 1876, page 289, El Dorado County Historical Society Museum).

The Pacific Mutual Life Insurance Company of California v B. N. Bugbey, Martinette Bugbey, and Ann Johns, In the District Court 11th Judicial District Court, (El Dorado County Judgement Book E, 1874, page 237, El Dorado County Historical Society Museum).

The Pacific Mutual Life Insurance Company of California v B. N. Bugbey, Martinette Bugbey, and Ann Johns, In the District Court 11th Judicial District Court, (El Dorado County Judgement Book E, 1877, page 295, El Dorado County Historical Society Museum).

The People of the State of California vs The Gold Run Ditch and Mining Company, In the Superior Court of the State of California, in and for the County of Sacramento, testimony of B. N. Bugbey, December 9th and 10th, 1881, Sacramento, Ca, California State Archives microfilm MF2:9 (46) Roll 4, Pages 4558 – 4599

W. R. Strong and Company v B. N. Bugbey, Sacramento County Court, 1875, (Civil Case Files 1850 – 1879, Case 3125 or 3126, Box 46)

Water & Mining Co. v Bugbey, (U.S. Supreme Court, October 1877)

Woods v Bugbey, California State Supreme Court, 1866, (29 Cal. 472).

Images

Natoma Vineyard, Residence of B. N. Bugbey, photographer J. A Todd, Sacramento, Natoma vineyard views, Calif. photographed by J.A. Todd, BANC PIC 1905.01574--A.

Maps

Plat of the Rancho Rio De Las Americanos finally confirmed to Joseph L. Folsom, U. S. Surveyor General by A. H. Jones, Dep. Surveyor, May 1857. U. C Davis G4363, S26-465,1857, U61, No. 3

Music

Bosworth, H. H., *Gungl's Railroad Galop*, (Published by L. R. Hammer, Sacramento)

Hardinge, J., *Railroad Kings Galop*, (Publisher M. D. Swisher, Philadelphia).

Yanke, Hugo, *Bugbey's Champagne Galop*, (Published by Hugo L. Yanke, Sacramento, California, July 4, 1870, Second Edition). John Hopkins, The Lester S. Levy Sheet Music Collection.

Benjamin Norton Bugbey

Yanke, Hugo, *Bugbey's Champagne Waltz*, (1871). John Hopkins, The Lester S. Levy Sheet Music Collection.

Archive and Online Material

1880 Report on History and Facilities of the Natoma Water and Mining Company, (California State Archives, Public Utilities Application No. 6975, January 2, 1923, F3725:7098-7101a)

B. N. Bugbey Railroad Refrigerator Car, January 9, 1883, U.S. Patent No. 270383

California Digital Newspaper Collection (CDNC), Center for Bibliographic Studies and Research, University of California, Riverside, http://cdnc.ucr.edu

- California Farmer and Journal of Useful Sciences
- Daily Alta California
- Los Angeles Herald
- Marysville Daily Appeal
- Pacific Rural Press
- Placer Times
- Red Bluff Independent
- Sacramento Daily Union
- Sacramento Transcript
- Sacramento Union
- San Francisco Call
- Santa Barbara Weekly Press
- Santa Cruz Weekly Sentinel
- Sonoma Democrat

El Dorado County Deed Books, Recorder Clerk office, microfilm

G. M. Cole Turn Table, September 17, 1861, U.S. Patent No. 33294

Land Park News, Lance Armstrong, October 13, 2016, Valley Community Newspapers, Inc.

Nathaniel Knight letter to Ambrose Knight, May 6, 1871, Folsom, CA. (Bancroft Library Call Number MSS 98/22 C).

Benjamin Norton Bugbey

Nathaniel Knight letter to Ambrose Knight, July 2, 1871, Folsom, CA. (Bancroft Library Call Number MSS 98/22 C).

Natoma Water and Mining Company Articles of Incorporation. (State of California, Department of State, California State Archives, March 28, 1922).

Pioneer Valley History Network, Western Massachusetts Pioneers Spreadsheet https://pioneervalleyhistorynetwork.org/project/gold-rush-stories/

Placer Herald, Folsom Historical Society Museum Archive

Sacramento County Deed Books, Online Index of Recorded Documents http://www.ccr.saccounty.net/DocumentRecording/Pages/Index.aspx

Thomasville Press, November, 1888

U.S. Department of the Interior, Bureau of Land Management, General Land Office Records. Accession CACAAA 013472, Bugbey, Benjamin N, 08/01/1894, Document 24666, California, Mount Diablo Meridian, Township 33 North, Range 6 West, Sections 26, 27, 34, 35, Shasta County.

Bugbey

1850 U.S. Federal Census Mortality Schedules, 1850 – 1885, Connecticut, Somers, Tolland, Eleazer W. Bugbey, Age 55, Death October, Occupation Farmer, Days Ill 28 with Fever

1860 United States Federal Census, California, Sacramento, Granite Township, p. 237, B. N. Bugb(e)y, Age 33, Birth Conn., M. J. Bugb(e)y, Age 23

1863 U.S. Excise Tax, California, Division 1, District 4, Assessor John Avery, B. N. Bugbey $145.35

1864 U.S. Excise Tax, California, Division 1, District 4, Assessor John Avery, B. N. Bugbey, Folsom, Auctioneer (2 months) $3.33

1864 U.S. Excise Tax, California, Division 3, District 4, Assessor John Avery, B. N. Bugbey, Salmon Falls, Manufacturer, 1,000 gallons wine, $60.00

1866 California, Voter Registers, 1866 – 1898, Benjamin Norton Bugbey, Sacramento, California, Age 38,

1867 Sacramento County Great Register, Bugbey, Benjamin Norton, Age 38, Occupation Vintner, Residence Granite, July 30, 1866

Benjamin Norton Bugbey

1868 California, Voter Registers, 1866 – 1898, Benjamin Norton Bugb(e)y, Age 40, Occupation Vintner, Residence Folsom

1869 Sacramento County Directory, Granite Township, Resident Voter Bugb(e)y, Benjamin Norton

1870 United States Federal Census, California, Sacramento County, Granite Township, Bugb(e)y, Benj. N, Age 43, Occupation Wine Grower, Value of Real Estate $10,000, Value of Personal Property $20,000, Birth Conn, Martinette, Age 26, Occupation Keeping House. Other occupants at the residence include: Amasa W. Mars (m), Age 37, Occupation Carpenter, Frank Duckahl, Age 30, France, Occupation Wine Cooper, James Butler, Age 35, New York, Occupation Champagne Maker, Sing Ah (m), Age 32, China, Occupation Laborer, Chee Ah (m), Age 30, China, Occupation Laborer

1871 Sacramento County Directory, Advertisement, Bugbey's Natoma Wines, Brandies and Champagnes.

1872 Sacramento Great Register Card, Bugbey, Benjamin Norton, Residence Granite Township, July 30, 1866

1878 San Francisco Directory, Bugbey, B. N., watchman U.S. Mint, dwelling 413 Fifth

1879 California, County Birth, Marriage, and Death Records, 1849 – 1980, B. N. Bugbey, Marriage, 1879, J. F. Wible, Book H, Page 348

1880 United States Federal Census, California, Tehama, Red Bluff, District 140, George H. Balis, Age 53, Adelia, Age 48, William, Age 22, Mary, Age 17, Edward, Age 14, Newton, Age 7, Benjamin, Age 2

1880 United States Federal Census, California, Sacramento County, Granite Township, Bugbey, B. N, Age 53, Occupation Fruit Grower, J(ulia) F(lorinda) Bugbey, Age 26, Wife, Occupation Keeping House, E(mma) F Bugbey, Age 30, Niece, Occupation At Home

1881 California, Voter Registers, 1866 – 1898, Benjamin Norton Bugbey, Sacramento, California, age 54, 21/2 Precinct

1882 California, Voter Registers, 1866 – 1898, Benjamin Norton Bugb(e)y, Age 54, Residence 21/2 Precinct

1899 Government and Military records, California State Roster, page 149, B. N. Bugbey, Office of License & Tax Collector, Sacramento County

Benjamin Norton Bugbey

1890 California, Voter Registers, 1866 – 1898, Benjamin Norton Bugbey, Age 62, 2228 N Street

1892 California, Voter Registers, 1866 – 1898, Benjamin Norton Bugbey, Sacramento, California, Age 65, 5 feet 8 inches, Eyes blue, Hair gray, Birth Connecticut, 2228 N Street

1893 Sacramento Directory, Bugbey, Benjamin N., residence 2228 N.

1896 California, Voter Registers, 1866 – 1898, Benjamin Norton Bugbey, Age 68, Eyes blue, Hair gray, Occupation: Insurance Agent, Birth Connecticut, 2228 N Street

1900 Sacramento Directory, Bugbey, Benjamin N, County Tax Collector Hall of Records, residence 2228 N

1900 United States Federal Census, California, Sacramento County, District 94 Sacramento Ward 9, B. N. Bugb(e)y, Age 72, Birth Connecticut, Parents Birth Unknown, Julia Bugbey, Wife, Born 1854, Age 45, No Children, Birth Illinois, Father Pennsylvania, Mother Illinois, Anna Wible, Sister-in-Law, Born 1852, Age 47, Birth Illinois, Father Pennsylvania, Mother Illinois

1902 Sacramento Directory, Bugbey, Benj N, County Tax Collector, residence 2228 N

1903 Sacramento Directory, Bugbey, Benj N, residence 2228 N

1904 Sacramento Directory, Bugbey, Benj N, residence 2228 N

1905 Sacramento Directory, Bugbey, B. N, Real Estate, residence 2228 N

1906 Sacramento Directory, Bugbey, B. N, Real Estate, residence 2228 N

1909 Government and Military records, California State Roster, page 255, B. N. Bugbey, Notary, Sacramento

1909 Sacramento Directory, Bugb(e)y, B. N., residence 1914 L

1910 Sacramento Directory, Bugb(e)y, Benj N., Notary Public, 1914 L, Residence Same

1910 United States Federal Census, California, Sacramento County, District 123, Sacramento Ward 9, Bugb(e)y, Benjamin N, Age 82, 1914 L Street, Primary Louisa Dickson

1914 California, Death Index, 1905 – 1939, Benjamin N Bugby, Birth 1827, Death 19 November 1914, Age 87, Sacramento, California

1912 – 1914 California, Voter Registrations, 1900 – 1968, Benjamin Norton Bugbey, Residence 1914 L Street, Sacramento, Ca, Party Republican, Occupation Notary Public

California Death Index, Column 1361, Julia Bugbey, November 21, 1918, Benjamin N Bugb(e)y, November 19, 1914

Connecticut, Hale Collection of Cemetery Inscriptions and Newspaper Notices, 1629 – 1934, Section 5, Row 1, Windsor Locks, Connecticut, Grove Cemetery, E. W. Bugbey, 8 October 1849, Age 56, Hannah L. Bugbey, wife of E. W., died March 7, 1880, age 85.

Connecticut Town Death Records, pre-1870 (Barbour Collection), Bugbey, Eleazer W., Born Lanesborough, Mass, Residence Sommers, Death October 8, 1849, Age 55

U.S., Appointments of U.S. Postmasters, 1832 – 1971, Eleazer W Bugbey, 14 October 1844, West Stafford, Tolland, Connecticut

U.S., Find A Grave Index, 1600s – Current, Eleazer W. Bugbey, Born 1793, Lanesborough, Berkshire County, Massachusetts, Death 8 October 1849, Grove Cemetery, Windsor Locks, Hartford, Connecticut, Spouse Hannah L. Bugbey

War of 1812 Pension Application Files Index, Soldier Eleazer W Bugbey, Widow Hannah L Norton, Bugbey, Marriage 18 July 1816, Discharge Date 31 May 1814, Death 8 October 1849, Somer, Connecticut

Ann Johns

1870 Federal Census California, El Dorado, Salmon Falls

1880 Federal Census California, El Dorado, Salmon Falls, 053

Map of the County of El Dorado, California: compiled from the official records and surveys, (Library of Congress https://www.loc.gov/maps/?q=el+dorado)

Mormon Island Relocation Cemetery (http://www.usgwtombstones.org/california/californ.html)

McGlashan

1850 United States Federal Census, Wisconsin, Rock County, Town of Plymouth, Peter McGlashan

1866 California, Great Voter Registers, Sonoma County

1866 – 1898 California Voter Registers, Sacramento County

Benjamin Norton Bugbey

1867, 1872 California Biological Great Book, Sacramento, Cosumnes, McGlashan, Peter, Age 63, Birth New York, Occupation Farmer.

1870 United States Federal Census, California, Sacramento County, Lee Township, Peter McGlashan, Age 65

1880 U.S. Federal Census, California, Santa Cruz, McGlashan

California, Wills and Probate Records, 1850 – 1953, Peter McGlashan, Sacramento, Wills, Vol A – C, 1857 – 1883.

Wible

1879 California Voter Registers, Sacramento County

1880 U.S. Federal Census, California, Sacramento, Brighton

Yanke – Mansfeldt

1864 Index to Marriage Certificates – Men, Sacramento County, CA, Hugo Yanke to Anna Sanderson, Book C, Page 49

1866 Sacramento Directory, Yanke, Hugo, Musician, Residence 81 4 Street, bds Tolls' Hotel, 190 K Street.

1871 Sacramento Directory, Yanke, Hugo L., Music Teacher, Residence 151 7th Street between N and O.

1880 United States Federal Census, California, Alameda, Oakland, Mansfeldt, Hugo, Age 36, Occupation Music Teach, Anna, Age 36, Wife, Oscar, Age 15, Theodore, Age 13, Mable, Age 7

1907 California State Library Biography Card, Mansfeldt, Hugo L, Hugo Leonhardt Mansfeldt, Father Birth Berlin, Father Occupation Medical Doctor, Mother Emilia von Rauch, First wife died 1886, second marriage 1891, San Francisco. Residence in state, Sacramento until 1871, since in San Francisco, corner of Fell and Shrader Streets, Died San Francisco December 31, 1931.

1922 Passport Application, City and County of San Francisco, May 19, 1922, Hugo Leonhardt Mansfeldt, Naturalized Citizen July 28, 1882, wife Hazel Mansfeldt born 1890, San Jose. Hugo Born Bromberg, Prussia (Germany), August 10, 1845, Father Gottfried Jahnke, Born Prussia. Immigrated from Bremen, April 1860

Index

13th Amendment to the U.S. Constitution, 228, 231
Ackley, W., 64
Addison, Stephen, 135, 171
Alford, W. H., 280
Allen, Robert, 27
Anthony, E., 35, 193, 300
Anthony, James, 60
Anti-Chinese, 94, 221, 222, 224, 227, 232, 236, 237, 252, 297
Applegate, George, 141
Ashland, 199
Assemblyman French. *French, C. G. W.*
Avery, Benjamin P., 117
Avery, John, 96, 112, 306
Baldwin, Thomas, 220
Balis, Adelia, 115, 144, 185, 307
Balis, George, 115, 144, 163, 185
Barton, W. H., 83
Bates, Dr., 61
Beal, Flora, 292
Beal's Bar, 15, 16, 93, 199
Beck, Robert, 64
Bee, Fredrick A., 220
Bell, Tom, 36, 291
Bennett, David, 171
Berry, Henry, 38
Bidwell, John, 105
Big Gulch, 16, 199
Bigelow, D. R., 170
Bigler, 60, 65, 95, 96, 97
Blanchard, George, 167, 191
Blowers, R. B., 245
Brown's Ravine, 69, 72, 142, 163, 165
Bryte, Mike, 134, 174, 212, 213, 218, 221, 223
Buckner, George W., 72
Bugbey, Eleazer Wales, 17, 18, 306, 309
Bugbey, Emma, 187, 195, 219
Bugbey, George, 44, 45, 61
Bugbey, Hannah Norton, 17, 309
Bugbey, Julia, 195, 219, 308, 309
Bugbey, Mary Jane, 22, 27, 33, 108, 109, 110, 115, 292
Bugbey, Nettie
  Martinette, 115, 144, 163, 171, 172, 174, 175, 178, 179, 180, 181, 184, 185, 187, 188, 189, 192

Benjamin Norton Bugbey

Bugbey's Champagne Galop, 123, 124, 142, 304
Bugbey's Champagne Waltz, 123, 142, 160, 305
Bundock, Henry, 197
Bundock, Samuel, 198
Burlingame Treaty of 1868, 220
Burns, G. A, 292
Burrows, Joe, 38
Butter Cooler, 196, 197, 198, 206, 207, 209, 212
Cadwalader, George, 63, 144, 198, 199
Caldwell, William, 141
Carpenter, G. J., 167, 168, 179
Casey, T. C., 249
Catlin, A. P., 62, 93, 102, 144, 164, 191, 198, 199, 200, 201, 202, 203, 218, 247, 251
Chalmers, Robert, 90
Champlin, George, 16
China Slough, 55, 68, 303
Christy, Edward, 47, 49, 65, 102, 103, 261, 274
Chung, Charley, 230, 231, 233
Clark, Mattie, 192
Clarke, Asa Bement, 19, 20, 30, 300
Cobwell, Augustus, 181
Coffroth, J. W., 44, 54
Coggins, P., 57
Cole, Gilbert, 134, 206
Condemned Bar, 16, 199
Coner's Flouring Mill, 116
Conley, M., 274
Conness, Senator, 96, 97, 99, 100, 117
Constable Krimball
   Krimball, William, 190, 191
Cooper, Ellwood, 180
Cooper, J. H., 141
Cornwall, P. B., 16, 45, 46
Craig, O. W., 90
Crocker, Charles, 59, 147, 302
Crossette, W. C., 185, 191
Culver, Leander, 274
D. O. Mills, 59, 60, 285
Dot, Lee Ah, 227, 228, 229, 230, 231, 232, 233, 234
Doy, Sing, 230
Dr. MacLennan, 211, 212
Drew, Moses, 173, 177, 189, 190, 192, 195, 218, 219, 220, 235, 252, 279, 286, 291, 292

Benjamin Norton Bugbey

Duroc Ranch & Vineyard, 72, 73, 76, 77, 82, 115, 127, 129, 132, 144, 162, 163, 171, 178, 210, 245, 274, 295
Dye, Troy, 189
Eberhardt, A., 90
Eoff, John, 177
Ewing, Frank, 37, 62
Favor, Frank, 39
Fielding, C. W., 248
Foley, John, 84
Folsom, Joseph Libby, 26
Fong, Wong Ah, 234
French, C. G. W, 62, 104, 166, 167
Fruit Growers Association, 117
Gafford, J. W., 37
Gay, Daniel, 37, 38
General Carey
   Carey, John T., 228, 229, 230
George, Henry, 264, 266, 268
Gim, Yu, 227, 228, 229, 230, 231, 233, 234
Gleeves, J. M., 247
Goosey, Thomas, 170, 179
Gozinger, George, 90
Griffith, S. W., 47, 49, 177, 182, 273, 303
Gwin, William, 42
Hamilton, Charles, 38, 72
Haraszthy, A., 90
Hardesty, Samuel, 69, 72
Harper, John, 274
Hart, A. L., 223
Hartley, H. H., 63, 84
Hastings, B. F., 59, 60
Haswell, G. C., 47, 49, 273
Heilbron, A., 134, 144, 173, 195, 213, 219
Hilborn, S. G., 224
Hinkson, A. C., 224
Hoag, I. N., 90
Hoag, W. M., 47, 49, 141, 261, 273, 274
Hobby, W. H., 198
Holl & Dunn, attorneys, 281
Hollister, County Supervisor, 51
Hopkins, Mark, 59
Hopper, P. J., 43, 44, 62, 83, 105, 131
Hoskins, E. D., 43
Houghtaling, T. H., 24, 27, 109
Howard Benevolent Association, 131

Hoy, Suey, 228
Hunt, John, 43
Ince, Annette, 60
Ingham, S. S., 56, 57, 66
Jackson, 23, 38
James, E. A., 170
Jenkins, James, 27
Johns, Ann, 135, 174, 175, 181, 182, 304, 309
Johnson, Grove L., 102, 103, 210, 221, 223, 250, 252, 279, 281
Johnson, Hiram, 12, 103, 281, 282, 283, 284
Johnston, George, 90, 128, 129, 130, 131, 133, 135, 140, 141, 142, 145, 153, 172, 206, 213, 248, 249, 295
Jones, C. T., 230
Judah, Theodore, 17, 26
Judge Adams, 167, 174
Judge Freer, 250
Judge Hoffman, 231, 232
Judge Hughes, 283, 284
Judge Johnson, 281, 282, 283
Judge S. S. Holl, 228
Judge Van Fleet, 228, 229
Justice J. Currey, 63
Kahl, Louis, 54
Kee, Frank, 230, 231, 233
Kee, Hong, 234
Keller, Matthew, 90
Krimble, William, 185, 219
King, Charles, 90
Knight, Nathaniel and Ambrose, 133, 148, 305, 306
Kurtz, W. W., 29, 60
La Rue, Hugh M., 104, 178, 219
Lamblett, Francois "Frank", 190, 191, 192, 219
Lansing, James, 43, 44, 46, 47, 49, 54, 57, 65, 84, 97, 98, 100, 131, 204, 205, 218, 261, 273
Lawson, Chris, 199, 200
Leidesdorff, William Alexander, 17, 24, 25, 26, 27, 134, 135, 163
Lewis, O. C., 185
Little Oregon Bar, 16, 199
Luce, Israel, 21, 29, 60, 273
Madden, John, 43, 45, 46
Marshall, Sylvester, 43
Matlock, W. L, 284
Mayo, Eli, 87
McAllister, Hall, 225

McClatchy, James, 21, 22, 29, 45, 46, 50, 51, 59, 60, 65, 66, 76, 84, 97, 98, 99, 100, 116, 130, 131, 144, 204, 261, 269, 273
McClory, 39
McConnell, Thomas, 84
McEwen, Warren Lee, 72
McGlashan, Charles, 171, 178, 184, 187, 188, 189, 221
McGlashan, Peter, 115, 144, 146, 156, 163, 171, 178, 309, 310
McKune, J. H., 45, 46, 54, 59, 60, 76, 84, 177
McLaughlin, William, 27
McManus, 44
McMitchell, Wyman, 65
Mechanics' Institute, 77, 93, 101, 141, 261, 274
Mette, Henry, 93, 163, 191
Meyers, 36, 38
Middendorf, Henry, 27
Miller, Dwight, 59
Miller, E H., 129
Miller, Frank, 59
Moody, William, 29
Moore, Richard, 192
Mormon Island, 13, 15, 36, 61, 62, 71, 72, 76, 83, 102, 104, 108, 164, 175, 182, 203, 218, 309
Morris, Speyer & Company, 178
Morrison, J. M., 281, 282
Mumford, F. S., 62, 71, 102, 103
Murphey, R. W., 135
Murphy, P. F., 50
Murphy, R. W., 170, 171
Murray, 39
Nagle, General, 90
Negro Bar, 16, 17, 24, 25, 26, 27, 28, 33, 164, 170, 199, 201, 202
Negro Hill, 76, 199
Nickerson, J. E., 90
Nickerson, J. R., 138, 141, 142
Norris, 87, 88
Nought, Jacob, 90
Nuttall, Charles, 135, 171
O'Hara, Jack P., 37
O'Neil, Charles, 37, 38
O'Neill, brick maker, 62
Odbert, John P., 205
Order of Chosen Friends, 205
Pacific Mutual Life Insurance Company, 170, 174, 175, 176, 179, 181, 182, 304

Palmer, Charles Theodore Hart, 134, 135, 149, 170, 174, 175, 178, 181, 187, 213, 301
Parker, J. E., 87, 228
Parker, John, 214
Perkins, Nathaniel, 129
Peterie, C. C., 64
Philip, J. M., 135, 174
Poole, Robert, 39
Price, William, 39
Putnam, George A., 273
Que, Ting, 228
Quigley, B. C, 104, 109
Redding, B. B., 47, 49, 57, 76, 84, 160, 261, 273
Rev. Wible
   Wible, Elias A., 188, 191, 196
Robinson, J. P., 46, 59
Rooney, John, 43, 46, 65, 84, 204
Rose Springs, 210
Rose, L. J., 90
Sacramento Pioneer Association, 60
Sacramento Savings Bank, 132, 170
Salt Bar Hill, 200
Sanderson, Annie
   Yanke-Mansfeldt, 121
Sanderson, C. J., 64
Saul, J. B., 273
Sawyer, Lorenzo, 76, 84, 224, 225, 226, 227, 230, 232, 238
Schell, A., 141
Schmidt, William, 130
Scofield, 38
Scott, Bill, 36, 37
Seavey House Hotel, 209
Section 5377 of the Revised Statutes, 228, 231, 240
Section 5519 of the Revised Statutes, 1874, 223, 224, 225, 226, 227
Seffer, Lazarus, 93, 94
Shattuck, William, 49
Sheriff Johnson, 283, 284, 285
Sheriff McMullen, 248, 281
Sheriff Stanley, 248, 251
Shingle Springs, 72, 77, 82, 144, 178, 210, 295
Shirland, E. D., 102, 103, 105
Simmons, Celia, 59
Sing, John, 220, 222
Sing, Mum, 134, 135, 174, 222
Sizer, Daniel, 29, 87

Slayback, Mancron, 213
Smith's Garden, 58, 59
Snyder, J. E., 90
Speyer, J. W., 135, 174
Stackhouse, 64
Stanford, Leland, 29, 53, 59, 60, 76, 129, 193, 252, 264, 271, 301
Starr, J. B., 27, 57
Stevens, John, 252, 253
Stewart, 56
Strentzel, J., 90
Strong, W. R., 177, 178, 182, 304
Stroup, L. T., 161, 162
Supervisor Gillis, 285, 286
Sutter, John, 17, 25, 27, 45, 52, 55
Swezy, G. N., 90
Symonds, George N., 54, 55
Texas Hill, 164, 202
Tray, Andrew, 93
Tullis, Aaron, 189
Tutt's Bar, 203
Vine Growers' and Wine and Brandy Manufacturers' Association, 141, 172
Wackford, William, 214
Waldo, Ned, 37
Wallace, Thomas, 178
Weed, Limers, 37
Weinrich, Charles, 284
West, George, 90
Wheeler, Charles and Frank, 116
White, A. H., 62, 68, 303
White, William S., 24
Wible, Elias, A., 187
Wible, Julia Florinda
  Bugbey, Julia, 192
Williams, George, 167
Williams, George C., 179
Wilson, B. D., 90, 141
Wilson, Pete, 259
Wittenbrick, Henry, 214
Wong, Ah, 227
Wood, Evarilla, 195, 219
Woodliff, Mary, 62, 68, 303
Woods, David, 62, 63, 64, 68, 69, 304
Wright, Catherine, 214
Wright, John, 30, 37, 300

Benjamin Norton Bugbey

Yanke, Hugo
  Mansfeldt, Hugo, 120, 121, 122, 124, 146, 147, 302, 304, 305, 310
Ye, Suey, 228
Yeager, Philip, 105
Yew, Chew, 56, 57, 66, 222
You, Gout, 233, 234, 235
Young, P. R., 28

www.ingramcontent.com/pod-product-compliance
Lightning Source LLC
Chambersburg PA
CBHW071109160426
43196CB00013B/2516